Top Left: Saipan, June 1944.

Top Right: Saipan, June 1944.

Lower Left: Courtesy of Philip M. Arne.

Below: Saipan, June 1944.

Second Marine Division

1940 - 1999

TURNER PUBLISHING COMPANY

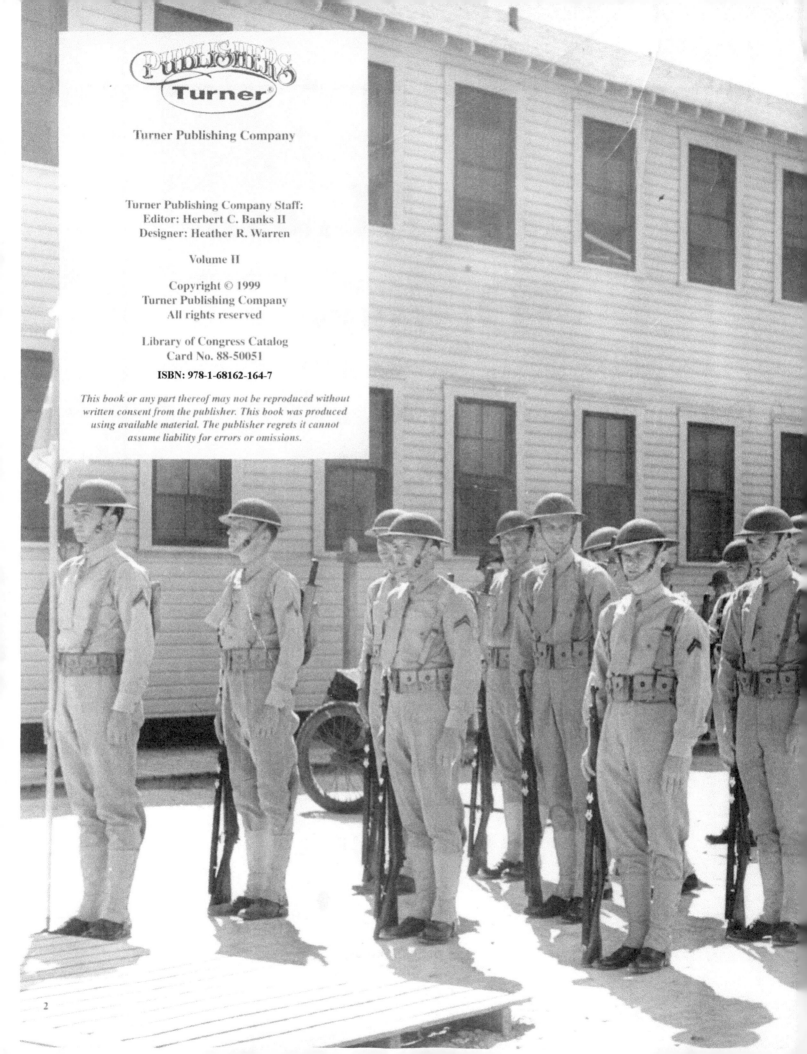

Turner Publishing Company

Turner Publishing Company Staff:
Editor: Herbert C. Banks II
Designer: Heather R. Warren

Volume II

Copyright © 1999
Turner Publishing Company
All rights reserved

Library of Congress Catalog
Card No. 88-50051

ISBN: 978-1-68162-164-7

1 Mar Div

TABLE OF CONTENTS

INTRODUCTION

Training, Travel, and Travails: The Story of the Second Marine Division.

You are about to read a few vignettes which trace the long and storied history of the Second Marine Division, based at Camp Lejeune, North Carolina.

This is the second volume of the Division's history. But, two volumes of history do not begin to scratch the surface of the Second Marine Division's significant accomplishments since its inception in 1941. What they do, however, is keep alive the memory of the thousands of Second Division Marines who have been killed or wounded in major battles like Saipan, Tarawa, or Desert Storm—and of those who have served in between.

Actually, this book is a tribute to those United States Marines who have been fortunate to have served in the Second Division and continue to do so today as members of the Second Marine Division Association (SMDA). There are over 7,000 members of the SMDA, most of whom served with or were attached to the Second Division at some points in their careers. The fact that they choose to continue their association with the division is a credit to the pride instilled in every Marine. Moreover, it is proof that the old saying, "Once a Marine, always a Marine," is as true today as it was back on November 10, 1775, when the Continental Congress authorized the formation of two battalions of Marines. That began a tradition of military service second to none in the United States.

U.S. Marines have a history of gallantry and loyalty to country that is unparalleled among military service veterans in general. Despite their centuries of noteworthy accomplishments, they have often gone about the serious business of protecting the United States without seeking glory.

Nevertheless, glory seems to find them. Of course, they deserve it. After all, they have earned their glory the hard way: protecting the liberty and freedom of millions of Americans. Second Division Marines are no exception to that viewpoint.

To be sure, not every Second Division Marine has served in combat or performed heroic acts that merit Medals of Honor or other military awards.

But, make no mistake about it: military life is not all about war and training. Second Division Marines, like their counterparts in other military services, do have fun, too. That fact is reflected in many of the stories contained in this volume. In total, the book is a journal of Second Division Marines' tales of training, travel, and travails. It is a collection of firsthand stories that anyone can appreciate, since it shows Marines as people as well as warriors. So, sit back and enjoy the anecdotes related by this peculiar breed of human beings: the members of the Second Marine Division Association, who have earned their places in the history they so vividly recount in this book.

THIS BOOK IS DEDICATED TO EVERY PAST AND PRESENT MEMBER OF THE SECOND MARINE DIVISION ASSOCIATION AND OF THE SECOND DIVISION. MAY THEY NEVER BE FORGOTTEN—AND BOOKS LIKE THIS WILL ENSURE THEY WILL NOT BE.

Art Sharp
Art Sharp

Marine landing teams rescues a downed pilot during Tactical Recovery of Aircraft/Personnel (TRAP) exercise, 22 February 1996.

8

THE HISTORY OF THE "HOLLYWOOD MARINES"

Second Division Marines can rattle off three important birthdays: their own, the Marine Corps', and the Division's—not necessarily in that order. Every Marine remembers that November 10 is the Corps' birthday. Most Second Division veterans know that February 1, 1941, is the division's birthday. Their own? Well, for dyed-in-the-wool Second Division members, their own birthdays take a back seat to the other two. That is not surprising. After all, both the Marine Corps and the Second Division have storied histories—and the history of one is the history of the other.

The Birth

Ironically, the Second Division, which is based at Camp Lejeune, North Carolina, was formed in San Diego, California. The Marine Corps combined the 2nd, 6th, and 10th Marine Regiments to form the Second Division, aka the "Hollywood Marines" and the "Silent Second." Not everyone is pleased with the latter, which has been a subject of controversy among Second Division veterans.

The "Hollywood Marines" And The "Silent Second"

There is no doubt whence comes the nickname the "Hollywood Marines." However, no one can say for sure where the name "Silent Second" derived. Theories abound. Here is one. Unit mottos are designed to not only reflect, but to help build esprit de corps within the current members of an organization. When organizations [individuals] have performed deeds worthy of note, and they have been written in the sands of time and the annals of history, there is no need to boast or brag. It is fact. Thus, the "Silent Second." BUT, just in case there are those who doubt, "Silent Second" is followed closely by "Second to None." And, that leaves no room at the top!

In other words, *we are the best*—and everyone knows it!

Mere braggadocio? One Second World War veteran who served in the Second Division, Battery A, 2nd Platoon, 2nd Special Weapons, Anti Aircraft, 6th Regiment, known as the "Pogey Bait Marines," recalled that at the beginning of the offensive attack against the Japanese at Guadalcanal, only a few small outfits of the Second Division took part in the operation. (See below.) The main forces were in New Zealand and other places training for their turn to take part while the First Division was taking its beating on the front lines. So, the Second Division guns were silent and being used only in training. The rank and file wanted to get in the action, but if they had known of their fate at Tarawa, they would not have been so anxious to have gotten in and lose their lives, as so many did.

Camp Paekakariki. E-2-8 New Zealand, 1943. 1st Wave Tarawa.

So, explained the veteran, it is no disgrace or slap in the face to be called the "Silent Second." It is exactly what they were at first in their role in the war effort to defeat the Japanese army. Their guns were silent no more when they made their mark in history at a place called Tarawa. As the old saying goes, "Silence is golden." So, too, is the reputation of the Second Marine Division.

There is no debate over the Division's other nickname. The term "Hollywood Marines" can be traced back to the 22nd Field Artillery Battalion of the Marine Corps Reserve, which trained at Camp Elliott near San Diego before WWII. The original artillery unit hailed from Los Angeles. Active duty Marines called them "Hollywood Reservists," since many unit members were involved in the movie industry. The name stuck when they were switched to active duty. Strangely enough, many of the active duty Marines became part of the "Hollywood Marines" when the two groups were merged to form the 2nd Marine Brigade. Ultimately, several more active duty units were added to form what is now known as the Second Division. It was commanded by BGen "Barney" Vogel, who was promoted to major general during a ceremony at Marine Corps Recruit Depot, San Diego. The ceremony marked the first time the Division formed on the parade deck. It was by no means the last. Thus began the history of the Second Division, which has long been one of the workhorses of the Marine Corps. Since its inception in 1941, the Division has participated in a wide variety of wartime and peace time operations. Its record is unparalleled in Marine Corps history. Let's take a look to find out why.

WWII

The Second Division did not have to wait long after its inception to see its first action. Shortly after the December 7, 1941, Pearl Harbor bombing, the Second Division began training intensely for operations in the South Pacific. It stayed at Camp Elliott under Spartan conditions. Many members slept outside because of a lack of tents. Showers were not always available. In fact, the only time some of the Marines could take showers was when they visited San Diego on liberty. The conditions prepared them well for the war in the Pacific.

A month after Pearl Harbor, the first elements of the Division set sail for the Pacific Theater, where it provided the first and last Marine Corps units sent into action, the 1st Battalion, 2nd Marines on Florida Island, where it was attached to the First Marine Division, and the 8th Marines on southern Okinawa respectively. The Division participated in several major battles during the four-year war: Guadalcanal, Saipan, Tinian, Tarawa, Okinawa...these were but a few of the places the Marines of the Second Division showed their mettle and brought glory to themselves and the Corps.

Guadalcanal

The first significant stop was Guadalcanal, where the Division took over from the bloodied but unbowed First Division. The combination of the Second Division and the U.S. Army Americal Division and 25th Infantry drove the Japanese off the island, but at a price. A total of 1,187 Second Division Marines were killed or wounded in the Guadalcanal area. What remained of the weary, disease-plagued Division sailed to New Zealand for rest, relaxation—and more training. (Almost 13,000 Division members had confirmed cases of malaria after leaving Guadalcanal.)

Kindness And "Kiwis"

The first ships containing Marines landed in New Zealand in June 1942. The landing began a love affair between U.S. Marines and New Zealanders that exists today. Second Division veterans still make pilgrimages to New Zealand every five years or so and many of the "Kiwis," as the New Zealanders are referred to lovingly, show up at the Second Marine Division Association's annual reunions. Movie aficionados may remember the movie *Battle Cry*, starring Aldo Ray and Van Heflin, which depicted the love affair between the New Zealanders and U.S. Marines.

Let it be emphasized that the Marines were not in New Zealand strictly for social

Taken on a 2-week hike through the hills around San Diego, CA. 1941.

purposes. There was still a war on, and Guadalcanal was but the first of many battles that had to be fought to wrest significant islands from the Japanese grip. Certainly, the fact that 20,000 New Zealand men were absent from the country to fight in other locations did not go unnoticed by the Marines. Thus, they protected the island and the women—although that did not make a lot of New Zealanders feel particularly safe. Over 1,500 New Zealand women married American servicemen during World War II. Many of them became widows as a result.

Tarawa: The Marine Corps' Finest Hour

MGen Julian C. Smith, the eventual founder of the Second Marine Division Association, assumed command of the Second Division on May 1, 1943. His was not a particularly healthy command. In fact, half the Division was replaced between Guadalcanal and Tarawa. Nevertheless, training continued in New Zealand. The Marines had a job to do—and they intended to do it well.

In October 1943, the Second Division sailed away from New Zealand en route to Tarawa, where it participated in one of the fiercest battles in military history. The

Marines landed on November 20, 1943. For all intents and purposes, the battle lasted three days. The Second Division suffered heavily. Of the 18,088 Marines and sailors who participated in the assault on the island—55 percent of whom were combat veterans—3,166 became casualties. Of those, 48 officers and 846 enlisted men were killed in action. Another 8 officers and 76 enlisted men eventually died of their wounds. It was a terrible price to pay. The Division's reward was a trip to Parker Ranch on Hawaii, more training—and more costly battles.

Shivering On Hawaii

The Second Division Marines who descended on Hawaii after the Tarawa battle appeared strange to the natives. Many were without adequate clothing. They could not have come at a worse time. The weather was cold, there was not enough water, despite the seemingly never-ending rain, and sleeping bags and blankets were in short supply. The Division really did not have enough supplies to make up for the shortages. Nevertheless, it survived, grew healthy—as healthy as a Division can get in wartime—and trained. Soon, the Second Division embarked again and headed for its next battle—which proved even more costly than Tarawa.

Saipan And Tinian

On June 15, 1944, the Second and Fourth Divisions made an assault landing on the island of Saipan. Four days later, the island was "under control." Once again, the Division suffered heavy losses: 73 officers and 1,029 enlisted men killed in action. Another 6 officers and 205 enlisted men died of their wounds. Moreover, 256 officers and 4,946 enlisted men sustained wounds. The total was 6,515, double the numbers of Tarawa. About two months later, the Marines captured Tinian, immediately south of Saipan. The Second Division sustained 1,077 more casualties. That was the bad news; the good news was that only one more major battle lay ahead for the Division.

Okinawa

By previous battle standards, Okinawa was not particularly costly for the Second Division. It suffered a total of 450 casualties, 58 of whom (1 officer and 57 enlisted men) were either killed in action or died later of their wounds. Okinawa turned out to be the Division's last major battle of the war. All totaled, it sustained 12,395 casualties—and etched its name indelibly in the annals of Marine Corps history.

A Military And Marine Milestone

The history of the Second Division cannot be told in all its glory without mentioning that in 1942, the Corps began recruiting African-American Marines. The Marine Corps had wasted little time after President Franklin Delano Roosevelt issued Executive Order No. 8802 on June 25, 1941, which allowed African-Americans to serve in the armed forces. The Marine Corps did not welcome the order with open arms. In fact, the Marine Corps Commandant at the time, Major General Thomas Holcomb, told the General Board of the Navy that "there would be a definite loss of efficiency in the Marine Corps" if it had to take "Negroes." Nevertheless, he relented. On April 7, 1942, the Marine Corps agreed to admit African-Americans. Four-and-a-half months later, August 26, 1942, 13 of the first 1,200 African-American Marine Corps recruits arrived at a place called Montfort Point, North Carolina. A new era in USMC history began that day.

It did not take long before the African-American Marines tested their combat skills. They helped their white counterparts beat back a Japanese counter attack on Saipan on June 15, 1944. Sadly, PFC Leroy Seals became a casualty that day. He became the first African-American Marine to die of wounds in battle. Shortly thereafter, the new Commandant of the Marine Corps, LtGen Alexander A Vandegrift, declared "The Negro Marines are no longer on trial. They are Marines period." From that day forward, the history of African-American and other Marines became one and the same.

Back To Lejeune—And Home

Members of the Second Division spent a brief time in the occupation of Japan after the war ended. Shortly thereafter, the Division was reassigned to Camp Lejeune, which has been its home ever since. Few Second Division Marines can say that they have stayed there for any great length of time, however.

Here, There, And Everywhere

There is hardly a time when Second Division Marines are not involved in peacekeeping missions somewhere. That has been the case since the end of WWII. The list of places they have served includes Palestine, Lebanon, Guantanamo, Dominican Republic, Beirut, Grenada, Panama, Somalia, Haiti, Bosnia, and Zaire. The Second Division maintains a constant presence in the Caribbean and Mediterranean Seas. Some members were absorbed into other divisions and fought in Korea and Vietnam. In 1991, the Division fought in Operation Desert Storm and wreaked havoc with the Iraqi forces. Let's look at a few highlights of the post-WWII years.

The Second Marine Division in the Post World War II Period 1945-1949

There have been many stories told about experiences in the Second Marine Division during World War II in the Pacific arena. There has not been much said about the division or its units during the post war period. This narrative should give all members of the Second Marine Division Association some information of the actions and whereabouts from late 1945 to 1949.

On August 6, 1945, the U.S. delivered the first atomic bomb to be exploded in combat on Hiroshima. Three days later, it dropped the second, this time on Nagasaki. On August 14, 1945, President Truman announced that a cease fire was in effect and that the war had ended. General MacArthur was designated SCAP and given authority to accept the surrender of Japan for the governments of the U.S., Republic of China, United Kingdom, and USSR. For the first time in four years, the Second Division was free from combat. It was not an ending, though; it was simply the beginning of a new type of mission. On September 2, 1945, Japan surrendered formally to the Allied Powers on board the *USS Missouri* in Tokyo Bay. The Marine Detachments of the *Missouri,* as well as Marine officers from Fleet Marine Force, Pacific, the staffs of CinCPac-/CinCPoa, and the Third Fleet were present.

Still On Saipan—But Not For Long

By the end of the war, the Marine Corps had reached a peak strength of 485,833. The major Marine ground commands in the Pacific consisted of Fleet Marine Force, Pacific, at Oahu, the III Amphibious Corps on Guam, and the V Amphibious Corps on Maui. The Second Division was based at Saipan. While the Marines waited, an advance reconnaissance party from the V Amphibious Corps—led by Colonel Walter W. Wensinger, Corps Operations Officer, and consisting of key staff officers of the Corps and the Second Marine Division— arrived at Nagasaki to prepare for the landing of the V Amphibious Corps troops supported by Army units.

On September 23, 1945, Major General Harry Schmidt, V Amphibious Corps com-

Survey Section. H & S Btry, 4th BN, 10th Marines 2nd Marine Division. Front Row L to R: Ward, Spillman, McGregor, Crofford, Bayliss. Back Row L to R: Ferry, Mead, Arnold, Vevsteeq, Bain. 1942, Camp Pahatinual. Wellington, New Zealand.

mander, established his command post ashore at Sasebo and took control of the Second and Fifth Marine Divisions. The 2nd and 6th Marines, Second Marine Division, landed simultaneously on the east and west sides of the harbor at Nagasaki for occupation duty and relieved the Marine detachments from the cruisers *USS Biloxi* and *Wichita,* which had been serving as security guards. The next day, General Walter Krueger, commander of the U.S. Sixth Army, assumed control of all forces ashore. The remainder of the Second Marine Division landed at Nagasaki.

Administrative changes occurred at a rapid rate. On October 1, 1945, a U.S. Army task force occupying Kanoya airfield—the only major Allied unit ashore in Kyushu other than the Second and Fifth Marine Divisions—was transferred to the command of the V Amphibious corps from the FEAF. On October 4th, the V Amphibious Corps changed the boundary between the Second and Fifth Marine Divisions to include Omura in the Second Division zone. The Fifth Division security detachment at the Marine air base was relieved by the 3d Battalion, 10th Marines, and the detachment returned to parent control.

By October 13th, all units of the 8th Marines, Second Marine Division, had established themselves in and around Kumamoto and begun the process of inventory and disposition. On October 27, the 2nd Battalion, 2nd Marines, Second Marine Division, assigned to the eastern half of Kagoshima, arrived at Kanoya from Nagasaki and relieved the U.S. Army task force there. Two days later, a motor convoy carrying the major part of the 1st Battalion, 8th Marines, Second Marine Division, moved from Kumamoto to Kagoshima City to assume control of western Kagoshima. On October 30, the 2nd Battalion, 2nd Marines, Second Marine Division, assumed operational control of the Army Air Force detachment manning the emergency field at Kanoya from a battalion of the 32d division, USA, and the battalion prepared for return to Sasebo to rejoin its regiment.

Second Division troops continued to move here and there—all anxious to return home to the United States. On January 31, 1946, the Second Marine Division relieved the 32d Division, USA, of duties in Yamaguchi, Fukuoka, and Oita Prefectures. At this time, the prefectural duties of the

major Marine units were: 2nd Marines, Oita and Miyazaki; 6th Marines, Yamaguchi, Fukuoka, and Oita; 8th Marines, Kumamoto and Kagoshima; 10th Marines, Nagasaki. Finally, by mid-year, they received the long-awaited orders to go home. On June 13, 1946, the 2nd Marines—responsible for the Oita and Miyazaki Prefectures—left Sasebo, Kyushu, bound for Norfolk, Virginia. The 8th Marines followed soon after. As quickly as they had moved into Japan, they moved out.

On June 24, 1946, the Second Marine Division headquarters left Kyushu for the U.S. A week later, the 6th Marines' Headquarters and Service Company and Weapons Company departed Sasebo, Kyushu. By July 2, 1946, the major elements of the Second Marine Division had departed for the U.S.

On July 12th, the Second Marine Division docked at Norfolk, Virginia, from Japan and proceeded to Camp Lejeune, North Carolina, where it arrived the following day. The reason it was sent to Lejeune was simple: the war may have been over, but threats to world security were not gone.

National security concerns were focused on the expanding communist threat in Eu-

WPNS Co. 6th Marines. Left Front; Arthur Tully, Joseph Pritz & Stanley Schreck. Rear left; Bert Spooner, Mike Taglarini. At Camp Tarawa, Hawaii. Spring of 1944.

rope and the Mediterranean region. In response, the Second Division was assigned to Camp Lejeune on the east coast of the United States instead of returning to southern California. Lejeune was an ideal place for the Second Marine Division to launch expeditions to the Mediterranean and Caribbean regions when needed. Many such an expedition set sail for both regions in the ensuing years.

Home—But Just For A Visit

The Second Division underwent changes as it settled in at Lejeune. On September 2, 1946, the 4th Marines (Reinf) (less one battalion) was returned to the U.S. from China to join the Second Marine Division at Camp Lejeune. Then, in a significant event on December 16, 1946, Fleet Marine Force, Atlantic, under the operational control of the Commander in Chief, Atlantic Fleet, was activated by the Commanding General, Second Marine Division, who assumed its command.

Any members of the Second Division who thought they would be rooted at Camp Lejeune for a long time were sadly mistaken. Between January 13 and March 28, 1947, the Second Division, commanded by Major General Thomas E. Watson, participated in amphibious maneuvers with the Fleet in Caribbean waters. Less than a month after their return, on April 15, 1947, Commandant A. A. Vandegrift announced that the Marine Corps was being reorganized into more flexible units and armed with more powerful infantry weapons. Marine units would be able to disperse by air, surface vessels, or submarines without administrative delay or loss of firepower. And disperse they did—often.

The Marine Corps and its Second Division began a new life after WWII. The reorganization of the Fleet Marine Force to gain mobility and peacetime utility was effected. Under the new "J" Tables of Organization, the new FMF eliminated the infantry regimental echelon within the brigade and division and provided for battalions. The new tables provided for a more economical use of service personnel. This translated into travel and a new approach to peacekeeping, one component of which was was what Second Marine Division members lovingly refer to as "Med Cruises."

The First Med Cruise Sets Sail

In January 1948, the Second Marines (Reinf) left Morehead City, North Carolina,

Japanese light machine gun, Okinawa. Courtesy of Don Tesiero.

on the Navy transports *USS Bexar* and *Montague* for assignment to ships operating in Mediterranean waters. This move initiated the Marine Corps policy of maintaining an air/ground force with the Sixth Fleet in the Mediterranean. Fleet Admiral Chester A. Nimitz implied the Marines sent to the Mediterranean served as a warning to Yugoslavia that the 5,000 U. S. Army troops in the Free Territory of Trieste were not to be molested. The Marines were to be divided among the carrier *USS Midway* and the cruisers *Portsmouth, Providence,* and *Little Rock.* Other Second Division units followed. For example, between February 20th and June 28th, 1948, the 8th Marines (Reinf) took on their role of the landing force of the Sixth Fleet in the Mediterranean. The Division rotated troops frequently in the Mediterranean region. The strategy proved almost immediately to be a wise one.

On July 18, 1948, a provisional Marine Consular guard was detached from the 21st Marines on board the *USS Kearsarge* at Tripoli and sent to Jerusalem to protect the U. S. Consul General there. That was by no means the first time Marines would visit the area. In fact, as subsequent events proved, the Palestine region would prove to be active—and deadly—for members of the Second Division. Before the region became a battleground for the Division, however, other units began frequenting the Caribbean. On March 2nd, 1949, U. S. Marines, soldiers, and three Canadian platoons made a landing on Vieques Island in the Caribbean as part of what was up until that point the largest postwar amphibious exercise.

(Note—The Canadian Company had been previously attached to the 8th Marines to prepare for and participate as a unit in FLEX-49.) That area, too, proved to be active for the Second Division as future events unfolded.

A World At War—Again

While Second Division Marines sailed to and fro in the Caribbean and Mediterranean Seas, the world returned to war. In 1950, a "police action" broke out in Korea which occupied the attention of the United States. Although many troops were dispatched, including large numbers of Marines, the Second Division's role was limited. The Division per se did not participate. Many members were attached to First Division units, where they performed with honor. The next major event involving the Second Division did not occur until November 1, 1956, when the Third Battalion, Second Marine Regiment helped evacuate Americans from Alexandria, Egypt. Less than two years later, the Division was back in the Middle East. On July 15, 1958, Battalion Landing Team crossed the beaches at Beirut, Lebanon. These episodes were the beginning of a series of incidents requiring the Division's services. Mobility became the Second Division's middle name—and its strongpoint.

From The Halls Of Montezuma To The Shores Of Tripoli...And Cuba...And Grenada...And...

The Second Division Marines in the 1960s were an active bunch. On October

2nd Platoon L. Co. 3rd Battalion. 8th Marine 2nd Division. Taken on Tinian after the battle. Jack Quinn is 7th from left on top row.

27, 1962, the Division and the 2nd Marine Aircraft Wing deployed during the Cuban missile crisis. In April 1965, 3/6 was lifted by helicopter from the *USS Boxer* to secure the American Embassy in Santo Domingo, Dominican Republic. These were but preludes to a growing number of small—but significant—missions over the next few years.

Tragedy In Beirut

October 1983 was a particularly sad month for the Marine Corps in general and the Second Division in particular. An event on October 23rd brought home in startling fashion what all Marines keep locked up in the backs of their minds: death is always an imminent possibility for peacekeepers. As do all servicemen and women, Marines run the risk of injury in death as part of their duties. Seldom, though, do peacetime Marines die by the hundreds. Unfortunately, death was the fate of 273 1st Battalion, 8th Marines on October 23, 1983, when a terrorist drove a truck carrying gas-enhanced explosives into their barracks in Beirut, Lebanon. The incident devastated not only the Division, but the nation as well. The Marines who sacrificed their lives will always be remembered. There exists a living memorial of 273 Bradford Pear trees along Camp Lejeune Boulevard, one for each Marine who died in Beirut. They serve as reminders that keeping the peace can be—and is—fraught with danger. Yet, such untimely deaths do not deter Second Division Marines, nor their counterparts throughout the Corps, from protecting the United States. That has always been their mission.

No doubt it will continue to be—and they will do it well.

Two Days Later, It's Back In Action

Only two days after their comrades died, Battalion Landing Team 2/8 landed at the eastern Caribbean island of Grenada at five a.m. to rescue 800 college students stranded there. Then, on December 20, 1989, the Second Marine Division began combat operations as part of the aptly named Task Force Semper Fidelis in Panama against General Manuel Noriega's forces. Such actions grew routine to Second Division units from that point on. Marines of the 22nd Marine Expeditionary Unit arrived via air in Monrovia, Liberia, on August 5, 1990, to help evacuate personnel from the American Embassy. On January 4, 1991, Marines evacuated 260 U.S. and foreign citizens from the American Embassy, Mogadishu, and Somalia, during Operation Eastern Exit. Three months later, on April 7th, the 24th Marine Expeditionary Unit participated in Operation Provide Comfort, a multinational relief effort to aid Kurdish refugees on the Iraq-Turkish border. That Marines were operating in the area at the time was no surprise. After all, the Second Division was one of the main participants in the legendary Desert Storm operation, which had begun only a few months earlier.

Desert Storm—
A War To End All Wars

Most of the Second Division was deployed to the Middle East in 1991 to com-

bat Iraqi forces. Units had started for the region as early as September 1990, when the First Battalion, Second Marine Regiment arrived in Saudi Arabia in support of Desert Shield—four months before actual hostilities began. Not all of the Division was available for duty in Desert Storm, though. As is often the case with the Second Division nowadays, its members are separated in diverse places. For example, on December 16, 1991, approximately 300 members of the Eighth Marines arrived at Guantanamo Bay, Cuba, to participate in Haitian humanitarian efforts for 6,000 refugees. The constant activity, though, is a blessing for Division members. At least they will never get bored. They certainly did not in Kuwait.

The first ground action in Desert Storm took place on January 17, 1991, when Division artillery fired rounds for thirteen minutes to eliminate an Iraqi logistics site and truck park. Twelve days later, ground troops swung into action. Second Division Marines skirmished against dozens of Iraqi vehicles located across their front. One Marine, Corporal Edmond Willis, a TOW gunner with the 2d Light Armor Infantry Battalion, recorded the first ground combat kill of the war by destroying an enemy tank. He added a second shortly thereafter. There was a lull in the action after that day.

Division Marines spent much of their time between January 29th and February 24th clearing mine fields and destroying long range targets. They did find time on January 29th to participate in the first major ground action of the "war" when they repulsed an Iraqi mechanized battalion. Their next major taste of action took place on February 24, 1991 when, with massive air support, First Battalion, 6th Marines, First Battalion, Eighth Marines, and Second Battalion, Second Marines initiated an assault on Iraqi forces in Kuwait. The Marine Corps Hymn blared over loudspeakers as the troops launched their highly successful assault. They, along with their First Division counterparts, breached Iraqi mine fields and spearheaded the Desert Storm ground offensive.

As the day ended, the Iraqis were in a serious state of disrepair. Large numbers of their vehicles and personnel were destroyed courtesy of the Second Division, whose losses amounted to one member killed in action and twelve others wounded. Three days later, Division Marines participated in their last action of the short war when they killed Iraqi snipers and other soldiers firing rockets at them. They destroyed an ammunition truck in the bargain. After that, they spent their time improving their positions, setting up firing ranges, and maintaining equipment in anticipation of further action. That action never came.

A Triumphant Return

The Division shipped captured equipment back to Camp Lejeune as trophies of war. Quickly, the troops also came back to their home base after a withdrawal to Saudi Arabia. By May 1991, the Division was home again, basking in its glory. Amazingly, almost 14,000 Iraqi soldiers had surrendered to Division personnel in what amounted to a four-day war. As usual, though, the Division paid a price. Six Marines were killed in action and 38 were wounded. Compared to other wars involving the Second Division, that was a small price to pay. But, one death is one too many to Second Division Marines, as it is to members of all the American military services.

The Beat Goes On

This brief history does not pretend to capture the full glorious history of the Second Marine Division. As you read this, Division members are involved in a variety of activities designed to keep their skills sharp and America free. From time to time they will perform heroic deeds that keep them in the limelight and let Americans know the Second Marine Division is working to protect their freedom. One such event was the daring rescue by a Second Division unit which rescued Air Force Captain Scott O'Grady from behind enemy lines in Bosnia on June 8, 1995. But, the Second Marine Division does not seek glory. Glory comes naturally to the Division, one of the finest fighting units in United States Marine Corps history. It has been since its inception in 1941—and will continue to be until peace becomes a reality throughout the world. May that day come soon. Until it does, however, the Second Marine Division will be there to do its part.

Kuwait March 1991. Left (standing) Lcpl. D. Wahl, Left (sitting) Cpl. Ancheta, Center (with glasses) Cpl. G. Ashe, Right (back) Lcpl. Hall.

Saudi Arabia. February 1991. G Co. 2/2. Typical living quarters during Desert Storm.

Second Marine Division Association
Association History and Information

PURPOSE OF SMDA:

The Association has two main purposes for membership. First, it is a means of re-establishing and/or maintaining contact with those who served with the 2D Marine Division or attached units. Second, to support a unique Scholarship Fund to assist in the education of dependents of the 2D Marine Division personnel.

MEMBERSHIP ELIGIBILITY:

The Association is incorporated as a civilian veterans organization open to anyone who served or Is serving in the 2D Marine Division or attached units or units in direct support of the Division. The annual dues are $15.00 and Life Membership is $100.00.

STATE CHAPTER
MEMBER ELIGIBILITY:

The By-Laws of the Second Marine Division Association cover State Chapters under Article XIII. Article XIII (c) provides "All Active members of organizations authorized by Article XIII must be members in good standing of the Second Marine Division Association" After the documents have been approved by the State and presented and approved by the National Staff, a State Charter will be issued. Chapter dues are set by each Chapter.

BACKGROUND SMDA:

The 2D Marine Division was formed early in 1941 and has served with distinction since that date in many areas including the recent action in the Persian Gulf. The 2D Marine Division is the direct descendant of the 21) Marine Brigade which was activated on July 1, 1936 and saw service in China in 1937 and 1938. As the prospect of war increased and the Marine Corps expanded, division sized organizations were created. Accordingly, the 2D Marine Division was officially activated on February 1, 1941 at Marine Corps Base, San Diego, Calif., dropping its earlier designa-tion as the 2D Marine Brigade. Individuals who served or are serving with the 2D Marine Division - an efficient, reliable fighting unit, seldom matched in military annals - are justifiably proud of their Division's accomplishments in the many battles of WWII, Peacetime, Cuban Crisis, Dominican Republic Intervention, Lebanon, Grenada and the Persian Gulf. Some of the Esprit de Corps of the USMC remained in each of them. The accomplishments were accompanied with inescapable loss of lives of thousands of our country's proudest and most honorable men. The Second Marine Division Association was created in order to honor the memory of the men of the 2D Marine Division who have given their lives in defense of this Nation and all men and women who have served under its colors since 1941. Some units of the Division served in all parts of the world many years before the forming of the Division. The USMC is built on tradition and heritage and so is the Association.

The Association Seal, as it appears on our stationery and publications, is the copyright property of the Association and was approved by our founder General Julian Smith. The Association is a national civilian veterans organization and was so incorporated as a non-profit organization. We do not use the Globe, Anchor and Eagle of the US Marine Corps on our official stationery but use our Association Seal. We are all former Marines, or attached, and have a lasting love for the Marine Corps, but we are a civilian organization.

ASSOCIATION HEADQUARTERS:

Camp Lejeune, NC, has been the home of the 21) Marine Division since July 1946. The Headquarters of the Association has been located on the Marine Corps Base, Camp Lejeune since the fall of 1989. The SMOA uses the facility known as the Marine Corps Base Historical Reading Room and is located in Building 1220 Marine Corps Base, Camp Lejeune, North Carolina. The mailing address is:

Second Marine Division Association
P.O. Box 8180
Camp Lejeune, NC 28547
Phone (910) 451-3167

The office is under the supervision of the Executive Secretary, Col. C.W. Van Horne, USMC (Ret). He is assisted by Ms. Erin Winner. Visitors are always welcome.

EXECUTIVE SECRETARY:

This position was created at the National Assembly in Knoxville, TN in 1989. Col. C.W. Van Horne, USMC (Ret) retired from the Marine Corps and joined the Association October 1, 1991. He has turned our National office into a National Headquarters. Executive Secretary Van Horne performs his duties under the direction and supervision of the National Staff and in consultation with the Association's President or Adjutant. Secretary Van Horne has the expertise and administrative background to be the ideal fit for the Executive Secretary's position. In addition to his many and varied military duties in 30 years of service he held several management positions. He received his Master of Science Degree in Management in 1973.

ANNUAL REUNION AND
GENERAL ASSEMBLY:

This well attended event moves to various regions of the US each year and the membership has expressed an overwhelming desire for it to be held just after the Labor Day week-end. The National Staff solicits invitations from local Chapters and then selects a site that falls in the parameters of the ByLaws of the Association. Details are carried in "Follow-Me."

BIRTHDAY CELEBRATION:

This event to celebrate the forming of the 2D Marine Division February 1, 1941 is held annually at Camp Lejeune. The Association Members are guests of the 2D Marine Division and participate in the celebration ceremonies. The National Staff has a staff meeting during the visit. The Association Military Awards are presented during the Anniversary Ceremonies. The Executive Secretary coordinates the Association activities with the 2D Marine Division.

"FOLLOW ME" NEWSLETTER:

The association newsletter carries reunion, meetings and SMDA news. The Editor welcomes news items. The newsletter has been upgraded and expanded. Executive Secretary Van Horne is becoming more involved and is bringing Camp Lejeune and current Marine news to each edition. The advertising of the PX Souvenir section has been expanded. Art Sharp, Editor, coordinates the assembly of all items.

SOUVENIR SHOP:

The PX Souvenir Shop is located at the National Headquarters. A mail order form is included in "Follow Me. "Additional items are constantly being added. The PX Souvenir Shop is an important part of each reunion.

LIFE MEMBERSHIP CERTIFICATES:

Certificates are given to members when they join as life members of the Association. The Headquarters of the Association has a supply of these that can be furnished to State Chapters. The State Chapter name can then be printed above the Second Marine Division Association for State Chapter use. These can be given by the State Chapters to Chapter Members when they join as Life Members.

SMDA - CHAPLAINCY:

The Association Chaplaincy is organized and operates under the supervision of The Association Chaplain and operates on four levels: National, Chapter, Group and At-Large. The reference is the USMC Operational Handbook FMFM-5-6 "Religious Ministries in the Fleet Marine Force - August 29, 1991." The mission is to bring God to Association members and members to God. The Chaplains work very closely with the 2D Marine Division Chaplains. The services are a very important part of all Meetings and Reunions. They are equally important on the Chapter level and

each Chapter should have a Chaplain. Condolence letters and telephone calls to communicate the Association's sympathy to those whose loved ones have passed on are handled by the Chaplaincy.

SMDA - STATIONERY:

Association stationery has been approved by the past several Administrations. The shoulder patch of the 2D Division on the left side with the Association Seal on the right. We are a veterans organization, and the stationery assists us in accomplishing this. We are also endeavoring to solicit younger members and want to present a standard business format. For Chapter use the name of the State Chapter can be printed in the center under "Founded by Lt. Gen. Julian Smith USMC 1949."

NOMINATING COMMITTEE:

This is a very important committee as they are the ones who select and recommend the slate of officers to be elected at the National Assembly Each Chapter supplies a delegate and an alternate to serve on the committee. The Nominating Committee Chairman is appointed by the President. The purpose of the Committee is to attempt to get the best qualified people to serve on the National Staff. The Chairman works very hard to set down guidelines to attempt to present the best slate to the National Assembly for the election. Correspondence and recommendations are received during the year. Meetings are held at the Camp Lejeune gathering and at the Annual Reunion. If at all possible all regions should be represented.

SECOND MARINE DIVISION ASSOCIATION ENDOWMENT FUND, INC.:

A corporation that operates under the umbrella of the Association. The Fund is operating under the Chairmanship of John R Nixon. A Board of Directors has been approved of some distinguished people. The purpose is to solicit major tax deductible funds - the corporation has been approved as tax exempt by the IRS. The President of the SMDA is a non-voting member of the board.

BOARD OF DIRECTORS:

Gen. Alfred M. Gray USMC (Ret); Mr. Robert L. Groves; Mr. Robert L. Hemmings; B. Gen. James Howarth USMC (Ret); Mr. Zell Miller; Mr. John P. Nixon; Mr. Eddie Owen; Mr. James Seale; Mr.

Robert H. Schultz; Mr. Arthur G. Sharp; and Col. C. W. Van Home USMC (Ret)

SMDA - MEMORIAL SCHOLARSHIP FUND:

The Board of Trustees administers the awarding of scholarships as provided by Article XIV - Scholarship Fund - of the Association By-Laws. The Fund is to be administered by a Board of Trustees, to consist of five members in good standing of the Second Marine Division Association appointed by the President and approved by the National Staff. The Trustees are to report annually to the Annual Assembly and to the National Staff upon request. The funds are requested from the Association Treasurer.

BOARD OF TRUSTEES:

Darrell B. Albers, Chairman; William E. Ashley, Member; Ralph Feck, Member; John M. O'Connor, Member; Steve Judd, Liaison to National Staff; B. Gen James Howarth, USMC (Ret), Chairman Emeritus; and Martin T. McNulty, Member

NATIONAL MARINE CORPS COUNCIL:

Past Judge Advocate Bill Rogal serves as the representative of the SMDA on the Council. The NMCC represents all the Marine Corps civilian organizations.

FINANCES:

The finances of the SMDA, Memorial Scholarship Funds, Endowment Fund, Inc. are handled by the treasurer. He seeks counsel from outside sources on investments, bonds, etc. All checks and transfer of funds written on any SMDA account require two signatures. At present the Treasurer, President and Adjutant have authorized signatures on file. The Executive Secretary has an operating account at Camp Lejeune and coordinates his activities very closely with the Treasurer.

SMDA AWARDS:

The Association presents two types of awards, Military and Civilian. The Military Awards are presented to members of the 2D Marine Division and the Civilian Awards to individuals or organizations who have performed outstanding or meritorious service for the Association.

SMDA CIVILIAN AWARDS:

These Awards are the appointment of the Association President. The Executive

Secretary assists in preparing the certificates and the Ladies pendant. The Awards are presented at the Annual Reunion. The Ladies Award is presented at the Ladies Luncheon and the Certificate of Award is presented to each recipient at the Men's or Ladies' Luncheon. The Distinguished Service Award is presented at the formal closing banquet.

THE HARRIOTTE B. "HAPPY" SMITH DISTINGUISHED LADIES AWARD:

In 1995, the national staff elected to change the name of this award to the Harriotte B. "Happy" Smith award, in honor of our First Lady Emeritus, and wife of our founder, General Julian Smith. The Ladies Award, originated in 1956, consists of a gold pendant on a gold chain. Also, beginning in 1995 the ladies honored will receive a framed Harriotte B. "Happy" Smith, Certificate of Award. The award is presented to individual ladies in recognition of their support of the SMDA. It is presented annually at the National Assembly.

The Certificate of Award: The Certificate of Award is presented by the Second Marine Division Association President to individuals and organizations that have performed an outstanding achievement and meritorious service for the Second Marine Division Association. This Award has been presented annually since 1956.

DISTINGUISHED SERVICE AWARD:

The Distinguished Service Award is the highest award any individual or organization can receive from the Second Marine Division Association. This Award is presented by the President, on behalf of the membership of the Second Marine Division Association to an Officer, Committee Chairman, or National Staff Officer who in the performance of his assigned duties provided exemplary service in the attainment of the Association's objectives. It is indeed a treasured possession of those few who have been selected to receive ft. This prestigious award was first given in 1987. Usually only two, but a maximum of three, are given annually.

The Distinguished Service Award is of parchment paper and is lettered in "Old English," or Calligraphic printing. This is also true. of the Certificate of Award. These parchment awards are in the custody of the Executive Secretary.

SMDA MILITARY AWARDS:

These awards are presented at the Annual Anniversary Celebration, February 1, at Camp Lejeune. The Commanding General 2D Marine Division presents the awards to the recipients, assisted by the Association President. It is the responsibility of the Executive Secretary to obtain the selections from the 2D Marine Division and to provide proper awards. The Commanding General makes the selections.

THE TARAWA AWARD:

The Tarawa Award is presented annually to the officer selected by the commanding general as the outstanding platoon commander of the 2D Marine Division for leadership excellence. The recipient receives a Marine Corps K-Bar fighting knife. When first offered by the Association, it was presented to the outstanding drill instructor of the year, or the "DI of the Year" in 1956 and 1957. It was not presented in 1958 and 1959. From 1960 until 1990 it was presented each year to the Squad Leader of the squad in the Second Marine Division that placed first in the "Unit Combat Marksmanship Competition."

THE MAJOR GENERAL CLAYTON B. VOGEL AWARD:

The Major General Clayton B. Vogel Award was established to the memory of the first Commanding General of the 2D Marine Division. The Clayton B. Vogel Award has been presented annually, since 1982, to a staff non-commissioned officer of the 2D Marine Division selected by the commanding general for leadership excellence. The recipient receives an NCO sword.

THE LIEUTENANT GENERAL JULIAN C. SMITH AWARD:

The Lieutenant General Julian C. Smith Award was established in honor of the founder of the Second Marine Division Association. The Julian C. Smith Award has been presented annually, since 1978, to a non-commissioned officer of the 2D Marine Division selected by the commanding general for leadership excellence. The recipient receives a Marine Corps K-Bar fighting knife.

THE JOHN HENRY BALCH AWARD:

The John Henry Balch Award is named for Navy Pharmacists' Mate First Class John H. Balch. During World War 1, while serving with the Sixth Marine Regiment in France, Balch distinguished himself by exhibiting exceptional gallantry, intrepidity and bravery in the face of enemy fire. He was awarded the Medal of Honor. This Award is presented to a Navy Corpsman who is selected for outstanding performance of duties. The selection is made by 2D Marine Division personnel, but the recipient must be a Navy Corpsman. The award has been presented since 1986. The recipient receives a Marine Corps K-Bar Knife.

Each of the recipients of the Military Awards receives a Life Membership in the Second Marine Division Association. The Executive Secretary works very closely with the Commanding General's office in the selection process and maintains the records of the recipients.

The Military Awards were not made in 1991 due to the 2D Marine Division being deployed because of the Persian Gulf War.

SMDA MARINE OF THE QUARTER AND NCO OF THE QUARTER:

The Executive Secretary presents an NCO sword to the NCO of the Quarter and a K-Bar knife to the Marine of the Quarter. The recipients. are selected by the Division and the awards are presented at a parade or battalion formation. They also receive a life membership in the SMDA.

MEMORANDUM OF UNDERSTANDING:

Negotiations of a contract (Memorandum of Understanding) with the Camp Lejeune Base is one of the more important things that Executive Secretary Van Home has accomplished for the Association. The Memorandum of Understanding (MOU) sets out the conditions under which the Second Marine Division Association (SMDA) is afforded access to and use of, facilities owned by the Marine Corps Base, Camp Lejeune. Our duties under the agreement are to assist in the establishment of the Marine Corps Base Historical Reading Room in furtherance in the Marine Corps Base, historical program. Agreement Is signed by the President of the Association and Commanding General Marine Corps Base. Original is on file in Association Headquarters.

AUTHORITY TO OPERATE AS A PRIVATE ORGANIZATION AT CAMP LEJEUNE, NORTH CAROLINA:

This letter initiated by Secretary Van Horne from the Commanding General, Marine Corps Base, Camp Lejeune (5760/

19 MWR dated December 3, 1991) addressed to Executive Secretary Van Horne grants the SMDA authority to operate as a private organization at Camp Lejeune, North Carolina. The Letter was, signed by James K. Van Riper, by Direction. Original on file in Association Headquarters Office.

AUTHORIZATION TO CONDUCT BUSINESS - SOUVENIR ITEMS:

This letter agreement initiated by Secretary Van Home from the Commanding General, Marine Corps Bass, Camp Lejeune (5370 PERS/mlu 15th January 1992) addressed to Executive Secretary Van Home grants the SMDA authority to conduct a souvenir business (PX) on Base. The Letter Agreement was signed by J. W. Hotry, by Direction and by C. W. Van Horne. Original is on file in Association Headquarters Office.

The 20 Marine Division Patch: The 2D Marine Division shoulder patch was authorized for wear by units which served with or were attached to the division in the Pacific during World War 11. Designed and approved in late 1943, the insignia is in the official Marine Corps colors of scarlet and gold. The insignia displays a spearhead-shaped scarlet background with a hand holding aloft a lighted gold torch. A scarlet numeral "2" is superimposed upon the torch, and the torch and hand is encircled by five white stars in the arrangement of the Southern Cross constellation, under

which the division's first World War If combat took place - at Guadalcanal. The wearing of unit shoulder patches by Marines Was discontinued in 1947.

ELECTED NATIONAL STAFF - STAFF APPOINTED OFFICERS AND COMMITTEE APPOINTMENTS:

All serve without salary compensation except the nominal fee paid to the Executive Secretary National

Staff officers can be reimbursed for telephone, postage, copies, etc., expenses incurred for the SMDA. All National Staff Officers and SMDA employees are bonded. The Elected National Staff Voting Officers are elected by the National Assembly The appointed National Staff Officers and National Committee appointments are made by the President for his term of office. He usually consults with other Staff members prior to the appointments.

Courtesy of K. Dean Hamilton.

Second Marine Division Association
Past Presidents

JULIAN C. SMITH*
1950 - 1951 (Hq-Hq)

JAMES P. RISELEY*
1951 - 1952 (H&S-6)

RAYMOND E. MURRAY
1952 - 1953 (Hq-2-6)

MICHAEL A. BOYLE
1953 - 1954 (Sig-Hq)

HUGO V. GENGE*
1954 - 1955 (H&S-2)

WENDELIN A. MARTIN*
1955 - 1956 (Hq-Hq)

SIDNEY 0. SHAPIRO*
1956 - 1957 (L-3-8)

JAMES E. HOWARTH, JR.
1957 - 1958 (Hq-Hq)

A. GUINN RASSURY
1958 - 1959 (A-1-2)

DAVID M. SHOUP*
1959 - 1960 (Hq-Hq)

ROBERT W. MEGGELIN*
1960 - 1961 (B-Tk)

ALFRED J. PEDERSEN*
1961 - 1962 (Hq-3-2)

JACK E. LEE
1962 - 1963 (Hq-3-2)

MITCHELL A. THOMAS*
1963 - 1964 (H&S-10)

JOHN J. HRUSKA, JR.
1964 - 1965 (Wpns-8)

MEYER I. SEGAL*
1965 - 1966 (A-Tk)

ADOLPH B. PATTERSON*
1966-1967(A-1-6)

WALTER S. BOROWSKI*
1967 - 1968 (E-2-6)

WILLIAM E. SCHEY
1968 - 1969 (H&S-1-10)

GEORGE J. FOX
1969 - 1970 (K-3-8)

HENRY R. MAST
1970-1971 (A-1-18)

GENE HOWARD*
1971 - 1972 (Hq-1-8)

ELDON H. LANDBACK
1972 - 1973 (Hq-Wpns)

HERBERT A. HUDSON
1973 - 1974 (Sig-Hq)

CARL E. EIDSON*
1974 - 1975 (E-2-2)

EDWARD M. CURRAN*
1975 - 1976 (E-2-8)

THEODORE A. JACH*
1976 - 1977 (Hq-1-8)

BERNARD KRUEGER
1977 - 1978 (D-2-18)

PAUL H. TURNER*
1978 - 1979 (C- 1-10)

IRVING L. BIRR
1979 - 1980 (C-1-8)

FRANK R. SLIVOCKA
1980 - 1981 (H-3-10)

ALBERT TIDWELL*
1981 - 1982 (A-1-8)

FRANCIS L DAY*
1982 - 1983 (G-2-8)

PETER A. PAVEL*
1983 - 1984 (E-2-6)

GEORGE T. GARDEN
1984 - 1985 (Wpns-2)

PETER MALOVICH*
1985 - 1986 (B-1-2)

THEODORE SUMMERS*
1986 - 1987 (K-3-8)

T. ROY THAXTON, JR.
1987 - 1988 (M-3-2)

ROBERT L GROVES
1988 - 1989 (G-2-6)

DARRELL B. ALBERS
1989 - 1990 (K-3-8)

JAMES C. COUNTISS
1990 - 1991 (2dCombSerGrp)

GRANT J. JOHNSON
1991 - 1992 (Hq-3-2)

CARROLL D. STRIDER, SR.
1992 - 1993 (A-1-18)

WILLIAM R. SMITH*
1993 -1994 (H&S-2-2)

WILLIAM F. GRAHAM
1994-1995 (B-1-2 - D-2-Med.)

ROBERT L ROBERTS*
1995-1996 (B-1-8&A-1-6)

CARL WIEGEL
1996-1997 (G-2-8)

ROBERT E. (CHICK) LEWIS
1997-1998 (A-1-18)

JACK P. HERNANDEZ*
1998-1999 (K-3-8)

ORVILLE (ED) GAMBLE
1998-1999 (B-1-10)

*Denotes Deceased

Past Reunions

1st	JOHN E. RENTSCH* .... 1950 Washington. D.C. Mayflower Hotel	13th ALVIN SIEGEL* .... 1962 Miami, Florida Americana Hotel
2nd	PHILIP L COCHRAN* .... 1951 Chicago, Illinois Sherman Hotel	14th ELI H. SOBOL* .... 1963 Denver, Colorado Denver Hilton Hotel
3rd	STANLEY R. ROBBINS* .... 1952 Boston, Massachusetts Steller Hotel	15th MEYER I. SEGEL* .... 1964 Atlantic City, New Jersey Claridge Hotel
4th	MICHAEL A. BOYLE* .... 1953 St. Louis, Missouri Steller Hotel	16th WILLIAM E. SCHEY* .... 1965 Chicago, Illinois Sheraton Chicago
5th	ORIEN W, TODD, Jr. .... 1954 San Diego, California U.S. Grant Hotel	17th EDWARD M. CURRAN* .... 1966 Los Angeles, Callibmia Hilton
6th	HOWARD L. STRAHAN* .... 1955 New Orleans, Louisiana Roosevelt Hotel	18th HENRYR.MAST* .... 1967 Winter Park, Florida Langford
7th	SIDNEY 0. SHAPIRO* .... 1956 New York, New York Hotel New Yorker	19th A. GUINN RASBURY* .... 1968 Houston, Texas Shamrock Hilton
8th	LOAL G. ARNOLD* .... 1957 Detroit Michigan Hotel Steller	20th ALFRED J. BORSHEIM .... 1969 Saint Paul, Minnesota Hilton
9th	A. GUINN RASBURY* .... 1958 Houston, Texas Shamrock Hilton Hotel	21st LOUIS BENOFF* .... 1970 Philadelphia, Pennsylvania Marriott
10th	ROBERT W. MEGGELIN* .... 1959 San Francisco, California Marines Memorial Club	22nd CARLOS L. REDDOCK* .... 1971 Biloxi, Mississippi Broadwater Beech
11th	JULIAN C. SMITH* .... 1960 Washington, D.C. Hotel Washington	23rd DALE M. RUSE* .... 1972 San Diago California Royal Inn at the Wharf
12th	ROGER P SCOVILL* .... 1961 Madison, Wisconsin Holiday Inn	24th HOWARD K. McKINSTRY* .... 1973 Madison, Wisconsin Sheraton Inn, Madison

25th HERBERT A. HUDSON 1974
Arlington, Virginia
Stouffers; Inn

26th STEVEJUDD* 1975
San Jose, California
Hyatt House

27th MICHAEL D. MINGOLELLI 1976
Boston, Massachusetts
Howard Johnson Motor Lodge

28th BERNARD KRUEGER* 1977
Springfield, Illinois
Holiday Inn East

29th HOWARD F KEOGH* 1978
Las Vegas, Nevada
Union Plaza Hotel

30th JAMES S. MOORE* 1979
Seattle, Washington
Seattle Hyatt House

31st FRANCIS L. DAY* 1980
Atlanta, Georgia
Century Center Hotel

32nd F WILLIAM BARROWS* 1981
Colorado Springs, Colorado
Antlers Plaza Hotel

33rd GEORGE T GARDEN* 1982
Cleveland, Ohio
Cleveland Marriott: Inn, Beachwood

34th NORMAN S. MOISE* 1983
San Antonio, Tom
Hyatt Regency

35th B. MARCUS RUBINSOHN 1984
Cherry Hill, Now Jersey
Hyatt Cherry HUI

36th HARLAND F"BUCK" DOUD 1985
San Diego, California
Hanalei Hotel

37th PETE PAVEL, JOHN CARRIGAN 1986
Orlando, Florida
Hyatt-Orlando Hotel

38th TOM GLYNN 1987
Minneapolis, Minnesota
City Center Marriott Hotel

39th ROBERT L. GROVES, ARTHUR E. OWEN 1988
Dallas, Texas
Fairmont Hotel

40th ROBERT L. ROBERTS, JOHN F McGIVNEY 1989
Knoxville, Tennessee
Hyatt Regency Hotel

41st DAVID W. DOWDAKIN 1990
Portland, Oregon
Red Lion-Jantzen Beach

42nd WILLIAM H. COLONA, JR. 1991
Norfolk, Virginia
Omni Hotel

43rd CARL N. WIEGEL 1992
Milwaukee, Wisconsin
Grand Milwaukee Hotel

44th WILLIAM J. HARE 1993
Denver. Colorado
Red Lion Hotel

45th FRANK TURSE, WILLIAM P BANNING, JR. 1994
King of Prussia, PA
Sheraton Valley Forge

46th JOHN O'CONNOR,,DARRELL B. ALBERS 1995
Long Beach, CA
Sheraton Long Beach

47th BERT DIEHL, TOM JAMISON 1996
Spokane, WA
Red Lion City Center

48th FRED FLAMMINI, MANNY RAYMOND 1997
Danvers, MA
Tara's Ferncroft Conference Resort

49th ED GAMBLE, JIM COUNTISS 1998
Biloxi, MS
President Casino Broadwater Resort

50th BOB CUNNINGHAM 1999
Kansas City, MO
Hyatt Regency Crown Center

2nd Marine Division Lineage

1936-1940

Activated 1 July 1936 at San Diego, California, as the 2D Marine Brigade, Fleet Marine Force

Deployed during August-September 1937 to Shanghai, China

Relocated during February-April 1938 to San Diego, California

1941-1957

Redesignated 1 February 1941 as the 2D MarineDivision, Fleet Marine Force

Elements deployed to Iceland, July 1941-March 1942

Deployed to the South Pacific during January 1942-January 1943

Participated in the following World War II Campaigns:
GUADALCANAL,
SOUTHERN SOLOMONS,
TARAWA,
SAIPAN,
TINIAN,
OKINAWA

Deployed during September 1945 to Nagasaki, Japan

Participated in the Occupation of Japan, September 1945-June 1946

Relocated during June-July 1946 to Camp Lejeune, North Carolina

1958-1984

Elements participated in the Landings in Lebanon, July-October 1958

Participated in the Cuban Missile Crisis, October-December 1962

Elements participated in the Intervention in the Dominican Republic, April- June 1965

Participated in Numerous Training Exercises throughout the 1970s and into the 1980s

Participated as part of Multinational Peace-Keeping Force in Lebanon, August 1982-February 1984

Elements participated in the landing on Grenada-Carriacou, October-November 1983

Elements participated in operation Just Cause in Panama,
December 1989-January 1990

Participated in Operations Desert Shield and Desert Storm August 1990-May 1991

Unit Citation

THE SECRETARY OF THE NAVY

WASHINGTON

The President of the United States takes pleasure in presenting the PRESIDENTIAL UNIT CITATION to the

SECOND MARINE DIVISION (REINFORCED)

consisting of Division Headquarters, Special Troops (including Company C, lst Corps Medium Tank Battalion), Service Troops, 2nd, 6th, 8th, 10th and 18th Marine Regiments In the Battle of Tarawa, as set forth in the following

CITATION:

"For outstanding performance In combat during the seizure and occupation of the Japanese-held Atoll of Tarawa, Gilbert Islands, November 20 to 24, 1943. Forced by treacherous coral reefs to disembark from their landing craft hundreds of yards off the beach,. the Second Marine Division (Reinforced) became a highly vulnerable target for devastating Japanese fire. Dauntlessly advancing in spite of rapidly mounting losses, the Marines fought a gallant battle against crushing odds, clearing the limited beachheads of snipers and machine guns, reducing powerfully fortified enemy positions and completely annihilating the fanatically determined and strongly entrenched Japanese forces. By the successful occupation of Tarawa, the Second Marine Division (Reinforced) has provided our forces with highly strategic and important air and land bases from which to continue future operations against the enemy; by the valiant fighting spirit of these men, their heroic fortitude under punishing fire and their relentless perseverance in waging this epic battle in the Central Pacific, they have upheld the finest traditions of the United States Naval Service."

For the President,

Acting
Secretary of the Navy

11-1-19

MEDAL OF HONOR

PFC Robert L. Wilson.

The President of the United States takes pride in presenting the MEDAL OF HONOR posthumously to

PRIVATE FIRST CLASS
ROBERT L. WILSON
UNITED STATES MARINE CORPS

for service as set forth in the following

CITATION:

For conspicuous gallantry and intrepidity at the risk of his life above and beyond the call of duty while serving with the Second Battalion, Sixth Marine Division, during action against enemy Japanese forces on Tinian Island, Marianas Group, on 3 August 1944. As one of a group of Marines advancing through heavy underbrush to neutralize isolated points of resistance, Private First Class Wilson daringly preceded his companions toward a pile of rocks where Japanese troops were supposed to be hiding. Fully aware of the danger involved, he was moving forward while the remainder of the squad armed with automatic rifles closed together in the rear, when an enemy grenade landed in the midst of the group. Quick to act, Private First Class Wilson cried a warning to the men and unhesitatingly threw himself on the grenade, heroically sacrificing his own life that the others might live and fulfill their mission. His exceptional valor, courageous loyalty and un-

wavering devotion to duty in the face of grave peril reflect the highest credit upon Private First Class Wilson and the United States Naval Service. He gallantly gave his life for his country.

/S/ HARRY S. TRUMAN

Colonel David M. Shoup

The President of the United Sates takes pride in presenting the MEDAL OF HONOR to

COLONEL DAVID M. SHOUP
UNITED STATES MARINE CORPS

for service as set forth in the following

CITATION:

For conspicuous gallantry and intrepidity at the risk of his own life above and beyond the call of duty as Commanding Officer of all Marine Corps Troops in action against enemy Japanese forces on Betio island, Tarawa Atoll, Gilbert Islands, from November 20 to 22, 1943. Although severely shocked by an exploding enemy shell soon after landing at the pier, and suffering from a serious, painful leg wound which had become infected, Colonel Shoup fearlessly exposed himself to the terrific, relentless artillery, machine-gun and rifle fire from hostile shore emplacements and, rallying his hesitant troops by his own inspiring heroism, gallantly led them across the fringing reefs to charge the heavily fortified island and reinforce our hard-pressed, thinly held lines. Upon arrival on shore, he assumed command of all landed troops and, working without rest under constant, withering enemy fire during the next two days, conducted smashing attacks against unbelievably strong and fanatically defended Japanese positions despite innumerable obstacles and heavy casualties. By his brilliant leadership, daring tactics and selfless devotion to duty, Colonel Shoup was largely responsible for the final, decisive defeat of the enemy, and his indomitable fighting spirit reflects great credit upon the United States Naval Service.

/S/ FRANKLIN D. ROOSEVELT

1stLt. William D. Hawkins

The President of the United States takes pleasure in presenting the CONGRESSIONAL MEDAL OF HONOR posthumously to

FIRST LIEUTENANT
WILLIAM D. HAWKINS
UNITED STATES
MARINE CORPS RESERVE

for service as set forth in the following

CITATION:

For valorous and gallant conduct above and beyond the call of duty as Commanding Officer of a Scout Sniper Platoon attached to the Second Marines, Second Marine Division, in action against Japanese-held Tarawa in the Gilbert Islands, November 20 and 21, 1943. The first to disembark from the jeep lighter, First Lieutenant Hawkins unhesitatingly moved forward under heavy enemy fire at the end of the Betio Pier, neutralizing emplacements in coverage of troops assaulting the main beach positions. Fearlessly leading his men on to join the forces fighting desperately to gain a beachhead, he repeatedly risked his life throughout the day and night to direct and lead attacks on pill boxes and installations with grenades and demolitions. At dawn on the following day, First Lieu-

tenant Hawkins returned to the dangerous mission of clearing the limited beachhead of Japanese resistance, personally initiating an assault on a hostile position fortified by five enemy machine guns, and crawling forward in the face of withering fire, boldly fired point-blank into the loopholes and completed the destruction with grenades. Refusing to withdraw after being seriously wounded in the chest during this skirmish, First Lieutenant Hawkins steadfastly carried the fight to the enemy, destroying three more pill boxes before he was caught in a burst of Japanese shell fire and mortally wounded. His relentless fighting spirit in the face of formidable opposition and his exceptionally daring tactics were an inspiration to his comrades during the most crucial phase of the battle and reflect the highest credit upon the United States Naval Service. He gallantly gave his life for his country.

/S/ FRANKLIN D. ROOSEVELT

PFC Harold G. Epperson

The President of the United States takes pride in presenting the MEDAL OF HONOR posthumously to

PRIVATE FIRST CLASS
HAROLD G. EPPERSON
UNITED STATES MARINE
CORPS RESERVE

for service as set forth in the following

CITATION:

For conspicuous gallantry and intrepidity at the risk of his life above and beyond the call of duty while serving with the First Battalion, Sixth Marines, Second Marine Division, in action against enemy Japanese forces on the island of Saipan the Marianas, on 25 June 1944. With his machine-gun emplacement bearing the full brunt of a fanatic assault initiated by the Japanese under cover of predawn darkness, aggressiveness, fighting furiously in defense of his battalion's position and maintaining a steady stream of devastating fire against rapidly infiltrating hostile troops to aid materially in annihilating several of the enemy and in breaking the abortive attack. Suddenly a Japanese soldier, assumed to be dead, sprang up and hurled a powerful hand grenade into the emplacement. Determined to save his comrades, Private First Class Epperson unhesitatingly chose to sacrifice himself and, diving upon the deadly missile, absorbed the shattering violence of the exploding charge in his body. Stouthearted and indomitable in the face of certain death, Private First Class Epperson fearlessly yielded his own life that his able comrades might carry on the relentless battle against a ruthless enemy, and his superb valor and unfaltering devotion to duty throughout reflect the highest credit upon himself and upon the United States Naval Service. He gallantly gave his life for his country.

/S/ HARRY S. TRUMAN

PFC Harold C. Agerholm

The President of the United States takes pride in presenting the MEDAL OF HONOR posthumously to

PRIVATE FIRST CLASS
HAROLD C. AGERHOLM
UNITED STATES MARINE
CORPS RESERVE

for service as set forth in the following

CITATION:

For conspicuous gallantry and intrepidity at the risk of his life above and beyond the call of duty while serving with the Fourth Battalion, Tenth Marines, Second Marine Division, in action against enemy Japanese forces on Saipan, Marianas Islands, 7 July 1944. When the enemy launched a fierce, determined counterattack against our positions and overran a neighboring artillery battalion, Private First Class Agerholm immediately volunteered to assist in the efforts to check the hostile attack and evacuate our wounded. Locating and appropriating an abandoned ambulance jeep, he re-

peatedly made extremely perilous trips under heavy rifle and mortar fire and single-handedly loaded and evacuated approximately forty-five casualties, working tirelessly and with utter disregard for his own safety during a gruelling period of more than three hours. Despite intense, persistent enemy fire, he ran out to aid two men whom he believed to be wounded Marines, but was himself mortally wounded by a Japanese sniper while carrying out his hazardous mission. Private First Class Agerholm's brilliant initiative, great personal valor and self-sacrificing efforts in the face of almost certain death reflect the highest credit upon himself and the United States Naval service. He gallantly gave his life for his country.

/S/ HARRY S. TRUMAN

SSgt. William J. Bordelon

The President of the United States takes pleasure in presenting the CONGRESSIONAL MEDAL OF HONOR posthumously to

STAFF SERGEANT
WILLIAM J. BORDELON
UNITED STATES MARINE CORPS

for service as set forth in the following

CITATION:

For valorous and gallant conduct above and beyond the call of duty as a member of an Assault Engineer Platoon of the First Battalion, Eighteenth Marines, tactically attached to the Second Marines, Second Marine Division, in action against the Japanese-held Atoll of Tarawa in the Gilbert Islands on November 20, 1943. Landing in the assault waves under withering enemy fire which killed all but four of the men in his tractor, Staff Sergeant Bordelon hurriedly made demolition charges and personally put two pill boxes out of action. Hit by enemy machine-gun fire just as a charge exploded in his hand while assaulting a third position, he courageously remained in action and, although out of demolition, provided himself with a rifle and furnished fire coverage for a group of men scaling the seawall. Disregarding his own serious condition, he unhesitatingly went to the aid of one of his demolition men, wounded and calling for help in the water, rescuing this man and another who had been hit by enemy fire while attempting to make the rescue. Still refusing first aid for himself, he again made up demolition charges and single-handedly assaulted a fourth Japanese machine-gun position but was instantly killed when caught in a final burst of fire from the enemy. Staff Sergeant Bordelon's great personal valor during a critical phase of securing the limited beachhead was a contributing factor in the ultimate occupation of the island and his heroic determination reflects the highest credit upon the United States Naval Service. He gallantly gave his life for his country.

Sgt. Grant F. Timmerman

/S/ FRANKLIN D. ROOSEVELT
The President of the United States takes pride in presenting the MEDAL OF HONOR posthumously to

SERGEANT
GRANT F. TIMMERMAN
UNITED STATES MARINE CORPS

for service as set forth in the following

CITATION:

For conspicuous gallantry and intrepidity at the risk of his life above and beyond the call of duty as Tank Commander serving with the Second Battalion, Sixth Marines, Second Marine Division, during action against enemy Japanese forces on Saipan, Marianas Islands, on 8 July 1944. Advancing with his tank a few yards ahead of the infantry in support of a vigorous attack on hostile positions, Sergeant Timmerman maintained steady fire from his antiaircraft sky mount machine gun until progress was impeded by a series of enemy trenches and pillboxes. Observing a target of

opportunity, he immediately ordered the tank stopped and, mindful of the danger from the muzzle blast as he prepared to open fire with the 75-mm., fearlessly stood up in the exposed turret and ordered the infantry to hit the deck. Quick to act as a grenade, hurled by the Japanese, was about to drop into the open turret hatch, Sergeant Timmerman unhesitatingly blocked the opening with his body, holding the grenade against his chest and taking the brunt of the explosion. His exceptional valor and loyalty in saving his men at the cost of his own life reflect the highest credit upon Sergeant Timmerman and the United States Naval Service. He gallantly gave his live in the service of his country.

/S/ HARRY S. TRUMAN

The President of the United States takes pride in presenting the MEDAL OF HONOR posthumously to

FIRST LIEUTENANT
ALEXANDER BONNYMAN, JR.
UNITED STATES MARINE
CORPS RESERVE

for service as set forth in the following

CITATION:

For conspicuous gallantry and intrepidity at the risk of his life above and beyond the call of duty as Executive Officer of the Second Battalion Shore Party, Eighth Marines, Second Marine Division, during the assault against enemy Japanese- held Tarawa in the Gilbert Islands, from 20 to 22 November 1943. Acting on his own initiative when assault troops were pinned down at the far end of Betio Pier by the overwhelming fire of Japanese shore batteries, First Lieutenant Bonnyman repeatedly defied the blasting fury of the enemy bombardment to organize and lead the besieged men over the long, open pier to the beach and then, voluntarily obtaining flame throwers and demolitions, organized his pioneer shore party into assault demolitions and directed the blowing of several hostile installations before the close of D-Day. Determined to effect an opening in the enemy's strongly organized defense line the following day, he voluntarily crawled approximately forty yards forward of our lines and placed demolitions in the entrance of a large Japanese emplacement as the initial move in his planned attack against the heavily garrisoned, bombproof installation which was stubbornly resisting despite the destruction early in the action of a large number of Japanese who had been inflicting heavy casualties on our forces and holding up our advance. Withdrawing only to replenish his ammunition, he led his men in a renewed assault, fearlessly exposing himself to the merciless slash of hostile fire as he stormed the formidable bastion, directed the placement of demolition charges in both entrances and seized the top of the bombproof position, flushing more than one hundred of the enemy who were instantly cut down and effecting the annihilation of approximately one hundred and fifty troops inside the emplacement. Assailed by additional Japanese after he had gained his objective, he made a heroic stand on the edge of the structure, defending his strategic position with indomitable determination in the face of the desperate charge and killing three of the enemy before he fell, mortally wounded. By his dauntless fighting spirit, unrelenting aggressiveness and forceful leadership throughout three days of unremitting, violent battle, First Lieutenant Bonnyman had inspired his men to heroic effort, enabling them to beat off the counterattack and break the back of hostile resistance in the sector for an immediate gain of four hun-

dred yards with no further casualties to our forces in this zone. He gallantly gave his life for his country.

/S/ HARRY S. TRUMAN

Distinguished Service Award

This is the highest Award any individual or organization can receive from the Second Marine Division Association. This Award is presented by the President, on behalf of the membership of the Second Marine Division Association, to an Officer, Committee Chairman, or National Staff Director who in the performance of his assigned duties provided exemplary service in the attainment of the Association's objectives. It is indeed a treasured possession of the few who have been selected to receive it. The Distinguished Service Award is presented at the formal closing banquet at the Annual Reunion.

The "Distinguished Service Award" has been presented as follows:

1987	SgtMaj Frank Turse, USMC (Ret.)
1987	T. Roy Thaxton
1988	Hugo V. Genge
1988	W. Wyeth Willard
1988	Robert L. Groves
1989	B. Gen James E. Howarth, USMC (Ret.)
1989	Geo. F. "Smoke" Powers
1990	Adolph Patterson
1990	William R. Smith
1991	Col. C.W. Van Horne, USMC
1991	A. Guinn Rasbury
1991	Peter A. Pavel
1992	Joseph J. Lawnick
1992	Carl Wiegel
1992	Jack P. Hernandez
1993	William F. Graham
1993	John P. Nixon
1994	Howard E. Frost
1994	Harriotte B. "Happy" Smith
1995	Carroll D. Strider
1995	William W. Rogal
1996	Darrell B. Albers
1997	Robert E. "Chick" Lewis
1997	Robert L. Roberts
1998	Jim Countiss
1998	Ed Gamble

156th PLATO

32

S. MARINE CORPS
DIEGO
943

— FIRST TO FIGHT

Tarawa

by Domenick D. Amadio

When the President spoke at a luncheon for 125 Medal of Honor winners, my thoughts turned to war and to one Marine who never got a medal. The year was 1943 and no one knows who he was. He came wading into the beach at Tarawa with a rifle held high over his head. When he hit the beach, he was one of only four left from the group of 20 Marines who had been dumped off the small blue Higgins invasion boat, 600 yards out on the coral reef beyond the shallow lagoon.

A Japanese machine gun had dropped all but those four men into the lagoon, dead or so badly wounded that they drowned with the 75 pounds of equipment on their backs. The Marine lay still for five minutes. His khaki started to dry out and turn light again, except where the blood oozed out near the shoulder.

Finally he raised his head. He could make out the Japanese machine-gun position concealed in a nest 100 feet to his right. It was four feet above him, behind a line of coconut logs that formed a barricade the length of the beach.

The Marine looked back. He saw men pile out of other landing boats off the atoll. He knew they were going to get it from the same machine gunner who got the men who started in with him. As the Marines waded closer, he could see bullets kicking up the water around them. The bullets came from the position just up the beach from where he lay. Some Marines were hit. First he saw their helmets, then their rifles, sink below the surface.

Marines on the beach with him who told the story saw him get to his knees. They knew what he was going to do even though they could see a sticky splotch of red where blood still flowed from the wound on his shoulder. He quickly pulled himself up over the log barrier so that he was on the sandy plateau above the beach, on a level with the Japanese gunners.

The others lost sight of him as he moved inland a little, behind a tangle of brush. Suddenly there were wild shouts in English mixed with Japanese. Then there was a short burst of machine-gun fire and, almost simultaneously, an explosion. Then, silence. When the other Marines made their way to the scene, there were pieces of two Japanese machine gunners blown apart by the Marine's grenade. In front of them there lay the Marine, cut in two through the middle by the last burst of machine gunfire as he hurled his grenade. Out in the lagoon, Marine reinforcements waded in safely. They never knew why the machine gun fire had stopped. The men who knew never had time to tell them. That's the way the battle for Tarawa began 40 years ago.

During the fight for one square mile of coral in the Pacific, 4,690 Japanese soldiers were killed, 17 were taken prisoner and none escaped. There were 1,026 Marines killed and 2,296 wounded. It was war at its disgusting worst and not all the Marines were heroes, either. There were huge pyramid-shaped cement barriers that the Japanese had built in the shallow waters to prevent landing craft from getting to shore. Some of the wading Marines stopped and hid behind the barriers, while the braver among them waded onto the beach in the face of enemy fire. It's always that way and who among us is certain what he'd do under the circumstances.

There were other horrors. One live Japanese soldier would lie among a pile of his own dead, wait until the Marines had passed by, then rise and attack them from behind. It led to the unpleasant Marine habit of firing their automatic weapons into any pile of dead Japanese they passed. There should be better ways to settle differences among us.

A Most Unforgettable Christmas

by Henry A. Gleich

Does anyone remember the USS *Mifflin* (APA-207)? I was first introduced to the lady on the bitter cold and windy day of December 2, 1945. She was riding high in the water, gently straining against the creaking hawsers that bound her to the pier. Paint was chipped, several rust spots speckled her side, and part of the "P" (in APA) was missing, but this lady was the most beautiful sight my eyes had ever beheld. She was to be charged with returning us to the West Coast—HOME!

An officer verified each man's dog-tag against a boarding roster before we were allowed to descend the metal ladders into the smelly bowels of the troop transport; we bribed a sailor to look the other way while we availed ourselves of their fresh-water showers. It was a sensation one might expect to experience only in paradise. Several layers of filth were removed, and for the first time in over a month, the penetrating warmth of hot water soothed our sore bodies. We returned to our hold with just enough time to get in line for the evening meal.

The next day, December 3, we noted an unusual amount of activity among the crew. The fretful hustle and a prevalent sense of anxiety should have alerted us as to what might be in store. Extra precautions were being taken to secure deck equipment. All loose objects were stowed below decks and cargo hatches were double lashed. By mid-morning lines were cast off.

The USS *Mifflin*, with her ship load of jubilant Marines, slowly wended her way down the channel of the busy port. Once clear of the harbor, speed increased and the ship's wake left a wide arc in the East China Sea as the bow of APA-207 was brought around to point south.

The ship intended to remain on this course for the night, steaming southerly, and keeping just beyond sight of the large Japanese island of Kyushu. Morning should bring us a few short miles west of the Satsunan Islands, and the treacherous passage through the Osumi Strait would be made in daylight. That, of course, was the planned route and schedule. It soon became apparent, however, that things were not going well, and our optimistic timetable was due for drastic revisions. High winds, a driving rain and huge waves shook every inch of the big ship. Rope lines, to serve as handholds for the crew, were strung along the deck. All hatchways leading on deck were dogged shut and troops were confined to quarters.

By morning (Tuesday, December 4) little doubt remained but that we were in the grips of a major storm. Mountainous waves pitched our ship about as if it were a mere child's plaything. Winds of incredible force whipped the seas into a frenzy, seemingly intent on sending the USS *Mifflin* to the ocean floor. Most all of the troops, along with a good many of the sailors, became seasick.

All day long the storm raged. Its fury continued through the night into Wednesday. I didn't entirely escape the terrible seasickness that struck down my fellow Marines, but I was spared the lasting violent convulsions that completely debilitated the troops and so many of the ship's company. By morning, although still quite unsettled, I felt strong enough to leave my bunk. Slowly, and deliberately, I made my way along the empty passageways to the mess-hall. The smell of greasy food certainly didn't improve my already queasy condition, but I was driven by an insatiable thirst. I filled my cup with juice and sat in a corner gingerly sipping the liquid, giving each temperamental gulp ample time to decide for itself whether or not it intended to stay down.

The mess hall was deserted. A Navy cook, working in the galley, came wobbling across the pitching deck and sat beside me. He told me he was the only cook still on his feet. Most of the crew were unable to report for duty. In view of the fact that I could at least stand and wasn't at the moment vomiting, I was recruited as his "assistant."

I was kept so busy I had no time to brood over my dizziness and unsteady stomach. It also gave me a freedom of movement about the ship I would otherwise never have enjoyed. One sailor led me to a point where I could observe the typhoon's terrible onslaught in action. It was a spectacle beyond description, and the most terrifying sight I had ever witnessed.

Normally, the bow rides effortlessly, 35 to 45 feet above the water line, but now, immense waves crashed high over the rail, washing the decks under several feet of water. Metal rails were twisted into grotesque sculptures by the powerful hands of Neptune. Each time the vessel plunged through one of the enormous swells, propellers flailed in the air, causing a trembling shudder throughout the ship that threatened to tear loose every rivet and weld. At other times, when the great transport climbed to the crest of a towering wave, the entire ship would quiver and shake, like a bass trying to disgorge a hook. It seemed impossible that anything could remain afloat, or long survive, under such severe punishment.

By Thursday, it seemed the typhoon's intensity had increased even more, yet the craft continued her defiant battle to remain afloat. A second seam opened mid-ship on the upper deck. A rivulet of water began trickling in and splashed noisily down the metal stairwell. It was frightening, but most Marines were too sick to care. I remember one retching private saying, "I don't give a damn how she does it, even if this tub has to crawl on the bottom from here to the West Coast. Just so long as she gets some of us home!"

Sometime during the night of December 6, the storm came to an abrupt end and Friday dawned on a different world. It was as though someone had turned a page in a picture book. The rains stopped and winds subsided. Swells remained unusually high,

New Zealand after Guadalcanal Island. Courtesy of Michael Wattik.

U.S. Marine - Cooks, Bakers, and Messmen of the Second Medical Battalion - Second Marine Division on Saipan Christmas Day - 1944.

but the USS *Mifflin*, and her courageous crew, persevered in an exceptional battle against a ruthless opponent. By noon the sun was making an effort to break through the cloud-streaked sky. In the distance we could see land. The ship had been driven within sight (and smell) of China. We were hundreds of miles off our intended course. Sailors immediately busied themselves repairing damage, and the gallant USS *Mifflin* turned to head for a point just north of Okinawa. In a day or so, we would pass through the chain of islands, into the Pacific, and on our way. Destination—HOME!

These old APAs could attain a speed of no more than 8 to 12 knots, so our daily progress was less than 250 nautical miles. As we sailed steadily, south and east, the weather became warmer and the breezes more gentle and soothing. Each day a few more men recovered from their terrible bout with sea-sickness and the pale starchy faces appeared on deck. For the next two weeks, we relaxed and basked in a lazy tropic sunshine.

Conditions returned to ship-board normal; except that the usual rivalry between Navy and Marines was absent. The reason

was, not only because we had shared so much during the past few days, but also because every Marine aboard the ship was aware that these sailors were very special. Many had extended their enlistment for the sole purpose of providing transportation to the veterans waiting to go home. They were part of what was known as "The Magic Carpet Fleet."

War-time restrictions were relaxed. There was no need for "blackouts" and the Marines were allowed to spend evenings on deck. Someone produced a harmonica and, at first, seven or eight men began harmonizing. They sang the songs popular in our day. The group quickly grew to 30 or 40 voices. A sailor with a guitar and a few more Marines with harmonicas joined in. It became a nightly event. Officers and enlisted men alike either sang along, or sat in quiet reverie, engrossed in the very personal thoughts awakened by the nostalgic sound of the melodies.

The evening of December 24 began as usual, but soon took on a more religious quality. Instead of the customary "pop" songs, we turned to spirituals and Christmas carols. One by one, the Marines and

sailors joined in until the entire ship became part of that devout serenade.

It was approaching "Taps," yet the caroling continued. Finally time arrived to draw the evening to a close. There came a long silent pause as we reluctantly prepared to descend into the stuffy holds. Suddenly, with the ship gently rolling through a tropic ocean, and guided by the "Southern Cross" shining so brightly in the sky, a solitary voice began the one hymn that, until now, had been avoided: *Silent Night!*

As though on command, every man quietly rose to his feet. They stood listening in reverent silence, a silence so profound that each heartbeat resounded in the ears like the beat of a drum. Then, almost imperceptibly, a faint singing was heard to come from below decks where the sick and injured were quartered. It began as a modest hum that steadily grew until everyone aboard joined to lend his voice to that of the lone singer. Three or four renditions of the beautiful hymn were offered to the star-filled heavens. As the strains of the last chorus faded, once more an emotional hush fell over the USS *Mifflin*. Only the rhythmic throbbing of the ship's engines punctuated the stillness. The spell was broken when, once again, the lone singer raised his strong clear voice, this time to chant a prayerful "AMEN!"

Time stood still. For perhaps a minute, no one stirred. Then slowly, without further word, the men filed off the deck and down into their respective holds, each thankful that under screen of darkness, their emotions could be concealed.

Next morning, the lights in the troops' hold blinked on and the shrill call of a bo'sun pipe roused APA-207 for reveille. The ship's commander, Navy Captain E.M. Waldron, made the morning's announcements himself. He wished everybody a "Merry Christmas" and canceled all the day's non-essential work details. He went on to say that Christmas Services would be held on the "After-Deck" before breakfast and the galley was preparing a "traditional" Christmas dinner to be served at noon. The Captain proceeded to read the menu. It started with turkey soup and included roast turkey with gravy, dressing, mashed potatoes, peas, celery stalks, hot buns and butter. The feast was topped off with plum pudding, ice cream and coffee. Assortments of candies, nuts, cigars and cigarettes would also be available. His report was received with a thundering cheer.

Volunteers rushed to help decorate the mess-halls and perform whatever chores were necessary to make ready for the holiday. Continuous music played over the PA system and, for the entire day, huge containers of punch were on hand down by the galley. Everyone entered into the Christmas spirit. By evening, sailors and Marines alike gathered on deck to rest their over-burdened stomachs and exchange tales of "Christmas back home."

We sang all the carols we were able to remember, but could never recapture the sentiment and deep emotional feeling of the previous evening. The night wore on and time for "Taps" was fast approaching. Suddenly the voice of Captain Waldron boomed over the ship's PA system. Once again he wished a "Merry Christmas to all!" then made a startling announcement. The ship had crossed the International Date Line from west to east! It was no longer Tuesday, December 25. We had traveled back to Monday, December 24. It was Christmas Eve and tomorrow would be Christmas Day 1945 all over again!

The Captain promised an exact duplicate of the previous day, and although resources were somewhat strained, the crew tried their creative best to fulfill that promise. A little water was added to the soup, portions were not as generous, the plum pudding was replaced by jello and most brands of cigarettes were absent. Nevertheless, everything was received with the best of humor and sense of gratitude. Bursts of laughter echoed the length and breath of the ship, as jokes about this "second Christmas" were repeated and passed around. All-in-all it was a most joyous "second" celebration.

Memories of those "two" Christmases endure with a clarity that belied the half century that passed. My sentimental souvenir will remain with me forever. When I hear people speak of "a special Christmas," my thoughts always drift back to my own experience in 1945: the improbable circumstance leading up to the day, the unusual setting, and the extraordinary feeling of a closeness to the real meaning of the observance. The initial caroling had been but an expression of our nostalgic longing for home and family, but the beautiful lyrics of *Silent Night* transformed that boatload of weary Marines into something more spiritual. The words took on a special meaning. The wounds of battles past, the humility endured during the last months in Japan, and the near disaster in the grips of a horrible typhoon all washed away. In place there came a tranquillity and inner serenity as though we were enveloped by the true gift of the Christ child. That Christmas evening, over a thousand comrade warriors stood shoulder to shoulder, yet for a brief moment each was alone in a venerate communion that brought a peace that cannot be described. Thanks to the incredible voice of that anonymous singer who led an entire troop transport in a rendition of *Silent Night,* it became an outstanding and a never to be forgotten Christmas.

I Made It Fine
by John C. Bruns

I knew that Saipan would be my first and last battle. I am not a superstitious person, but I knew that I would be wounded and not killed in that assault. This hunch started bothering me long before we headed for Saipan.

One day I was having a wart removed from my trigger finger when I said to the doctor, "It would be a darned shame if I had this arm blown off, making you do all this work for nothing." The doctor just laughed.

Later on, I wrote my mother a letter telling her not to worry about me. I warned her that I'd be coming home without one of my limbs but promised her I would be okay. I even bet some of my buddies in the company that I'd be going home after the Saipan Campaign.

Marine 81 MM mortar crew on front lines fighting Japs. Corp. Michael Judiscak of Laveta, Colorado, Pfc. Neil Lorimer of Highland IL, Pfc. Walter V. Mountain, of Evergreen AL, Pfc. Michael Wattich of Library PA. Pfc. Jasper Coker of Seabrook, Texas, Pfc. Harold Gass of River Rouge, MI, and Pfc. James R. Boswell of Hearside, TX.

Summer of 1945 on Saipan. 81 mm mortar Plt. members H.Q. Co. 3rd BN. 6th Reg. 2nd Div. Courtesy of James Montgomery.

About the first of August the battalion regrouped in an area north of the 2nd Marine Division cemetery and stayed there until the next assignment. We left in February 1945.

To this day I still like bananas.

A Series Of Good Fortune
by Robert Rhea Cowan

Upon joining the 2nd Marine Division in Saipan (as a ship's platoon of replacements for Camp Pendleton), I found life on an island had few comforts. It is not easy to carry a 20 pound back-pack plus two blankets and an M-1 rifle in 90-100 degree heat. The Marine Corps, however, accustomed us to these conditions as we prepared for landing on Okinawa.

The regiment landed and fought with valor, then went back to Saipan for preparation of the big job, landing in Japan. Prayer became a daily event. The Marine Corps used its skills in preparing the division for Japan with squad, platoon, battalion, regiment and division maneuvers. Then the big day came and we boarded the ship, feeling no joy for the invasion of Japan.

We had been fully loaded for a week when the ship's radio announced an atomic bomb had been dropped on Nagasaki, and we would disembark to return to our original quarters on Saipan. Our prayers were answered and our lives saved.

Within a month we were on our way, not to landings, but to military occupation of Nagasaki. We covered the areas where our landings would have been held, often by Japanese horses. This series of good fortune seems hard to believe when considering other Marine Corps landings in the South Pacific.

An Unwanted Diet
by Ralph R. Crosiar

I am sure that many of those who took part in the Guadalcanal Campaign remember those old C-rations. They came in wooden cases, packed 24 cans per case. The selection was always the same, eight cans each of meat and beans, meat and vegetable stew and last, but not least, meat and vegetable hash.

I, as the runner used most often by our lieutenant, was seldom on hand when the rations were doled out. Not really "doled" out, as everyone took their pick, first come, first served. The result was always the same. My choice, whenever I was off

I was in the first wave of the assault on Saipan. I knew I'd get hit, but I didn't know when. As I was making my way up the beach around eleven o'clock in the morning, I found a foxhole and jumped into it, holding my helmet on with my right hand. That's when a Japanese mortar hit me in the right arm and took it clean off at the elbow. Thank goodness the shell didn't go off; I picked up my arm and ran to the aid station and was back in the States before I knew it. I spent about nine months in naval hospitals, where doctors amputated my arm at the shoulder and where I learned how to write with my left hand. But just like I promised my mother, I made out fine.

Searching For Bananas
by Canara G. Carruth

The summer of 1944 I was a young Marine in the 2nd Armored Amphibian Battalion, attached to 2nd Marine Division, headed for combat. This being the battalion's first operation for most of the personnel, all were gung-ho, which changed after going ashore on the island of Saipan.

Starting at Green Beach, going north toward Garapan, we were the extreme left flank ending up at Marpi Point. After witnessing the killings and terrific loss of lives with the water red from blood, D Company moved back to a bivouac area below Mount Tipo.

Another tank buddy and myself decided to go up on Mount Tipo or Hill 789 to search for bananas that were not shot up from the recent combat. When we arrived we found some that were in good condition, so we cut two stalks each and were preparing to go back to camp. My buddy asked in a loud voice if I had a weapon; I said no then asked why? His reply was he was looking a Japanese right in the eyes. No more questions; both of us started a rapid descent with the Japanese firing at us. We were running as fast as we could and the ground was flaring up under our feet. We finally outdistanced the Jap's firing and made it back to the bivouac area where we examined our bananas and found no damage.

on a "run" when the rations were put out, was all that was left—meat and vegetable hash.

I am sure, too, that you who were there recall that we had to eat those rations cold to avoid giving our positions away to "Tojo's" troops. That meat and vegetable stew might have been passable when heated, but cold, they were pretty awful. Hungry as I was, it was still hard to consume a can of the stuff and that is where the unwanted diet kicked in. Between the lousy cold meat-vegetable hash and frequent bouts of diarrhea, I lost over 20 pounds in the less than two months that we were on Guadalcanal.

My conclusion after this experience was that whoever selected meat and vegetable hash to be a part of the C-Rations of those days certainly should have been forced to eat them cold for a minimum of two weeks before their finalizing of that selection. I feel sure that they might have made a different choice. I, for one, certainly thought that the powers that be improved the rations when they went to the K-Ration.

Two Celebrations Then Spam
by Ralph R. Crosiar

Our unit of the 6th Regiment boarded the troop transport, *Feland*, in Wellington for the trip to Tarawa for that invasion. Since it was a few days before Thanksgiving, we were served our Thanksgiving turkey and its trimmings before our arrival off Tarawa- the only time that I can recall ever eating Thanksgiving dinner early.

When we were picked up by another troop transport a few days later, we were then taken to Hawaii. I am sorry to say that I no longer recall the name of that transport. Suffice it to say, they had not served their Thanksgiving dinner early, so we were the recipients of that meal also. Thus, we had two Thanksgiving dinners that year. Thank the Lord for that as the reader should understand from the rest of this "tale."

Aside from the food and fixings for that dinner and the Navy beans for Saturday's "Traditional" breakfast, the ship's stores were almost empty save for a generous supply of "Spam." The result was an almost constant diet of Spam for the few days it took to reach Hilo, where we left the ship. While I did not lose weight as with my earlier "diet" of meat and vegetable hash, I certainly lost my desire for a Spam dinner. Even yet, it is not among my favorite dishes.

Memorable Moment From Tarawa
by Ralph R. Crosiar

William K. Jones, Lieutenant Colonel (Retired), was our battalion commanding officer on Saipan. He was also the ranking officer of the unit I was in, above platoon leader, during my time in the 2nd Division. He had written a book, titled *A Brief History of The Sixth Marines*. He told of the wounding of Captain George Krueger on Tarawa by a sniper hidden in the top of a coconut tree.

This brought back my memories of moments before that happened. My unit, 1st Platoon of Dog Company, a heavy machine gun platoon attached to A Company, passed Krueger with his B Company air-cooled machine guns. He looked over his shoulder, saw me and asked how it was going, calling me by name. As I turned to go on I noticed movement among some fronds on a downed coconut caused by the firing of a weapon under it. I started to look for the sniper but was ordered to "Come on" by a non-com. I cannot help but wonder if that was the sniper who wounded Krueger. It was definitely very close to the same time.

Krueger was our platoon leader when I joined the 6th. He had a photographic memory as indicated by his ability to recall everyone's name after their first contact. He was one officer that I shall always think of with pleasant memories. A second one, Captain Durfee of A Company was another, although I was only in his unit a short time. I recall one time when my issue dungarees were getting a bit threadbare, and as he wore the same size and for some reason had extras, he had a pair of them issued to me. He was killed on Saipan. As any of us who served with the 6th through Guadalcanal, Tarawa and part of the Saipan campaign

(L to R) VMO-2 Saipan 1945. Robert A. Deal, John Bailey, and Sgt. Mike.

WPNS CO. 6th. Marines Mid November, 1945. On trucks going to docks at Nagasaki, Japan. Veterans returning stateside. Truck with 3 Marines. Left; Mike Taglarini, center; unknown. sitting; Ed Halligan. Front truck: sitting in center over MP's head; Harold Pryor. sitting with elbow on tailgate; Bert Spooner.

knows, we all have many more memories but this is the one that I choose to submit herewith.

Three Short Stories
by Richard A Cruickshank

•One time at a general inspection a friend and I were assigned head duty. They inspected the head twice, finding faults of one kind or another. The third time we tied all the stool lids together. When they opened the door, I yelled attention and my friend pulled the string. When all the lids stood up the inspecting officer looked in and all he could say was "'aw to hell with it" and walked off.

•Another time I was on duty in the orderly room when a friend came in. We started discussing telephone wiring. We somehow got carried away and drew diagrams on one wall, starting from the central office to the phone. Needless to say, we spent the next day painting the whole room.

•One time at the rifle range, the day before qualifying day, my buddy broke the range record with his 45 and I with my carbine. We were so happy and ready to do the same the next day when it would count that we went to the beer garden to celebrate that night. Needless to say, we were lucky to even qualify the next day.

A Corporal for 30 Seconds
by Bill Day

I was born January 8, 1924, enlisted in the service in December 1942 and was sent to San Diego Recruit Depot in January 1943. I was assigned to Platoon 108, Serial #801311.

My best buddy, Jack Redman, was selected for Sea School, but our friendly DI said "No way, you are out to Camp Mathews (Rifle Range) for a month of mess duty." Oh Boy, Camp Pendleton is just up the road. There, we went through Engineer School and learned to fight the ever-burning bush fires out in the boonie, fought battles with poison oak, learned how to build bridges, blow up things (demolition), camouflage and stevedoring (guess). We also loaded a bunch of ships. I was promoted to private first class, which lasted all the war.

September came along and I guess we knew all we needed, because I became Replacement #26. At the end of Broadway we were greeted by a large crowd, "Go get 'em Marines." Two and a half years later the crowd had all gone and we knew the war was truly over.

We went on to the South Pacific, New Caledonia and then to New Zealand, where we were scattered out to various units. I went to H&S Company, 18th Engineers. My best buddy was killed on Tarawa (I wasn't there) and I still miss him. We continued on to Hawaii, Saipan, Okinawa and sailed around China Sea. They finally figured the Japanese navy was done and sailed back to Saipan. We were all loaded for next invasion when we were told the bomb was dropped and the war was over. Thank God.

Since we were all packed, they sent us to Nagasaki, Japan, and we were almost the first ones in. The A-bomb had destroyed the industrial area (not main part of town as many do-gooders want to say).

In December we were on our way back to good ole USA and hit San Diego on Christmas Day. I went to Tent Camp Two then on to Great Lakes where I was offered corporal rank if I re-enlisted. I said "No thanks, I've seen all I can stand for now, ship me home." So I was a corporal for 30 seconds, just long enough to sign out.

Grasshoppers In The Pacific
by Robert A. Deal

After graduating from boot camp at Parris Island in the summer of 1943, I was trained as an aviation machinist mate. I left the East Coast by train for Miramar NAS California on September 8, 1944. I then departed by transport ship for Hawaii. There I was on standby for assignment to a B-26 tow target outfit. (Because the B-26 silhouette closely resembled that of the Japanese twin engine "Betty" bomber, it was used to tow targets in the Pacific.) While there I volunteered for duty on Saipan and flew in on a C-54 transport.

On our approach we were fired on by our own troops (at that time the Japanese still controlled the air space over the Marianas). As we were landing I looked out the window and saw burning tanks and knee-deep mud. The driver of the truck that took us across the mountain to East Field (later named Kagman Point by the Navy) told us to keep our M-ls handy since we had to travel through an area where some Army nurses were killed the day before.

At East Field I was assigned to VMO-2, an observation squadron whose duties included artillery spotting, directing naval gunfire, transporting personnel and evacuating wounded. Our pilots flew Stinson L-5 "Sentinels" (these were larger and more powerful than the Army's L-4 Piper Cubs). These unarmed, fabric covered monoplanes were called "Flying Grasshoppers" by the Marines. Since they were able to fly slower and lower over the targets than the more powerful Navy planes, our pilots were better at pinpointing and calling in artillery fire on Japanese positions.

In the Saipan Campaign, the first American plane to land on Marpi Point Field was a VMO-2 "Grasshopper" flying off of a CVE (escort carrier). On a later mission, one of our pilots, Lieutenant Gordon Lopez, and William Fitzsimons, an artillery spotter with the 10th Marines, noticed some Japanese crawling onto one of our tanks. They made several low passes trying to scare them off and even fired at them with a pistol. When

they landed soon afterwards, they found aviation fuel leaking from the wing tanks where they had been hit by Japanese ground fire. (Fitzsimons was awarded the Air Medal on August 3, 1995) We lost two pilots on Saipan. One was hit by enemy fire and had to bail out too low for his parachute to help him. Another was on a mission when he encountered a sudden downdraft, causing the small plane to crash.

March 1945 found us en route to Okinawa where again a pilot from VMO-2 landed the first American plane on the island April 2. We performed reconnaissance and artillery spotting missions over Okinawa until the middle of April when we were ordered back to Saipan. One of our planes flew the body of Ernie Pyle, the famous war correspondent, to Saipan after he was killed on Ie Shima April 18.

In September 1945 we sailed from Saipan to Nagasaki, Japan on the USS *Marvin H. McIntyre*. Coming into the harbor we passed the giant Mitsubishi factory

November 14-23, 1951. Jack Middleton, Ed Dwyer, John Sousa.

Courtesy of A.G. Sharp.

demolished by the atomic bomb. Eventually based at Omura, a Japanese transport fighter field, we flew reconnaissance and familiarization flights as well as transporting mail and important passengers. One of these VIPs was Danny Kaye, the actor, who was a little uneasy about flying in our small planes. We also flew Igor Sikorsky of Republic Aircraft over Nagasaki to view the destruction done by the atomic bomb. A Marine transport pilot who flew into Omura regularly was the famous actor, Tyronne Power. He was a regular guy and a real gentleman. You would never have known he was a big star. Instead of some easy stateside duty assignment, he was at the front.

Finally, one of the more humorous things that happened while we were in Japan: There were very few "air worthy" enemy planes on the base. Some even looked like experimental aircraft. Not willing to risk our pilots to fly these planes, we used Japanese pilots to test them. While they were in the air, there were F4U Corsairs flying above them. The F4Us were armed with live ammo with instructions to shoot them down if they tried to leave the area, and the Japanese were made aware of this. They kept complaining about the "lumpy" parachutes they were given. Further inspection revealed that the silk chutes had been removed and the packs had been stuffed with rags. It seems the GIs wanted the silk to bring home with them.

Memories of Tarawa
by Herbert H. Deighton

These are my memories of Tarawa from the prospective of 54 years later. The 2nd Battalion, 6th Marines boarded the *J. Franklin Bell* in Wellington harbor after nine beautiful months in New Zealand. The New Zealanders had been wonderful to us and it was hard to leave.

The convoy left on November 1. We stopped at the island of Efate, New Hebrides for a practice landing on November 6. The 6th Marines had been designated as reserve.

The morning of November 20, the *J. Franklin Bell* pulled into the transport area with the rest of the convoy. We had our early breakfast and sat around our compartment, waiting and waiting. Word came back from the beach that our fellow Marines were in trouble and needed help. It was very frustrating. Early afternoon word was given that we would be landing on Green Beach the next morning, so we in the Intelligence section were given the job of making dozens of map overlays of Betio. I have never seen a map with so many enemy fortifications.

We worked most of the night making overlays. Breakfast, D+1, then we were told that the battalion would not land on Green Beach but was being sent to land on Bairiki, the next island of the atoll from Betio. The Japanese had been seen escaping across the sand.

At low tide the sand between islands is dry. After an early lunch of spaghetti, we boarded the landing craft and while bobbing around in the LCVPs a lot of that spaghetti came back up and was all over the landing craft. An hour and half later, as we were approaching Bairiki, a machine gun in a bunker opened up on us. The rounds hitting the ramp sounded like hail on a metal roof. A glance over the gunwales and a Kingfisher observation airplane from a battleship or heavy cruiser dropped a bomb, which was a direct hit and ended the machine gun fire.

Once ashore an examination of the bombed bunker showed not only a direct hit, but the Japanese had left a gasoline can

November 14-17, 1951. Jim Kennedy, Jim Hoard, Bob Huson, Ed Dwyer, and Joe Kolodrubitz.

November 14-17, 1951. John Chnuelowski, Roy Ivey, Jim Kennedy, Bob Huson, Jim Hoard.

near the entrance that caught fire and burned everything. The island was overrun in a couple of hours, and we even got a couple of prisoners.

We had a Japanese language interpreter who was of Mexican heritage and when the Japanese prisoner was brought in to the Command Post, he was so excited he began questioning him in Spanish.

D+1 evening an OP, along with a machine gun squad, dug in on the east end of the island. While digging in, a Japanese came racing past us out on to the dry sand and darkness. All we could do was to holler "halt." Next morning, D+2, a patrol went out across the dry sand to the next island, Banraeaba.

There were no Japanese, just one vicious dog. One of the guys had to shoot it. It is a very naked feeling to be out on one of those sandspits with no cover for 100 yards in any direction. Back to the Command Post and the battalion is ordered to Betio.

We boarded the LCVPs. Headquarters Company landed at the end of the pier and the rest of the battalion landed on Green Beach. We dug in across the airstrip behind Black Beach 2 for another sleepless night. AM, D+3, the battalion was ordered to re-embark aboard landing craft at the end of the pier and land on the island of Eita, the fourth island up the atoll. We started running across signs of Japanese, but the natives told us they had headed north along the atoll. We bivouacked near the Bonriki village at the bend in the atoll. We were told not to drink the water from the wells as the Japanese might have poisoned them.

On Thanksgiving Day, November 24, we had a K-Ration dinner. We were off early the next morning reconnoitering each island, sometimes walking between islands on dry sand and other times in high tide and water up to our chests. About 10 islands up the atoll we dug in for the night. On November 26 we moved out bright and early.

Two of us from the 2 section were sent out to reconnoiter Maranenuka village. As we were creeping around an old church, we heard a voice say in English. "Would you gentlemen like a drink of water?" It was an English nun, who had stayed on when the Japanese showed up at the start of the war, and the natives had helped to keep her from being captured. We got our drink of water and the information that the Japanese had been through there the day before. The natives were friendly and overwhelmed with joy to see the British officer with us who had been the commissioner of the Gilbert Islands before he and his group fled just before the Japanese arrived.

Each village we went through was clean and orderly. Some were deserted and some of the natives stood along the road clapping and greeting us with big smiles. The natives were a great help during this time, and all the young native boys would carry our packs for us. When we took a break, they would climb the coconut trees and cut down some of the coconuts, then cut them open and let us drink the cool, clear, delicious liquid from the green fruit. I do not think I have ever had anything that was as thirst quenching.

During one of our breaks a white-haired older gentleman approached us and told us his story. He was a Scotchman who had jumped ship at Tarawa a number of years before. He had a native wife and three children. He was a very happy man and glad he had jumped ship. His most prized possession was a small library of English language books. He asked us for any books we had, but we had none.

The islands of the northern half of the atoll were fewer in number and longer, so we covered almost the remainder of the atoll on November 26. The battalion dug in on a skirmish line across the lower third of the next to last island, Buariki. After the Command Post was set up, myself and two other men and one of our native boys went swimming in the lagoon. We knew there were native women about, so three bashful Marines borrowed some native grass skirts and when they got wet they weighed a ton. About that time we asked the native boy if there were any sharks in the lagoon and he said there were lots of them. We came out of water in record time.

Later that afternoon the natives from the nearest village came and gave us an impromptu show, doing their native hula-like dance and singing, keeping time by using our ration boxes as drums. They would sing American songs, *You Are My Sunshine*, etc. The most memorable was six young (4-6 year olds) girls in grass skirts doing a dance. Unfortunately, the battalion commander made us break it up, saying we made too good a mortar target. He was right, as a patrol from E Company was sent out and ran into a Japanese patrol. There was a brief firefight and several Marines were wounded. The Japanese probed our lines all night, but no Marine casualties.

Next morning, November 27, the battalion moved out in a skirmish line across the island, G Company on the right and E Com-

Ed Dwyer and "Little Joe" Kolodrubitz aboard the APA36 USS Cambria.

pany on the left. Shortly after moving out they found the Japanese positions. The Japanese held their fire until the Marines were almost on top of them. The vegetation was thick and the fight was at close range. With the first rounds, I dove behind a coconut log and soon found I was in the wrong place. The log was an old rotten one and the rounds were coming through as if it wasn't even there. I got up and made a mad dash for a living coconut tree and better cover. As I came to a stop, there, about three inches in front of my nose, was a piece of cloth and a pile of Jap feces.

After several hours all the Japanese (175) were killed; 2nd Battalion 6th Marines had 32 killed and 59 wounded. Once again the natives had helped by helping to care for the wounded at the aid station. Later that afternoon, as we in the 2 section were going over the Japanese bodies for intelligence information, one of the patrols from G Company almost blew us away thinking we were Japanese; whew, another close one.

One more island to go, Naa, the very northern tip of the atoll. November 28, we got a little advance support before we moved out across the sandspit. Two Corsairs, a half dozen strafing runs and a few salvos from a destroyer's 5-inch guns. We found no Japanese, only some well shot up buildings. Anticlimactic. Back to our Command Post on Buariki to wait for landing craft to take us across the lagoon to what we had hoped would be a ship and out of Tarawa.

The landing craft arrived late in the af-

Liberty in Oran. September 14, 1951.

ternoon and by the time we started across the lagoon it was dark. The convoy of landing craft was caught in the middle of the lagoon as the tide went out. There were landing craft scurrying every which way but soon all the water in the lagoon was gone; 2/6 spent the night out in the dry lagoon. Some of the men took their ponchos and spread them out on the dry lagoon floor. The tide started to come back in before sunrise and there was a lot of fast reboarding of the landing craft.

We arrived back at the island of Banraeaba midmorning, third island up from Betio, to find that we had been designated as garrison troops. I got dengue fever during the Christmas-New Year time. It was one miserable time. Two/Six stayed there from November 29, 1943 until we sailed for Hawaii aboard the *Prince Georges* on February 1, 1944 to join the rest of the division.

A Good Man
by Philip J. Doyle

The Marine Corps "got a good man" when Toivo Henry Ivary transferred over from the Navy Air Corps after totaling out a trainer plane by running into a cement mixer while trying to land in a crosswind. Hank was a survivor. Three years as center for the Ohio University football team, a plane crash and then volunteering for assignment to a raider battalion after Quantico.

A clerical error in his orders put him in a Radar School in the California desert where the Hollywood tough guys were making a movie during the day, having a few drinks and playing poker at night. After a few sessions Hank padded his wallet with some of Humphrey Bogart and John Wayne's money. When the orders error was discov-

ered, he was shipped out to New Zealand where he joined G-22 as the 1st Platoon leader.

Hank staked me into the poker games after I joined G-22, and for several months before shipping out to Tarawa, we both packed fat wallets on leave in Wellington. Aboard the *Zeilin,* two days before landing, all the poker playing officers sat in a full day session of a one-winner-take-all game which ended with Captain Warren Morris tapping my stack in a five card stud hand with both of us holding aces wired. They say his wife bought a new house for $16,000 with the purser's check Lefty sent home.

When we made the attack on Tarawa, Hank and I were in tracs in the third wave. As we got close to the beach Hank's trac took a hit and veered off into the cove on the right of Red Beach 2. I shall always remember Hank standing up in his trac waving to me as it moved away.

The point at which he landed was probably the most heavily defended on the beach. Against this the seawall afforded the only protection, but none against the grenades being thrown over. Hank was kicking them into the water until one went off just as he kicked it and shattered his right leg.

Thinking he was going to die anyway, Hank dragged himself up to hang on the wall where he could spot the point from which the grenades were being thrown and he would shout out the target identification such as three o'clock, one o'clock, ten o'clock, so that his men could jump up and fire in that direction.

After some time Hank became so weakened from loss of blood he fell from the wall. Later that day an ammo trac, which had gone off course, came in to the cove. The casualties were put on and brought out to the ship where Hank's right leg was amputated. For his action and total disregard of his own safety, Hank was awarded the Navy Cross.

After being brought stateside, Hank was transferred to the Navy Hospital on Mare Island where we resumed our life-long friendship. Hank moved to Berkeley, California. I was in law school at the University of California and Hank also entered the law school. We both practiced law in Oakland, California, for many years.

Hank was as proud to have been a Marine as any I've ever known. He never complained of his wounds and even though he later suffered a very disabling illness, he "hung on the wall" to give his wife and five

children the best protection he could provide without regard for his own interest. For this the Lord above will surely add a heavenly star to his Navy Cross.

Two Of My Memorable Experiences
by Jess W. Green

In 1941, before Pearl Harbor, the 8th Regiment had been formed and we went on a 180-mile hike. Us cooks would set up our galley at the next expected stop and have chow ready for the troops. Some of the land we went through and over belonged to Bing Crosby, who had a training race track, thorough-bred horses and a ranch house near one of the overnight areas where we set up our galley.

After our chores were done that evening, several of us walked about a quarter of a mile to his horses and training track. Bing Crosby came out where we were looking at the horses. He had a three or four days beard and said he was there for relaxation. He joined us for a short time observing the horses, which seemed to enjoy an audience. Being high spirited, some were kicking up their heels, bucking and neighing, and while doing so were expelling gas. One of the guys in our group, never missing an opportunity for personal comment, stated "I have always heard a __ horse was never tired. I guess this proves it." This comment really tickled Crosby and we all had a good laugh.

On Guadalcanal in late 1942 we were bombed daily by the Japanese, and many times the bombing was done by a lone solitary plane. The air raid siren went off one day and everyone scampered to our bombshelter inside a small cave near our bivouac. I was busy with some chore at the time and felt no immediate need to rush, but when the plane got close to our area it released an extra fuel tank and it sounded just like a bomb falling. Needless to say, I headed for the bomb shelter where the other men were. As I was running on this little narrow native path one of the large harmless lizards that were common on Guadalcanal suddenly appeared in the middle of the path and stood up on his front legs about one foot high, sticking his tongue out. Hearing the bomb-like sound of the falling fuel tank and confronted with a hostile looking creature, even though the creature was harmless, I jumped over the lizard and never broke stride. The men in the bomb shelter were laughing and saying "Ole Green can really move. We thought you were airborne for a minute. Humor does not solve all difficult predicaments, but it seems to offer some relief.

The Gales Of November
by David C. Gummere

The U.S. Marine Corps is an organization steeped in tradition. Each year, to celebrate the founding of our Corps, November 10, 1775, we conduct ceremonies, partake in revelry and celebrate with a birthday cake. Two hundred and one years later that tradition was about to continue, but with a few slight variations. During early November 1976, major elements of the 4th Marine Brigade were once again returning to the United States as part of an amphibious convoy crossing the Atlantic Ocean. We had just completed the Marine Corps' first brigade-level deployment to Europe since World War I. As a member of Lieutenant Colonel John H. Gary's 2nd Tank Battalion aboard the USS *Manitowoc*, a landing ship tank (LST), I was part of this historic expedition en route to our home base of Camp Lejeune, North Carolina. After months of tromping through Norway, Denmark and West Germany we were happy to be headed home and expressed our gladness to the Navy by engaging in every imaginable form of interservice rivalry possible.

Yet, as we neared the end of our venture together, the captain of our ship deviated from the Navy's series of well-natured pranks against us and surprised everyone. He directed his wardroom's chief mess steward to prepare a grand birthday cake in honor of our Corps' birthday. Appreciative of the gesture, we also called a halt to our escapades. The trip home was beginning to look rather boring, that is until we neared the treacherous coastal waters called Cape Hatteras, also referred to as the "Graveyard of the Atlantic."

We began to experience a drastic drop in barometric pressure, and the weather rapidly began to worsen. The seas increased in height and the wind began to produce a "siren song" as it blew through the lines and masts aloft. The sailors aboard our LST were well aware of what the eerie music represented and took frenzied steps to prepare the ship for the worst. Still, the excited activity failed to dampen our festive spirit for the upcoming birthday celebration. The chief mess steward had completed his culinary masterpiece in record time, and the LST captain quickly, but ceremoniously,

presented the cake to our battalion commander before returning to more urgent duties on the bridge. However, since it was not yet November 10, our commander directed the gift be set aside until we could reach port and disembark on Sand Island at Morehead City, North Carolina. Afterwards we would return to Camp Lejeune and use the cake for our official ceremony. As the battalion guard officer I was given the unenviable task of safeguarding the cake from hungry admirers and transporting it ashore when we reached our port of debarkation. But, as it turned out, the cake was temporarily to be the least of my worries.

Several thousand yards from our ship aboard the amphibious squadron command vessel, a Navy commodore was assessing the weather situation. He was a seasoned veteran of the tempestuous Atlantic storms and quickly ordered all ships to take evasive measures to ride out the heavy weather. This tactic would delay our arrival at Morehead City, but it was critical to the survival of the ships in the convoy. We were in no position to argue.

Meanwhile, in our ship's wardroom, the chief mess steward, ever protective of his cake, advised me that he was willing to secure the masterpiece and keep it from being damaged until we went ashore. I gladly accepted his invitation and moved on to more pressing tasks.

In the LST's communications room a well-intentioned radioman picked up a stateside music broadcast from a faint radio sta-

tion out of Virginia. Thinking the music would be a welcome distraction from the storm, the ship's captain agreed to broadcast the music throughout the vessel over the 1MC speaker system. The first and only song we heard before the signal was lost was ominous: The *Wreck of the Edmund Fitzgerald*, by Gordon Lightfoot! The mood was set, but not for the revelry we had anticipated.

As the seas increased we began to take green water over our bow. Green water meant trouble. Each time the LST's bow disappeared below the surface of the ocean the stem rose majestically upward exposing the massive bronze propellers churning in the air. Huge green walls of water took turns smashing into the superstructure causing our vessel to shutter uncontrollably. As the ship's long body twisted, the stress on the metal added a ceaseless metallic groaning noise. Teeth-rattling vibrations occurred each time the bow slammed back against the surface of the water and disappeared from sight. Sailors and Marines alike were thrown violently against bulkheads and passageways as we futilely attempted to brace for the next shock wave.

If that was not bad enough, our flat-bottomed vessel also had a tendency to roll to each side. A device called an inclinometer, located on the bridge, measured our rolls and reported continual readings of up to 65 degrees. Initially, the wide-eyed looks on the faces of the Navy officers were a topic of humor among the Marine offic-

Company B Med. assembled for a photograph on January 26, 1946.

LCAC hovercraft close on beach during MARFORLANT Capablities Exercise, 22 Feb 1996.

ers. But, the levity quickly passed when the ship's navigator explained to us that our particular class of LST was not designed to withstand rolls in excess of 45 degrees. We risked capsizing. Now sailors and Marines alike began to turn a shade of gray that rivaled the color of the ship.

Soon we all heard new noises. The battalion's M60A1 main battle tanks located on the well deck below began to strain at their chains. Crews of volunteers led by Lieutenant Colonel Gary fought to brace the 60-ton camouflage monsters with wooden shoring and prevent them from shifting their weight and capsizing us or breaking loose and rupturing the hull. Two amphibious tractors (LVTP-7s), each weighing 13 tons, had already broken their chocks and rammed the ship's massive stem gate before being brought under control. My personal worry as I moved between vehicles was to ensure our headquarters trucks had not broken loose. Each was secure, but the

contents in the rear of some of the trucks had minds of their own.

Topside the massive walls of water continued to pummel the exterior of our ship. Canvas tops were ripped from trucks, supplies stored in the rear of the exposed vehicles were washed into the sea, and many deck components were torn away from the surface of the LST. The wave troughs grew so large that lookouts aboard other ships in our battered convoy reportedly sounded alarms as they watched our vessel disappear from sight without reappearing on the horizon. Excited reports were circulated that we had gone to the bottom. Fortunately it was not so!

After two interminable days of fright, seasickness and injury, the storm passed and the sun appeared. We soon made port and tied up at Sand Island. Morehead City never looked so good! We had endured enough of Poseidon's revelry for one year. The most amazing fact was that our cake had miracu-

lously survived the ordeal. Now, after all this, I was not about to let anything happen to that damn cake. As ordered, I gave it my personal attention as we discharged our tanks and other damaged vehicles from the storm-battered LST.

It was after dark when we finally arranged our vehicle convoy and began the final slow journey along the coastal highway en route to Camp Lejeune. I followed the cake into the rear of a large 5-ton canvas-covered truck as one of the final vehicles in the long motorcade. Unfortunately, our driver was unable to start his engine. When he did bring the 5-ton to life he was apparently anxious to regain his position in the convoy and sped down the road. But, as luck would have it, he located the one remaining obstacle to our journey, a large pothole, courtesy of the North Carolina Department of Highways. Our truck hit the pothole, and the resulting jolt propelled our prized cake into the air, over the tailgate of the truck, and squarely into the road just as the last truck in the convoy smashed it flat! The Marines in the back of our truck howled with laughter so hard that I could not help but join in. Of all the things to happen, our cake was gone and I was in trouble.

Upon reaching our destination I explained the incident to our battalion commander. From what I recall, he took a dim view of the situation and improperly expressed a few adjectives and made a vague reference to something about my fitness report before dismissing me. If we were ever on good terms, that cinched it! Gordon Lightfoot's *Gales of November* came early. The 10th of November we were back home at Camp Lejeune, and, as tradition demanded, we conducted our ceremony, partook in revelry, but somehow missed out on our cake that year.

The above was written while I was living in Europe in 1995, but was never published.

Direct Hit
by Clarence Hargis

I had served with Charlie Cone in Mortar Platoon F-2-6 at Tarawa. Charlie was a fine sergeant in charge of 60 mm mortars and knew how to get the utmost from his men without being real pushy or too GI. The guys liked and respected him.

Charlie wasn't satisfied with the mortars, as he wanted to be a rifleman and thought he would see more close at hand action in a rifle platoon, so after Tarawa he transferred to the 3rd Rifle Platoon of Fox Company.

Fox Company and the 3rd Platoon landed at Saipan on the left flank of the beach in the first wave. The Japanese attacked Fox Company's lines three times the first night, blowing charge on the bugles and shouting "Banzai" and "blood for the emperor." Charlie Cone finally got the action that he so much wanted. His platoon leader was lost on the first day, so he was put in charge of the platoon and served as its leader from the "beachhead" until the end of the battle at the end of the island at Marpi Point days later. Fox Company was pretty well expended by morning, suffering many casualties, but repelled the Japanese in their fanatical charges.

We had only skeleton manpower as we later moved on toward the end of the island. It was hard to keep contact with fellow Marines on the left and right as the casualties had been high.

The Mortar Platoon was behind Charlie's 2nd Platoon as we moved on across the is-

land. I had only one man left in my squad, but we still carried the gun, ammunition, sight (gun) and binoculars. Charlie's platoon was up ahead, pinned down and needed mortar fire. Some Japanese had entered some type of building. Charlie had sent a runner back to my squad with description of target and had determined the azimuth by degrees on his compass to target and sent the distance back by yardage, 100 yards, I think. We adjusted the gun to his calculations and fired the first round. Normally we would have to adjust the elevation and deflection and fire a couple more rounds to get on target, but no, the runner appeared and said the first round of H.E. had been a direct hit and that all the Japanese had been killed. So finally, Charlie had his day as "forward observer" for 3rd Squad Mortars and as a rifle platoon leader.

The Mortar Platoon acted as rifleman, ammunition carriers, stretcher barriers and runners, whatever it took to annihilate the Japanese.

Near the end of the Saipan Campaign, the Japanese officers were assembling in the hills for orders for their final banzai charge. The mortar platoon was circled around the Fox Company Command Post. That night, July 4, 1944, seven Japanese officers came wandering into the 3rd Squad's area. Hughes was on the right in a foxhole by himself. Paul Cretinon and I were in a two man foxhole. Hughes challenged them with a "halt," thinking they might be Marines, as they were behind the lines. They broke and ran and were charging straight towards mine and Cretinon's foxhole, and we started firing. We could see them holding their sabers as they ran. Seven were in the group. All were dead the next morning. Two had jumped in a hole and had committed hari kari by holding grenades to their heads. They were headless when we saw them the next morning. We had thought that when they were tapping the grenades on their helmets that they would throw them. Some of the Marines in the Command Post got sprinkled with the skulls and debris. I remember the moon was so full and bright that night that we could see as though an illuminating flare had been fired.

We finally got some replacements just before we reached Marpi Point, the end of the island where we had them cornered. The Japanese, men, women and kids, would hold hands and jump from what was later called Suicide Cliff to the rocks below.

After the Saipan and Tinian battles, we trained on Saipan for the invasion of

Okinawa. We then returned to Saipan. We were training for the invasion of Japan proper when the war ended. Instead of going into Nagasaki, Japan as fighting Marines, we went in as occupational troops.

Before leaving Saipan months after the battle, one could look down from Suicide Cliff and see thousands of skeletal remains. They were bleached white from the salt water.

Charlie Cone and I make most of the reunions. I always look forward to seeing him. We reminisce about the good times and the not so good times. One of our favorite topics is the Foxton hike in New Zealand.

The *Blume Fontaine*
by Clement Vernon Henderson

The name only has meaning to 2,200 Marines and 400 Navy personnel who boarded this Dutch East Indies tub in August 1944. Supposedly, the *Fontaine* was the last ship to escape Manila harbor when the Japanese took the Philippines. Somehow, the ship and its all Indian crew wound up as a transport ship in the service of the United States. The scuttlebutt was that the owners were paid one dollar per day for chow and one dollar per day for billet for each man transported overseas. The ship was designed to carry an absolute maximum one thousand troops, so you can imagine the conditions with 2,600 on board. The men on the destroyer escorts in our convoy thought they were on the *Queen Mary* as compared with us.

After completing a third radio school at Lejuene and a quick cross-country train ride to Pendelton, I was placed in a unit designed as a replacement for overseas divisions. We weren't told where we were going or what division we were to join. "Just fall in and keep your mouths shut." A bus ride from Pendleton to San Diego harbor put us in position to board the *Blume Fontaine*. I wasn't expecting a luxury liner, but this small ship looked like something from the 18th century.

The unit I was with was placed in the second deck below. Bunks ran from the deck to the overhead, stacked eight high. You had a choice of sleeping on your back or your stomach. If you wanted to change, you had to get out of your bunk and slide back in; there wasn't room to turn over. We were told to get in our bunks and to stay there until further orders. The Marine Corps was not noted for giving out a lot of information when transporting troops during war.

My company had the "honor" of being selected for guard duty for the duration of our journey. Little did I know that in a short time I was going to become the ship's number one target for "Man Overboard," a situation that lasted for 38 days. My first post on guard duty was in the hold that housed 400 Navy personnel. Half were white and the other half black. Integration 55 years ago was not accepted and each group of men was hostile to the other. I had a full-time job keeping peace and the crowded situation in the fourth deck below didn't help. After a couple of days, tempers were very short, and I had to break up several disagreements. Conditions over the whole ship were so bad that an order was put out that no knives could be carried top-side. I had several run-ins with swabbies while enforcing the knife order, but I was able to win without calling for assistance.

When we stopped briefly at the Hawaiian Islands, I was on duty and the only one in the area that night. The OD came and told me that he had heard about my skirmishes with the swabbies and thought I must be pretty tough. I told him that I had just carried out my orders. He indicated that there was a bad situation top-side and he wanted to move me to that station. With so many men aboard the small ship, meals were a major problem. Colored chow-cards were issued and used to determine the order for meals. Every five days the order in which each color would eat was posted. It took all day to feed two meals to the enlisted men. When you got up in the morning you got in line to eat. When you finished eating your first meal, you got in line for your second meal. For the entire trip, the meals consisted of potato soup and beans. If potato soup was served for the first meal, beans were served for the second meal. The next day the order was reversed. In order to eat, you had to line up top-side, go through a hatch and down a ladder into a small chow hall. At the most, the chow hall accommodated about 25 men at a time. The temperature in the chow hall was at least 110 degrees. My need for food was solved at the first meal when I saw sweat running down the cook's arm into my bowl of soup. For the entire trip, I survived on canned cream, designed for use with coffee, that I swiped from the table.

My station on guard duty was at the hatch entrance to the chow hall. I had to make certain the chow card was in the posted order. If the red cards were eating, and a yellow card appeared, I had to kick

the chiseler out. Sometimes this amounted to a physical confrontation with the guy and his friends also shouting profanities at me. Phrases such as "There will be a SOB thrown overboard tonight," and "You'll be the first SOB in my rifle sight when we hit the beach," were common. The OD usually watched this show from a small platform on the deck above us. I told him not to be hesitant in drawing his weapon if a group decided to execute the "man overboard threat." I had no desire to swim in that shark infested Pacific Ocean while watching my convoy disappear at 18 knots per hour. Had this happened during the daylight, I'm sure one of the destroyer escorts traveling with the convoy would have rescued me. But then, I would have been a guest of the Navy, and that would be worse than being on the *Fontaine*!

I know I didn't make many friends on the *Blume Fontaine*, but I'm sure those of you who made that trip to Saipan in September of 1944 will remember me. I was that Louisiana Cajun chow-line guard!

Oklahoma, Oklahoma, New Jersey
by W. Mike Hewitt II

On February 27, 1991, my unit, the second battalion of the 2nd Marine Regiment (2/2) had stopped its advance through Kuwait at the western outskirts of Kuwait City. We had reached our initial objectives and were currently ordered to block all access to or from western Kuwait City. This was a fairly easy task because Kuwait is a desert country and in order to travel quickly one must use roads or highways that have been built into the dessert.

Though our present orders did not seem to be too difficult, they were very important. By the 27th of February, what was left of the Iraqi army in Kuwait was in full retreat. The Iraqi army and Iraqi looters were fleeing Kuwait City along a major highway leading westward out of Kuwait towards Baghdad. This passage was already made difficult by thousands of tons of Iraqi military hardware littered along the highway. Since the Gulf War had started our air forces had been wrecking havoc on Iraqi units using this thoroughfare. This highway had already become known as the "Highway of Death."

Nevertheless, 2/2's mission was to interdict any traffic going to or escaping from western Kuwait City. To accomplish this we established an ambush along the east-west highway that spanned from

Baghdad to Kuwait City. (Though 2/2 was [is] an infantry battalion we were mounted in Amtraks and had tanks and HUMV mounted TOWs in support). We moved up on-line about 700 yards from the southern side of the highway. On either side of us were bombed-out buildings that helped to hide our position from anyone traveling on the highway. Outposts were placed in the bombed out buildings to provide early warning of any incoming targets. The one weak spot of our position was that the northern side of the highway sloped down away from the road creating dead space (space we couldn't cover with our direct fire weapons). To counter this weakness our 81 mm mortars were set up to range this area. We also had Cobra helicopters on call to help destroy any threat that tried to make use of this area.

During the day and night of the 27th, 2/2 successfully interdicted a number of Iraqi vehicles trying to escape Kuwait. Sometime in the morning of the 28th we received word that two trucks were headed eastward (towards Kuwait City) on the highway and would soon be in our ambush zone. The infantrymen manning M-60 machine guns and the Amtrak gunners using .50 cal. machine guns and Mk. 19 automatic grenade launchers were poised behind their weapons ready to fire. I remember the gunner on the Amtrak I was sitting on yelling to other gunners that he would take the targets out well before anyone else because, as he said, he was, "just too good of a gunner!"

When the two target vehicles came into view a dozen machine guns began to erupt. Tracer bullets could be seen pouring downrange towards the targets. Amazingly the trucks were not hit with our initial bursts. The trucks realized they were being shot at and increased speed; our gunners kept up their fire and tracers were flying in front of the vehicles, between them, behind them, below them and over top of them. Miraculously the bullets were missing the trucks. (A few hours before these same gunners had handily destroyed a number of the same type of targets.)

Suddenly the alert driver of the lead vehicle swerved his truck off the north side of the highway. The second vehicle followed suit. These two trucks had escaped our bullets and were presently safe out of view of our direct fire weapons. As the mortarmen were preparing to take over our assault we heard voices coming from the direction of the escaped targets. Our gun-

ners had stopped firing and we could clearly hear someone on the north side of the highway yelling, "Oklahoma, Oklahoma, New Jersey! I'm from America, don't fire." We were all a little surprised and wondered if this were some kind of Iraqi trick. A moment later a couple heads appeared over the north side embankment and again we heard American state names being yelled. After a few seconds of silence about six people emerged onto the highway from the north side embankment with their hands in the air. One of them shouted," We're Americans; we're from CBS."

We quickly but cautiously dispatched some heavily armed HUMVs out to get a closer look at these people and their vehicles. What the lieutenant commanding the HUMVs discovered was about five men and one woman. Indeed, they were Americans - CBS reporters! It was truly amazing that they survived our ambush. I imagine they had quite a story to tell afterwards.

Saipan - July 1944
by Jodie Howington, F/3/6

Fox Company 2nd Battalion 6th Marines had been on the front lines for days, pushing the Japanese toward the north end of the island of Saipan. Everyone was sleepy, tired, dirty, and hungry. It felt like we had nothing to eat but K-Rations for weeks. When Company G came up to relieve us, Fox Company fell back to rest a little, clean up some, take on replacements and replenish the ammo and supplies. The Mortar Platoon, of which I was a member, and some of the other guys whose names I remember: Clarence Hargis, Jesse Repaul, Dick Meadows, Paul Cretinon, Randolf Longford, Jack Teague, Ed Rivers, Van Winkle and Price, decided to have a Bar-B-Q.

We had found a place, a farmhouse, thatch roof, water cistern, a couple of chickens (which went fast) and some pigs wandering around. We were getting ready to heat some water to clean and butcher one of the pigs for the Bar-B-Q when this lieutenant walked up and asked us what we thought we were going to do. We told him we were going to butcher and Bar-B-Q a pig. He thought a minute and said he didn't think he would eat a pig as they had probably been eating dead Japanese. Needless to say, the Bar-B-Q was canceled, and believe me, K-rations never tasted so good.

The *Morning Star*
by Jack F. Igo

This is a story about myself and the *Morning Star*, a 14-man outrigger canoe. It happened during my service in the Marine Corps in World War II and in the South Pacific near the island of Espirito Santos of the Hebrides chain. But I need to go back a little to relate what brought me there. The first retaliation against Japan was the invasion of the island of Guadalcanal. Our part in the invasion was that two tanks landed on Tulagi, the headquarters island just off of Guadalcanal. We were to support Edson's Raiders. They landed on the far and rugged end of the island, and we were to join them about halfway to their objective.

We landed cold turkey on this beach, not knowing if the raiders had gotten that far as yet. They had gotten that far and a lot farther as it turned out, and they had a guy sitting on the beach waiting to show us where to go. We stayed there in support using up all our gas and ammunition. Someone decided to send us back to our ship after we had been there about 72 hours with just rations and no sleep. When we got to the ship, they told us that while we slept, they would get our two tanks cleaned up and ready for further action. They could have sent two different tanks, but didn't because we had the experience.

We slept so soundly that we didn't even hear the great battle of Savo Island, where the Japanese sank six of our cruisers, and they could have come in and sunk all the transports, including ours. Everything was ordered out of there, because when daylight came, the Japanese might realize what sitting ducks we were.

We sailed to Espirito Santos, where we began a frenzied effort to unload our ship, getting supplies just on shore. Our ship had to run somewhere else to get more supplies for the troops that were left on Guadalcanal. Our unit, C Company, 2nd Tank Battalion, stayed right there. Who else stayed, I do not know. We ended up standing guard over these supplies stacked up on the beach for the first month or so.

The natives turned out to be Tonganese copra workers. All little people, they dressed alike with their white slacks and black jackets. They were scared to death of us at first. One of them had been a galley worker on an ocean going vessel and could speak some English. We can call him Sam for now.

We found the *Morning Star* on the beach, covered with palm fronds. It was really a beautiful boat hollowed out of a log with the name carved on both sides in the front. As time went on, we got to know our way around and could understand Sam a lot better. He invited my friend and I to gamble with them one night and we were to go to one of the small houses in their quarters after dark. We went and what an experience. The house was full of just men with a couple of women serving, and it was so full of smoke or something that you could hardly see. These people were small (about half our size) and they made room for us way in the back. The action was in the center of the room where there was a small rug. They had a small aluminum pan with a lid and into the pan went coins about the size of a nickel with one side painted white and the other painted black. You then bet odd or even, black or white. You could bet odd white or even white or you could bet odd black or even black. One of the natives had to bank each game, and when that was done, they threw the disks at which time pandemonium broke out. They seemed to know who won or lost, but the conversation that went with it was something. The first time that it happened, we tried to get out of there. We were betting 25 cents each time and there were not that many times.

As food for the guests, they had tea where they would hand you a tea kettle of sorts with a spout and you were to drink from that spout. I wouldn't have drunk from that spout for any money, but my friend did and he swore it was just tea. He even ate some small cakes and pieces of raw coconut. We made that trip just once, which was enough for me. I lost 75 cents. If they hadn't told me, I would have no way of knowing, even though I was there.

It was later that I learned that we could buy the boat. They wanted $10 for the boat and $100 for the sail. They said they could make another boat, but couldn't get another sail. I had four dollars, and it took six other guys to come up with three more dollars. We finally bought the boat for $7. We had no idea how we were going to make the boat go. We finally moved it from the beach area to our new place in a coconut grove on a fairly large and deep river.

The day we were to sail the boat to the new area, all seven of us had some shape of board to use as a paddle. That sucker was really hard to move. Then we got out into the bay currents and they moved us at will. We ran into three ships which threatened to shoot us out of the water. We could hear them telling us not to get any closer or they

Saipan June, 1944.

Saipan June 1944.

Betty Hutton and friend entertained us very well. That helped out a lot.

Saipan June 1944.

The Japs treated these people like dogs - when we would find them in caves, we would have them come out and share our rations. It made us feel good to be protecting them.

would sink us or something. We were so tired paddling the boat that we would just as soon they did sink us.

Where the river ran into the bay there was a naval station there with a phone. And four of the guys called our base and got them to send a truck for us. Three of us managed to get the boat up the river to our landing area. As tired as we were, we figured that would be it with our boat, and that we had made a bad investment. Later, we went down and painted it camouflage green and hid it in the reeds.

Some time passed, and we were just marking time, really, and having a lousy time of it with food. We had plenty of papayas, mangos, bananas, coconuts, and some lemons and grapefruit of very bad quality. Everyone had a still in his tent. It was called kooly-how and you made it out of anything that would ferment. Everyone had a giant stalk of bananas hanging up in his tent. Natives, who used to be head hunters, would come through our area carrying a long bamboo pole with as many as 10 stalks of bananas hanging from it, and you could get a whole stalk for a pack of cigarettes. Our meals were usually made somehow out of Spam. They would call it by different names, but you always just tasted the Spam.

It was about this time that the major called me in to see him. Everyone wondered what I had done so wrong to get the commanding officer on my case. He asked me about the boat, where it was and why we didn't use it. I told him that it was just sitting up in the reeds and was too much boat for us to handle. He said, "Jack, would a four cylinder Evinrude work on that boat even though it comes to a point in the river?" We kicked it around a bit and decided to work on it. Seems that all tank units have iron and iron cutting equipment and it didn't take long to build a steel bracket on the rear and attach the motor to it. We tried it up and down the river until we had it working just great. Sunday was to be its maiden voyage. The four who had left us at the beginning were no longer shareholders, so the three of us made the first trip that Sunday. We each had on a sweat shirt, a pair of cut-off pants to make shorts and a pair of old shoes. We had to carry a weapon by orders and we had water and rations. We took off and it was great. It went very fast and made for a good time. We went to one island that we heard had watermelons. There were none there, so we went to another island and it was there that we found millions of juicy tangerines and all ours. The Frenchman who

owned them even gave us sandbags for carrying them and helped to fill our boat so full I thought we would sink any number of times. We made it and at the naval station called our camp to send a truck to the boat landing. They wouldn't do it at first, but eventually did. We ended up with every tent getting two bags of tangerines. It helped, but we needed to do much better. The next trip, six of us went and we started back when the bay was a little choppier, and we ended up sinking out there. We were trying to figure out what to do when a navy boat called to us to grab a line they would shoot to us. We caught the line and were dragged out of what turned out to be a mine field. That trip, we came back with nothing and further trips were in doubt.

About a month later, we went again with just three of us. I had an idea this time and wanted to try it. None of us wore any rank and I made the other two just keep quiet and say "Yes, Sir" to me if I gave them an order. I was going to try to go aboard ship and scrounge. The other two were scared to death, and so was I really. We went to a cruiser and requested permission to come aboard and it was granted. We went on board and I told the officer on the deck we needed to work out some kind of a trade for supplies, like bananas and tangerines for any kind of food that they could spare. He told me to wait a minute and he would check. I started drinking cold water until I almost got sick. We had had nothing cold since we got on the island. The officer of the deck came back and asked me what I could use. I was flabbergasted and didn't know how to answer him. I told him that we had 40 men, including officers, in our unit and had been eating nothing but Spam and rations for eight months. He asked me how I could carry anything in that small boat. For starters, he gave us lots of fresh home-made bread and some pies. With that he gave us all the butter we would need for that much bread. He told me to come back the next day and he would have some other stuff boxed up so we could carry it in the boat. He had no use for any bananas or tangerines; they were just willing to help. We hurried back to camp and called for the truck again and this time had no problems. That night we had Spam again, but this time we had just about enough hot bread and butter. The officers were overjoyed and the CO told the first sergeant to keep me off any duty rosters until he told him differently, and if I needed any help to turn loose any of my crew I might need. He did that when I told

him that they wanted me to come back the next day for more. About this time, I was very popular with everyone coming to my tent to tell me what I should try to get. The cook gave me a want list, like instant potatoes and instant milk. Guys needed shaving gear, cigarettes, and chewing tobacco. I put Homer in charge of the PX detail and he would take orders from the guys and get their money to pay for it.

On one trip our Lieutenant decided to go with us and he agreed that I was the man in charge and he would do as I told him and just say "Yes, Sir." Everything went beautifully and I imagine he came back and reported to the CO. We were just scrounging, which is in every Marine's soul. The Navy did everything they could for us and no questions asked. One occasion, I brought back a whole side of beef. Many times I had lots of ice cream packed in dry ice so that it was still frozen when dished out. We brought back ice packed in dry ice so we could have iced tea for supper. We were able to find out when new ships were coming in and where they were coming from so we would know if their supplies were in good shape. Those that were coming in from a long patrol, we left alone. Their larders would be down. We kept trying to fix the boat so it would hold more.

We tried to shop at cruisers. All entrances to the bay were mined, and I believe that cruisers were the biggest ships that could get in there. A lot of days we would just go out and give sailors a ride in our outrigger and give them a chance to take pictures. Usually, one of us would take about six of them on a short run about the bay. The other two of us would stay aboard and drink cold water and anything else they would give us. We could always get hot coffee and most of the time, a doughnut or a sweet roll to wash down with it. Or we would shop at the PX. Twice, we were just given the ship's candy ration for that day. Now we are talking about 15 or 20 boxes and they just gave them to us to share with our group. The Navy was very good to us in those days and we loved them for it.

If there was more than one ship at anchor and we were giving rides, those not getting rides would beg us to come over so some of them could ride. They wanted to take pictures to send home. We finally got smart and repainted the boat white and the raised letters *Morning Star* painted bright red. That made a lot better picture to send home. In all of that time I never did get a picture of *Morning Star* for myself, but I

Indians with the Marines on Saipan landed with the first waves to hit the beach. Left to Right, Corporal Oscar B. Iithma, Gallup, New Mexico; Private First Class Jack Nez, Fort Defiance, Arizona; and Private First Class Carl N. Gorman, Chimle, Arizona.

surely can see it in my mind. It got to the point that we no longer tried to carry food in our craft. We were busy giving rides all day. The three of us were with the boat all day, almost every day. We would get messages from certain ships asking if the boat would be available on such and such a day and between the hours of such and such. We tried to make every request and it paid off, because it resulted in the ships sending us every kind of supply. They would send it to the naval unit at the head of the river who would call our office and a truck would be sent to pick it up. Those were really happy days for the three of us and the boat. And what made it even nicer, our other members didn't resent us because of what the boat was doing for all of us.

However, all good things are bound to come to an end. We were fixing to move and get back into the war. I was told to bring the boat to the maintenance dock and there

the motor was removed. We then just pulled the boat back up into the reeds. I could have sold the boat for plenty, but never had a chance. We began loading up to go. Some brought the stuff down to the beach and some loaded from the beach to the small boats going to the big ship then unloaded from the boats to the hold of our big ship. I was on that detail, and therein lies another great war story that could come later. It depends on the reaction to this little true tale. The next one would be called the New Zealand episode.

Carrol's Capers
by Henry H. Jandl Jr.

We had an ex-Army fellow from South Carolina by the name of Carrol in our battery and he liked to drink. He got happy when he was drunk and always wanted to do something for the people he liked.

One night at about 0200 to 0230 he stole all the ice-cream he could carry out of the mess hall and went around the barracks waking up everybody he liked to give them a box. He couldn't wake Meriwether so he put a box in the sack with him. In a little while that woke him up.

•Another caper he pulled off was when we were in the Med. Carrol and John Rushton, one of the boys from the gun section I was in, got lit up and missed the last liberty launch. Carrol decided that Rushton needed something to eat, so we got into one of the food lockers aboard, opened up a box of hams, unwrapped them all and took the biggest one with idea of swimming ashore with it to give Rushton something to eat. Somebody on watch spotted him. They got to chasing him and he ran up to the foredeck and disappeared. He crawled down the hause pipe on the anchor chair, stuck his head up and said, "Pee pie, here I am." They

Pfc. Carl Gorman (358512) of Chimle, Arizona, Navajo Marine, who manned an observation post on a hill overlooking the city of Garapan while the Marines were consolidating their positions on the island of Saipan.

caught him and he spent the rest of the night in the brig.

A Memorable Train Journey
by Roland K. Jennings

This is an account of a train journey taken while serving as a member of the occupation forces of Japan. The 10th Marines arrived in Nagasaki on September 23, 1945. They were given the responsibility of patrolling the inland city of Isahaya, only minutes away. Approximately six weeks later, they were transferred back to the port city of Nagasaki. Guard duty assignments consisted of stationary posts, roving posts, or a combination thereof. The four to six hour shifts could be down-right tedious, or in some cases exhilarating, according to the luck of the draw.

It was late in December 1945, when Private First Class Jones and myself were cho-sen to escort a supply train from Nagasaki to Miyazaki, home of the 2nd Marine Regiment, some 240 miles away. The average temperature of Kyushu for December ranges from 30 to 40 degrees fahrenheit, much cooler than what we were accustomed to in the Marianas. Marine personnel had been issued shoe paks (a combination rubber/leather boot) with removable felt insoles, along with sheepskin coats to combat the cold weather. The upcoming journey was not my first trip by rail however. Several weeks earlier, myself and another Marine escorted a supply train from Isahaya to Nagasaki, a distance of 21 miles. We rode in the cab of the locomotive, sharing space with the Japanese engineer and fireman. The trip, made under cover of darkness, was rather uneventful but a truly unique experience.

Late one afternoon, Private First Class Jones and myself were taken to the Nagasaki rail yard with instructions to occupy a box car well back from the locomotive. Fortunately, the car chosen was lightly laden, allowing us ample room to move about. Later that evening we would rearrange the sacks of foodstuff to form a pallet for our sleeping bags. After viewing our spartan like accommodations, I had a hunch it was going to be a trip that would test our survival skills. I think my buddy Jones had already anticipated our plight, as he managed to acquire a five gallon, open top, square tin container, and filled it with small lumps of coal at the rail yard before we boarded.

It was nearly dark when we got underway. The route we would follow was along the coastline bordering the inland sea until we reached Kagoshima, then cross country to our destination, Miyazaki. Jones and I settled down in our sleeping bags hoping for a little shut eye. I soon drifted off despite the clattering of the wheels against the steel track. Sometime later, I awoke with a start. Apparently the train had stopped directly in front of a public address loudspeaker at a railway station. A young Japanese woman was vigorously announcing arrivals and departures, or we presumed as such. My buddy was also wide awake. This point, prompted by the falling temperature, was the time to try our makeshift coal burning stove. As soon as the train left the station, we ignited our cache of coal. As smoke and soot from the flames began to curl upward and fill the interior of the box car, we cracked the door open a few inches hoping for a chimney effect.

This worked to a certain degree and also provided a source of badly needed fresh air. There would be no more sleep for us two private first classes the rest of the night, as we remained huddled near the fire absorbing the added warmth. At daybreak, as the train approached Kumamoto, about half way into our journey, we disposed of the stove. As we did, we discovered there was a large hole burned through the thick wooden floor where the tin container had stood. We could peer through the opening and see the blur of the road bed below. The edge of the hole was still aglow so we used our water filled canteens to douse the burning embers. Under the circumstances, I feel we were very fortunate or lucky, but desperate people do desperate things. After all, when your 19, you are invincible.

Upon our arrival at Kumamoto the train left the main line and pulled onto the siding. Little did we know this was going to mean a five-hour layover, something we had not anticipated or been advised of. When the train came to a halt, we made our way to the station washroom to clean up. Judging from the appearance of our faces, they had become the sole depository for the soot generated by the coal fire. Jones and I resembled a couple of hobos for sure. The only light areas showing were the squint marks or crow's feet around our eyes and mouth. Fortunately, we were able to remove most of the grime.

There was not a visible sign per se, saying, "No English Spoken Here," but it would have been most appropriate. Many people we encountered in Nagasaki could speak limited English, but there appeared to be a void here in Kumamoto. My buddy had no interest in trying to converse with the Japanese attendants, so it was left up to me. I had managed to learn basic Japanese since my arrival from Saipan three months ago. Also, I carried with me, TM 30-641, a Japa-

Tunga River Gudalcanal. We really enjoyed this day.

nese phrase book, issued by the War Department to occupation personnel. After repeated attempts I was able to determine the train would not leave until 1300 hours. As Jones and I were relaxing in the station waiting room, our train began to move about on the siding. A quick glance was exchanged, the only communication needed before we bolted out the door and climbed aboard the slowly moving boxcar, just in case my G-2 regarding the departure time was erroneous. How would you explain losing a train? As it turned out, the yardmaster was only realigning the cars to their proper position prior to continuing on to Miyazaki. At 1300 hours we were on our way again. Today the skies were clear. The temperature was quite mild for December in stark contrast to last night's bone chiller. Since we would be traveling in a southern direction, we opened the boxcar door fully to take advantage of the warm afternoon sun. The miles rolled by quickly. Soon the shadows began to lengthen. Our trek was nearing an end. About 1600 hours, we reached the coastal city of Kagoshima, then headed in an easterly direction toward Miyazaki, about one hour away.

It was dusk when we arrived at the station, to be greeted by Military Police from the 2nd Marines. They were a welcome sight as it had been over 24 hours since we had seen an American. My buddy and I were driven to their barracks nearby. After enjoying an evening meal and a hot shower, we were ready to relax a bit before hitting the sack. Kibitzing was in order until we were too weary to continue. We arose

early the next morning, after a good night's rest, and made our way to the mess hall before picking up our gear and heading for the train station. Only this time, we boarded a passenger train sharing a coach with Japanese civilians for the return trip to Nagasaki.

Troop Transport "Lurline" June 1942
by Harold Lysene, PFC, BARman

Just fresh out of boot camp, this 18-year-old Marine is boarding ship for a "free vacation" overseas. Off we go on "the good ship lollipop," 5,000 trigger-happy gyrenes. We are supposed to relieve tired, sick Marines on Guadalcanal. Fourteen days later we cross the Equator, and stop over at Samoa. We struck camp and set up guard stations along the beach road, because they tell us the enemy would like to be here too.

Now the fun begins. Early one morning a truck full of sailors came sailing down the road. It so happens that two of us are armed with Browning automatic rifles. As the truck approaches they spot us two Marines waving our heavy artillery around and it's "mayday, mayday." In seconds there are 10-15 sailors unloading and standing at attention. I guess you know, we felt like a couple of 4-star generals.

Marines On Board
by Harold Lysene, PFC, BARman

Dateline January 7, 1942: About 30 of us boarded a train out of Seattle, Washing-

1 Jan 1943. Guadalcanal.

ton heading for San Diego, California and "boot camp." The Army was drafting, so we (my uncle and I) volunteered for the Marines. Our thinking was that smaller units and better training, etc. would give us a better chance of survival, which may have proved to be true, because 50 years plus I am one of the survivors.

After crawling around the Camp Elliot training grounds, we went on to Camp Matthew's Rifle Range. Six months later the transition from "Civy" to "Gyrene" was complete. Somehow during that time I became a "volunteer" BAR man.

Now we are ready to board a troopship. The Matson Line ship loaned one of their ships named the *Lurline*. It had been renovated to haul 5,000 18-year-old leathernecks anywhere Uncle Sam needed them. Out at sea the picture is like this: The bunks are four deep. It seems like those prone to seasickness always got the upper berths, because undigested meals gravitated to the lower berths; needless to say, I camped on deck.

For 14 days we snaked across the Pacific Ocean with little or no escort. I guess the Japanese were all tied up at Guadalcanal. We were supposed to be replacements, but I think we were so seasick they dropped us off in British Samoa for some R&R! It so happened that the 7th Marines secured the "'Canal," so we stayed to guard the island for the next 18 months. Then it was back on board and the high seas again. But, you know, one never gets used to it, because the guy in the top berth was still the lucky one.

South Seas Visit To Betio, Tarawa
November 20-23, 1943
by Eldon M. (Mike) Meyer

At 2200 hours, November 20, 1943, we were in an amphibian tractor headed for the beach at Betio, Tarawa. It was black and we could see nothing. Moonrise would occur in three hours at about 0130. We hoped for signs of activity on the beach and a welcoming party to show us where to put our equipment until we got our bearings.

We were 16 Company I Marines, a radio operator, one lieutenant, and two drivers on that amphibian tractor. All except the drivers had been on the water since 0645 hours and anxious to get ashore.

During the day, in other landing craft, we had started several runs to the beach, only to be driven back. Then, in daylight, we could see what was happening. Now in the dark, we grew apprehensive as the tractor got closer to the shore.

There had been 94 of us with the lieutenant that left the Monrovia at 0645 hours in a tank lighter. We were driven back on our first two attempts to land. The tank lighter next to us just blew up and disappeared. In our group, we lost several men, wounded when the ramp was let down. We turned to the relative safety of the lagoon and transferred the wounded to a boat going to a hospital ship. We tried to get to shore five or six more times in smaller groups and smaller boats, each time turning back. In the afternoon, the Control officer needed our tractor for critical supplies, but not men, he said. He put the 18 of us on a supply boat

close to a buoy used as a marker for boats going in and out, to wait there until he could get us into shore.

Waiting was almost agonizing. Every time a boat came close, we anticipated this could be our turn, but by dusk, as a dim light on the buoy turned on, our chances to move in seemed more and more remote. Stars became brighter, some island fires were visible, and an occasional tracer was seen. It was about 2115 by my government issue watch when a control boat came out to us and the navy officer asked how many. Our Lieutenant said 18. The officer drove away. In 40 minutes, he returned with an amphibian tractor. We transferred our equipment, packs and my radio to the tractor. The control officer told our lieutenant, "About 800 yards to the left and then to shore." To us, it was a relief. Waiting was over.

Our feet would soon be on solid ground, but we would have felt better if it had not been so black. We sat or stood in the well deck. To our right we could see a couple of small fires on the island. We felt the tractor turn to the left, to go about 800 yards in the dark. It seemed like an hour, but took only five minutes before our tractor turned to the starboard and headed in. We were fairly close to the beach, as it seemed like only a minute or two when our treads hit the ground and a shell exploded on the front of the tractor. Gun flashes came from three sides and high, like riflemen in trees. The driver yelled, "Beach," and about six men went over the side.

The sergeant yelled, "I'm hit" and fell back on Leland and myself. By the time we got out from under the sergeant, the tractor was backing out into the lagoon. The lieutenant and another man jumped on the side of the tractor and climbed inside as we got underway. The sergeant never woke up. Sixteen of us including the sergeant and the drivers returned to the buoy. A control boat found us and took the two drivers who had been hurt in the explosion and the sergeant to the nearest ship. Our longest night finally became morning.

The remaining 13 of us started again for the beach. At 0530 hours a tractor and two new drivers took us to the long pier. There, the shore party officers needed the tractor for supplies and no one wanted to lose it to anti-boat fire taking men into the beach. It was not safe to move on top so we went along the west side of the pier in the water, from neck deep and over my head, to knee and ankle deep.

A short section of pier had no side boards

On Guadalcanal January 1943. Joe E. Brown and Johnny Marvin entertaining the troops.

When we turned to go east (to our left) 800 yards, we really should have turned west. That way we would have come to a beach with our Marines instead of Japanese Marines. After reading that book my hopes were renewed that I might get in touch with some of the men I had known at Tarawa.

In 1992 three former members of Headquarters Company, 3rd Battalion, 8th Marines, 2nd Division, organized a reunion and 33 Marines attended (10 I knew from New Zealand and Tarawa). At our second reunion, I told my experience in that night landing, and standing in front of me was one of the four men who went over the side on that dark night on Betio and made a world record dash west to the American lines. Luck was with me in finding some of the others. A corporal was killed at Tinian and our lieutenant died in an observation airplane crash at Saipan. I finally got in contact with the Marine who was knocked down by the sergeant in the amphibian tractor. I am thankful for my three and one half years as a Marine in World War II. I have utmost respect for those men, my friends, Marines, corpsmen, sailors, who overran that impossible island, Tarawa, and the many other islands in our Pacific War. The experience described above and the people I see there have become my purpose for attending those 3rd Battalion, 8th Marine, 2nd Marine Division reunions.

One Lucky Marine
by Kenneth H. Mosher

I joined the Marines in June of 1939, enlisting at the Marine recruiting station in San Francisco, CA. Following boot camp and sea school, I was assigned to duty aboard the USS *Maryland* (BB-46), a battleship. After two years of sea duty I was transferred to the 8th Marines, B Company, where I took part in the Guadalcanal Campaign. Following the Guadalcanal Campaign I was commissioned 2nd Lieutenant and transferred to Company G, 2nd Battalion, 8th Marines, 2nd Marine Division. In the battle of Tarawa I landed in the assault in the second boat wave with a portion of my platoon on the right flank of the battalion, alongside of the big pier. Immediately upon hitting the beach, Major Crowe, Battalion CO, ordered me to take a group of Marines, about 25 to 30, and report to Major Chamberlin, Battalion Executive Officer, who had landed on the left flank of the battalion front. Company F had landed in that zone of action.

to walk on. To keep my radio dry, I put it up on the pier where someone could pick it up later. We were shot at from the beach, from the sunken ship to our right and from some destroyed landing craft and amphibian tractors. We were also shot at from beneath the pier.

On reaching the shore, I was sent to Headquarters Company area and the others were assigned to another line company. I mentioned my dry working radio on the pier to a sergeant and he immediately sent me out to get it. Another two hours in the water, carrying the radio on top of the pier for about 60 feet, and bringing it to where I had seen the sergeant. I could not find him and never saw him again, but gave the radio to one of our squad leaders who took it to a communications center.

With my radio and my lieutenant gone, I became a runner, a water carrier, an ammunition carrier and a messenger. On the third morning, there was an explosion on the air

strip to my right and a thumb-sized shell fragment buried itself in my upper right arm. The corpsman patched me up and sent me to the USS *Doyen* where the shrapnel was removed from my arm. I spent six months touring navy hospitals through Aiea Heights near Pearl Harbor, through Oak Knoll, Sampson, Brooklyn Navy Yard and Camp Lejeune. At Camp Lejeune, among other activities, I played baseball and helped rehabilitate my arm until I was re-assigned to active duty, meaning, ultimately, the invasion of Japan. I was on Guam when the atom bombs shortened the war.

In the ensuing years I have wondered about the attempt to capture that tail of Betio with 18 men and about the men who had been in that group. I began collecting books about the battle for Tarawa. In 1991 I found the book *76 Hours, The Invasion Of Tarawa* by Eric Hammel and John Lane, that on page 135 described my part of the battle and helped solve some of the mystery for me.

Major Chamberlin ordered me to place my men in a skirmish line directly to the rear of Company F to support them in the event of an enemy counterattack from the east end of the island. That portion of the island had not been landed on by our assault forces. This action placed me in a position close to the beach, enabling me to observe the east end of the island.

The first night I placed two men to a foxhole. This allowed one man to rest while the second man could remain alert. About midnight I observed a small group of men in a close huddle about 50 feet from my position. I knew that was close to where my men were located. I thought at first it was my men, but I had told them not to move around after darkness, to remain in their positions. So, I challenged them with "Who's there?" No response. Then again I challenged with "Open up or I'll blast you." They broke and four men dropped to the ground. The other three ran toward the beach, right past my position. As they passed by toward the water, I and the sergeant (who had been wounded previously) cut loose with our weapons and shot all three. They all fell into the water.

Those that hit the sand could easily be seen as the sand was light and though there were other bodies laying around, dead Marines or enemy dead, I had the idea that those who hit the sand were playing possum. I knew that the enemy wore split toe shoes,

so I told a couple of my men to feel of their feet and if they had on split toed shoes to shoot to kill. Two were killed and the third one we took prisoner by knocking him in the head with a rifle stock, then tying him up with a mortar lowering line.

A shot was fired real close and a person stood up. I told the corporal to take him prisoner also. He said, "Let me stick him, lieutenant, let me stick him." I again ordered him to be taken prisoner, to take him to the water's edge, strip and search him, then tie him up. The subject then walked to the water's edge and stripped himself naked. I told the men to watch carefully, that the man appeared to understand English. The corporal said again, "Let me stick him lieutenant." As he said that, the subject then suddenly blurted out, "I'm a Marine! I'm a Marine!" What a shock that was. We had almost killed him. I asked his name, his rank and the unit he was with. He told me he was a member of a tank crew and that his tank had been disabled. I asked his tank commander's name which he gave. I recognized the lieutenant's name. I ordered the Marine to dress and remain alert the remainder of the night and in the morning to return to his unit. In the morning he was gone. He was "one lucky Marine."

The incident of the "Lucky Marine" took only about two minutes. All that time he was unable to speak; I assume because he was in a state of shock. He had awakened dur-

ing the commotion and found someone lying beside him. He shot him with a 45 pistol then stood up. That is when we almost shot him. At least he lived through the first night! I never did know if he survived the battle of Tarawa or not. I am certain if he did survive and is still alive he would remember that night. I would really like to make contact with anyone who remembers that incident, especially that "Lucky Marine." I retired in 1975 as a lieutenant colonel and another lucky Marine.

Why I Am Me!
by Erwin C. (Bud) Nielsen

It was the fall of 1943. I was 17 years old, born to a family rich in everything that counted, but poor in every other respect. My friends had electric trains, summer vacations, family outings, roast beef on Sunday, but we had love, a mother that cared, a sister who always helped, and a father I did not see much of.

In some cases this might have developed a feeling of insecurity, but not in my case. I merely assumed that there were those in the world destined to have things and those in the world destined not to have things, and we belonged to the latter category. I suppose what I really had was an inferiority complex. My best recollection was that we were not quite as good as some of our friends and neighbors with automobiles,

This is gunner Lund's (far right) Platoon B-1-8 returning from our patrol near the Point Cruz area. Notice flat helmets and .03 rifles. Guadalcanal November 1941.

nice backyards and console radios. As a result, I certainly was not a leader, but placidly a follower.

Money was important, not to get ahead in the world necessarily, but just to pay the bills, put food on the table and see if the lights worked when you turned on the switch. This was a way of life. It did not bother me. I accepted it and as a result started working at a very early age.

After my sister married, Mom and I moved to San Jose. I quit school just after starting the 11th grade and the two of us decided to make a go of it. I went to work for John Urzi in a service station and garage in San Jose. When I eventually left there, I was the head mechanic and ran the place in his absence. (Not too bad for a 17 year old). Mother had bought an old house on 7th Street and we were taking in boarders.

This was the war years. Everyone was caught up in it in some fashion. Our customers had plenty of money to spend, as pay in the defense plants and ship yards was really good. But making money was never my highest priority, nor is it now. I wanted something more, I guess. I wanted acceptance, to be looked upon and be respected, to be at least as good as the next guy and maybe someday even stand out in a crowd.

I remember going to the Santa Cruz beach one weekend with a buddy of mine. I can't remember his name, but he was still in high-school and on the football team. Girls, of course, were important. I had a couple of girlfriends, nothing very serious, but after all who can be too serious at 17. I lived with a great big doubt. How could I, a local grease monkey, who had not even finished high-school and from a poor family, ever impress the real cute girls.

We were out walking along the boardwalk. I remember it was Saturday afternoon. The battle for Guadalcanal was over and the U.S. Marine Corps had its first batch of heroes. A good share of them were spending their liberty here in Santa Cruz, walking down the boardwalk in their dress blues, campaign ribbons on their chest, and at least one girl in one arm and sometimes two girls in two arms. What a sight! People's heads turned, watching, smiling with pride and admiration in everyone's eyes. They were the best. They were all heroes and just to be in their presence was awesome!

Therein lies the answer to all my hidden desires. They symbolized everything that really mattered to me at the moment. Call it hero worship, call it anything you like, but

Dead Japanese on Guadalcanal 1942.

Jap Stuts - Tanambogo.

I knew at that moment that was for me. By joining the U.S. Marine Corps, I could become what I had never been. I could be as good or better than anyone else. All I had to do if they would take me was pass their physical examination, endure their boot camp, go to war, and come back alive - a piece of cake.

Years have passed since that day. God watched over me and I did come back and spent a lot of time doing the things that I wanted to do. Sure, I started out as a mechanic. There is nothing wrong with that, and I subsequently bought an automobile repair business. Then one day I decided that I would

like to become a lawyer, so I went to night law school and eventually started my own law firm. I became a rancher, etc. etc. When I think back, somewhat with amazement, I realized all of my accomplishments. I don't mean to imply that they have all been great, but whatever they have been, large or small, they can be traced back to one Saturday morning in the fall of 1943 at the U.S. Marine Corps Recruit Depot in San Diego, CA.

I was a member of Platoon 67, who had just completed boot camp. We had been knocked about physically and mentally, torn apart, convinced that we were individually not worth a damn, that we were the scum of the earth, that only our drill instructor and the U.S. Marine Corps could rescue, rehabilitate and reincarnate each of us into something that the Marine Corps "may" be proud to call its own.

We were standing at attention. The Marine Corps band was playing the Marine Corps hymn. Our khaki shirt and trousers were starched and pressed to perfection. We had survived a holocaust and were entering the real world. The world of each of us as a United States Marine, one in which we were as good as, or better, than anyone else. There was nothing that we could not do or accomplish. The world and the war were given to us on a silver platter. We were prepared to accept it, to deal with it in any manner necessary. We had learned the meaning of pride. We had been taught the meaning of Semper Fi (forever faithful). We were members of an exclusive fraternity and would be members of this fraternity for the rest of our lives.

Pride. We were proud to wear the Marine Corps uniform. Saluting the flag was a privilege; hearing the Marine Corps hymn caused a lump in our throat. The pride we had was founded on something that we were and what we had done. It was not vanity; we did not look for admiration or praise. On the contrary, it was a type of pride which could never solicit admiration or praise. It was self-respect, a clearly worthy feeling. It was self-esteem. Perhaps a more generous estimate may be of our own character and abilities than we were entitled to, but nevertheless, we had it.

We were tough and we knew it, and it turned out to be true. We fought battles. Some died, some lived. But we always won. We were part of an indestructible team. No job or no task was too large or too difficult. My life had been sculptured and shaped. If I wanted something bad enough I could have it. I only needed the desire. I recall graduation from Lincoln University in San Francisco in 1956. 1 had finally completed all of my law studies. I was the class valedictorian, graduating Magna Cum Laude, a real honor for a kid like me. It was made possible by God and the U.S. Marine Corps.

During my years as a lawyer, I developed a sort of reputation among many in the San Jose legal community, taking cases no one else would. Cases that did not look like winners, when the chance of recovering any money was highly doubtful. "Go see Bud Nielsen" was not an uncommon suggestion. None of these cases ever made me wealthy, but they provided the most stimulating form of satisfaction, starting with nothing and turning it into something. The ability to challenge the odds when everything seemed to be against you. All of this can be traced to that sun-filled Saturday morning in San Diego, when God and the U.S. Marine Corps made me a man.

My First Overseas Guard Duty
by Bill Ogden

My first guard duty in New Zealand was a farce! I still wasn't sure that there were no Japanese around. I was placed across the road from camp and told to guard the motor transport compound. It was pitch dark, cold and a wee bit frightening. I heard a sound! I anxiously looked across the road to see if it was time for my relief. It wasn't. I again heard the sound! I quickly closed the gap and again waited for the sound. I heard it! In my mind I decided that I was doing the honorable thing and was prepared to give my life for my country. I quickly moved forward and ran directly into my enemy. The enemy turned to me and said, "Moooooooooo." It was a black New Zealand cow!

Joey, The New Zealand Parakeet
by Bill Ogden

Shortly after arriving in New Zealand, a kind New Zealand lady brought her pet parakeet, Joey, out to our camp. She left him there so that he could help "keep us happy." The CO could not properly get out of keeping Joey so he graciously accepted him. Joey lived with the troops! He went to chow, to the movies, to the showers, and even sat in on the nightly poker games. As the men would stand and shave in the morning, Joey would run back and forth along the shelf holding the shaving gear and would look at his image in the mirror and bark out orders.

No one realized the completeness of Joey's vocabulary until the kind lady returned a couple of months later to pick up her pet. As Joey began to conjugate Marine verbs and to spout out his magnificent repertoire of unmentionable adjectives, the camp emptied until only the kind lady, the CO and a very salty bird were left.

Runner
by Bill Ogden

Most Marines find humor in any and all situations. The night before we hit Tarawa, I was designated a "runner" (don't ever become a runner!). A staff NCO would sit at the desk in the stateroom where a full colonel and a lieutenant colonel usually slept. He would take operational messages from the bridge and the runner, a private (me), would run these messages to the various holds of the ship to the platoon leader or company commander to whom it was addressed. These officers seemed hard to find because we were practically on the equator and the heat was so unbearable that they would strip to the waist and would be lying on the deck with their men. You couldn't tell an officer from an enlisted man. However, it was significant that I could wake up any man and he knew exactly where I could find his commanding officer.

Guadalcanal 1942-43.

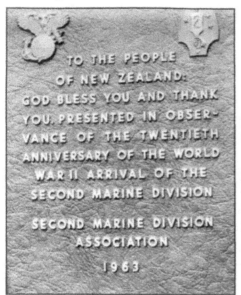

The colonel and the lieutenant colonel slept topside where they could get some breeze (something we weren't allowed to do). The staff NCO was very "Gung Ho" and "by the book" and also somewhat nervous - a perfect person to tease in practicing my sick humor! I was tired of standing and messages had slacked off when I decided to lie down on the lieutenant's colonel's bunk. I reached up and put the colonel's cap on my head and our staff NCO almost died. I took the cap off so he could breathe again when the lieutenant colonel walked in. I slithered and sprung to a position of attention and, to this day, I cannot remember how I put his cap back onto the hook. He went to the desk, asked a question, picked up something that he had come down for and turned to leave. As he passed me, he said, "I don't see how you can stand it down here in this heat" and left. I immediately collapsed on his bunk, but as I reached up for his cap, the staff sergeant said, "Don't you dare!"

Almost Killed At Tarawa
by Bill Ogden

Before leaving Betio and returning to a ship, I was assigned the duty of building a fire in our bivouac area. That way we could have hot coffee and heat our rations. I dug the hole and thought that I had cleaned out all of the Japanese ammunition. I had taken out 250 to 300 rounds. However, as we sat around the fire with the lieutenant colonel (same one whose cap I had worn), shells still left in the hole overheated and began exploding. We all fell backwards in order to keep from being hit. The lieutenant colonel accused me of trying to kill him whereas

all of us were sitting around the same fire. Oh, the humilities of war!

2nd Battalion, 8th Marines Drum & Bugle Corps
by James A. Ogilvie

Lieutenant Colonel J. Cody, CO of the battalion, had called for volunteers from the battalion and I was with Company F, 2/8 when answering his call. In his office the first day he conducted an audition for me by giving me a set of shelterhalf poles to play rudiments on his desk, then an old trumpet "mouth piece" to blurt out some lip sounds and I was hired on as the drum major/director.

I was given the pick of the battalion to form a 13 man drum and bugle (six buglers, one scotch bass drum, two side snare drums and two tenor drums). The battalion adjutant was dispatched back to Norfolk for the equipment and was able to get six new G/D bugles (one valve), five old drums donated from the school of music, and one new bass drum. I made up the drum majors baldric (white cross over shoulder strap) with the battalion's battle honors scrolled on it with a Marine emblem at the top. A drum majors mace, made from a broom stick with a silver sugar bowl atop/w emblem, and a dog chain wrapped around it.

The D&B was carried on the roster as the flame section of H&S Battalion (which no longer existed), but we were the security section for headquarters and the colonel's body guard in the field.

Lieutenant Colonel Cody sent Battalion Sergeant Major M. Hardiman and myself TAD to the Jamaican Regiment so that I could learn the mace movements of quick

and slow time marching. After selection of the corps, long hours on the windward air field were put in on marching formations, and learning the necessary songs and drum cadence for parades and reviews. Our uniform consisted of sea-going blues for formal outings and utilities with white "pith-helmets" and guard belts for daily colors and guard mounts.

The Corps played "hell-cat reveilles," morning colors (with the battalion present), parade and reviews each month, along with formal mess nights for the battalion's officers and SNCOS each month. We were invited to play at the naval dependents grade school, Brown & Root Construction Company on the base, and many of the naval commands. The most memorable event was when the battalion was ordered to leave Guantanamo after several years as a supplemental defense force for the Marine barracks, and return to Camp Lejeune. Lieutenant Colonel Cody had the battalion form, colors in front, the battalion staff, D&B Corps, and Companies H&S, F/G and H in trace marching from Camp Buckley to the ship at the dock in Mainside, Guantanamo. The drums beating, colors flying and troops with fixed bayonets made an unforgettable sight to all the naval personnel and Cuban/Jamaican workers on the base. When our ship arrived at Moorhead City and we were trucked to Camp Geiger (Lejeune), the battalion formed outside the gate of Camp Geiger in the same manner. The regiment had companies from the 1st and 3rd battalions, as well as our Company E Regimental Commander and representatives from Division Headquarters to welcome us back. We marched in, colors flying, drums beating, aligned in front of Regimental Headquarters, the D&B did a "Soundoff," and we played our colonel's slow march for the last time as we marched in front of him and finally marched off to the *Marines Hymn*! The 2/8 Drum & Bugle Corps had to be disbanded. I got a few of the buglers and one drummer into the Division Drum & Bugle Corps through auditions. The battalion drums, bugles and the Drum Majors Baldric & Mace were retired to the regimental display case in headquarters.

Hell-Fire & Damnation
by Noal C. Pemberton

"Move out1 Over the wall! Keep low! Look sharp!" I'm not sure who gave the order, but over the wall we went! Right into the middle of hell-fire and damnation! I joined Fox Company in New Zealand in August 1943 as a replacement from the U.S. After much extensive training with the "Old Salts" who had already been through combat duty (Tulagi, Guadalcanal, etc.), including hand-to-hand combat, bayonet, knife fighting, etc., and several practice beach landings around the New Zealand area, the 2nd Marine Division was deemed ready for combat.

All combat gear was readied and loaded aboard the troop transport ship *Zeilin* and we said good-bye to New Zealand and headed out to sea to "destination unknown." After several days at sea and another "practice landing and invasion" at the New Hebrides Islands, then several more days at sea, we were finally briefed on the "destination unknown" - Tarawa Atoll (Betio), Gilbert Islands.

We were told the island was about two miles long and about 500 yards wide and it was occupied and defended by up to as many as 5,000 Japanese Imperial Marines. It was heavily fortified with a variety of weapons, including some big coastal artillery guns; however, we shouldn't be too concerned, because they said, it would be a "piece of cake" for the 2nd Marine Division to take this island from the Japanese. The reason for this optimistic prediction was that our Navy was going to bombard Tarawa with everything they had, up to and including the 16 inch guns of our battleships. Aircraft carrier planes would bomb and strafe and some Air Force planes would saturate the island with 500 pound bombs and maybe 1,000 pound bombs. After all this bombing and shelling, they figured most of the Japa-

nese would be dead, wounded or badly shell-shocked, and all we would have to do is walk in and dispose of a few shell-shocked survivors, and we would have the island secured in no time at all.

About midnight the night of November 19, 1943, the galley crew of the *Zeilin* fed us a big meal of steak and eggs, and wished us good luck. About daybreak the morning of November 20, the fireworks really began! The Navy really put on a show. A huge armada of warships, from minesweepers to destroyers to cruisers to battleships, were throwing everything they had on the island of Tarawa. Planes from aircraft carriers were swirling around the island like a nest of mad hornets, dive-bombing and strafing. Before long the island was awash in flames and black smoke obscured parts of it.

Pretty soon we were ordered to "prepare to disembark"! We donned our battle gear, climbed down the side of the *Zeilin* on rope netting into an amtrak and headed toward the island. (Incidentally - this activity itself was not nearly as easy as it may sound - because the ship was rocking and rolling from rather big waves and the amtrak was really bouncing and banging against the ship and then swinging several feet away from

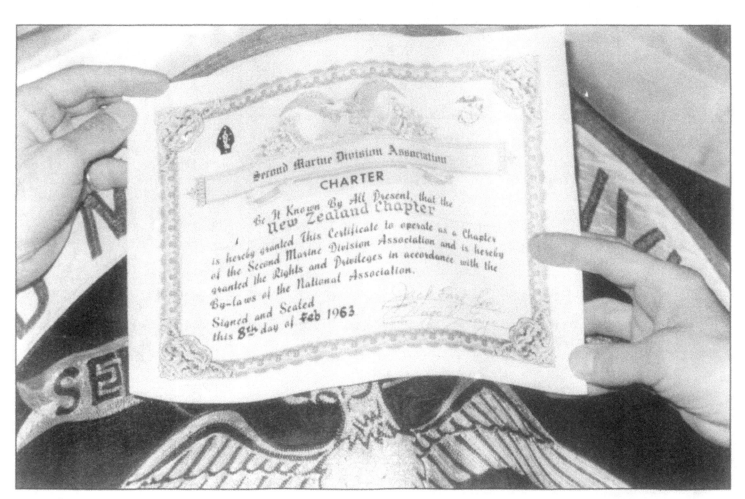

Front Row Left to Right: Richter, Loftus, Ernest Petri. Back row: Sullivan, Nickerson, Steele, and Tackett. Courtesy of Ernest Petri.

1stLt. Robert A. Hall, Adjutant; Sgt. Major Ehlen. 3rd BN 2nd Marines on Saipan.

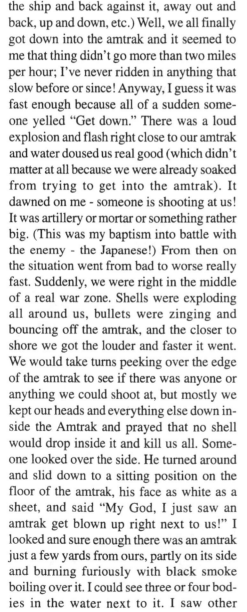

the ship and back against it, away out and back, up and down, etc.) Well, we all finally got down into the amtrak and it seemed to me that thing didn't go more than two miles per hour; I've never ridden in anything that slow before or since! Anyway, I guess it was fast enough because all of a sudden someone yelled "Get down." There was a loud explosion and flash right close to our amtrak and water doused us real good (which didn't matter at all because we were already soaked from trying to get into the amtrak). It dawned on me - someone is shooting at us! It was artillery or mortar or something rather big. (This was my baptism into battle with the enemy - the Japanese!) From then on the situation went from bad to worse really fast. Suddenly, we were right in the middle of a real war zone. Shells were exploding all around us, bullets were zinging and bouncing off the amtrak, and the closer to shore we got the louder and faster it went. We would take turns peeking over the edge of the amtrak to see if there was anyone or anything we could shoot at, but mostly we kept our heads and everything else down inside the Amtrak and prayed that no shell would drop inside it and kill us all. Someone looked over the side. He turned around and slid down to a sitting position on the floor of the amtrak, his face as white as a sheet, and said "My God, I just saw an amtrak get blown up right next to us!" I looked and sure enough there was an amtrak just a few yards from ours, partly on its side and burning furiously with black smoke boiling over it. I could see three or four bodies in the water next to it. I saw other amtraks, some sitting still, apparently hav-

ing been hit by artillery from shore. Several Marines were jumping over the sides of their amtrak and wading toward shore, but some would go under water and not come up. I'm sure a lot of them drowned, probably a lot hit by bullets and shrapnel from shore. Sergeant Bailey kept yelling at the rest of us to "stay down unless you want to get your heads shot off." Of course not, so we hunkered down as close as we could to the bottom of the amtrak, and the farther we went the louder the battle noise got. (All this time the Navy ships were still shelling the island and many planes were still bombing and strafing the island.)

Finally, after what seemed to me like at least seven eternities, our amtrak lurched a few times and came to a sudden jarring halt as if it had hit a big tree or huge boulder. Well, it had indeed hit something solid! - the log seawall on Tarawa!

Lieutenant Barr yelled: "Everybody over the side but keep low!" We bailed out and played like a bunch of leeches hugging that seawall! (The sea wall was similar to a modern day "retainer wall" along the lower side of a sloping yard or garden, except it was built with coconut logs instead of railroad ties or landscape timbers. The wall was about four feet or so high (my wild guess) and was constructed specifically to prevent any type of landing craft such as the U.S. Marines used, amtraks, half-tracks, tanks, etc., to actually get ashore. Our amtrak went in just a little way to the right of the long pier and landed on Red Beach Two. As I looked in both directions along the beach, our amtrak was the only one of the first wave which had gotten out of the water and

to the sea wall. The others were scattered from a few yards out to hundreds of yards out and there were lots of bodies in the water, some dead and some still alive trying to make it to shore on the coral reef amid the blizzard of artillery and mortar shell explosions, rifle and machine-gun bullets. Not for long, though, because the Japanese were saturating that beach with everything they had: artillery, knee mortars, grenades, rifles, machine-guns, etc., and I wouldn't be surprised if one or two of them were even lobbing coconuts at us! (Laugh if you want to, but this may not be as impossible or impractical as it may seem at first thought, because during the next several hours, quite a number of Japanese snipers were killed in the palm trees, and most of them were tied to the tree so they wouldn't fall out when shot and give away their secret to us (the secret of snipers hidden in the palm fronds and tied to the tree). As soon as I figured this out, I told every Marine I could to blast the top of every coconut tree within range that had any palm fronds left on it. We did this and kept doing it as we moved inland and we saw several Japanese fall a few feet and just hung there because they were tied in. (If they ran out of ammo they might have tried throwing coconuts!) Lieutenant Barr gave the order to "move out, over the seawall"! We did and immediately for me it was total madhouse confusion, strictly a matter of self-preservation. We were just trying to stay alive, immediately glancing around for a place to hit the ground with some sort of cover in front of us and simultaneously firing at anything that moved. We were in the first wave to land on Red Beach Two, so everyone on the inland side of that seawall was the enemy. After a few minutes we sort of got ourselves back together and started moving forward one or two at a time, zig zagging a few feet and hitting the ground or jumping into a shell hole. Fortunately for us, all the shelling and bombing had provided us a pretty good supply of ready-made foxholes. Tarawa was flat except where the Japs had built up their pillboxes, bunkers and gun emplacements, etc., and those bomb and shell holes were really life savers.

We got to a small pile of scattered rubble, apparently the remains of a small building which had been destroyed by bombs, and we got pinned down by a steady barrage of rifle and machine gun fire and grenades coming from both our flanks as well as from our front. A few of us (maybe five or six) had gotten several feet ahead of the rest of the front line when we got as far as this building rubble, so both our flanks were exposed to enemy cross-fire. After a while, a few more Marines began to move up on both sides of us and gradually we began to inch forward again. Suddenly, for a few minutes, there was an almost quiet lull in the shooting, and for a minute or two I just lay there against the inland side of a shell hole and gasped for breath. Then, I remembered I had a canteen of water on my cartridge belt so I gulped down a few swallows of water.

Then someone said "Let's go." Immediately, two of our Marines, a black-haired Irish kid named O'Hare and a blond-headed kid named Bailey (I think, not Sgt. Bailey), jumped up and ran forward just a few feet when a Japanese machine-gun opened up and just riddled those two guys. It spun them both around facing me. I will never forget the bewildered looks of amazement on both their faces as they crumbled apart and fell in a hail of bullets. (They were maybe 10 or 15 feet from me). Miraculously we spotted two Japanese machine guns (woodpeckers we called them because they fired so fast). If I remember correctly, they were 6.5 mm and fired much faster than any of our machine guns). We quickly silenced those two plus two or three snipers and then were able to move forward a few more feet.

A little further inland we encountered a large bunker which was spewing machine-gun (woodpecker) bullets at us from several porthole like slits. Wow! Could combat possibly get any worse? Apparently so! We learned later these bunkers were constructed of steel reinforced cement walls several feet thick, had honey-comb type passages, were several feet high (I guessed about 12 to 20 feet), were covered outside and top with several layers of coconut logs, sand bags, etc., and the whole thing covered with tons of loose sand. They looked like huge, giant ant hills, except they were oblong and paralleled the beach so the machine-gunners inside could swivel the guns from side to side and cover every inch of the area in front of the bunker. There were several of the bunkers, but only this one in the direct front of our part of the F Co. front line, to the best of my memory.

The noise of battle, so intense, so furious, so deafeningly loud, made it extremely difficult and almost impossible to maintain any communication or control, but someone somehow got word back to send up some flamethrowers. Well, finally, after what seemed to me a long, long time, one guy did get up pretty close to us with a flamethrower. After a lot of shouting back and forth from shell hole to shell hole, several of us in unison popped up just enough to clear the top of our holes and started pumping bullets into the slits in the bunker which kept the Japanese from firing long enough for the guy with the flamethrower to run up the sloping side of the bunker and shoot a stream of fire into one of the slits. We did this until all the machine guns were silent. Also the bunker had two or three air vents in the top, and some of our guys got up there and dropped grenades down through those vents. Believe me, I am firmly convinced that flamethrower guy, I have no idea who he was, saved a lot of Company F lives, including my own.

I have no idea of what happened during any given time frame because it was just one long continuous hellish battle, but sometime during the afternoon we made it across the fighter strip and into a large revetment (a tank trap or storage area for ammunition or fuel or something) between the fighter strip and the bomber strip. It must have been 25 or 30 feet across by 40 or 50 feet long and four or five feet deep. Was it ever a welcome place! Finally, I thought to myself, a place where we'll be safe from enemy bullets and if we're lucky maybe we can spend the night here. We were able to rest there quite a while, taking turns firing at Japanese on our right flank, across the southeast or southern end of the fighter strip. They were firing at other Marines who were zigzagging from shell hole to shell hole across the fighter strip, as we had, coming to join us.

Finally, by late evening, we had at least 40 to 50 and possibly more Marines in the big revetment. I had no idea what had happened to most of F Company, from Captain Morris to Lieutenant Barr, Sergeant Bailey, to Corporal Turner, etc., but I figured most of them had been killed or wounded. Lieutenant Sanford was the only officer I knew of at that time who made it to the big dugout. He soon got us somewhat organized and decided this was the best place to spend the first night on Tarawa. (Best and only choice, I thought!) Lieutenant Sanford had defensive positions set up around the dugout, with half of us on alert and the other half trying

Camp Lejeune, N.C. Drill Team. Kenny Adams - 2nd from left.

to sleep, or at least get some rest, changing places every three hours or so. Fortunately the Japanese didn't attack our position that night, but they did make some noise, a few screams and yells, I figured just to keep us awake. A Japanese plane flew over about the middle of the night and dropped a few bombs but not very close to us. I sure didn't sleep any and I doubt that anyone else did. I was still plenty scared and staying alive was still foremost on my mind. If the Japanese did attack, I would be awake and ready for them. Next morning, November 21, we started to get ready to continue our attack across the bomber strip to the beach on the other side of the island. A few guys from the weapons platoon had made it to the dugout with a couple of 30 caliber air-cooled machine guns. When they took inventory they discovered they were almost completely out of ammo! The plan was to set up the two machine guns to give us riflemen covering fire as we dashed across the bomber strip. Then, we would cover them while they brought the machine guns across. Of course, this could not work with no machine gun ammo! Immediately there was a call for volunteers to go back across the fighter strip to the beach and bring back some belts of machine-gun ammo. (I've never in my life heard such profound silence as followed that request!) My first thought was: "He's got to be kidding, right?" Wrong! He was dead serious, and I knew of course he was absolutely right. I knew several of us would surely die trying to cross the bomber strip, which was much wider than the fighter strip, if we didn't have covering fire from the machine guns.

Well, after a long period of silence, I did what I have told myself many times since was the stupidest thing I've ever done - I volunteered. (That was the first and last time I volunteered for anything in the U.S. Marine Corps!) Another Marine, William "Bill" Roberts, volunteered. I don't remember which one volunteered first, but the two of us decided we could do it. We shed everything except our rifle and ammo belt to be able to carry back as much ammo as possible and we took off, one running a few feet and diving into the nearest shell hole, then the other, etc. As soon as we left the dugout a Japanese machine gun opened up on us from somewhere to our left, across the southeast side of the fighter strip. As soon as one of us jumped out of a hole and ran he started firing, and as soon as we dropped into another hole, he stopped. The next one would jump and run and he started

Unidentified Marines in bunker at Tarawa.

Commander Gene Tunney, USNR, former Heavyweight Boxing Champion of the world, examining a Japanese skull orchard in a cave on Saipan. On his right 1st Lt. Robert A. Hall and Lt. Col. Wall Layer of 3rd BN 2nd Marines.

firing. His bullets followed us all the way across the strip and he never touched either of us, unbelievable as it may sound, but I believe to this day that a lot of his bullets were hitting right between my feet as I ran.

As we approached the beach, we came out right by the main pier where I had landed on Red Beach Two the day before. We started asking everyone we saw for 30 caliber machine gun ammo belts. We started walking along the beach, to our left along Red Beach Two, and I could not believe my eyes at the masses of bodies lying all along the beach as far as we could see. Literally hundreds and hundreds, most of them dead, some already bloated and stinking from the blazing hot tropical sun, but a few were still alive. Here and there a corpsman was treating wounds and applying bandages. We finally found some guys with a machine gun and some ammo, but they wouldn't give us any ammo because they needed it themselves, they said. We explained our situation and our position between the fighter and bomber strips and our group in the dugout waiting for us to bring them ammo for their two machine guns so we could continue our attack to the beach on the other side of the island. We finally convinced them to let us take some ammo, so Bill and I each wrapped four belts of ammo, crisscrossed around our shoulders, and headed back. We retraced our steps back to the pier and back the same way we came so we wouldn't get lost and maybe come out on the fighter strip much closer to the Japanese machine gunner, just in case he was still alive by now. We got just past the rubble of the building where O'Hare and Bailey got hit yesterday and we stopped for a few minutes to catch our breath. That ammo was heavy and the sun was blistering hot.

We were lying on our backs in a depression between some logs. Even though the beach itself was pretty much secured by US Marines, there was still an occasional shot or two from Japanese snipers who had been bypassed or somehow survived yesterday's advance by hiding or pretending to be dead as we went by. Anyway, we were still keeping as low as possible and being as cautious as possible. I looked up at a big tree right by our hole and right above our heads several feet was a coconut. I said to Bill, "Bill, I see water!" Bill said, "Oh no, he's cracked up; he's gone crazy, I knew that ammo was too heavy for a little guy like him, and between the heavy ammo and the sun he's gone plumb crazy." I said, "No Bill, I'm not that crazy, watch this," and I lifted my M-1 rifle, took careful aim, squeezed off one shot. Down came that coconut and almost hit Bill on the head. Bill shouted, "What the hell you trying to do - kill me." I said, "No Bill, just getting us something to drink." He looked at me with a very amazed expression and said, "Now I know for sure you're crazy! I'm going to call a corpsman." I said "No Bill, I'm okay; watch this." I took my Marine knife (which, incidentally I had left on my ammo belt when we left everything else in the dugout) and cut and chipped the outer hull off and then bored a little hole in the stern end and turned it up and took a few sips of coconut milk, I

handed it to Bill and said, "Here Bill, have a drink of fresh water." (While on the beach, someone had offered us a drink of water which we gladly accepted, but it had almost made both of us sick because it tasted more like gasoline than water. Apparently someone had hurriedly filled gas cans with water to send ashore from one of the supply ships without first rinsing out the gas cans.)

Bill took a few sips of coconut milk and said, "I saw you shoot that coconut off that tree and open it up and I'm drinking this coconut milk, but I still don't believe it. But, this sure tastes better than that gasoline those guys gave us back at the beach!" Well, that coconut milk was not water and it was warm, but it was nourishing and gave us enough of a lift to start the dash back across the fighter strip to the dugout.

Bill said, "Since you found water for us in this dry burning sand and maybe saved my life, I'll go first." I said, "Okay Bill, but remember, go fast, keep low, zigzag, and dive into the first hole you come to, just in case that dam "woodpecker" is still alive." Bill took off and ran several feet and dived into a shell hole and all was quiet. I took off and ran just a few feet when, believe it or not, that damn Japanese machine gun started spraying bullets right under my feet just like the first time. But I dove into a hole and was not hit. Scared half to death again but still alive. Bill jumped out and took off and sure enough the "woodpecker" started pecking but he didn't hit Bill either. Well, believe it or not, Bill and I both made it across the field to the dugout, one hole at a time and machine gun bullets between our feet every step of the way. (I, to this day, still wonder why someone there in our dugout or someone on either side of us didn't spot that Japanese machine gun and take him out, but I guess that was just one of many, many unanswered questions about the battle for Tarawa.)

No sooner had Bill and I both gotten back into the dugout than some of the machine gunners grabbed our belts of machine-gun ammo and set up the two guns and we heard the words, "get ready to move out across the bomber strip to the beach!" I couldn't believe my ears; move out? Bill and I had just barely 'moved back in' about two minutes ago and they wanted us to immediately go charging into the enemy again? We had been 'moving out' all morning-back across the fighter strip, to the beach, begging for ammo, witnessing hundreds of dead and dying Marines, back to and across the fighter strip loaded with ammo, worn to a

complete frazzle, so thirsty we couldn't swallow, our lips swollen from the dry, burning sun, unable to even crawl another inch, totally exhausted. Move out? No way! I thought, just shoot me right now, right here where I lay and get it over with! Surely it would be much easier than trying to fight and shoot our way across the bomber strip and to the far beach! Well, while everyone else was preparing to move out, someone gave us some water. Someone, I think it must have been Lieutenant Cooper, who, with a few other F Company Marines, had joined the gang in the dugout while Bill and I were back at the beach. Fortunately, the final order to "move out" was delayed for a short time as the officers made sure everyone in the dugout knew exactly what the plan of attack was, where we were heading, our objectives and that everyone had plenty of ammo and was ready. This delay gave Bill and me time to get a few minutes rest and get our breath back. So we decided after what we went through yesterday and this morning this next charge should be a "piece of cake." We were ready to go. Piece of cake? We discovered soon after that a "piece of cake" and Japanese bullets did not mix at all!

When the order was finally given by Lieutenant Sanford to move out, we all, except the machine gun platoon (what there was left of it plus two machine-guns,) took off in a skirmish line across the bomber strip, again from shell hole to shell hole as we had across the fighter strip. However, this time we drew very little enemy fire, because, we soon discovered, the bunkers on that side of the island, between the airstrip and the beach, were facing the beach (Black Beach Two) same as the ones on the other side of the island were facing Red Beach Two wherever we came ashore yesterday, November 20, 1943. We cleared the airstrip and set up defensive positions to provide cover while the guys with the two machine guns came across, and then we advanced to a long, deep, rather narrow tank trap that ran parallel to the beach. Then the battle started again!

We were in front of those bunkers and the Japanese opened up on us with machine guns, rifles, grenades, and everything they had! We lost several more good Marines right there in that tank trap. Several were wounded and I'm pretty sure (though not positive) that was where Lieutenant Cooper got shot in the jaw and was evacuated back across to Red Beach Two. Two other Marines close to me in the tank trap (I can't

6th Con Section, Quantico VA. Fall 1950. L to R: Sgt. Carlson, Jean, Hank Jandl and Vanner.

Camp Lejeune N.C. L to R: Front: H. Doren, Carroll, R.C. Wilson, Hank Jandl. Back row: Carpenter, H. Glasser, Ball.

remember either of their names) got shot, one right through the cheek and the other right in his private parts. After several minutes of intense firing from both sides, a few of us were lucky enough to get several hand grenades into their machine guns and knock them out. We were than able to get to more of their bunkers. With concentrated firing and tossing grenades in, we silenced most of them in the next few hours.

Finally, we appeared to have accomplished our objective of establishing a front line clear across the island from Red Beach Two to Black Beach Two, in effect, cutting the island in half. The island was by no means secured yet, but we seemed to have the upper hand. After a few more "get'em out of the bunker" skirmishes, we got the word to establish perimeter defense lines to start digging in for the night. (The night of November 21, 1943). This we did. Apparently, we had silenced most of the Japanese, at least most of the machine guns, because it was fairly quiet our second night on Tarawa and I was able to even sleep a few short naps.

Next morning, November 22, 1943, we conducted a mop-up operation, eliminating the few remaining live Japanese, checking all the pillboxes, bunkers, etc. Finally, we received word that the island of Tarawa had been officially declared secured! We had done it! We had taken the island of Tarawa from the Japanese! We had sent a message to Japan - Don't mess with the USA!

One really unbelievably funny thing happened the morning of November 22: a few of our tanks had been brought ashore. One of them, the *Colorado*, was moving slowly along the Black Beach side of the bomber strip, supporting our mop-up operation, when all of a sudden a Japanese with a sword in his hands ran out of the bunker and started hacking and slashing at that tank as though he thought he could just cut it into little pieces with his sword! We were all too shocked and amazed to shoot for a while. We started laughing and just watched as he hacked at the right side of the tank several times and then walked around behind it hacking furiously as he went. Finally someone said, "Let's stop that nonsense before he disables that tank." I suspect that several dozen bullets did indeed stop him.

Later that day, November 22, F Company, plus other units, lined up and marched back across the island to go back aboard a ship to go, as it turned out, to Hawaii. As we approached the pier where we had landed November 20, we passed an American flag hoisted several feet above the ground on a topless coconut palm. Believe me we all gave that flag a really snappy and proud salute! (See page 146 of *Follow Me*, the story of the 2nd Marine Division in World War II).

As I recall, there were 76 of us F Company Marines who were able to walk off of Tarawa, out of about 200 or so who went ashore on November 20, 1943. (See page 147 of *Follow Me*). Several of us had been wounded and left some blood on Tarawa, mostly shrapnel wounds, I think. I still have a piece of shrapnel from a Japanese knee mortar about as thick as a pencil lead and about one-half inch long imbedded in my left wrist bone and a pinhead size piece in the flesh of my left arm about four inches below the shoulder. I got hit just a minute or two after I jumped out of the Amtrak and got against the seawall when we first hit Red Beach Two, just to the right of the main pier. When we got to Hawaii the medic told me to leave it alone and it would eventually work its way out (rather than surgically remove it). Well, I left it and 52-1/2 years later I'm still waiting for those two pieces of shrapnel to work their way out of my body! HA! Good joke on the doctor!

I didn't get a Purple Heart or any compensation for those wounds, but I survived the 72 hours of Tarawa, I'm still alive 52-1/2 years later and I thank God for that! (See page 122 of *Follow Me*, first sentence, upper left.) I did receive a Purple Heart later (in Japan) for wounds received in action on Saipan in 1944. After 52-1/2 years, my recollection of names, times of day or night, and exact location, etc., are not as clear as I wish they were, but hopefully this brief sketch of some of my memories of Tarawa may be of some help to some of the other survivors of the F Company battle for Tarawa. (A footnote to emphasize how well the Japanese had planned and constructed those large bunkers, and how most of them survived all of the shelling and bombing:) The third day, November 22, 1943, just before we left the island, I sat on an unexploded 16 inch shell from one of our battle wagons and ate a can of C-ration hash. That 16 inch shell had made a direct hit on the front of a bunker, went through several layers of sand covered coconut logs and the nose chipped a hole out of the steel reinforced concrete wall only about 12 inches around and about six inches deep. Of course, we had no idea why it did not explode on impact, but a projectile that large traveling that fast would have penetrated all the way through almost any structure except those bunkers.

One final footnote: As the author of *Follow Me* so aptly stated on pages 111 and 112, and I quote: "What happened in those 76 hours, and in the five days that followed them, is a story that never has been told, and never will be told. A number of writers have tried to tell it, but they have failed, in the last analysis, because concentrated battle experience of the sort Betio provided simply cannot be communicated. It has to be lived." And I add my heartfelt amen to that profound and true statement!

Tarawa D-Day
by Robert H. Rogers

Ever since Tarawa, my thoughts as the company commander of E-2-8 reoccur to me from time to time concerning the problems encountered on D-Day. What a difference that first day on Betio would have been if we had had access to the small radios available today. After reviewing written accounts of Tarawa, it appears that communication was also a critical problem for others up to and including the Division Commander.

E Company's mission was to land with its men in the first three waves on D-Day in the right (western) sector of Red Beach #3. The plan called for my leading platoons to be disembarked inland on the taxi strips and continue their advance across the island. The company's zone of action presented different problems from those encountered on other landing areas and not apparent prior to D-Day. The wide open space between the juncture of the two taxi strips produced a hazardous route for all to negotiate safely. It separated troops in the interior of this island from their company support units, the battalion command post, resupply and medical services on the beach.

My amtrack in the third wave was delayed in its approach to the beach when it was partially disabled by enemy fire. After landing and reporting to my battalion commander, his only order was to get E Company off the beach. No information was received concerning my company units that had already landed. The small group of E Company mounted the coconut wall without delay to move inland, clearing Japanese still in the trenches nearest to the beach. The men had formed a skirmish line by the time we advanced across the wide open

Front: R.C. Wilson. L to R: Parks, Paddy Graincer, Joe Potokwpc on USS Rushmore.

junction of the taxi strips. As we entered the palm tree area in the middle of the island, we cleared the Japanese from this area. We found a long trench that gave us good protection from enemy fire until I could determine our next course of action. My TBY radio operator had been lost somewhere between the beach and our inland position. With no radio, my ability to communicate with my battalion commander was limited to use of runners. As we looked about in all directions, we saw no friendly troops in our area.

Not long after reaching this inland position, we saw a small Japanese tank moving from left to right in front of us. Without anitank weapons, I decided to let it pass, as it was too far away to our front. There was no evidence of friendly troops on my right flank in the 2nd Marines zone of action. On my left flank well to the rear, F-2-8 was held up by a large fortification near to the beach. At this time, it was important to know the location of other E Company troops, as it appeared that only Japanese forces were ahead of us. A runner was dispatched to the battalion commander on the beach with a request for the location of my assault platoons. My message included information of Japanese positions we had observed behind the large fortification in front of F Company.

By afternoon my return to the beach was necessary when the two runners, dispatched at different times, had failed to return. The route back was across the wide open taxi space. Puffs of smoke from an automatic small arms weapon followed my heels to the center of this area, and I took cover in a

shell hole about five feet deep. After a rest, I started to exit the hole toward the beach. As half of my body was exposed, I felt the pressure of a hand on my left shoulder, and a voice that said, "Get back!" As I retreated backwards into the shell hole, just as my eye level reached the rim of this hole, I saw many puffs of dust on the ground from automatic small arms fire. This volley of enemy fire would have been received in the middle of my back. There is little doubt in my mind that I would not have survived that first day on Betio if the warning had not been received. I can not explain the hand on my shoulder or the voice I heard as I was alone in the shell hole.

Later it was learned that my leading platoons had disembarked from their amtracks inland on the taxi strip and moved rapidly to the north side of the main landing runway near the south side of the island. There they met and successfully turned back Japanese troops. My executive officer, Lieutenant Edmonds, was with these men, as his amtrack had been in the middle of the first wave to coordinate their initial movements. He was also forced to return to the beach later that morning for essential information when his two runners, both sent at different times, failed to return. Lieutenant Edmonds was wounded that first day and evacuated before my return to the beach later that day.

The two leading platoons of E Company had suffered over 40% casualties, including the death of both their officers soon after landing. Even with these casualties, radio communication between all E Company units and its company commander might

well have produced vastly different results that first day. With the ability of the company commander to coordinate the company's full strength, the option to continue the attack would have been possible. Consolidation of a better all-around defense for the evening of D-Day would have resulted. These E Company's movements could also have been coordinated by Battalion Commander Major Crowe based on his knowledge of the location of friendly troops. Fortunately, D-Day on Saipan was very different. The 2nd Battalion 8th Marines were assigned an assault role again with E-2-8 in the initial waves. My radio operator was killed soon after landing and the radio on his back destroyed. An artillery shell struck him in the chest as he followed me off the beach. Control of E Company units was realized not long after landing, in spite of a heavy concentration of incoming Japanese artillery fire. Communication with my company units and battalion was possible without a radio, because of the trees and cover that allowed us to move about. It was not like Tarawa, where Marines were killed by long range small arms fire, wherever they stood or sat.

In the planning stages, Colonel Shoup had requested that 7th Air Force drop 2,000 pound "daisy cutters" to kill the troops near the beaches and level the few wooden buildings offering concealment. The request, approved by Smith, was never fulfilled. Weeks later he found out why. A flight of 24 Liberators (based at Funafuti, several hundred miles to the south) had been assigned the mission, but the pilots were inexperienced and the first bomber, flown by the squadron leader, splashed into the water at the end of the runway. The next four made it safely into the air, but the one after that crashed. The rest of the pilots, 18 in all, simply refused to take off. The four in the air attempted to carry out the mission and dropped their bombs, but not on Betio. It has never been established what their target was, but most probably was Mariana.

TS Or Not TS -
That Is The Question
by William C. Saltzer

In as much as no one knew for sure what lingering effects there would be after dropping the A Bomb, we, the Marines, were given the wonderful opportunity to find out when General MacArthur sent the 2nd Marine Division to Nagasaki.

When he and the Army saw that we survived, probably to their chagrin, we were shipped off to the farthest end of Japan, Kanoya, which had been a Naval Air Station on the southern end of Kyushu. Ironically, this was the area that the 2nd was scheduled to hit as part of the 5th Amphibious Corps a few months hence in the penultimate invasion of Japan Operation Olympic.

Being the only interpreter left in the 2nd Battalion, I got a lot of unusual duties which were unique, gratifying, challenging, sad and humorous. My first assignment was chief of the honey dippers and cleaning the benjo (head) at the former POW camp at Nagasaki. However, things got better and a humorous one has stayed with me over the years.

The surrender required the Japanese to submit lists of weapons, equipment and ammunitions and where it was located. One of our primary duties was to find and destroy it. On one of these missions I went out with a squad to the town of Shibushi, where there were artillery emplacements in the hills on both sides of Ariake Bay. Several former Japanese officers were assigned to us for this effort and one of them impressed me; Captain Hashimoto, a former artillery officer who had been stationed in the area. He was about 25, single, and in the military all his life, even as a youth in military school. For obvious reasons he was confused and concerned about his and Japan's future. He was anxious to learn English and thought he might like to become a journalist. I wanted to improve my Japanese so we spent much time discussing, the best we could, our present and future situations. We never spoke about the war and what happened and why, which was quite different from some of my earlier experiences with Japanese POWs on Saipan. At the time, one of our favorite expressions, except for the "F" word, which was used for almost everything and anything, was the term TS (sanitized to tough situation). Mashimoto had picked up on this and was perplexed because it seemed to be used in all settings and circumstances. He finally asked me to explain its meaning, which challenged my limited military-style Japanese. I could tell from body language and his face that I was not getting through in either the literal or figurative sense. We had been in Shibushi for several days when a jeep roared up one day from some other outfit, the 18th Marines I think, and told us that we were in their territory and to leave. Our lieutenant checked with headquarters

back in Kanoya and we were told to stay and finish our job. After some heavy back and forth they left. That night or the next, two jeeps showed up with guys in MP armbands and told us we could not leave the compound and parked themselves at the gates of the school yard we were staying at. A turf war already. I guess the big war was over too long for some. The lieutenant said he would check it out again, but to cool it and stay in the area for the time being. Hashimoto was taking all of this in with a sly grin. After 10-15 minutes he got up, stretched and deliberately walked over to the gates and between the MPs, looked back at us and said "TS Marines" and left!

About an hour or so later he returned

with the local specialties: roasted sweet potatoes and sochu (white lightning made from sweet potatoes), about the only thing they had in that part of Japan. After a bit of ribbing him and ourselves, we all sat down on the ground with "Hashi," the ex-captain, and had a good laugh. Later, I accused him of putting me on that he did not understand TS and all its subtle ramifications. He smiled and said, "Saruzasan wakarimasita, we Japanese have many sayings one of which is shigata-ga-nai." My education had been broadened. Thereafter, many times, that Japanese phrase helped get me out of many tough situations when I was stuck trying to understand or explain something in Japanese or English.

Unidentified Marines.

L to R: Repetski, J. Sibley, G. Johnson, Carrol Meryweather. Greek soldier standing.

To Open A Tunnel
by John M. Sheehy

I was in the Marine Corps during the time of World War II and was on the island of Tarawa in November 1943. My serial number is 311191. I was in Company A of 18th Engineers, which was a demolition flamethrower outfit at that time. I didn't get in on Tarawa until the afternoon of the second day (November 21, 1943). I was so scared that I got in a hole and was practically numb. I cleaned my rifle and my pistol. By the next morning I was in pretty good shape.

We had a lieutenant by the name of Rentel. There was a block house, one of the coconut log type, that had a tunnel that emptied into an anti-aircraft gun pit and perhaps linked to the seawall because the gun pit was only about 30' from the seawall. Rentel took a demolition flamethrower squad up there to attempt to blow up the tunnel at the blockhouse. He left word for me to come up. By the time I got there, Rentel and his crew were gone. Two of the Marines were shot up, but the only one I remember was Tschida, who had been shot in the hip.

My flamethrower was down in the hole and I didn't have the nerve to jump in there and try to get it. There were a few infantry men there hanging down over the seawall. I threw in with them and they had a lieutenant among them. There were only 15 or 16 people left out of probably what had been his platoon. He called us all back off of the top next to the tip and threw a couple of hand grenades in there. Then he hollered, "Everybody up." I ran up and there was a coconut tree on my right as I went up. I was right on the edge of that machine gun pit. The pit was probably 25 or 30 feet across. It had been meant for anti-aircraft. They didn't have a weapon mounted in it.

I threw my rifle to my left. As I got to that tree there were two Japanese coming across the pit. One of them ran at me with a bayonet. When he hollered "Banzai" I shot him. I have often wondered had he not hollered "Banzai" would I have shot in time. That was my first encounter with the enemy. The other one fired on a Marine who was coming up on my left. Fortunately, that Japanese missed and that Marine went back over the seawall. The Japanese and I stood there and looked at each other for what seemed a long time, but probably wasn't over a couple of seconds. He cracked the bolt on the rifle and when he did I shot him.

I had not kept track of the amount of ammunition left in my rifle. At that time that was the last shell and the clip flew out. With an M-1, when the clip flew out it rang like a bell. Another Japanese came out of the tunnel on his hands and knees. I had a 45 pistol that I was carrying on half cock. All I had to do was pull the hammer back. He saw that I was still armed and he tried to go back. I shot him in the hip and when he went down I shot him in the head. I didn't know what else to do.

I was pretty well protected by the tree. This young lieutenant came up and squatted down and looked up that tunnel. I yelled at him "Get away from there, there's Japanese in there." He said "I know." About that time I heard a rifle crack and he went down. I ran around the pit, grabbed him by the hand and pulled him down to the seawall. They had shot him through the throat and he was dead. I still had that tunnel on my mind. I wanted to complete what Rentel had started to do if I could. About that time a light tank that was armed with a 30 caliber machine gun and a 37 caliber tank gun showed up on a rise. They had a telephone on the outside. I ran up and pulled the telephone off and I think the man who was running it was a lieutenant by the name of McMillan. I had met him when we were going to Guadacanal. We had not been good friends but we had always recognized each other when we met. I asked him if he could put machine gun fire in that tunnel so I could get down in the pit and get my flamethrower. I had the erroneous idea that I could burn that tunnel with the flamethrower. Probably the flamethrower wouldn't have worked anyway, but he said he couldn't and that if I would wait there he would send me someone. I got down where I could watch the edge of that pit, so that no Japanese could sneak up and shoot me from the edge of it. After a while a half-track with a 75 mm gun came along and I told them what I wanted to do. There were two men in it and one of them said, "Where is this tunnel?" I pointed it out to him and they squared their half-track off with the tunnel and started firing detonating shells into the tunnel. It took three or four shells to blow the lid off of the tunnel. The final shell they put right into the block house.

Those block houses had a maze door. If I remember right, I was only in one of them, but I think it had three turns before you got into the main room. The main room was probably 20 or 25 feet by 40 or 50 feet. It was all made with coconut logs and it had a coconut log roof built like an old western ranch log cabin. It was all covered with sand. When they got through there was no more tunnel or block house. So Rentel's mission had been completed.

It was not my doing that did it. I was just one of the people that happened to be involved and be at the right place to help. This took place where Red Beach 1 and Red Beach 2 joined, which would have been to the west of the long pier. It would have been right on the edge of what was known as the "Pocket," which was the most deadly defense that the Japanese had.

Late To Arrive - Soon Put Down
by Bertrand L. Spooner

The 2nd and 8th Marines had been landed on 20 November 1943. We, the 6th Marines, were 48 hours overdue. Colonel Jones' 1st Battalion went ashore on Green Beach around 4:00 p.m. on D+1. About 10:00 a.m. the next morning, Lieutenant Colonel Kenneth McLeod landed his 3rd. Battalion 6th Marines behind Jones on Green Beach. I consider myself very lucky to have been attached to 3-6 with elements of Regimental Weapons Company. Otherwise, I might not be writing this. I guess you could consider us the final reserve troops available to take the island. Our other Combat Team 2nd Battalion, 6th had already landed on Bairiki, the adjoining island, to slam the door shut on any Japanese who tried to make it across the connecting sand bar.

By the time we were actually committed the following morning, we had tanks and flamethrowers with us. Now we were able to advance along the Black Beach south shore. Some engineer turned his torch on a bunker loaded with ammo and when it blew, a chunk of coconut log tried to take my right leg off. It spun me around and knocked me down. I was hit on the kneecap and for a stunned minute or so I thought that my leg was gone. It was the end of normal walking for weeks to come. Two or three days later a tank lighter took us from the pier out to the APA USS *Harris*. I knew I was in trouble when we pulled up to the landing net. I waited until I was the last Marine in the boat, then made my attempt to climb. Since I could not bend my knee at all, the effort was wasted. I just shook my head and stood there. Up on the deck of the *Harris* there was a naval officer who was looking for people like me. He had the ship's ladder lowered. The boat pulled up to the ladder, the crew helped me on to the first step, and

Native Woman on Guadacanal poses for picture.

I began my one-legged climb. When I reached the deck a Navy Corpsman took me into the sick bay where X- rays were taken and the knee was bandaged. One of the corpsmen helped me down to my compartment.

How fortunate I was that our company first sergeant was with us and had not gotten off the ship at Tarawa. I was quite surprised when he tried to put me on compartment guard duty the next day. Our corpsman had to tell the top that I could just about stand up.

After arriving at Camp Tarawa in Hawaii, the first sergeant kept assigning me to various chores. I went to our company sick bay for no duty chits. Finally the petty officer in charge went to see the first sergeant. A week or so passed and I was again assigned guard duty by the top kick. Since I could walk a bit without bending my knee, I decided to hell with it, and Weapons Company got its one-legged guard.

A funny thing, with all the dead and wounded I saw at Tarawa, I had a guilty feeling about being disabled. A Purple Heart was not awarded to me.

The Coconut Tree Man
by Bertrand L. Spooner Jr.

Our front line was advancing up the coast toward Garapan. Ahead of us was a coconut grove. I was behind a BAR fire team admiring the team work and the fearless ap-

pearance of the team. They advanced slowly, walking upright. In the center was the BAR man. On each side were his assistants, spaced about 10 feet apart. The BAR man was working over the ground in front of the team. When he emptied a clip of ammo he released the magazine and tossed it to his teammate on one side or the other. While his empty magazine was in mid-air his assistant would be tossing a full magazine to the BAR man. It was pure combat poetry in motion. The automatic rifle never seemed to stop chattering.

As we got nearer to the coconut grove the gunner shifted his work to the tops of the trees. Marines had long ago learned the lesson about Japanese snipers and machine gunners tied into tree tops. The slugs were slapping into the palm fronds, and pieces of them were falling to the ground. While our entire front line advanced there was a lot of lead tearing into that coconut grove.

The line had approached to about 100 feet from the nearest trees. Suddenly a Japanese soldier burst out of a coconut tree top and ran down its slanted trunk! Everyone was quite a bit startled, watching a man run down a tree, but recovered by the time he reached the ground. He didn't get more than two steps further when he was hit by a hail of fire. In another minute or two we had entered the grove. Like everyone else passing there, I paused and looked down at the crumpled lifeless form. For just a moment I felt remorse for this man who had been such a fine athlete he could run down a tree. A pity he had to die. Then, I wondered how many Marines he might have killed and continued on my way.

The Weather Changes
by Bertrand L. Spooner Jr.

We approached a valley. Hills surrounded the cane fields on both sides. Ahead was the cliff and plateau. In the afternoon we paused at a thin line of trees which separated the cane fields. Within minutes Japanese mortars found us. They were apparently pre-registered on the line of trees because their mortarmen were able to drop the shells right on top of us. I heard the first rounds flutter down, then the flat kr-rump as they landed. Several came in and Marines were hit. I was on the deck, but those fragments buzzed by quite close. It was safer to continue forward.

Late in the afternoon someone got the bright idea to move our platoon of 37 mm

guns up a road on our right. Just at sunset we reached the top of a hill; four trucks, pulling the guns behind them and gun crews riding in the trucks, were loaded with ammunition and other weapons and were strung out in a row on top of that hill with the sun setting behind us, just like ducks in a shooting gallery. I guess this was intended as our night time position because the trucks stopped.

Mike Taglarini and I were sitting among the gear about three feet apart. The Japanese 77 mm field gun on the opposite hill put a round between Mike and me and it exploded on the road bank less than 15 feet away. About the time the second round came in, both of us were on the road. We hit the deck running, downhill, away from the trucks. More shells came in. The Japanese gunners were only two or three feet high from hitting their targets, but didn't hit a single truck. Before they could correct their range two things happened. The sun went down behind our hill, and a radioman passed information back to our artillery, which began to shell the hill where the Japanese had their guns. When the shelling stopped, we moved our trucks and guns off the road and dispersed them.

We took up positions in holes the Japanese had dug down hill from the road. After dark I fell asleep sitting up in my hole. It began to pour buckets of water. Rain that fell on the road ran down the hill and into our holes. After a while I was almost chest high in water; it ran in the back of my hole and out the front. I went back to sleep. No Japanese moving around this night. At first light we emerged, covered with muck, soaked to the skin and shivering. The rain had stopped for a while.

One Red Meatball
by Bertrand L. Spooner Jr.

It was just after daylight on April Fool's Day April 1, 1945. My platoon from WPNS-6 was below deck in the bow compartment of our APA, and we were waiting orders to disembark. I had a guard posted at the bulkhead door of the well deck. I was standing with the guard when the Japanese kamikaze planes struck our transport fleet.

In the midst of all the anti-aircraft fire and noise, I could hear aircraft engine noises. Suddenly a Japanese dive-bomber came into view, going over us at about ship superstructure height. Not a single gun on our APA was firing at the plane. Like a slow motion picture at the movies, the plane hung there in my eyes and memory. I saw the huge red meatball on the wing on my side. I saw the pilot sitting in his cockpit. He had a helmet on his head that looked like the old time football helmets. He was wearing goggles and had a white scarf around his neck. As he passed over the ship he turned his head and was looking directly at me. Just a fraction of a second, then he was gone, passed over us and headed toward another APA. I believe that ship was the USS *Hinsdale*. The image of the plane and pilot is etched forever in my mind: the wing and its red meatball and the pilot who turned and looked right at me.

The Story Of A Flag
by Earl L. Stout

This flag was obtained on July 5, 1944 at about 10:30 a.m. as we, Company A of the 1st Battalion 2nd Marine Division were headed down from the east side of Saipan by the Mt. Petosukara zone via Kababerra Pass to the west side and the ocean and the general area of Black Beach 1 and 2 possible landing and invasion sites. It was a relativly quiet and uneventful day; a distant shot could be heard now and then, but nothing to get too excited about. I was walking along with another hospital corpsman when we came upon a dug-out that was open on one side, with an incline to drive a tank in under cover, The roof was coconut logs and palm fronds and was even with the ground surface and not too apparent, unless you were on the incline side. We stopped and looked in and all looked normal. On the back wall was a screen of blankets held up to the ceiling and hanging down. As we were just about to leave, I noticed that the blankets were jiggling and moving as though they were being held up by a nervous hand.

I prodded my buddy and lifted my carbine and opened fire into the screen, which dropped after the first few rounds hit in. This revaled three Japanese solders, in uniform, sitting on a dirt ledge or shelve and armed with a hand grenade. The one on the end was already hit by one bullet that I had fired. The one in the middle was the one with the grenade which he was doing his best to strike and set off. I directed my fire on this person and motioned for the other to come forward, which he did. We took him prisoner. We left with one who did surrender and turned him over to the Marines who had come back to in-

vestigate all the firing going on behind the "front."

Returning to the dugout, I finished off the two badly wounded men, as the one with the hand grenade started in trying to set it off as soon as he saw me. Maybe for hari-kari or maybe to take me, too. This is the person that had this flag on his body and his heart was full of the Japanese rules of Bushido. Only 736 prisoners of war were taken, and of these 438 were Koreans.

Tarawa Statistics
by M.F. Swango

The land battle of Betio Island, Tarawa Atoll, began at 9:10 a.m. on November 20, 1943. It ended 76 hours later on November 23. The conquest of the entire Tarawa atoll was completed at 8:00 a.m. on November 28. In that time 1,090 Americans were killed and another 2,311 wounded. The Japanese garrison of 4,960 lost all men except 17 soldiers and 129 Koreans who were taken prisoner.

In its issue of December 6, 1943, *Time* magazine said: "Last week some 2,000 or 3,000 United States Marines, most of them now dead or wounded, gave the nation a name to stand beside those of Concord Bridge, the Bon Homme Richard, the Alamo, Little Big Horn and Belleau Wood. The name was Tarawa."

The book, Follow Me, the story of the Second Marine Division in World War II, said: "What happened in those 76 hours and the five days that followed them is a story that never has been told, and never will be told. A number of writers have tried to tell it, but they have failed, in the last analysis, because concentrated battle experience of the sort Betio provided simply cannot be communicated. It has to be lived."

In every combat veteran's subconscious mind lurks the memory of one terrifying incident, one close brush with death that will forever transcend all else. For the rest of his life this one memory will form the basis of his most hideous nightmares. He will awaken in the small, dark hours of the night and reflect on God's plan for those who will die and those who will be spared and granted the gift of continuing life, the priceless heritage to die of old age.

The memory of this experience will never fade and will remain vivid in every detail throughout his lifetime. Seldom will a day pass that he will not pause for a moment and say, "Thank you God, but why me?" He will reflect and possess a deeper appreciation for that which has been bestowed upon him.

The memory that has forever altered my life is that of the assault on Tarawa, 76 hours of incredible horror, death and destruction. Even today I can close my eyes, envision the torn bodies, hear the mind-numbing sounds and smell the pervading stench of death. I will live with this until the day I die.

Nearing the end of boot camp training at the Marine Corps base in San Diego, Cali-

Israel Aronovitz, Silver Star recipient at Tarawa. Killed in action at Saipan by shellfire. June 15, 1944.

Cpl. R.R. Crosiar (341681) received Purple Heart on 3 August 1944.

fornia, I was given a questionnaire listing various assignments and instructed to select my first and second preferences. My first choice was to become a member of a tank crew and my second choice was to be a radio operator. I never really believed that those who controlled our destinies were ever guided by these questionnaires, but, to my surprise, I was assigned to radio school. At the completion of my training I was sent to Oceanside, California, to become a member of the First Medium Tank Battalion assigned to the Second Marine Division. I couldn't have been more pleased.

The Sherman tank, a 33-ton behemoth powered by twin Chrysler diesel engines and armed with a 75 mm cannon, a 50 caliber and two 30 caliber machine guns, was the largest tank in the Marine Corps arsenal. Our battalion was the first and we were generally regarded as experimental. If we were to win back the Pacific islands now occupied by the Japanese, we would need juggernauts with fearsome firepower to spearhead the attacks. The Sherman tank was such a weapon and it was awesome. In training we lumbered about the California hill-country at speeds up to 30 miles per hour. Surrounded by 3 inches of armour steel, we could crush anything in our path. We believed that nothing could stop us.

Unless you have been inside a tank, buttoned up with all hatches closed and peering through the limited vision of a periscope, you cannot imagine what it is like. One who is even slightly afflicted with claustrophobia would exit screaming at the close of a hatch. It is dark and the quarters are extremely cramped. The driver and bow gunner sit at a lower level while the tank commander, radio operator and turret gunner are squeezed into the crowded turret, or fighting compartment, as it is called. Ventilation is provided by the fans of the huge diesel engines. Air is pulled through vents located strategically about the hull and turret and exhausted through the engine compartment. When the 75 mm cannon is fired, the engines must be kept running at a minimum of 2000 RPMs or the acrid smoke will accumulate within the fighting compartment and quickly suffocate the crew.

I knew almost immediately that I did not like being within a tank and I determined that, at the first opportunity, I would request another assignment. The opportunity came sooner than I had expected.

Considering that tanks are slow moving, cumbersome and in combat conditions, nearly blind, it was determined that the bat-

talion should be complemented with a reconnaissance platoon. The platoon would be composed of a half-track and four jeeps, all radio equipped. They would scurry ahead of the tanks, guide them and generally direct their fire. This was for me. I volunteered, was accepted, and assigned to a jeep as radio operator.

I enjoyed this element of freedom away from the dark enclosure of the tank. We were always dashing about ahead of the tanks, scouting the terrain of the beautiful hill country of Southern California. Ah, but little did we know the horrors that lay ahead.

Our first combat mission was to be an assault on tiny Betio Island of the Tarawa Atoll. Betio was only two-and-one-quarter miles long and 800 yards wide at the widest point. What possible use could be made of our reconnaissance vehicles in so small an area? Obviously none. This sandy little island was so small and the attack strategies so unique that it would be impossible to use any of the mechanization of our reconnaissance platoon. We were destined to be afoot and in the worst possible manner.

The Tarawa Atoll is actually a coral reef with small sandy patches emerging at intervals to form islands. The largest was called Betio and it was heavily fortified. What was going to make our assault unique was the fact that Betio was surrounded by a coral shelf extending on the north side, from which we would attack, some 800 yards. At low tide the water within the shelf would be approximately 3 to 4 feet deep. The initial waves of infantry, carried in amtraks, or alligators, as they were sometimes called, would clamber over the edge of the reef and proceed to the beach or seawall. The remaining waves of infantry would be carried in Higgins boats. They would be dumped at the edge of the reef and would have to make their way through the water to the seawall in the face of withering fire.

Facing us now was the difficult task of getting the tanks ashore. Obviously, they would have to be dumped at the edge of the reef and make their way to shore much as the infantry. But how? The depth of the water would fill the tank, drowning the motors and shorting the electrical system. Perhaps even the crew members would be drowned in the process. The tanks would somehow have to be transformed into semi-submersible vehicles capable of traversing water at this depth.

During the weeks prior to the invasion, we were in training on the island of New Caledonia. The tanks were fitted with cus-

tomized sheet metal stacks extending six to eight feet above the ground. One of the stacks would provide air intake for the engines; the other would allow the exhaust to exit. Then every opening below the anticipated water line was sealed with a tar-like substance. We now believed these lumbering Sherman tanks would safely negotiate the reef.

But what of the reconnaissance platoon? What function would we serve? Ah, but we had not been forgotten. It was planned that prior to the physical assault the island would be bombed by planes from our carriers and shelled by the 16 inch batteries of our dread-naught battleships lying offshore. It was logical, therefore, to assume that a number of the bombs and shells would miss the island and pock-mark the shelf of the coral reef with huge craters.

Our tanks, traversing the 800 yards across this reef, would be unable to see the craters through the limited vision afforded by the periscopes. A drop into one of these craters would not only eliminate the tank but the crew would surely drown. The tank would drop like a rock and the external pressure from the water would not allow the crew to open the hatches and escape.

This is where our reconnaissance platoon would fit the strategic pattern. Prior to the assault by the tanks, and immediately following the initial waves of infantry in amtraks, we would be landed at the edge of the reef facing Red Beach 2. Each of us would carry three orange metal floats about the size of a soccer ball. The floats would be fitted with a five-foot section of rope which would, in turn, be attached to a small metal anchor weighing about five pounds.

We were to spread out in a horizontal line and begin walking toward the beach. Upon encountering a crater we were to mark it with a float and continue on. This would, in theory, provide a safe corridor for the tanks. Once the tanks were safely ashore, we were to follow them in and make ourselves available as back-up crew members. Considering the amount of time we would be in the water and exposed to enemy fire, it was acknowledged that our casualty rate would be extremely high. But the die was cast and I had the uneasy feeling that we were designated expendable.

Prior to enlisting in the Marine Corps and while reading the daily news accounts of their heroic struggle on Guadalcanal, I often wondered what it would be like to go into combat. What does a Marine think of when he is about to confront the enemy face

Both Sgt. O'Dell and Lt. Powers, with equipment borrowed from the Army, developed a highly-successful Boxing Program for the 3rd Bn., 10 Mar., 2nd Marine Division after the Tawara campaign. Sgt. Fay O'Dell was a highly-rated amateur boxer in the Southwest. Prior to enlisting in the Corps, Lt. Jim Powers was Boxing Instructor at Father Hogan's Boys' Camp at Saratoga Lake, N.Y. and boxed for Temple University.

to face? Realizing that his life could come to an abrupt end on this particular day, what are his priorities of thought? Does he think of his loved ones at home? Does he wonder how he will react in the inevitable moment of confrontation when he must act quickly or die? How will it feel to kill a fellow human being? 1 would soon know.

Having been awakened at 4:00 a.m., we hurriedly dressed and made our way to the mess hall where we tried to choke down a last hot meal before disembarking. On deck we prepared to climb down the rope ladder into the bobbing Higgins boat that would transport us to the edge of the coral reef. We entered the boat in predawn darkness and rendezvoused with other similar boats. Then we circled, awaiting the signal to make our assault.

In the distance we could hear the thunderous roar of the big 16 inch batteries of the battleships as they pounded the little atoll relentlessly. Their sound was punctuated by lesser concussions emanating from the cruisers and destroyers. Overhead, we watched the slow arc of the huge projectiles, glowing in the darkness, in groups of three as they appeared to float to their in-tended target. Then came the awful impact as they performed their deadly mission.

Later, dive-bombers screamed in out of the post-dawn twilight in deadly precision, delivering their lethal salute to the bunkers below. Only at the last instant would they terminate their full- throttle dive and streak off into the smoke-filled sky from whence they came. It occurred to me that I was privileged to witness one of the most awesome and terrifying scenes of the war.

In the first gray light of dawn the massive silhouettes of the ships of war began to appear all around us. From our vantage point they stretched as far as the eye could see. The sun appeared on the horizon and began its climb into the sky and still we circled. Some of the men became sea-sick and I felt pity for them. What a way to begin the most tragic and possibly final day of their lives.

We watched as the circle of amtraks began to form a horizontal line, then start their move to the island. They were soon followed by two other waves. This was it.

I have no way of knowing what the other men in my craft were thinking, for there was little or no conversation. They sat with impassive faces, each with his inner thoughts. As for myself, I was both curious and apprehensive. Enough of this endless circling in the choppy water. I was anxious to get on with the task at hand.

Soon the signal came. The Navy coxswain maneuvered our boat into alignment with the other craft within our circle, opened the throttle wide, and we raced for the reef.

I believe that God has provided many, not all, of us with a mental defense mechanism that will kick in (in times of stress), allowing us to continue with the duties at hand without being paralyzed with fear. Some do not make use of it. Strangely, at this particular time I found it possible to allow myself to become a spectator on this small boat, racing to its destiny with hell.

It was a strange feeling. I looked about at the faces of my friends and observed their individual reactions. To me, somehow, I was not in mortal danger here, but they were. Their casual attitude of a few moments ago had changed. They were tense and I could tell that each of them was thinking, "Hey, this is for real. This is not just another damned maneuver. We're about to confront the enemy and we are going to kill and be killed, and it's starting to happen right now."

Ahead we could see the land mass rapidly approaching. And between us and the beach or sea-wall, we could see the turbulence at the edge of the reef. This was our destination. This is where we would begin our assignment. In the seven or eight hundred yards between the edge of the reef and the beach, we would attempt to plot a safe route for the tanks that would follow. How well we were able to perform our task would mean life or death to our friends within those tanks. It was an awesome responsibility.

It was believed that the pre-invasion pounding by our bombs and shells would largely neutralize the island defenses, thus allowing our infantry to quickly establish a secure beach-head. Unfortunately, this did not happen. The bunkers and pillboxes were so heavily reinforced that they withstood the heaviest hits. The Japanese had merely holed up. When the shelling stopped and the amtraks came into view, they were waiting. The three initial infantry waves suffered dreadful casualties. Those who survived were pinned down and fighting for their lives. Attention of the shore batteries and machine gun emplacements was barely diverted from the activities of our reconnaissance team.

As we approached the edge of the reef, projectiles and machine gun fire began ripping through the bulkheads of our landing craft. Several of our group fell to the deck wounded. There was no time to administer first-aid and we began dividing the floats of those who would not be leaving the boat. The Navy coxswain who piloted our craft was a very brave man. He never wavered for a moment and rammed the fragile craft solidly onto the edge of the reef. It was imperative that we get into the water as quickly as possible. To pause even for a few minutes would provide the Japanese machine gunners with a stationary target and we would surely die. We cast a parting glance at our wounded comrades and plunged over the side of the boat and into the shoulder deep water.

Sergeant Zirkle, who was in command of our little group, lay bleeding on the deck of the landing craft. He would not be going with us and we were on our own. It didn't matter, for we knew quite well the grim task that lay ahead.

We would have only a limited amount of time in which to lay our floats, for the big Sherman tanks, each in its individual landing craft, were circling impatiently, awaiting the signal to charge the reef. It was our mandate not to lose a single tank in a hidden bomb crater. We must not fail.

From the beginning it was apparent that the floats were not going to work. The ropes became soggy with salt water and could not be separated from each other. We also believed that the anchors were too light to hold the floats in place. The wash from the first tank to pass them would cause them to drift out of position. We therefore abandoned all the floats at the location of the first crater.

We spread out in a single line, spacing ourselves as far apart as possible while still being able to see any crater, that may appear between us. At each crater one man would remain to wave the tanks safely by. The closer we approached to the island the more intense the enemy fire became. The small arms and machine gun fire appeared as giant raindrops in the water. Occasionally, what I estimated to be a 30 millimeter projectile, perhaps larger, would come somersaulting across the water leaving a frothy wake. Grimly, I observed that each time I surveyed our little group there were fewer of us. A man would simply sink beneath the water and not be seen again. I prayed that when my time came the wound would be instantly fatal. It would be a horrible death to be mortally wounded and drown while thrashing about in the chalky water.

Our tanks were watching for us as they plowed through the water, exhausts roaring, like some terrible denizens of the deep. Occasionally one of the tank hatches would lift slightly and the hand of one of our buddies would wave a friendly salute from within the dark confines.

Finally all the tanks had passed. Most of them made it in. A few met with mishap or drowned out and were abandoned in the water. Our task was done and we had been instructed to follow the tanks in and serve as replacements for the crews. In theory this would be no problem. Practical application of the theory would be something else.

Throughout D-Day the island was literally a no man's land. There were no specific lines drawn and a particular area of the beach would be occupied for a time by our Marines and later by the Japanese. Radio communication had broken down and chaos reigned. To merely proceed directly to the nearest beach (Red Beach 2) would have been suicide. What to do?

I looked about for other members of our group and only a handful were left. Gradually we drifted apart, each to his own initiative as to how he would survive and find our battalion. I tried to keep moving about so as not to provide a stationary target. It was also my intention to move close enough to the beach to enable me to determine if it was occupied by friend or foe. If I could be certain that those figures scurrying about on a particular section were our men, I would make a dash for it.

In time I drifted into an area I believed to be off Red Beach 1. I spotted a wrecked amtrak at what seemed to be a strategic distance from shore. Perhaps if I climbed aboard this vehicle I could get a better view

Left to Right the Marines are: Pvt. Samuel F. Hunger, 21, of 3415 Melrose St., Philadelphia, PA., Pfc. Fred Del Russo, 21, of 395 N. 7th. St. Newark, N.J., Pfc. Derwood Deans, 20, of Route 2, Wilson, N.C.; Gunnery Sgt. Ernest E, Smith, 26, of Cochrane, Georgia, and Pfc. ___ ___, 2514 South Main St., Rockford, Illinois. Picture was taken on Saipan.

(L to R) George Lampoon (Whale), Ed Dwyer, Jim Kennedy (Pudge), Jim Rentz (Rebel) and Jim Hoard (Nose). Naples, Italy Dec 21, 1951 - "The Rainbow."

of conditions on the beach. One end was jutting out of the water at a rakish angle and, at the highest point, a 50 caliber machine gun was mounted. The breech of my 30 caliber carbine had long since rusted shut from being immersed in the salt water and I was without a weapon of any kind. That big machine gun would provide me with some degree of comfort.

As I pushed my way through the water I could see a man on the opposite side of the amtrak. It appeared that he and I both had the same plan in mind. Each of us were staying as low in the water as possible and just our heads were visible. It was therefore impossible to determine if he was American or Japanese. He was perhaps 40 or 50 feet closer to the amtrak than I and it was obvious that he would arrive first. I did not like the odds. If indeed he were Japanese I would be at his mercy. I turned and proceeded to put some distance between the two of us.

I had no watch and therefore had no way of knowing the time of day. But it appeared to be late afternoon and time was running out. At high tide I would be in deep water and would have to go ashore regardless of conditions. Furthermore, I could not allow darkness to catch me off shore. Going in during the night time could get me shot by one of our own men. Disaster awaited behind every option.

I had been eyeing the rusting hulk of a ship that had apparently been wrecked on the reef years ago. The hull extended far out of the water. I edged closer. It could provide a haven at high tide and possibly a vantage point from which to view the beach. In desperation I headed for it.

I had reached to within perhaps 100 yards of the ship when it erupted into a gigantic ball of flame. I could feel the heat and impact against my head, and later, a jolt of underwater concussion impacted my body. I was momentarily stunned and confused. What could have caused this? Then I turned and began making my way from the ship as quickly as possible.

I later learned that word had reached our command that the ship was infested with Japanese snipers. With their advantage of being able to fire from an elevated and oblique angle they were taking a deadly toll on our forces. One of our destroyers was called in to shell the hulk and its occupants to oblivion. Perhaps the snipers had been happily watching my approach.

What now? Time was running out and I would have to make my move for the beach very quickly, regardless of who was in possession. I knew that I had received more than my share of good fortune this day. Any one of those thousands of projectiles hissing into the water about me could have terminated my life. I could have taken a machine gun bullet in the Higgens boat as had some of my comrades. The snipers in the wrecked ship could doubtless have picked me off had they not waited for a closer shot. The odds were now against me. Perhaps the next roll of the dice would be my last. But I could procrastinate no longer. I began edging my way toward the forbidding atoll and to my God-given destiny.

If only I had a weapon. The carbine that still hung from my shoulder with the breech rusted shut from hours in the briny water could serve me no better than a club. I smiled in grim humor as I contemplated the

morbid fact that I was no more than a pathetic Neanderthal in a battle fought with sophisticated weaponry.

Behind me and above the cacophony of battle I could hear the increasing roar of a motor. I turned to see an amtrak bearing down on me. The driver throttled back and yelled, "Hey Matey, you look like you could use a ride."

Indeed I could and those were the kindest words I had heard all day. I scrambled aboard and we charged the beach at full throttle. Soon I had found my battalion and what happened in the days to follow is another story.

Up Against A Wall
by Daniel A. Villarial

Here's an incident that took place in the month of July 1948 in the harbor of Haifa, Israel, during the Arab-Israeli war of 1948.

Those U.S. Marines of the 2nd Marine Regiment, 2nd Marine Division, FMF BLT 21, 6th Task Force, aboard the USS *Marquette* (AKA-95), after unloading 6x6 trucks, jeeps and other supplies needed by the UN Command in Haifa, Israel, were now heading for the open sea from the enclosed harbor of Haifa. Before doing so, a civilian harbor pilot had to come aboard our ship and guide it through the opening of the sea wall.

Several of us U.S. Marines, including the writer, were on the starboard side of the USS *Marquette* when we noticed that our ship wasn't turning to the opening of the sea wall. As we were yelling "turn the ship," we rammed into the sea wall that stopped our movement, at the same time splitting the bow of our ship causing the ship to lose all our fresh water supply. With the sea water coming in, work parties were formed to get our ammo to the drier parts of our ship; no ammo was lost, but it was handled very carefully.

After the damage was assessed, we set sail for Athens, Greece, for repairs. Once we arrived, tied up and repairs started, port and starboard liberty was granted to the Marines and the ship's company that lasted for three weeks. The rubble and destruction of World War II was still visible. At that time, we were the occupation forces in the Mediterranean Sea area of World War II.

Later, on August 24, 1948, I and 62 other U.S. Marines of the 2nd Marine Regiment, 2nd Marine Division disembarked in Haifa, Israel, and we became the first United Nations Peace keeping force in the world.

Music On The Front Lines
by William M. Wente

Does music on the front sound strange? It happened like this. We came in to Red Beach on Saipan on June 15, 1944. (We being 1st Battalion 6th Marines). It was the second afternoon and our line had been adjusted several times in the last several hours. The trouble was to our right in the Lake Susupe area, where stiff resistance was causing a delay in moving forward. So our line was not advancing and we had been having relatively light resistance. I and my foxhole buddy found ourselves near a farmhouse that had been vacated and most of the contents left behind. To our left in the next hole was a machine gun crew from another company. At this point, we were less than 12 hours from the impending Japanese tank attack that was to hit our company head on. Nothing going on and all quiet at this part of the front. We rummaged through some of the contents of this house and found a phonograph and many records which we proceeded to play, finding music and singing in the Japanese language. Quickly we would go from one record to another till we found a very familiar tune. The singing was in Japanese but unmistakenly the tune was My Blue Heaven. We must have played that record 25 times."Just Molly and me and baby makes three; we're happy in my blue heaven." This is a story that as far as I know has never been told farther than the squad I was in.

A footnote to this would be: The machine gun crew was killed in the tank attack and my buddy and I took over then until morning. We were not wounded and both made it home to raise families after the war. I will not go into the tank battle, as it has been described many times before. One thing I have found out in later years though is that Charles Merritt and Herbert Hodges, who were credited with many tank kills with the bazooka, are both now passed on.

Meeting Dad In The Strangest Places
by R.D. Werneburg

My story is not about battlefield encounters; it is about a poignant and memorable experience for me while serving with the 2nd Marine Division in the South Pacific during World War II.

My dad was a carpenter's mate first class with the 94th Seabee Battalion during World War II. We were both serving in the South Pacific Theater at the same time. We finally established each other's location shortly after the Tarawa Operation. The 2nd Division had started a training camp on the big island of Hawaii and Dad's Seabee Battalion was working on a Navy base on the island of Oahu. Dad managed to obtain a three-day pass and hitched a ride to come visit me. My battery commander, Captain Edwin Kittrell, was kind enough to issue me a pass to spend a couple of days in Hilo, Hawaii, with my father. I was only 18 years old and had been overseas about 10 or 11 months and was plenty homesick. Our visit together was a tremendous lift for me.

Believe it or not, but an almost identical situation happened to Dad and me several months later. Dad's Seabee unit was on Guam and our division was based at Saipan. We were fortunate enough to meet for the second time overseas and enjoy some more priceless time together.

God Was On My Side
by John J. Wetterer

I was 22-years-old and married five days when preparing to go overseas. My wife left her Long Island home and missed me at Quantico, but finally managed a phone call before we embarked at Norfolk. I spent the

Med Cruise 6th Task Fleet. Haifa, Palestine. Aboard USS Marquette AKA-95.

next three years thousands of miles from home.

We sailed aboard the troopship, Kenmore, which was hot and uncomfortable. Quarters deep in the ship were woefully inadequate, bunks were stacked five deep and ventilation and showers and sanitary facilities were poor. The tropical heat for the next three months was brutal. Passing through the Panama Canal, crossing the Equator and being initiated as a Shellback broke the monotony.

We finally disembarked and spent time in New Caledonia. The natives and customs of the French population and the fact the higher echelon of "brass" was stationed in Noumea at the time was interesting, at least to me. Also, Noumea was the training ground for the first medium tank of the Pacific War, the General Sherman. This tank was not exceptionally large but seemed awesome at the time and was destined for great action with the 5th Amphibious Corps.

It must be about 1500 miles from Caledonia to Auckland, New Zealand. We took about three to four days, arriving in the later part of February 1943. We eventually left for Wellington by rail. The trip was picturesque. We met up with the rest of the 2nd and we, the 18th Marine Engineers, were bivouacked in Judgeford Valley. One of our greatest pleasures was the milk, steak, eggs and beer (although warm).

In April and May it started to get cold and we welcomed the issuing of heavier green winter service uniforms and new combat equipment. Around September we started more intensive training (amphibious), but a friend and I still found time to leave Wellington for the first day spring meeting at the Trentham Race Track. Program lawn music, marches and waltzes...it was a fine day.

The end of October we began boarding transports. Mine, I believe, was the Virgo. We sailed out November 1 with the scuttlebutt we were going to retake Wake Island. In retrospect, this might have been easier.

As it was, the invasion was to be Betio Island of Tarawa Atoll, code name "Helen" and occupied by Japanese Imperial Marines Naval Landing Force. D-day was November 20 and I was a bit apprehensive, although we became more confident by the barrage of naval bombardment by our battleships and cruisers. Their shells lit up the sea with great flashes and the noise was unimaginable. We had all been awake for hours, but we were not to go ashore for many, many hours while they were having an awful lot of trouble ashore. The operation was having problems: the reefs, stiff opposition and faulty communication were playing havoc. Yes, the Marines were pinned down on Red Beach with small protection by the sea wall. It would appear the Japanese raised even more cain with the later waves.

Strategy, I don't know. There was so much confusion the first couple of days at the point of departure that we of the 3/18 went ashore a bit early. On D+2 we came ashore near Red Beach long pier. In retrospect it was good, because later our fellows did a fine job with the heavy equipment.

Nothing had prepared me for the devastation, all the bodies, and all the death. The water was bloody, bright red in places. A Marine rule is never to take time to help a buddy, but I am sure where there is crying and praying, this rule is broken. Our pier was not as difficult as it might have been

Frank Drapczynski.

due to earlier efforts by men like Lieutenant Hawkins. My contribution might have been small, but I sure had walked in the company of brave men. I was revulsed at the sights of body parts and bobbing, bloated Marines next to the pier. Even at this early time of the landings, being a degree off the Equator, the sweet, sickening smell of death was unbelievable and seemed to invade everything.

Then again, now, after almost 55 years, I am still disconcerted when I think of Betio. After the island was secured we moved to "Ella" in the Atoll. Intelligence had reported activity. All I managed was a bad case of Dengue where everything hurts, even the back of your eyeballs. While I was sick, the natives in the village were having a dance which I sure hated to miss.

The next move was a couple of hundred miles voyage to Hawaii. The transports were worse than ever, smelling of sweat, blood and Betio. We dropped wounded off at Pearl to be sent to a naval hospital. We disembarked at Hilo and trucked 50-60 miles to a cold Camp Tarawa. I do remember the orders by Headquarters not to bother us, probably because we looked like haunted, weak scarecrows. We eventually came around, though, with good rest, food and a 2nd Division rodeo at Parker's Ranch. Later, I must have been feeling good because one day I invited a young Texan out of camp to fight. All I succeeded in accomplishing was a beauty of a black eye which I sported around for days.

By spring, training became more intense. Marches, landing practices on Maui, etc. We didn't know it at the time, of course, but undoubtedly we were getting ready for the Marianas. For this I was under command of Lieutenant Colonel R. Lloyd. We finally embarked in May 1944. En route we stopped at beautiful Eniwetoc with the 4th Division. This island was a forward rendezvous area and we had no occasion to disembark.

On June 15, we watched the cruisers and destroyers hurling shells into the beach. D-day promised to be a fine day, weather-wise, as the battleships and cruisers continued firing as they had for days. We watched them hurling shells into the beach and hills and watching the Navy and Marines carrier planes strafing and bombing. Much later, our shore party was finally put ashore on Green One, late on D-day. We dug in for the night, with little safety, for rest, as we were near the Charon Konoa.

One fairly unnerving incident occurred on or around this time. One of the fellows

John Chnulowski, and Ed Dwyer. Crete, November 19-22, 1951.

was tying a shoe lace in a foxhole when an unexploded shell from Mt. Tapochan blew off his leg. Since we were unable to treat injured on the beach, he was evacuated to a hospital shop where I understand he died, probably from shock. As I say, the night was brutal between the small attacks and threats. At least we weren't told we were "The Island of Walking Dead Men," as we were told on Betio.

By D+1 we were well beyond the rail line that ran from the sugar factory at Charon Konoa to larger Garapan. By about D+7 we were well on the way up the mountain. We by-passed a number of caves and ravines. It was in a cave that I confiscated a large regimental flag and Japanese album which I still have. I also got a fairly minor hit in the head, although the records classify it as "laceration of the scalp."

Something slightly annoying on our trek up "Tapioco" was the number of defenseless cows hit and the large pig killed by apprehensive triggers. It's a cardinal rule to know what your rifle has in its sights.

It was somewhat later, about D+10, I believe, that the 2nd and 4th Divisions on the flanks and the 27th N.Y. Army Division in the center had a large banzai attack near Tanapag Harbor. The Army was driven back and the 29th 2nd Division Artillery had to replace them. This precipitated Lieutenant General (Howling Mad) Smith sending Army General R. Smith back to Pearl. I believe they had different ideas on how to advance.

Much later, coming down from our point on the mountain was very arduous. We were

tired, dirty, with well worn uniforms and under a lot of pressure, not only from the enemy but conditions, mosquitoes, etc. We were physically and mentally exhausted (at least I was). Around the 4th of July, we were all but finished. The units were greatly mixed up and Saipan was secured on July 7; but additional days were spent mopping up caves and pockets of resistance.

Interesting at this time was the fact you could look across at Tinian. Also, I learned my brother-in-law's destroyer was impudently patrolling between the two islands.

On July 25, time had passed and the 2nd Division came ashore on Tinian in force on a clear fine morning. Shortly after, we were pelted by rain from a typhoon. The battle for Tinian ended officially in nine days, but mopping up took weeks. In my estimation it was an easy invasion. For the 100 or so men lost or the young Private First Class Wilson, who sacrificed his life and who posthumously was awarded the Medal of Honor, it was bad. In the long run, Tinian proved to be invaluable. On August 5, 1945 the B-29, Enola Gay, left the island to bomb Tokyo.

This recital has been difficult. I've tried not to be too garrulous in attempting to put some of my experiences on paper, and I hope I've succeeded. Other than that, the only thing I know is the good Lord must have been watching over me those years overseas. Otherwise, I truly don't know how 5I could have survived.

Semper Fi!

This was their base and town. Submarines and lots of sea planes. We leveled the town and for weeks they still came out of town living like rats and snakes.

There were quite a few planes that hauled the Japanese troops and merchandise from the mainland. About 7 to 10 looked like the one on the left.

The island was volcanic and had many holes the Japanese could stay in. They had local women with them. They had been working on fortifications for around 20 to 30 years - The local people were starved, beaten and abused.

U.S. Marines in action at Saipan.

U.S. Marines coming ashore at Saipan.

Monument for Camp Tarawa site on Parker Ranch. Waimea Hawaii.

March 28, 1998. Color Guard at dedication ceremonies Camp Tarawa Hawaii. With monument in background.

1065th PLATOO

U.S. MARI

84

M.C. SAN DIEGO
42

FIRST TO FIGHT

KENNETH M. ADAMS, born Oct. 6, 1938. Entered the service in October 1955 at Morgantown, WV. Assignments included Parris Island, SC. Recruit training, Camp Lejeune, NC. Assigned to I-3-6, L-3-2, B-1-2 2nd Marine Div. (Wpns. Plt.). Embarked on Mediterranean cruise in 1957 (Operation Deepwater - assigned to USS *Olmstead* APA-188). HQ USMC, Henderson Hall, Arlington, VA. Discharged in October 1959 with the rank of corporal. Adams was awarded the Good Conduct Medal.

Retired from the Arlington, VA police department as a master police officer/detective. Presently a magistrate in Fairfax, VA.

Member in the American Legion, Veterans of Underage Military Service, FOP, and Masonic Order. He and his wife, Patricia, have three children: Kenneth, Bruce and Stephanie; and one grandchild, Rachel.

JOHN M. ALCORN, born in Beattyville, KY Jan. 3, 1923. He was raised in Lexington, KY. After graduating from high school he enlisted in the USMC Aug. 28, 1942. He was to be in Plt. 729 at San Diego boot camp. After boot camp he was assigned to Jacque Farm for tank training. He sailed as a replacement in late 1942. Arriving in New Zealand he was assigned to Co. B, 2nd Tank Bn., with deactivation in Apr. 1943. Reassigned to Co. A in Oct. 1943. Assigned to Co. A-1, 2nd Amphib. Tractor Bn. sailing to Samoa. The company received 50 new amphibians for the landing at Tarawa. He was also at Saipan, Tinian and Okinawa. Returned to States with the battalion which was deactivated Nov. 29, 1945, at Camp Pendleton, CA. He was discharged Dec. 7, 1945.

At the outbreak of the Korean conflict he was called by the Army as second lieutenant. In May 1951 he was assigned to Co. E, 35th Inf. Regt., 25th Div. in Korea.

He was sent to Vietnam in 1967 to the 4th Trans. Command and later reassigned as operation officer in Qui Nhon Support Command. He had two tours of duty in Germany. During his military service he was awarded three Bronze Stars for valor, Purple Heart, three Army Commendation Medals, 11 Battle Stars and Good Conduct Medal. He retired as lieutenant colonel in 1970.

After retirement he entered the USPS, retired again as postmaster of Midway, KY. Resides in Lexington, KY with his wife, Cynthia

G.; daughter, Pamela Layell; and two granddaughters, Andrea and Allissa Edmondson.

JAMES L. ALEXANDER, born Sept. 10, 1918, in Load, KY. Enlisted in the USMC Jan. 13, 1942, at Charleston, WV. Left there for Parris Island for six weeks basic training. Went to Quantico, VA to shoot rifle range. While there he was selected for small arms instructor and remained there until June 1943. Left Quantico for Camp Lejeune and then to San Diego. In September 1943 he sailed on the SS *Typhoon*. Went to Hawaii in November 1943 and spent Christmas day at Pearl Harbor. Then joined 6th Marines on Hawaii Jan. 6, 1944. After training there they sailed on LST 131 for the invasion of Saipan and Tinian. He went in the third wave with Motor Plt., Co. C. Sixth day on Red Beach he was wounded and received the Purple Heart for shrapnel wound. He still has a piece of the metal in his back. Sailed on the *Manifee* 202 for Okinawa. Back to Saipan, then to Nagasaki and Sasebo. From there to San Diego where he was discharged Jan. 12, 1946. He was promoted to corporal while on Saipan.

Memorable experiences: Battle of Saipan, Tinian and Okinawa. Too many to write.

He and his wife, the former Omah H. Skidmore, have two children, Connie and James Douglas. Civilian activity as maintenance man with General Motors.

DOMENICK D. AMADIO, KIA Tarawa 1943.

STANLEY R. ANDERSON, born in Evanston, IL Feb. 2, 1929. He enlisted in the USMC in September 1946. After boot camp at Parris Island he was assigned to the 2nd Pioneer Bn. and later to the 16th Marines at Camp Lejeune. His unit participated in the division's maneuvers on Culebra and Vieques Islands in the Caribbean area during 1947-48.

After his discharge in 1948, Anderson joined the USMCR and attended college.

He was recalled to active duty in September 1950 and was assigned to the 2nd Shore Party Bn. at Camp Lejeune. He saw service in the Mediterranean area during his tour of duty when his platoon was assigned to the 2nd Bn., 6th Marines (BLT). He was discharged in August 1951 as a staff sergeant and returned to college.

He married Jeanell Prewett in September 1964 and they have one daughter, Sharry. Anderson was employed as an aeronautical engineer in the aerospace industry for 38 years and retired in 1990. He resides with his wife in Duluth, GA.

VIRGIL P. ANDERSON, born May 28, 1923. Enlisted in the USMC April 9, 1945. Assignments included Parris Island, Camp Lejeune, Courthouse Bay, Camp Pendleton, 2nd Engr. Bn., Kokura Japan, 6th Regt., and Saga Japan. Discharged Aug. 26, 1946, with the rank of private first class. Anderson was awarded the Asiatic-Pacific Campaign Medal and Occupation Medal.

Earned AB degree at the University of Nebraska (Omaha) in 1948 and JD degree at Creighton University School of Law in 1952. Employed as attorney-at-law and associate counsel, California State Automobile Assoc., 1953-58; manager, Governmental Affairs Dept., 1958-88; retired in 1988. He married Edna Pedersen in 1948. They have two children, Edward and Janet; and five grandchildren: Elizabeth and Hilary Anderson and Emily, Sarah and Andrew Nitschke. Membership in Sutter Club, Sacramento, CA; Rotary Club, Sacramento; and numerous awards and resolutions from the California State Legislature, and California Highway Patrol for contributions to Motor Vehicle Laws & Traffic Safety. Served as secretary, Motor Vehicle Conference, state of California 1960-88.

PHILIP M. ARNE, born July 4, 1923. Enlisted in the service Jan. 21, 1942. Assignments included San Diego, American Samoa, Guadalcanal, New Zealand, Tarawa, Hawaii, Saipan, naval hospital at Pearl Harbor, Floyd Bennett Field, Brooklyn and Camp Lejeune. He was discharged Jan. 22, 1946, with the rank of corporal. Arne was awarded the Purple Heart (D-Day, Saipan).

Memorable experiences: Location - Fungusal Bay; players - He and Rosie (age 12-15). Rosie's legs were so short that they called her "Low Butt."

The Marines discovered a pipe running continuously from who knows where. The water was cold and clean. With just four 4x4s and some burlap bags they made a shower.

As he was showering one day Rosie walked in. While filling her pail she looked him up and down two or three times. Then, with a full pail, and a little smile, she walked out.

Civilian activity as a police officer in New York City July 1, 1955-Dec. 9, 1976. He met his second wife, Rena, in 1942 and married her in 1994. She is a New Zealander, but that's another story. He and his first wife, Marjory (deceased), had two children, Barbara and Richard; and four grandchildren: Samantha, Richard Jr., Gregory and Stephanie.

EDWARD F. BAKER, born in Elmira, NY in 1939. He enlisted in the USMC in September 1956. After boot camp at Parris Island, SC he was assigned to B-1-8. He served on the Caribbean cruise where he received mountain training in Vieques, PR and jungle training in Panama. In 1958 he served on the Mediterranean cruise in Beirut, Lebanon. While in the Corps Baker received the Armed Forces Expeditionary Medal, the Good Conduct Medal and the Mediterranean Cruise Ribbon. He also earned the Sharpshooter and BAR badges. Baker was discharged from the Corps in Sep. 1958 as a private first class and remained in reserved discharge status until 1962.

In 1963 Baker married Patricia Hancock and they have two children, Brenda Moore and Edward Baker Jr., and one grandchild, Danyelle Moore.

Baker joined the Carpenters in 1966. In 1980 he was elected business manager of the Carpenters' Union Local #532 in Elmira, NY and is presently overseeing and finding work for 250 carpenters.

Baker is currently a trustee of the Carpenters Pension and Welfare Plan and is the apprentice coordinator for Local 532's apprentice program. He served two terms on the United Way Board, is a member of the Town of Veteran Planning Board, Government Affairs Committee Chemung County Chamber of Commerce, Southern Tier Central Regional Planning and Development Board, a charter member of REDEC and president of the Southern Tier Building and Construction Trades. In 1984 Baker received a certificate degree in labor relations from Cornell University after completing a three year program.

R.H. (PETE) BARNES, born March 11, 1925. He turned 17 in March 1942 and joined the Marines two months later, May 21, 1942. Went through boot camp at San Diego, Plt. 424.

Went to Camp Elliott for additional training. Sailed for New Zealand in November 1942. Early in 1943 they (the 2nd Div.) went to Guadalcanal. He was in the 6th Marines, Co. 3 of the 2nd Div. He became a runner and about the only message he delivered was the password, which they had a new one just about every night. They always used words the Japanese found difficult to pronounce. One evening while taking the password up to front-line, Japanese machine gun began firing. The picture shows the wounded being brought back. Barnes is in the upper left with shorts on. He saw the photographer taking the picture. The picture is in the book *Follow Me!*, story of 2nd Marine Div. in WWII by Richard W. Johnston, Random House, New York. Went back to New Zealand for additional training for the Tarawa invasion. It was this time (the second time in New Zealand) that he met the First Lady Eleanor Roosevelt. They were in the Allied Service Club in Wellington, New Zealand. She came over to Barnes and another Marine (see picture) and began giving Barnes the history of the 6th Marines, and the fourragere in particular, how the French had presented it to the 6th Marines during WWI. After a period of training they invaded Tarawa. Then to Hawaii where they were preparing for the invasion of Saipan. It was in Hawaii, while loading ships for the Saipan invasion, that he dropped a large box on his foot and broke it. He was in the Army hospital in Hilo for awhile. Then transferred to the Naval Hospital in Pearl Harbor. Back to the States in late 1944 where he spent his remaining time in Camp Lejeune, NC. He was discharged May 21, 1946.

Barnes was awarded the Presidential Citation Guadalcanal, three ribbons and two stars for Guadalcanal and Tarawa.

Civilian activities include Harding University, Searcy, AR in 1950; Post Graduate School, Memphis State. Two years with Nashville Motor Div., 30 years with Colgate Palmolive Co., and eight years at Kimberly Clark. He married Nita Thompson Aug. 18, 1945; they have four children: Hal, Vicki, Steve and Mary Linda; and six grandchildren: Brian, Joel, Adam, Shelby, Kathryn and Erik.

VERNON E. BARTELS, born in Maynard, IA in 1925. Upon graduation from high school he enlisted in the USMC in August 1942. After boot camp in San Diego he was assigned to HQ Co., 2nd Anti-tank Bn. and sent to New Zealand. He landed on Tarawa and was wounded on the second day of the battle. PFC  Bartels was medically separated in December 1944 from the Corps because of his wounds.

He married Ruth Heller in January 1946, had three sons and celebrated his 50th wedding anniversary last year. He drove a semi-truck for several firms in Waterloo, IA until his death Dec. 14, 1996, of a heart attack.

BRUCE G. BARTON, born in Detroit, MI in 1928 and enlisted in the USMC in the summer of 1946. After boot camp at Parris Island he was sent to the 2nd Marine Div. at Camp Lejeune, NC and assigned to a combat intelligence team (S-2) of HQ Co., 2nd Bn., 8th Marine Regt.

After training in various base schools and at the Army/Navy Amphibious Intelligence School at Little Creek, VA he received his MOS of 636. From there it was field and office training including maneuvers in the Caribbean. It was train, train, train since the Cold War was emerging.

Near the end of his enlistment he was transferred to the Marine barracks, U.S. Naval Shipyards at Charleston, SC where he served in various garrison guard duties. He was discharged with the rank of corporal in August 1948.

He is a lifetime member of 2nd Marine Div. Assoc. and has had several articles about his experiences while in USMC published in *Follow Me* the 2nd Marine Div. Assoc. quarterly paper.

After separation he returned to college receiving a Bachelor's degree in civil engineering in 1952. He worked in various engineering positions until he formed his own company (Thunderline Corp.) in 1960 which was to specialize in the manufacture of rubber and plastic automotive parts. It also produced an unique rubber pipe seal (LINK-SEAL) which is one of many patents he was awarded during his career.

He sold his business in 1989 and has retired to Charlevoux, MI and Singer Island, FL with his wife, the former Shirley Jean Wilson. They have two children, Bruce Jr. and Tracy, and enjoy three grandchildren.

GRAHAM BARTON, born in Detroit, MI Oct. 31, 1928. With his twin brother, Bruce, he left for boot camp at Parris Island Sept. 13, 1946, where he was a member of Plt. 359.

After boot camp he was assigned to HQ 2-8, Intelligence Section, at Camp Lejeune.

After infantry training the 2nd Div. shipped out to Little Creek for amphibious work with the cadets and midshipmen and then moved out to the Caribbean in February 1947 for maneuvers on the island of Culebra. This was called Operation Camid.

In late 1947 he was transferred to 4th Regt. and helped reform this famous unit into the 2nd Div. and the 1st Bn. Landing Team (BLT) with a new type of table of organization. The 2nd Div. then left for the Caribbean for maneuvers on the Island Vieques. He was promoted to corporal.

In the spring of 1948 he was promoted to sergeant with permanent warrant and transferred to the Naval Gun Factory in Washington, D.C. and attached to the Shore Patrol Unit. He was discharged in August 1948 and received the WWII Victory Medal.

After discharge he entered college receiving a BSME degree in 1953 and was then employed as an engineer at Michigan Oven Co., retiring as their executive vice president in 1989.

He married Betty Perona in 1952 and they have two sons, Greg and Mike, and two grandsons, Sammy and Joey.

Restoring military vehicles, hunting, fishing and mountain hiking are his major interests.

LEO BASSETTO, born Sept. 13, 1922. Enlisted in the USMC Nov. 17, 1942. Accomplishments include a successful carry out chicken business, Lee's, from 1959-76. Retired to Wisconsin and opened a restaurant in 1978.

He married Dolores in 1951; they have six children: Bill, Tom, Jim, Steven, Donna and Linda; and 13 grandchildren: Bridget, Brianne, Cara, Gina, Julie, Tom, Taylor, Janean, Natalie, Ann Marie, Karson, Alexander and Madeline. He is presently retired and living in Wisconsin, God's country.

PETER A. BEAUCHAMP, enlisted in the Reserves in May 1950 while a high school student in New York City. Korean War started in June and his unit was activated in August. Went from Ft. Schuyler, Bronx to Lejeune. Twenty of them transferred to NAS Quonset Point, RI. Reenlisted in regular Marines in June 1951 (made corporal). In July 1951 was at Pendleton, Tent Camp, IL. 14th Draft aboard USS *Noble* to Korea in October 1951. 1st Plt., G-3-1 November 1951-October 1952. Returned to USA aboard USNS *Marine Serpent*.

November 1952, Camp Lejeune, 2nd Marine Div., F-2-2 (made sergeant); N-4-8; ATA Plt., Wpns. 1-8. Little Creek, VA, three Vieques,

PR cruises, one Mediterranean (attached C-1-8). Discharged from Wpns. 1-8 in June 1955.

Medals include Good Conduct Medal, Korean Service Medal w/3 stars, United Nations Service Medal, Presidential Unit Citation, Korean Presidential Unit Citation, Navy Unit Citation, Naval Occupation (Europe), National Defense Service Medal, and Sharpshooter Medal.

Life member G-3-1 Korea, 1st Marine Div. Assoc. Member of 2nd Marine Div. Assoc., Marine Corps League and VFW. Divorced with two sons, one daughter, one granddaughter and one grandson. Employed as designer by Harris Corp. (aerospace/communications) in Palm Bay, FL.

RICHARD R. BERTONI, born in Ann Arbor, MI Nov. 18, 1923. Inducted into the USMC Thanksgiving Day, Nov. 27, 1942. Completed boots (Plt. 1128) in San Diego. Graduated from Communications School (telephone) and was assigned to the replacements in the 2nd Div. (H&S-3-10). Action at Tarawa and Saipan with the 3rd Bn., 10th Marines at Saipan. On July 7, 1944, nearly 4000 Japanese soldiers in a surprise element in the greatest Banzai attack of the war. While bringing ammunition to isolated units, he drove a jeep through heavy machine gun and rifle fire. Was awarded the Bronze Star Medal for combat in the Banzai attack. He remained in the area until he was seriously wounded.

His parents received notice that he was killed in action when he was really in a naval hospital in Hawaii. Was discharged from Great Lakes Naval Hospital in Jan. 1945 with the rank of private first class. He declined all promotions.

Attended school on the G.I. Bill and graduated with a major in accounting. Was married to a beautiful and wonderful woman, Jennie, for 50+ years and has four beautiful children: Michelle, a physical therapist; JoAnne, a registered nurse; Denise, a registered nurse; and Robert, a physical therapist; and five grandchildren: Kurt, Erik, Anthony, Daniel and Jolleen. They endured several family sorrows. One son died at birth and another in a car accident at the age of 29. He resides in Ann Arbor and belongs to many Veteran's organizations and is presently active in the Washtenaw County Corps League.

HENRY G. BLACK, born Jan. 21, 1920. Enlisted in the service Sept. 1, 1938. Assignments/locations/positions included Pearl Harbor, 2nd Marine Div. HQ Co., 2nd Tanks, San Diego Marine Base, Camp Matthews, Reykjavik Iceland, New Zealand, Saipan, and El Toro Air Station. Discharged Nov. 13, 1946, with the rank of staff sergeant. Awards/medals: Good Conduct, Asiatic, Foreign Land, Presidential Citation and Sharpshooter.

Memorable experiences: Action against enemy, Marianas Island. Started cooking ca-

reer at Pearl Harbor in 1939 at the Marine barracks.

Black belongs to Masonic Lodge 732, Citrus Heights, CA, Shriner of Los Angeles, Order of the Eastern Star, White Shrine, VFW, and Ham Radio. He and his wife, Mary E., were married May 10, 1942. They have three children: Dennis, Donald and Michelle; and three grandchildren: Carol, Jennifer and Kelly. He is a retired locksmith.

ROBERT J. BRAMLETT, born Jan. 13, 1922, in New York City. Enlisted in the USMC in September 1942. Finished high school in 1941, worked in industry before boarding train for Parris Island, SC. After training at New River he was posted to C-1-20, 4th Div. In May 1943 he was transferred to Camp Pendleton, CA to join the 24th Replacement Bn. In July 1943 the battalion was shipped to New Zealand where he joined E-2-18, 2nd Div.

Saw action at Tarawa, Saipan and Tinian. Sailed to Okinawa in April 1945; not needed. After the A bombs, the division sailed to Nagasaki for occupation duty. Robert was transferred to Sasebo to join the 5th Div. to get ready to sail stateside. Bramlett was honorably discharged as a corporal at Bainbridge, MD Jan. 17, 1946.

He attended Penn State and Price School of Journalism and Advertising and spent the next 35 years in journalism, advertising and public relations.

His first wife, Constance Curry, died in 1975 without issue. He married Nancy Iredale in 1979 and has had a ball ever since. He has three stepchildren: John, Anna and Thomas; and four step grandchildren: Elizabeth, Alice, Christopher and Daniel.

JESSIE E. BRISTER, born in September 1919 in south Mississippi. Attended public school and junior college. Enlisted in the Corps in October 1940. Boot camp in San Diego, then to C-1-10, later to B-1-10. OCS at Samoa, then A-1-10. After Guadalcanal and Tarawa, back to C-1-10 as executive officer. Wounded at Saipan. Released to Reserves in January 1946 as captain. Put on retired list in February 1958 as lieutenant colonel. Received Letter of Commendation for Tarawa, Silver Star for Saipan, Purple Heart and three Presidential Unit Citations.

Feels he owes his success in Corps to the enlisted personnel with whom he served, and support from Bob Carney, Joe Stewart and E.P. Rixey, along with good friends John Stone and Harry Dickinson. After release, worked as railroad conductor in Southern California, supervisor in Venezuela, then operated small business in Jackson, MS. Retired in 1977, settled in Brandon, MS where he helps care for ailing wife, Patty.

CHARLES GETRICK BROWN, born April 16, 1924. Grew up in Livingston, MT. Enlisted in Spokane, WA and was sworn into the Corps for four years Oct. 24, 1941. Went through boot camp in San Diego with Plt. 166. After boot training was assigned to G Btry., 3rd Bn., 10th Marines at Camp Elliott after completion of Telephone Linesman School.

Boarded the *President Jackson* in San Diego while the *Presidents Adams* and *Hayes* were also loading to what was to become the 2nd Marine Bde. The practice landings are well remembered, especially at Coronado.

Enroute to the South Pacific they crossed the Equator July 10, 1942. His big shellback certificate is framed on his den wall yet today. Also enroute their convoy put into the Friendly Tonga Islands. The *Hornet* (he thinks it was the *Hornet*) had steering problems and they all got to go ashore on Tonga Tabu. This is where many Marines learned what the coconut runs were all about. The *President Jackson's* heads were filled to over flowing that night.

Landed on Tulagi first day, Aug. 7, 1942. Then to Wellington New Zealand, departing Guadalcanal Jan. 30, 1943.

Fondest and most alive memories of overseas were the liberties in Wangonier, New Zealand, one of the world's really nice cities, with the world's really nice people.

In MOB 4 at Silverstream, New Zealand with malaria again, met Mrs. Roosevelt as she came through the wards. A few days later Joe E. Brown came through, they were all standing by their bunks if they could. Joe E. saw Brown's name on the bunk, stuck out his hand and said, "Hi, my name is Brown too," as if he didn't know. They learned later that day he had been notified that his son, a fighter pilot in the Air Corps, was down, and missing in the South Pacific.

Went ashore at Tarawa the second day, survived, and on to Camp Tarawa on the big island. To Saipan and ashore the first day. Once Saipan

was secured, 5-N-10 was loaded aboard ship again and alongside the *Rocky Mound*, sailed to Guam. Was a forward observer during all this time, got to go ashore the first day again.

After a furlough home to Montana he landed in the Marine base hospital in San Diego where he met pharmacy mate 3/c Frances G. Peitz. Father Cronin, base chaplain, performed a beautiful wedding ceremony in the base chapel March 9, 1945, and 53 years later they are still holding hands.

After a son, Charles Thomas and daughter, Deborah Anne and 46 years as a union teamster he's mostly retired and fully involved with catching, and releasing, nature's gift to us, the rainbow trout. Their home is near Sumner, WA but surely loves and enjoys all of the beautiful northwest. They also have one grandson, Jefferey.

Memorable experience: While on duty at the observation post atop the hill on Tulagi above King George playing field, BGEN Rupertus, his staff and Chaplain Willard would run for their coconut log revetment whenever the air raid alarm sounded. One night the general was bringing up the rear as they hurried for protection. While Rupertus was buckling on his helmet he turned to Brown, smiled, and said "Speed is not my counterpart, tis endurance!"

HAROLD E. BROWN, born June 16, 1922. Enlisted in the Reserves, 10th Marine Bn., in New Orleans, LA Feb. 12, 1940. Active duty began Nov. 20, 1940. Served with Cos. F-2-6, H-2-6 and HQ-2-6. Military locations and stations included Iceland, 1941-42; Camp Elliott, Linda Vista, CA; New Zealand, 1942-43; Hawaii, 1943-44. Served during the invasion in 1944. Was wounded in action on Saipan June 16, 1944. Received Purple Heart in 1945.

After discharge in San Diego, CA worked for the post office in National City, CA 1945-54. Worked for Safeway Stores in June 1955. In 1961 was employed by Mayfair Markets until retirement Dec. 31, 1983.

While in New Zealand was a messman in serving Mrs. Eleanor Roosevelt upon her visit there. She met each messman that served her for a luncheon. Served under the command of MGEN Raymond L. Murray, COL LeRoy P. Hunt Jr. and also COL Nutting.

Married Elaine Richards Nov. 12, 1944. They had six children, one every two years, four girls and two boys. All are still living except his lovely wife who died in 1985. Remarried in September 1987 to Florine. He also has 18 grandchildren and two great-granddaughters.

JOSEPH B. BROWN, born in Wichita Falls, TX June 10, 1918. Joined the Marines Sept. 4, 1940. Called to active duty Nov. 6, 1940. Served in 2nd Bn., 8th Marines from Nov. 6, 1940-Aug. 1, 1944, with Cos. E, HQ and F. Boarded ship

Jan. 6, 1942, to Samoa, Guadalcanal, New Zealand, Tarawa, Hawaii, Saipan and Tinian. Wounded June 18th on Saipan (not bad), then on Tinian Aug. 1, 1944, in hand to hand combat by bayonet. Wrested bayonet from enemy and used on him. (Brown has the bayonet in his possession.) In hospitals in Hawaii, Seattle, WA and Corpus Christi, TX. Awarded the Silver Star, Bronze Star and two Purple Hearts.

Married Margueritte Sick Sept. 25, 1944. They have three children: Darlene, Darwin and Dean; six grandchildren: Park Johnson III, Michelle, Tiffany, Misty, Emily and Ryan; and two great-granddaughters, Autumn Jamae and Whisper Dawn. Discharged at Corpus Christi Naval Air Base Oct. 11, 1945, as platoon sergeant. Worked one year with Texas Highway Engineers, 22 years with Halliburton Co. and 14 years with Baker Oil Tools. Retired and loves to travel.

MARCUS R. BROWN, born in Wichita Falls, TX May 28, 1916. Joined Marines Sept. 4, 1940. Called to active duty Nov. 6, 1940. Served in 2nd Bn., 8th Marines from Nov. 6, 1940-August 1944 with Cos. H and HQ. Boarded ship Jan. 6, 1942, to Samoa, Guadalcanal, New Zealand, Tarawa, Hawaii, Saipan and Tinian.  Wounded on Tarawa Nov. 20, 1943. In hospital in Hawaii. Rejoined the division on Hawaii for Saipan-Tinian operation. Was discharged in 1946 at San Francisco, CA as sergeant.

After discharge started college at Texas A&M, was finishing his third year of veterinary medicine when killed in motorcycle accident. He married Venti Carl (Dooley) Bruno and had a daughter, Debra, born two weeks after his death.

JOHN C. BRUNS JR., born Dec. 13, 1923, in Baltimore, MD. He graduated early from high school in order to enlist in the USMC Oct. 5, 1943. After boot camp at Parris Island and basic combat intelligence class at Camp Lejeune, Bruns participated with HQ Co., 3rd Bn., 6th Marines, 2nd Marine Div. in the first wave of the assault on Saipan, where he lost his right arm to an enemy mortar. 0He recuperated at the San Diego, Mare Island and Philadelphia naval hos-

pitals and was honorably discharged Jan. 26, 1945, with a Purple Heart.

Bruns and his wife, Eileen, were married April 12, 1947. They have two daughters, six grandchildren and four great-grandchildren. After working for 35 years for the IRS and 10 years in retail, Bruns retired and now devotes much of his time to the American Legion, VFW, DAV and Kiwanis.

JOHN F. BUCHALSKI, enlisted in the USMC Nov. 26, 1946. After boot camp at Parris Island (Plt. 448) he was assigned to Camp Lejeune, F Co., 21st Marines and later reassigned to F-2-2. Overseas tours included Marine Barracks, Pearl Harbor; Guam; Puerto Rico; and Cuba. Sea duty aboard the USS *Toledo* (CA-133) in Korea (three campaigns). Stateside assignments in Barstow and Long Beach, CA. Short assignments to Hollywood for USMC publicity with movie stars. Finished tour of duty and discharged at the Marine Corps Recruit Depot, San Diego, CA Nov. 25, 1951. After nine months of civilian life he re-enlisted in the USAF Sept. 17, 1952, for training at Sampson AFB, NY. Upon completion of training he was assigned to Shaw AFB, SC to the provost marshal office as an air policeman/investigator. While in the USAF he had three tours of duty in Germany (13 years), twice awarded the Air Force Commendation Medal while assigned to SAC. Was the first staff sergeant to be assigned the duties as first sergeant and later promoted to tech sergeant. Was assigned to HQ A&AFES in Munich, Germany as an administrative supervisor performing covert intelligence for the OSI. Retired from the USAF in 1974. Started a new career in civil service as chief of police and later worked for the Army as OPSEC intelligence officer and physical security inspector. Prior to retiring from civil service he has received five Army Meritorious Civilian Awards and the Army Commanders Award. Listed in *Who's Who in American Law Enforcement* 1983 and 1986. Has 35 years of service as a volunteer in scouting, was awarded the Silver Beaver and the St. George Award for service to the youth and is a Woodbadge member.

Buchalski is married to the former Ingeborg G. Nadler of Marienbad, Czechoslovakia, daughter of Dr. and Mrs. Ernst Nadler. He has three children: Carol, Martina and Thomas, a U.S. Army major; and three grandchildren. Buchalski is a graduate of the University of New Hampshire and St. Anselm's College with a degree in criminology and criminal justice.

CARL H. BUCK, born Sept. 15, 1912. Enlisted in the USMC Sept. 21, 1932. On Aug. 5, 1943, crossed Equator to New Zealand on Dutch ship. Part of team hit Tarawa Nov. 20, 1943; then to Hilo, HI Dec. 28, 1944; hit Saipan June 6, 1944. Discharged Feb. 11, 1962, with the rank

of chief warrant officer third class. Buck was awarded four Bronze Stars and ribbons.

Memorable experiences: Saving lives on Saipan in 1944 and receiving Letter of Commendation from GEN W.T. Clement for saving a man's life.

Civilian activity included restaurant owner for seven years; taught foods at Seattle Community College for three years; and taught high school for three years. He and his wife, E. Jeanette, have two children, Collene and Richard; and five grandchildren: Andrea, Jeffrey, Bethany, Jordan and Brian.

JOSEPH T. (BUZLEGKI) BUZA-LEWSKI, born July 8, 1923. Enlisted in the USMC July 8, 1941. Assignments/locations/positions include Parris Island, Quantico, Camp Elliott, 18th Engr., Wellington New Zealand, 1942 action, 2nd Marine Div., Tarawa, Saipan, Tinian, and Okinawa. Discharged Aug. 28, 1945. Buzalewski was awarded the Bronze Star Medal and Presidential Unit Citation.

Was acting squad leader in July 1944-July 1945 without benefit of rank or pay (sergeant). Served as flame thrower, 1st Bn., Demolition Plt., 6th Marines.

Memorable experiences: A quote from his team demolition man, PFC Eli Whitney Hudson, born in Harlem County, KY. "Stick with me kid, the Japanese woman who will sire the soldier who is to kill me hasn't been born yet." He was true to his quote. He went back to the U.S. after Saipan and met his death in a training accident. He was a man without fear.

Buzalewski and his wife, the former Irene M. Imroczek, have three children: Elaine, Robert Thomas and Lisa; and four grandchildren: Jennifer, Luke, Lauren and Theodora.

WILBUR L. CALCUTT, born in 1929. Enlisted in the USMC in September 1946. Boot camp at Parris Island, SC. Afterward assigned to 2nd Marine Div., DUKW Co., 2nd Amphib. Tractor Bn., Camp Lejeune, NC.

Participated in amphibious maneuvers twice in the Caribbean waters. Also Little Creek, VA and Onslow Beach at Camp Lejeune. Separated from the Corps in September 1948. Joined the Reserves and was called back in November 1950. Served 14 months active duty this time in 2nd Amtrac Bn. at Courthouse Bay, Camp

Lejeune. Maneuvers again on Vieques Island in Caribbean. Discharged as a sergeant.

Calcutt was married to Ann Wood in October 1954 and has two girls, Donna and Sylvia and a boy, Jim. He also has four grandchildren and they reside in Pinehurst, NC.

Calcutt is a retired truck driver of 32 years with McLean Trucking Co. and Milliken Co.

FRED B. CAMP, born April 20, 1927. Enlisted in the USMC April 20, 1945. Assignments/locations/positions included Parris Island, Plt. 242, boot camp, Camp Lejeune, Camp Pendleton, Philadelphia Naval Base (man gate), Pearl Harbor, and Sasebo Japan. Left Japan for Norfolk with 2nd Marine Div. Discharged Aug. 21, 1945, with the rank of private first class at Quantico, VA. Camp's awards include the Good Conduct Medal, Pacific Theater Operations and Occupation of Japan.

Memorable experiences: D.I. for young Marines 1977-78.

He and his wife, Rita K., have eight children: Fred, Ron, Frank, Rita, Jim, Joe, Chuck and Rob; and 20 grandchildren (and counting). Civilian activities in electronics as test equipment engineer and foreman of electronics and maintenance. Retired Feb. 1, 1990, after 48 years with Philco T.V. and Ford Motor Co.

LOUIS ALEXANDER CARR, born Nov. 30, 1921, in Medora, IN. After graduating from high school in May 1941 he enlisted in the USMC in July 1941. Following boot camp at San Diego he was assigned to M-32. Left States in June 1942 on USS *Adams*; saw action on Guadalcanal Aug. 7, 1942-January 1943. Assault and capture of Tarawa, Nov. 20-24, 1943; Saipan Marianas June 15-July 9, 1944; Tinian, Marianas July 24-Aug. 1, 1944; domestic duty in San Diego; Camp Elliott; Camp Tarawa; Kalmath Falls, OR; Philadelphia, PA. Foreign duty in New

Zealand January-October 1943. Discharged Aug. 10, 1945, Depot & Supplies, Philadelphia, PA.

Married Marge Baldwin of Michigan Nov. 30, 1946. They have two children, Jon and Leanne (Carr) Fader, and two grandsons, Mick and Matthew Carr. Widowed in 1993. Civilian occupation: Worked in construction 1945-53. Retired from Kalamazoo City Fire Dept. in 1977 after 24 years.

RAYMOND E. CARTER, born April 9, 1928. Enlisted in the USMC in January 1947 and served with the 2nd Marine Div. Assignments/locations/positions included Camp Lejeune, Oceanside, CA, AGC #8 Mt. Olympus, LST 1163, Operation Nomex, Labrador, Norfolk and Quantico, VA, USMC Radio Station, Lejeune, HQ Co., 2nd Bn., 2nd Marines, FMF & H&S Co., 10th Marines FMF, radio teletype operator. Discharged in October 1951 and joined the USMCR. Carter was awarded the Good Conduct Medal, unit awards and Honorable Service Award.

Very active in Marine Corps League and MODD past commandant. Civilian activity as production supervisor for Bendix/Allied Signal for approximately 30 years. He and his wife, Anne, have two sons, George Allen and Raymond Edward Jr., and four grandchildren: Amber, Jermy, Ashlet and Tiffany. Presently retired. Plays lots of golf and does volunteer work.

WILLIAM P. (BILL) COFFIN, born May 22, 1923. Enlisted in the service Sept. 25, 1942. Assignments/locations/positions included G-3-10, forward observer on Tarawa and Saipan. Also 3rd Bn., 10th Marines was changed to 2nd, 155mm howitzer for Saipan, Guam and Iwo Jima. Discharged Oct. 3, 1945, with the rank of corporal.

Worked for various Department of Defense organizations in contracts administration. Also was contracting officer for HQ, USPS. Retired in 1986.

He and his wife, Kathleen, have three children: William, Robert and Kathleen; and five grandchildren: William, Mary Beth, Patricia, Andrew, and Elizabeth Anne. His son, Bill, is a retired commander of the USN and grandson, Bill, a graduate of the U.S. Military Academy, is a retired captain of the USMC.

THOMAS A. CONNORS, born in Pueblo, CO in 1924. After graduating from high school and attending college for one quarter he enlisted in the USMC in 1943.

Following boot camp he was assigned to the Japanese Language School at Camp Elliott until being assigned to 81mm Mortar School under MGYSGT "Waxy" Watkins, also at Camp Elliott.

After Mortar School Connors was sent overseas in December 1943 and joined H Co. (later to be HQ Co.), 2nd Bn., 8th Marines on the island of Hawaii. He saw action at Saipan, Tinian, Okinawa and Iheya Shima. The enemy had evacuated Iheya Shima before the landing, but the assault bombardment was very real!

Following the battle for Okinawa, the 8th Marines returned to Saipan where Connors was chosen to attend Officers Candidate School at Camp Lejeune, NC. On the way back to Camp Lejeune, the war ended and he was discharged Sept. 13, 1945, as a corporal.

Connors married Helene Gobel in July 1952 and seven children were born of this union. He graduated from the University of Denver with a degree in environmental science and zoology. Connors was a food and milk inspector for the Pueblo Health Dept. and was also an air pollution control specialist for the Colorado Dept. of Health in Denver.

He and his wife are grandparents of seven children and great-grandparents of six children. They are members of the Colorado Chapter of the 2nd Marine Div., are retired and live in Lakewood, CO.

ROBERT G. CONWAY JR., born in Albany, NY April 26, 1951. He is the son of Robert G. and Kathryn Kelly Conway. One of his brothers, Nicholas B., of Helena, MT is also a former Marine (2nd Light Armd. Vehicle Bn., 2nd Marine Div.). He attended Christian Brothers Academy in Albany, NY, graduated from Dartmouth College (AB degree in 1973) and received a JD degree from Albany Law School of Union University in 1976. During the summer of 1975, while attending law school, he completed Officers Candidate School at Quantico, VA and was commissioned a second lieutenant Aug. 15, 1975. Following graduation from Law School in 1976 he attended The Basic School at Quantico, VA and The Naval Justice School in Newport, RI. He reported in June 1977 to HQ Co., HQ Bn., 2nd Marine Div. where he was assigned for four years to the Office of the Staff Judge Advocate. From 1981-82 he was assigned as a judge advocate to the 3rd Marine Div. and to the 3rd Force Svc. Support Gp. in Okinawa, Japan where his father had fought as a naval officer during WWII.

During the next 14 years he was assigned to legal and staff billet at: Marine Corps Base, Camp Lejeune, NC; The Judge Advocate General's School, U.S. Army, in Charlottesville, VA; Marine Corps Air Station, Cherry Point, NC; HQ Marine Corps, Washington, D.C.; and, the Eastern Area Counsel Office, Camp Lejeune, NC. He advanced in rank to major and retired from the USMC July 31, 1996. His personal decorations include the Legion of Merit Medal,

the Meritorious Service Medal and the Navy Achievement Medal.

He and his wife, Lynda, were married Dec. 15, 1979, at Camp Lejeune, NC; and have one son, Phillip. Since retirement from the USMC in 1996 he has been counsel to the New York State Division of Military and Naval Affairs in Latham, Albany County, NY. He resides in Glenmont, NY.

ROBERT L. COOK, born in St. Lois, MO Aug. 4, 1920. Reared in East St. Lois, IL. Joined the CCCs in 1937, stationed in Highland, WI. Spent time in Chicago, IL 1939-40. Joined the Marines January 2nd after Pearl Harbor attack. Boot camp in Camp Elliott CA, Plt. 38. Assigned to D Co. for one month then assigned to Regt. Wpns. Co. Military specialty: demolitions. Acting mess sergeant in New Zealand after Guadalcanal. Active in demolitions on Tarawa. Transferred to Pearl Harbor after injury. Did guard duty in Pearl until sent Stateside in early 1945. Sent to duty at Jacksonville Naval Air Station. Discharged from that station Sept. 20, 1945, with the rank of corporal.

Civilian occupations included barber/beautician, sales, industrial worker, woodworker and writer. He and his wife, Mary Lou, have one son, Terrence D. and two grandchildren, Brian D. and Jamie Lyn.

JAMES V. COTTON, *Photos only, no bio submitted.*

ROBERT RHEA COWAN, born Dec. 25, 1921, in Summit, NJ. Enlisted in the service July 1, 1943. After boot camp at Parris Island entered OCS as second lieutenant, joined 2nd Marine Div. on Saipan. Platoon leader in Saipan and Tinian. Promoted to first lieutenant followed by landing at Okinawa and occupation of Nagasaki with 3rd Bn., 2nd Marines. Korean conflict called back to Reserves, active duty at Camp Lejeune. Honorable discharge USMC Aug. 18, 1951.

Cowan was awarded the Asiatic-Pacific Campaign Medal w/star, American Area Medal, Presidential Unit Citation and WWII Victory Medal.

Memorable experiences: Having duty of the day with his platoon and being asked by the commanding general, "Can you handle the 2,500

91

Japanese prisoners of war being unloaded in Nagasaki!" Cowan said "yes" figuring the odds were even.

Civilian activity as financial advisor in New York City for the Penn Mutual Life. He and his wife, Catherine (Kitty), were married May 20, 1950. They have one daughter, Carol A.

KENNETH H. CRONE, born July 16, 1920. Enlisted in the service March 17, 1942. Commissioned second lieutenant July 18, 1942. After commissioning he attended the 10th Reserve Officers Class. Left Quantico Oct. 12, 1942, and joined A-1-6 as a platoon leader. Participated in the battles of Guadalcanal, Tarawa, Saipan, Tinian and Okinawa. Wounded at Saipan and received the Purple Heart and the Bronze Star w/Combat "V." He was the last officer to leave the 1st Bn., 6th Marines that had sailed to the South Pacific in November 1942. One thing he will remember, out of many experiences ... on Tinian, when they were attacking, part of his duties as HQ Co. commanding officer was to perform liaison with the units on the flanks of their battalion. He was in the front lines when he saw two flashes approximately 1500 yards to their front. It was two Japanese guns rolling out of a cave to fire at a battleship close to Tinian Town harbor, and after firing, rolling back into the cave. He received permission to radio corps artillery and give them the information needed to fire on the guns. He gave the map coordinates, they bombarded the cave and silenced the guns. They had hit the battleship, which he later learned was the USS *Colorado*. He also learned that a sailor on the ship, who was a neighbor of his in Kansas City, was killed in this action.

Discharged Nov. 15, 1945, with the rank of captain. Crone was awarded the Purple Heart and Bronze Star w/Combat "V."

Civilian activity as president and CEO of Roycraft Industries in Saginaw, MI. He and his wife, Coletta, have six children: Stephen, Mary Anne, Rita, Maureen, Paula and John; 10 grandchildren; and two great-grandchildren.

RALPH R. (ROLAND) CROSIAR, born in 1914, in Star, ID. Moved with parents to Oregon in 1928. Engaged in agricultural work, one summer on Forest Service Lookout, before WWII. Enlisted in January 1942 and served four years in the Marines, 2nd Div., 6th Regt. with

two years in the South Pacific. Took part in Guadalcanal, Tarawa and Saipan campaigns. Wounded during landing at Saipan. Remainder of enlistment doing guard duty, Whidbey Island Naval Station, El Toro base. Also on ship's detachment, *W.G. Haan*.

Since discharge lived in California until moving to Oregon in 1965 where he raised sheep and cattle until retirement. Now resides at Marian Estates in Sublimity. He and his wife, Laura, have two sons and three grandchildren. Has followed an active interest in history of his area, doing a study of the U.S. post offices within Polk County, OR.

RICHARD A. CRUICKSHANK, born Dec. 31, 1930, in Del Norte, CO. Entered the USMC May 3, 1948. Boot camp at San Diego, Telephone School at Camp Del Mar, Camp Lejeune, Korea and back to San Diego as D.I. Other locations included Inchon, Seoul, Wonsan, Majon Ni, Hagaui-Ri and Koto-Ri. Discharged May 2, 1952, with the rank of staff sergeant.

Cruickshank was awarded the Bronze Star w/V, once removed, Purple Heart, Presidential Unit Citation w/2 Bronze Stars, Good Conduct Medal, National Defense Service Medal, Korean Service Medal w/1 Silver and 1 Bronze Star, United Nations Service Medal and the Korean Presidential Unit Citation w/1 Bronze Star.

Memorable experiences: He was fortunate enough to serve with Big Foot Brown, Chesty Puller and many others.

He and his wife, Shirley A., have eight children of which four were in the Marines (with one still in at New River), 17 grandchildren and one great-grandson. Civilian activity with Lincoln Telephone Co. for 31 years.

EARL E. CUMMINGS, born at Meridian, ID in 1922. He graduated from Melba High School, Melba, ID in 1941. On Aug. 18, 1942, he enlisted in the Marines and went to boot camp in San Diego, CA, trained as a tank crewman and amphibian tractor crewman in the 2nd Marine Div., completing  a 16 weeks course in tank crewman and also ranger tactics for eight weeks.

He was awarded the Bronze Star and a citation "for meritorious achievement," while serving as a crewman of a Marine amphibian tractor battalion on Tarawa, Gilbert Islands, Marianas, on Saipan and Tinian, Marshall Islands.

He was separated April 24, 1945, as a corporal. Upon returning home, he continued on the farm. In January 1947 he married Evelyn Kiester at Marsing, ID. They have three children: Robert, Renee and Reva; and seven grandchildren: Sarah, Austin, Hannah, Hailey, Chet, Markus and Rebecca. In 1950 he became a cattleman, raising registered Herefords and later "Tarentise" cattle, which is still his present occupation.

ORVAL CUTSHAW, born Nov. 23, 1923, in Elkhart, IN. Enlisted Feb. 13, 1945, in the Marine Infantry, San Diego, CA. Served in New Zealand with D-1-2. Participated in invasions of Tarawa, Saipan, Tinian and Okinawa; occupation of Nagasaki, Japan. Discharged Feb. 13, 1946. Cutshaw was awarded a Unit Citation - Tarawa.

He graduated from Purdue University in 1950 with a BSCE degree. Worked for the city of Dayton, OH as engineer-manager - Allegan, Branch, Barry and Emmet counties 1954-89.

Accomplishments: Secretary and president, Country Road Assoc. Michigan, Northern Michigan CRA, and Petoskey, MI Kiwanis Club. Served on Education Board, City Planning Commission, Charter Commission - Petoskey. Elder of Presbyterian church.

He married Betty McDowell June 7, 1947. They have four children: Gregory, Barbara, Nancy and Peggy; and eight grandchildren. Retired, ARC Disaster Service member. Resides in Petoskey, MI and spends winters in Treasure Island, FL.

BILL DAY, born in Springfield, IL Jan. 8, 1924. Raised in Decatur, IL and now resides in Houston, TX. Enlisted in December 1942 at Springfield, IL. Went to boot camp at San Diego in January 1943.

Short and sweet, from boot camp to Nagasaki Japan in a short two and one-half years.

Was not there but lost best buddy right off, Jack Redman Tarawa, his name is in book *Tarawa*.

To New Zealand with H&S Co., 18th Engrs. To Hilo, HI, Saipan and Okinawa. Back to Saipan then to Nagasaki Japan. Left in December and back to San Diego Christmas Day.

Back to Decatur and started school at James Milliken University where he played all sports and earned 11 letters. Then went into sales and transferred to Houston, TX with Brown Foreman Distillers in 1957. Hates cold, loves the southern weather. Has been married and is now divorced. He has one son, one daughter and grandchildren.

Day has received all his Purple Hearts. Best of all, thanks the Lord, he is a heart transplant recipient as of April 2, 1986.

JOHN DECKER, born Oct. 23, 1949. Enlisted in the service in December 1967. Served with E Co., 2nd Bn., 6th Marines. Military locations include Camp Lejeune, NC. Was grenadier for 1st Sqdn. Discharged in December 1988 with the rank of master sergeant.

Decker was awarded the Purple Heart, Navy Achievement Medal, Navy Commendation Medal, Combat Action Ribbon, Vietnam Campaign Medal, Vietnam Service Medal, National Defense Service Medal, and Good Conduct Medal w/1 Silver and 2 Bronze Stars.

He and his wife, Dianna (Baker), have two children, Shanna and John.

HERBERT H. DEIGHTON, born in Park City, UT Sept. 9, 1923. Lived in Los Angeles, CA from 1925-36 and La Habra Heights, CA from 1936-42. Attended high school in Whittier, CA. Enlisted in the USMC July 3, 1942. Boot camp at San Diego, then to Camp Elliott. Shipped out to Wellington, New Zealand Oct. 20, 1942, with G-2-6. To Guadalcanal Jan. 4, 1943, on the USS *President Jackson*. Left on same ship Feb. 19, 1943, for Wellington. Nov. 20, 1942, in Tarawa with 2nd Section, HQ Co., 2nd Bn., 6th Marines; Saipan, June 15, 1944, with HQ-2-6; Tinian, July 26, 1944, with HQ-2-6. Returned to U.S. Jan. 4, 1945. Duty at MCRD San Diego and NAS North Island Feb. 12, 1945, to discharge July 2, 1946, with the rank of sergeant.

Three years of college, four years at Northwestern University Dental School. Dental practice from 1953-89 in Escondido, CA. Was married for 25 years, single 15 years, and now married to a lovely New Zealand lady. Lives in New Zealand part of the year and California part of the year.

JAMES R. DELORENZO, born May 6, 1927. Enlisted in the service Nov. 27, 1942. Assignments/locations/positions: Lake Hurst, NJ Naval Air Station. 8th Marines, Okinawa; 2nd Marines Saipan and Nagasaki, Japan. Discharged July 19, 1946, with the rank of corporal.

Memorable experiences: Was with the first occupational troops to land in Nagasaki after the atomic bomb.

Worked in heavy equipment in Massachusetts and New Hampshire for 42 years. Now retired and living in Florida. He and his wife, Virginia, have been married 51 years. They have one son, three daughters and eight grandchildren.

FRED DEL RUSSO, born Dec. 3, 1924, in Newark, NJ. On March 18, 1943, he began boot camp at Parris Island, SC. After graduation spent six months on guard duty at Bayonne, NJ naval depot. He shipped overseas via New River, NC and the Panama Canal to Camp Tarawa on the big island of Hawaii. In June 1944 participated in the invasion of Saipan; in July, Tinian; and in 1945, Okinawa. At the war's end participated in the occupation of Nagasaki, Japan. Del Russo was honorably discharged Jan. 7, 1946, with the rank of private first class.

Memorable experiences: His regimental weapons company 37mm anti-tank gun crew had been involved in some heavy fighting on Saipan. At dusk one evening, in the town of Garapan, they set up their gun in a sandbagged defensive position at a crossroads opposite a bombed out brewery. Later they heard shrapnel plunking off their gun shield. In the darkness Japanese troops had sneaked into the brewery and for a few hours they traded throwing grenades across the road. Still later they heard glass shattering in front of them. At dawn, much to their surprise, not only was their position strewn with pieces of shrapnel, but also much broken glass ... apparently drunken Japanese had run out of grenades and heaved empty beer bottles at them!

He worked as a retail sales manager for Sears Roebuck for 33 years, retiring in 1987. He has been marred to his wife, Mary, for 55 years. They have seven married children: Susan, Cheryl, Glenn, Dawn, Joanne, Marilyn and Mark; and 18 grandchildren.

WILLIAM GERALD DEMOSS, born June 1, 1926. Enlisted in the USMC June 28, 1944. Assignments/locations/positions: Boot camp, San Diego, CA June 6, 1944; advanced training, Camp Pendleton, CA; Pacific Theater, Oct. 11, 1944-July 6, 1946; Okinawa Campaign Jan. 9, 1945; occupation and repatriation of Japan (Nagasaki, Kryukyu Island) Sept. 25, 1945-June 24, 1946. Discharged July 31, 1946, with the rank of sergeant.

DeMoss was awarded the American Campaign Medal, Service Medal, Asian Clasp, Japan Occupational Medal, Navy Occupational Medal, and Bronze Star (Okinawa Campaign).

Memorable experiences: Observed devastation sight after Atomic Bomb detonation at Nagasaki, Japan.

Civilian activities/occupation: Active BPOE (Elks) member; active Marine Corps League and Devil Dogs; PGA golf professional; construction superintendent, 30 years with McAfee-Guthrie Pipeline; Arizona Mounted Patrol.

He married Jesse Lucille Blankenship in October 1946. They celebrated their 50th Wedding Anniversary in October 1996. He has five children (including triplets): Gary, Jenni, Randy, Rodney and Rebecca; 14 grandchildren: three step grandchildren; and two great-grandchildren. DeMoss passed away March 18, 1997.

JAMES C. DIMITRIADIS, born Feb. 3, 1921. Enlisted in the USNR in 1943. Served as signalman and participated in nine invasions. Discharged in November 1945 with the rank of signalman second class. Military locations included Kiska, Tarawa, Saipan, Tinian, Pelleliu, Guam, Philippines, Leyte, Okinawa, New Guinea and Japan.

Memorable experiences: First wave attack on Tarawa, getting caught on coral reef.

He and his wife, Judith (deceased), have five children and 10 grandchildren. Grew up in the restaurant business. Dimitriadis is presently retired.

PHILIP J. DOYLE, born March 1, 1918, in Neola, IA. Discharged with the rank of first lieutenant. He received the Purple Heart and Silver Star.

He and his wife, Patricia Jane, have two children, Sharon and Christopher. He presently resides in Moraga, CA.

FRANCIS JOHN DRAPCZYNSKI, born June 19, 1945, in Philadelphia, PA. Entered the service June 18, 1963, in Philadelphia. Served with 2nd, 8" Howitzer Btry., 2nd Field Arty. Gp., For. Troops, FMFLant, Camp Lejeune. Honorably discharged Feb. 22, 1969, with the rank of corporal.

Drapczynski was awarded the Vietnam Service Medal w/2 stars, Armed Forces Expeditionary Medal, National Defense Service Medal, Good Conduct Medal, Republic of Vietnam Campaign Medal and Rifle Marksman Badge.

JOHN M. EARDLEY, born Nov. 21, 1922. Enlisted in the service July 2, 1942. Boot camp at San Diego, CA; 12 weeks Radio School; sent to San Francisco, Dept. of Pacific, 12th Naval Dist.; reassigned to Camp Pendleton in September 1943; sent to Hawaii to join 2nd Marines. Participated in invasion of Saipan and Tinian, Marianas Islands. Discharged Nov. 7, 1945, with the rank of private first class.

Eardley was awarded the Presidential Unit Citation, American Campaign Medal, Asiatic-Pacific Campaign Medal and WWII Victory Medal.

Memorable experiences: Contacted spinal meningitis in boot camp and almost died; yellow jaundice on Tinian and sent to hospital in Hawaii and then to Great Lakes Hospital. Twin brother was hurt on Guadalcanal, was paralyzed and died at the age of 37.

Graduated from the University of California-Berkeley and University of Colorado Pharmacy School. Owned pharmacy in Los Gatos, CA. Employed as pharmacist for 34 years.

He and his wife, Elsie, were married Jan. 13, 1945. They have two children, Cynthia and Julie, and two grandchildren, Tyler and Julianne. Has been a ham radio operator for five years.

ALVY EDWARD EBERLE, born near Vibbard, MO in 1925. One morning early in August 1943 he said his good-byes to the family, walked underneath Old Glory that his father frequently flew on special occasions, then crawled into the family Model A and his father drove him to the local bus station. As he leaned to say good-bye, he noticed tears rolling down his father's cheeks. He had never witnessed that before, and will never know if it was pride, sorrow, or a little of both.

He was on his way to become a U.S. Marine. With which he felt his patriotic wishes could best be served. Then came boot camp at San Diego and Hawaii where he was placed in the 4th Bn., 10th Marines.

In early June 1944 he remembers sailing out of Pearl Harbor alongside the battleships *Oklahoma* and *Arizona*. The *Oklahoma* lay on her side. The *Arizona* sank upright and Old Glory still flew from her mast. This was a reminder of the reasons why they had to do what they were about to do.

After a zigzag course came his first action against the enemy at Saipan. Then Tinian and later Okinawa.

He says there's a lot to remember about Saipan. The shell fire, screaming rockets, loss of comrades, the banjai attack. Also remembered the throwing of nearly 100 rounds of ammunition into the breach of a howitzer while standing in ankle deep mud and water with dengue fever of near 103°. This was done while shelling the tiny island of Maniagassa.

From Saipan linger the visions of hundreds of Japanese and natives jumping from cliffs. Whole families holding hands and walking into the sea to their deaths rather than surrender. You then realized they believed the propaganda of how vicious the Marines were.

As for the dengue fever, which he twice had, he still gives thanks to the corpsman that repeatedly came by, took his temperature and gave pills.

He remembers (off Okinawa) the sight of anti-aircraft tracers and explosions sent skyward against the suicidal air attacks as more spectacular than any Fourth of July fireworks.

In September 1945 he, along with the division, was deployed to participate in the occupation of Nagasaki. This was not long after the second atomic bomb was dropped.

The bomb area was devastated, but he believes that had it not been for the bombs his chances of returning were not great. Also that there would have been many, many more killed on both sides than the bombs themselves had killed.

He received an honorable discharge Jan. 9, 1946, three days before his 21st birthday.

The next day he crawled from a taxi cab a short block from home. With sea bag in hand he began the short walk. It would be a surprise. A few children seemed to come out of the woodwork, saying hello, and walked along. They were intrigued with the rifle range medals. He thought if only they knew the meaning of the three ribbons that were pinned just above. Then he heard those joyous words, Ed is home, Ed is home.

He finally settled in Liberty, MO and retired from the post office after 33 years.

He and his wife, Bonnie, have two children and two grandchildren. A member of the Masonic Lodge and worked several years with the Boy Scouts, taking the older ones on three wilderness trips near Yellowstone.

He keeps in touch with members of the 4th Bn., has attended several reunions and hosted one himself. He finds he still has pride in the men he served with and thinks the reunions are a reminder that once a Marine, always a Marine. The character, hardships and memoirs of those men will always be remembered. His lingering thought - God bless them.

CLIFTON (CLIFF) FARRIS, born Oct. 5, 1925. Enlisted in the USMC Aug. 20, 1943. Military locations/stations were recruit depot, San Diego, Camp Elliott, CA. Shipped out December 21 and arrived on Hawaii Island Dec. 25, 1943. Assigned to L Co., 3rd Bn., 2nd Regt., 2nd Marine Div. Was assigned a Browning auto-

matic rifle after firing for record with it (BAR). Said good-bye to his M1 rifle.

He was in the Saipan and Tinian Island campaign of the North Marianas Island. Was wounded on Saipan and still has a piece of hand grenade in his left temple. Was at Okinawa and went to Nagasaki, Japan for garrison duty. He was transferred to 5th Marine Div. at Sasebo, Japan for his return to the West Coast. He was at sea during the Christmas season of 1943 and was enroute home Christmas of 1946.   Was dis-

charged Jan. 9, 1946, as a corporal at Camp Lejeune, NC.

Honors that he cares to mention: He is the Marine who was photographed in prayer at "The Statue of Christ, on The Cross" at the Chamorro Cemetery on Saipan during the battle June 20, 1944. His picture was in *Look* and *Life* and others, including *Follow Me* when Hugo Genge was publisher. The correspondent sent him pictures after the war. He was 18 years old at this time.

He was selected by the governor of the Northern Marianas Islands to return for the 50th Golden Anniversary of the invasion of Saipan, as their special guest, and also his wife, Odean. He was to be special guest at all events and ceremonies. He represented all American warriors who fought for the capture of Saipan, the 162,000. This included the 2nd Marine Div., the 1st Bn., 29th Marines, the 4th Marine Div. and all Navy personnel attached to all Marine units. The 27th Army Div., the entire 5th Fleet, the Carrier Task Force 58th, the Coast Guard and the Army Air Corps 7th Air Force. If he could have selected any honor, it would have been the one which the Saipanese people bestowed on him. The special guest of honor, Cliff Farris. His first trip (1944) was paid by the Marine Corps for his services. His second trip (1994) was paid by the Saipanese. His last trip was paid by himself to say thank you Saipan. This was in June 1997. The following is a quote from Farris: "Saipan, I shall always remember you and its people! I shall always be your special guest! I now know the meaning of Royal Treatment!"

ALVIN D. FERRY, born in Nebraska Jan. 31, 1924. The family moved to Washington in 1929 and there he was raised and went to school. He left Washington in January 1942 for boot camp in San Diego where he was a member of Plt. 45. After boot camp he was assigned to the 10th Marines at Camp Elliott. When the 4th Bn. was activated he was assigned to the H&S Btry., Survey Section. In November 1942 the unit sailed to Wellington, New Zealand. After participating in the Tarawa, Saipan and Tinian campaigns he returned to the U.S. and was married to Grace Ruth Hicks Jan. 31, 1945. They have five children: Teresa, Carol, Alvin, Cathy and Jeff; and 17 grandchildren.

Alvin was a professional land surveyor and civil engineering technician during his career with the U.S. Forest Service.

PETER J. FLAHERTY, born in New York City April 30, 1938, to Peter and Anne Flaherty both born in Ireland. Raised in the Riverdale section of the Bronx. Attended St. Margaret's Grammar and Cardinal Hayes High schools, also in the Bronx. After graduating high school enlisted in the USMC Sept. 18, 1956. Assigned to Plt. 329 at Parris Island. Trained as a basic Marine (MOS 9900). Won Sharpshooter's Medal at the firing range. Graduated Dec. 10, 1956.

In order to be home for Christmas, shipped out to Camp Geiger for "intensive Marine training." After Christmas leave, reported to H&S Co., 2nd Bn., 10th Marines at Camp Lejeune, NC. Assigned as a truck driver-heavy duty. Main function was to transport (tow) 105 howitzers from the Gun Park to firing ranges such as Fayetteville, NC. Participated in the first amphibious assault to launch 88mm mortars from aircraft carriers to locations behind enemy lines. He and the captain he was driving were "captured" by the enemy (8th Abn.) as soon as the delivery helicopter headed back to the carrier. Participated in Mediterranean cruise in 1958. They motor convoyed to Moorehead City where they boarded the USS *Heritage*. They practiced landings in Turkey. Visited Spain and Italy on liberty but wound up doing guard duty on a beach in Lebanon with no ammo. Was a member of the 10th Marines for two years.

"Put in for" and received a transfer to Camp Elmore, Norfolk, VA. Reported to Svc. Co., HQ & Svc. Bn. Spent his last year driving officers to different locations on the Norfolk naval base and surrounding Norfolk area in staff cars (MOS 3531). (Visited Camp Elmore when the association had its annual celebration in 1991.) Awarded the Good Conduct Medal and Presidential Unit Citation. Discharged Dec. 16, 1959.

Returned to civilian life. His family had moved to Hastings on Hudson, NY. Started a career with Consolidated Edison Co. of New York in 1964. Retired to sunny Florida in Jan. 1997 with his significant other, Debbie Olmo, after 32-1/2 years of service in the electric utility industry.

Has two daughters, Robin and Angela. Angela is married to John Buschini and has a son, John and three daughters: Jennifer, Erin and Olivia. Robin has a son, Ryan.

FRANK C. FLORES, born Nov. 25, 1924. Enlisted in the service Dec. 2, 1941. Assignments/locations/positions: 2nd Marine Div., 2nd Defense; HQ, Filter Center. Discharged Dec. 9, 1945. Flores was awarded the Good Conduct Medal.

Civilian activity: Local politics, Optimists International and Scouting (BSA). He is a certified dental technician and retired laboratory owner. Flores has four children: Juan, Frank, Cecilia and Albert; and seven grandchildren.

Memorable experiences: One disturbing occurrence he recalls happened after they had shipped out of San Diego, CA March 6, 1942, on the *President Garfield*. At the time it was the first troop-bearing ship to cross the Pacific Ocean without a convoy, so they were all alone.

It was the seventh or eighth day out; the skies were incredibly clear and sea calm. Someone on board reported to the bridge that he had heard a faint voice hollering, "Help!" Their ship's captain passed the word to keep their ears and eyes open and to report anything they saw. He then ordered the ship's engines be turned off. They stood motionless on the deck, listening, squinting their eyes over the sea in hopes that they might find the someone who was hollering for help. The ship was deathly quiet for a long time. His skin crawls when he thinks of that faint, ghostly voice hollering "Help ... Help!" They all heard it, but none of them could find the man or woman who was hollering it. For about six hours they stayed in that general area, until they could wait no longer. The captain ordered the ship's engines to start-up, and they recommenced their journey to Samoa.

Those hours of silence and faint voice are still on his mind to this day, and he often wonders who it was they couldn't save.

PAUL FLOYD, born Aug. 25, 1927. Enlisted in the service Dec. 30, 1944. Assignments/locations/positions: Parris Island, Camp Lejeune, 83rd Replacement Draft to Guam and Japan. Assigned to G Co., 2nd Bn., 2nd Regt. Returned to U.S. via USS *Lavaca* through Panama Canal to Norfolk, VA. Discharged Aug. 22, 1946, with the rank of private first class at the age of 18. Floyd was awarded the Victory Medal, Japanese Occupation Medal and Asiatic-Pacific Campaign Medal.

Memorable experiences: Served during Korea and as battalion commander in Vietnam. Will never forget that he was a Marine.

Graduated from the U.S. Military Academy with the class of 53. Served in the U.S. Army from June 2, 1953-July 1973. Retired from the Army with the rank of lieutenant colonel.

JAMES R. FORD, born Feb. 7, 1933. Enlisted in the service Feb. 10, 1953. Assignments/locations/positions: Plt. 68, MCRD, San Diego; P Co., 3rd Bn., 2nd Inf. Tr. Regt. T-6-2, Camp Pendleton April 30, 1953; B Co., 1st Bn., 9th Regt., 3rd Marine Div.; A Co., 1st Bn., 2nd Marines, 2nd Marine Div. Discharged Feb. 10, 1955, with the rank of corporal.

Ford was awarded the Korean Service Medal, United Nations Service Medal, National Defense Service Medal, Marksman Badge-Machine Gun Expert.

He and his wife, Phyllis, have two children, James and John; and four grandchildren: Jennifer, Jeffrey, Jordan and Justin. Civilian

activity in West Texas oil field. Employed by Reed Tool Co., bit sales for oil field. Presently retired.

KENNETH W. FORS, born May 23, 1925, in Drake, ND. Enlisted in the USMC Sept. 25, 1943. Assignments/locations/positions: Boot camp at San Diego; Camp Elliott; replacement to B Co., 1st Bn., 2nd Marines on Hawaii after Tarawa; invasion of Saipan; Navy hospital, Pearl Harbor. Discharged as a private first class Dec. 3, 1945. Fors was awarded the Purple Heart and Bronze Star Medal. Served as platoon runner, military police at Pearl Harbor and Honolulu.

Memorable experiences: Was in V-12 program at Colorado College when WWII ended. Recognized by governor for pioneering work in pre-retirement planning.

Earned Master's degree in social work from the University of Denver in 1951. Employed in psychiatric social work in VA hospital in Topeka, KS and private practice in marriage, family and child counseling for 30 years in Sacramento, CA.

He and his wife, Donna, have five children: Karen, Steven, Kristen, Renee and Janee; and five grandchildren. Presently retired and is a community service activist in Sacramento.

BERNARD J. FREDERICKSON, born Dec. 31, 1923. Enlisted in the service Jan. 18, 1944. Military locations included Asiatic-Pacific area, Hawaii, Saipan, Ryukya, Nagasaki, Japan. Served with Anti-tank Unit, Special Wpns. Discharged Mar. 27, 1946, with the rank of corporal.

Frederickson was awarded the Expert Rifle and Presidential Citation for 2nd Marines occupation duty.

Memorable experiences: Meeting his Marine buddy, Joe, after 50 years and also friends through years with Rob Bird.

A grim and bitter memory of the invasion of Okinawa is Easter Sunday morning, April 1, 1945. 3,000 or more Marines left Saipan on USS *Hinsdale* on their way to Okinawa. For six to seven days they had a convoy to protect them. A quarter mile from the beach, they started to unload, a suicide plane hit and blew out the side of the ship. Didn't have his life jacket on, wasn't scared but passed two guys who were. Lights out, motor out, ship sinking, ships burning, planes burning, massive confusion. Two Navy planes flew in between them and the Japanese on the beach, leaving them a smoke screen. Had to go down a rope ladder or jump to get into the Higgins boats or LSTs, from getting sucked under the ship. Spent hours in the China Sea, back to Saipan, where the Nips had invaded their tents while they were gone.

He and his wife of 54 years, Irma, have five children: Jim, Dan, Chet, Peg and Jeff; and eight grandchildren: Andrea, Trica, Christopher, Jenny, Luke, Jake, Tara and Trey.

HERBERT RAWSON GAGE,

born Aug. 29, 1923. His descendant colonial family arrived in the New World in 1630 with the Sir John Winthrop fleet from England, today known as Boston Harbor. A direct descendant of GEN Thomas Gage (British army at the time of the beginning of the Revolutionary War where cousins fought cousins) and BGEN Joseph Summer Gage (Civil War). Enlisted in the USMC in WWII. Served with the 2nd Marine Corps Div., boot camp training in San Diego, CA. Served in the Pacific and in September 1945 went ashore Nagasaki, Okinawa and Saipan, Japan for nine months. Honorable discharge at Great Lakes, IL in August 1946.

CPT Todd advised all Marines to go out and get involved in the community.

First month after being discharged his application was accepted into Masonic Lodge, American Legion and VFW. He took an active part in the last 51 years, along with other organizations and through the years received many, many citations, honors and appointments.

CPL Gage holds membership in 28 organizations including Shrine and Crippled Children. He holds life membership in 13 organizations: American Legion, VFW, American Disabled Veterans, Free and Accepted Masons, Scottish Rite 32nd Degrees, Cooties Pup Tent #2, VFW National Children's Home, Sons of the Union Veterans (Civil War), Marine Corps League (Capital Detach.) in Lansing and elected Marine of the Year and 2nd Marine Div.

Served as commander of Post #174 and served as 4th Dist. commander of the American Legion. A past chef de gare of Kalamazoo Voiture #161. Served as grand correspondent of Michigan and Alt. Cheminot Nationale, served six years as grand voiture Nurses Training chairman. Gage has served as correspondent of Voiture #161 for 29 years and only missed two promenades in that length of time. Served 16 years on Selective Service Board. Years of service on the Ft. Custer National Cemetery Advisory Board and a volunteer of the Battle Creek Veterans Hospital with over 2400 credit hours. Gage donated 13 gallons of blood to the American Red Cross, voted over 170 times since 1946 in Kalamazoo, MI, a Republican that speaks his mind.

Serving as state commander of the Consoli-

dated War Veterans of Michigan and in the 60s when the Communism party was looking down our throats, took training in civil defense and served as a police reserve and many more.

Gage has enjoyed the Veterans and organizations throughout the years and gained many many friends and their support.

ROBERT L. GEORGE,

born in Tahlequah, OK July 26, 1924. He joined the Corps one day before his 17th birthday in 1941. He went through boot camp in San Diego and was assigned to Plt. 97. He was then assigned to Camp Elliott, CA.

They were the first convoy to leave the West Coast after Pearl Harbor Jan. 6, 1942. Their destination was American Samoa. From there they went to Guadalcanal, New Zealand, Tarawa, Camp Tarawa in Hawaii, Saipan and Tinian.

After 33 months and four major battles he returned to the States in Nov. 1944 and was discharged July 25, 1947, with the rank of sergeant.

George was awarded three Presidential Unit Citations - Guadalcanal (1st Div. attached), Tarawa and Saipan. Memorable experiences: Returned to New Zealand in April 1996 and found town of Pahatanui-Camp long gone.

He and his wife, Shirley, were married in November 1947 and have three daughters: Leslie, Lynn and Gail; four grandchildren: Paul, Michael, Jennifer and Holly; and two great-grandchildren. They now live in Sacramento, CA after retiring from retail sales.

CURTIS E. GILMORE,

son of an Irish emigrant was born in Johnstown, PA Nov. 3, 1928. He was the youngest of six children, five boys and one girl, four of which served in the armed forces of the U.S. (two Army, one sailor, and he as a U.S. Marine). Gilmore enlisted in the Marines while he was in high school. Then the Korean conflict came and he was activated. He took boot camp at Parris Island, SC in 1950 in Plt. 267. At Marine Barracks, Camp Lejeune he studied the T/Os and T/As and then went to the Marine Corps Forwarding Depot at Portsmouth, VA. At Portsmouth he worked with inspectors of naval materials in connection with the acceptance of commercial contracted and service furnished materials for Marine Corps consumption. This included the preparation of assault rations for the Marine Corps.

After the Korean conflict Gilmore was released and he returned to his wife, Mary Ellen, in Johnstown, PA and they had three children: Linda, Curt and Kathleen. Today they are blessed with six grandchildren: Amie, Jason, Ryan, David, Carrie and Renee.

WILLIAM P. GILTON,

survivor of Tarawa, Saipan, Tinian, Okinawa and Nagasaki Japan, was born July 25, 1921, at Russell, KY. At age two his family moved to a small farm in southern Ohio. At age 15 he left home, without permission, and traveled to the East Coast, then south, crossed the south to California, north to Washington State, then to a small town in northern Utah.

Worked in this small town for over a year. He picked tomatoes, topped sugar beets, cooked in a restaurant, was night clerk in a hotel and was a pin setter in a small bowling alley. One day he decided to go home. He traveled across the northern states back to Ohio arriving home at age 17. Worked various jobs in this small river town and at age 19 he went to work for the Chesapeake and Ohio Railway. At age 20 he joined the USMC July 15, 1942. Boot camp at Parris Island, trained at Camp Lejeune, Radio School at Quantico, went to Camp Elliott and Camp Pendleton, CA. Shipped out of San Diego in February 1943 and arrived in New Zealand and was assigned to the H&S, 10th Arty. of the 2nd Marine Div. about April 1, 1943. Trained in New Zealand and left Wellington at the end of October 1943 arriving at Tarawa, Gilbert Islands Nov. 19, 1943. Early morning November 20 he, and three other radio operators, were ordered on deck with full combat equipment including their radios. There were four Higgins boats that came alongside their ship and one of them was ordered into each boat. They were to be forward observers for H&S, 10th Arty. After talking to a Marine in the landing craft he learned he was with men of the 2nd Bn., 2nd Regt. and they were headed for Red Beach 2. They never got there.

Their boat hung up on the coral reef about 500 yards off shore. There was a lot of fire coming their way from shore. Rifle, machine gun, mortars and anti-boat guns. They didn't know where to go but they all knew they couldn't stay in the boat so they went over the side and into the water. At that point their organized attack became every man for himself. He was lost and alone. After a few hours taking cover where he could he finally hooked up with eight or 10 Marines taking cover behind a disabled Amtrak about 200 yards from shore. In late afternoon the fire from shore had slackened some and these Marines decided to try to make it to the sea wall. They started ashore in water about waist deep so he decided to go with them. Someone was yelling "spread out," numerous times and they did. He has no idea how many of them got to the sea wall. His radio was ruined. He had no way to do what he was ordered to do. He spent the first night, second day and second night as a rifleman. On the third afternoon he finally found an officer and three or four men from his outfit near Red Beach 3. On November 24 they left Betio and went to another island in the Tarawa Atoll chain. Stayed there four days and boarded ship and went to Hilo, HI and to the Parker ranch. There they built a camp and named it Camp Tarawa. They trained there until May 1944 then went to Saipan for the assault on Saipan in June 1944. About a week into this battle the communications officer of H&S, 10th told him to go, after dark, to the beach and rest awhile. He was resting on the beach when a man came up to him and asked if his radio worked, Gilton told him yes and he said to come with him. They joined a group of Marines about 30 yards away. He told Gilton this group was going on a patrol and needed a radio operator and he was to go with them. Gilton did so. About two hours later they were behind Japanese lines, in a ditch, between the beach and a sand road leading to Garapan. About half the Marines in this patrol crossed the road, the remainder of them stayed in the ditch as ordered. About an hour later the Marines came back. They were preparing to return to their lines when a Japanese supply and ammo dump blew up near their position. Due to the light from the fire they could not leave the ditch. They were trapped. He then began to call for help on the radio, he received no response but kept calling and giving their position. What seemed like an hour or two they heard a battle being fought between their position and their front lines. In a few minutes several of their tanks appeared, some in the road and others in the trees off the road. It sounded as if they were firing every gun they had. They found them and covered their withdrawal to their front lines. Thanks to Charlie Co., 2nd Div. Tank Bn. they were safely back, all of them. In November 1990 he and two of his buddies attended the 47th reunion of the Tarawa survivors in Chicago, IL. This was the first military reunion he had ever attended since being discharged 45 years earlier. At this reunion they met a man that was driving one of those tanks that night on Saipan. After a short discussion and between the two of them telling the story about that night he wandered off somewhere. He was gone before Gilton could get his name. His brothers and he looked for him the rest of the evening but he was not to be found. Just like that night on Saipan. As soon as he got them back safely he was gone on another mission. His brothers call him the "phantom tank driver."

Later in the Saipan Campaign, about the end of the first week of July 1944, the Japanese united for a last stand. A Banzai attack. They broke through the front lines and hit the 10th Arty. head on, about 6,000 Japanese in all. Gilton had just been relieved on his forward observer position and was headed back to the Fire Direction Center. He was in the area of the 105mm guns when it started. He took up a defensive position in one of the gun pits and became a rifleman again. That day the gunners of the 10th Arty. made history. They lowered their guns to the point blank position. They fired into the ground in front of the oncoming Japanese so the shells would explode. Then came the impossible. The gunners who were cutting fuses for air burst finally were cutting those fuses to explode four-tenths of one second after it was fired, 50-60 yards in front of the gun. That was never done before and to Gilton's knowledge has never been done since.

The attack was finally stopped and the entire Japanese force was wiped out.

His next campaign was Tinian Island. After that came Okinawa, then after the atomic bombing of Japan he was sent to Nagasaki and Isiaha Japan. Then home and discharged Dec. 22, 1945. During this past March 1998 he traveled to the big island of Hawaii to attend the monument dedication ceremony held March 28, 1998, near Waimea, HI. This new monument marks the site of Camp Tarawa which was built by the 2nd Marine Div. after the successful invasion of Tarawa in the Gilbert Islands Nov. 20, 1943.

The 2nd Marine Div. trained there for the battles of Saipan, Tinian and Okinawa.

The erection of this monument was primarily due to the untiring efforts of Mrs. Alice Clark, an Hawaii native, who serves as chairman of the Camp Tarawa Historical Foundation. Had it not been for her, this would never have happened. The construction of the monument and the subsequent ceremony was the culmination of years of work by Mrs. Clark, the residents of Waimea, HI and many others. Gilton salutes you, Mrs. Alice Clark, for a job **Well Done**.

There were over 1000 people in attendance, mostly consisting of grateful residents of Waimea. Also in attendance was Color Guard, Marine Forces Pacific, the Marforpac Band, commanding general 2nd Marine Div. 1998, commanding general FMT Pac 1998, mayor, county of Hawaii, Parker Ranch trustees and the gracious host, Mrs. Alice Clark.

While in Hawaii Gilton had the opportunity to meet Wilfred Billey, Navajo code talker, survivor of Tarawa, Saipan, Tinian and Okinawa. Also met Manuel Aviles, Amtrak driver and Jay Lopez, 18th Engrs., all 2nd Marine Div.

WALTER L. GLADBACH, born March 27, 1923, and raised on farm at Mendon, MO. Enlisted in January 1944, went to boot camp at San Diego, Plt. 142. Sent to Radio School, graduated, sent to Camp Pendleton. Left Pendleton in November 1944 and arrived in Saipan in January 1945. Assigned D-2-10. Saw action at Iheya Shima and Okinawa. Arrived at Nagasaki, Japan Sept. 25, 1945. Assigned H&S-2-10 as MP radio jeep driver. Left Japan June 19, 1946, on USS *Olmstead*. Discharged at Great Lakes Naval Base July 31, 1946, as corporal.

Civilian activity: December 1947 worked for Atchison, Topeka and Santa Fe Railroad at Chicago, IL as signal foreman. Married Wanda Mae Hunt in February 1950 and lived at Willow Springs, IL and worked signal maintainer job there. Moved to Laplata, MO in 1957. Retired in March 1983 due to thyroid and heart trouble. He has seven children: Rita K., Anne C., James H., John L., Alvin W., Norine E. and Christeen L.; and 15 grandchildren: Chandice, Chesston, Cody, Caleb, Bryce, Michael, Mallory, Nathan, Melanie, Sonya, Christopher, Jeremy, Chadwick, Emilia and Rachel.

HARRY GOOCH, joined the 2nd in New Zealand in October 1943 in time to go on maneuvers. They embarked on the USS *Sheridan* AP. The ships at this time did not have covers over the discharge holes from the "heads." Cargo nets were used to enter landing crafts and also to climb back aboard ship. Some of these nets would be over these holes as they were climbing back aboard ship. One time, someone was using the head, which no one was suppose to. One fellow, James C. McLaughlin, was under the discharge hole and heard the waste coming. He ducked but was covered. A big gob landed on top of his helmet and some went between his backpack and jacket. He didn't smell too good, and it is a good thing he never found out who the person was that used the head at that time. The rest of them got quite a chuckle over it.

The next time they went aboard these ships the discharge holes were covered. The troops at present don't have this problem. McLaughlin now lives in Washington.

WAYNE M. GORE, born May 1, 1939. Enlisted in the service June 4, 1957. Assignments/ locations/positions: Plt. 141, "D" Co., 2nd Bn., Parris Island, SC, "Dam Neck", VA, 1957, "Little Creek", VA, 1957, "USS *Des Moines* CA-134", Quantico, VA. Discharged June 6, 1960, with the rank of E-4. Gore was awarded the Armed Forces Expeditionary Medal for Beirut-Lebanon invasion July 1958 and the Good Conduct Medal.

Memorable experiences: Parris Island and seeing 27 countries while in the USMC. His hitch in the Corps was the best decision he ever made.

He and his wife, Donna G., have three children: Jim, Steve and Matt; and three grandchildren: Elizabeth, Evan and Benjamin. Civilian activity as manager of a "truck load" trucking company. Raised in Rich Creek, VA; moved to Florida for 13 years; settled in Ohio.

CARL NELSON GORMAN, born Oct. 5, 1907, in Chinle, AZ and died Jan. 29, 1998, in Gallup, NM. Educated in government and mission schools. He enlisted for "special" duty in the USMC. Inducted May 4, 1942, he was in the all-Navajo Plt., developers, as a pilot project, of the Navajo language code. As a Navajo code talker (G-42) he served on Guadalcanal, Tarawa, Saipan and Tinian. Evacuated from Saipan and hospitalized. He served with H&S, 6th and was discharged Sept. 29, 1945.

He G.I.'d at Otis Art Institute in Los Angeles, becoming a well-known Native American artist. In 1990 he received the Honorary Degree of Doctor of Humane Letters from the University of New Mexico, following years spent in the fields of Navajo and Native American history, culture, art and education. He belonged to the Navajo Code Talkers Assoc., the 2nd Marine Div. Assoc., the Marine Corps League and the VFW. He has been honored by the Marine Corps with the Meritorious Public Service Award.

TED L. GRANT, born in St. Louis, MO March 27, 1918, to Lovelace and Etta Spears Grant. He joined the Army in 1936 and served at Jefferson Barracks. Oct. 16, 1940, he joined the Marines and went to San Diego. He went with the 10th Marines to Camp Elliott where they lived in 6-man tents while buildings were being constructed. Later he joined the 2nd Special Wpns. Div. In November 1941 he was injured in a truck wreck and was hospitalized when Pearl Harbor was bombed.

In the summer of 1942 the Army opened Camp Hood for tank destroyers at Killeen, TX. Grant was one of eight sergeants and LT Pena in the first class. The night after they arrived SGT Grant met Ruth, his future wife. Grant was in the convoy to New Zealand in the fall of 1942.

SGT Grant was with the 2nd Div. in Hawaii until they sailed to Saipan in 1944. He was evacuated from Saipan to a naval hospital in Hawaii. In September 1944 he arrived at the naval hospital in Oakland.

He became a civilian in January 1945 and he and Ruth Squyres married March 2, 1945, in Lufkin, TX, where they made their home. Grant retired from Temple-Inland in 1983. He became a life member of the 2nd Marine Div. Assoc. He and Ruth were married 53 happy years; he celebrated his 80th birthday March 27th. They have a daughter, Carol Faviell; son-in-law, Richard; and grandsons, Christopher and Jonathan Faviell. He looked forward to this book but died May 15, 1998.

JESSE WAYNE GREEN, born Jan. 11, 1923, in Dunn, LA, a farmer's son. Enlisted in the service Nov. 13, 1940. Boot camp at San Diego, CA, then attended Cooks, Bakers and Butchers School. Duty stations included San Diego, Camp Elliott, Samoa, Guadalcanal, New Zealand, Tarawa, Hawaii, Saipan, Klamath Falls and naval hospital, Seattle. He was discharged June 18, 1945.

Green was awarded the Rifle Marksman Award, Pistol Sharp Shooter Award, two Presidential Unit Citations and other Pacific Operations Ribbons (five in all).

Attended business college after discharge. Worked in timber veneer and plywood industry in office, plant manager and quality supervisor. Married Margie Chandler Dec. 18, 1944, in Winnfield, LA. They have two wonderful children, Carolyn (Green) Cole and Gary; and four grandchildren. Member of Masonic Lodge 1956 and Scottish Rite 1962.

Although legally blind at age 75, God has blessed him wonderfully with a second wife, Kathryn Lyons Green. He is proud to have been a Marine and he loves his country. Above all else he is proud to be a Christian and he credits a praying father for his return to the good ole USA.

BURGESS GREER JR., born in New Orleans, LA Nov. 16, 1920. After enlisting in the USMC in November 1937 he was assigned to foreign service in Iceland and was discharged in November 1941. With the outbreak of war Greer re-enlisted in 1942. When asked what branch of service he was enlisting into, his response was "once a Marine, always a Marine." Greer served in New Zealand, the Gilbert Islands, the New Hebrides, the Hawaiian Islands and the Marshall Islands. While serving as a sergeant with Co. G, 2nd Bn., 8th Marines, he saw combat action on the Tarawa Atoll and Saipan. Experiences which shape a lifetime were made while in combat. During the invasion of Tarawa Greer saw his buddies bleeding and dying while only 500+ yards from shore. On June 27, 1944, on the island of Saipan, he became one of those seriously wounded. He received a medical discharge June 30, 1945, in New Orleans, LA and was the recipient of the Purple Heart, American Defense Medal, Presidential Unit Citation, Good Conduct Medal, American Campaign Medal, WWII Victory Medal and the Asiatic-Pacific Campaign Medal.

Greer married Josephine Pittari in June 1943 and has two daughters, Patricia and Cynthia. He retired from the Louisiana Dept. of Health where he worked as a registered food and drug sanitarian for 28 years.

DAVID C. GUMMERE, born in Indiana; raised in Michigan. Enlisted in 1969 and began active duty in 1970, serving in WestPac Ground Forces and CONUS. Appointed W-1 in 1975. Attended TBS, assigned to Force Troops, FMFLant and 2nd Marine Div. Left active duty in 1977, attached to USMCR while working for a U.S. Government agency. Assigned to 3rd Marine Div. as infantry officer in 1979. Assigned to 1st Marine Div. as infantry officer in 1980. Designated as intelligence officer in 1982; assigned sea duty with Amphib. Gp. 2 in 1983. Served at LFTCLant, Little Creek and NMITC, Dam Neck, VA as course director and on special assignments 1985-89.

Served as intelligence officer for U.S. Atlantic Command until retirement in March 1992. Earned the rank of chief warrant officer 4. Lived in Europe through 1995. Completed numerous infantry, intelligence, Airborne and special operations courses. Awarded Joint Service Commendation w/OLC and Navy Commendation Medals. Earned MS degree in education from Old Dominion University. Married with one daughter. Resides in retirement in northern Michigan.

AUBREY D. GUNTHER, born in Quincy, IL Dec. 7, 1928. After high school he enlisted in the USMC in September 1946. Boot camp, Plt. 371, 4th Recon. Bn., at Parris Island led to being stationed at Camp Lejeune, assigned to "A" Co., 2nd Tank Bn. The division maneuvered on Culebra in the Caribbean in March 1947. In January 1948 he made the very first Mediterranean cruise. He was discharged in August 1948 with a rank of sergeant and remained in the Reserves.

Gunther was called back to active duty in October 1950 during the Korean conflict, returning to the "A" Co., 2nd Bn. He made his second Mediterranean cruise in the spring of 1951 and then to Vieques in October for maneuvers in the Caribbean.

Gunther was awarded the Presidential Unit Citation, Good Conduct Medal, WWII Victory Medal, Navy Occupation Medal and Marine Reserve Medal.

After being discharged in November 1951 with a rank of staff sergeant, Gunther remained in the Reserves until 1955. He married Nancy Pacatte in 1956 and returned to the family farm, was blessed with sons, John and Jim, and retired as a rural mail carrier for the USPS in January 1993. Presently lives on a farm in Camp Point, IL.

CHARLES W. HALL, born in Fulton County, GA June 30, 1928. Enlisted in the USMC in October 1945. Received boot training at Parris Island, SC with Plt. #640.

Shipped overseas to G Co., 2nd Bn., 8th Marine Regt., 2nd Marine Div. on Kyushu Island in draft #92 as a barman.

Shipped again to A Co., 1st Bn., 4th Marine Regt. and K Co., 4th Bn., 4th Marine Regt., 6th Marine Div. in Tsingtao, China as MOS 604 machine gunner.

Shipped to Shanghai, Guam, Kwajalein, Johnson and Wake Islands and to Pearl Harbor and then to Stateside.

Stateside served at Parris Island, SC, Camp Lejeune and Norfolk, VA.

Overseas again to A-T Co., 1st Marine Regt., 1st Marine Div. in Korea.

Stateside to Camp Pendleton, CA; Albany, GA; Camp Lejeune, NC; and Huntsville, AL. Back to Albany, GA and Parris Island, SC and recruiting in Atlanta, GA.

Shipped to Okinawa and to 9th Mountain Bn., Dong Ha, Vietnam.

Ships served on were USS *Comet, Gage, Renville* and *General Black* and *Breckenridge*.

Retired in 1968 as a gunnery sergeant 3516. Attended college and taught as a vocational high school teacher. Retired again after 17 years.

Married Betty J. Ford in December 1953 in Dekalb County, GA. They have three children: Edith, Glenn (served in Marines) and Trace.

ROBERT ALLEN HALL, born in Birmingham, AL Sept. 2, 1914. Graduated from Law School at the University of Alabama in 1937 and began the practice of law in Dallas, TX. Was assistant district attorney in Dallas County when he enlisted in the Marine Corps in June 1942. Graduated from Officers School in Quantico, VA as a second lieutenant and joined the 2nd Marine Div. in New Zealand. Participated in the following battles: Tarawa, Saipan, Tinian and Okinawa. Awarded the Purple Heart, Bronze Star, Presidential Unit Citation, Asiatic-Pacific Medal w/4 stars and Victory Medal. Retired as a lieutenant colonel in 1958.

Memorable experiences: He is small of statue and weight. (He obtained a waiver of his height from the commandant to join the Marines.) After graduating from Quantico as a second lieutenant he was sent to New Zealand to join the 2nd Marine Div. He was assigned to a machine gun platoon in M Co., 3rd Bn., 2nd, as platoon leader. The company commander introduced him to his platoon and left. He made a few remarks that he was glad to be aboard and they were going to defeat the Japanese etc. A voice came out from the rear ranks and said, "And a little child shall lead them."

After WWII served as assistant attorney general of Texas and district judge in Dallas, TX. Was national vice-president of the Reserve Officers Assoc., representing the Naval Services. A widower he has one daughter, Jane Gamble Hall. Retired he lives at Lake Kiowa, TX.

KENNETH DEAN HAMILTON, born Sept. 7, 1919, on the family's farm near Preston, KS. The son of W.Z. and Hazel Hamilton. The family moved to Dodge City, KS in September 1922 for his dad to get work with the Atchison, Topeka and Santa Fe Railroad. Hamilton grew up with his younger sister, Donna Jean, in Dodge City, attending and graduating from high school, the junior college and a business college. He married Norma Jean Lembright Dec. 21, 1941, two weeks following the Pearl Harbor attack. He was employed as the staple goods stock manager at a local grocery store when he enlisted in the USMC, being sworn in at Kansas City, MO March 11, 1942.

His boot camp training took place at San Diego, CA. There he qualified for rifle marksman and pistol sharpshooter. He continued his training in San Diego attending Radio School at the main base. He became a radio operator assigned to Signal Co., 2nd Marine Div.

Hamilton's discharge papers list his foreign and sea service from Oct. 20, 1942-Jan. 15, 1945, as follows: Nov. 10, 1942 - New Zealand; Nov. 28, 1942, New Caledonia; Dec. 12, 1942, Guadalcanal; Feb. 27, 1943, New Zealand; Nov. 22, 1943, Tarawa; Dec. 14, 1943, Hilo, HI; June 22, 1944, Saipan; July 25, 1944, Tinian. He participated in action against the Japanese on Guadalcanal, Tarawa, Saipan and Tinian.

He returned to the U.S. Jan. 19, 1945. After a month furlough he was stationed at Corpus Christi, TX with the 1st Guard Co. NATTC on Ward Island doing guard duty of course. July 9 the same year he was sent to Camp Pendleton, Oceanside, CA for preparations for overseas duty a second time. The war ended making this deployment unnecessary. He was discharged Sept. 25, 1945, having reached the rank of corporal sometime before that.

Hamilton returned to Dodge City to pursue his dream of becoming a wheat farmer in southwest Kansas. He and his wife were selected as a Kansas State Master Farmer and Master Farm Homemaker in 1981. They are the parents of five children: Carol Jean Martin, Louise Tegarden, Ken Hamilton, Nancy Hampton and Terry Hamilton all of Dodge City.

The Hamiltons have nine grandchildren, several step grandchildren, one great-grandson and several great-grandchildren. Two grandsons, Todd and Tony Hamilton, enlisted in the USMC 1995 and 1997, respectively. Both are presently stationed at Camp Pendleton. It was a great thrill for Hamilton to observe the graduation of each at the same site of his training and on the same parade ground where he had marched so many times himself.

He and Norma Jean returned to New Zealand in 1978 with the 2nd Div. Pilgrimage. Hamilton was so pleased to see the plaque at Paekakriki commemorating the camp at McKay's Crossing where he had been stationed. It was at Camp Anderson in Wellington that he had received word of his first child born June 12, 1943. He was a victim of malaria and was recovering there at the time.

Hamilton died unexpectedly March 11, 1998, at his farm home south of Dodge City at the age of 78. *Written July 3, 1998, by Norma Jean Hamilton.*

CLARENCE E. HARGIS, born in Hope, AR Jan. 29, 1924, and moved to Garland, TX in 1926. He attended schools in Garland and played football, ran track, pole vaulted and played on the baseball team for the Garland High School Owls.

He joined the Marines Jan. 9, 1943. Went through boot camp (Plt. 29) in San Diego, CA. Was transferred to Flat Marine Force for advanced training at Camp Elliott. Fired expert on the rifle range at Camp Matthews.

Was shipped overseas June 5, 1943, to New Caledonia on the converted French luxury liner *Reaushombeau*. It traveled alone and traveled a zigzag course going overseas. COL James Roosevelt was forming a new Raider Bn. and the 18th Replacement was assigned to him. The Raiders were disbanded and Hargis was sent to New Zealand in August and joined the 2nd Marine Div., just back from Guadalcanal. From there he saw action with F-2-6, 2nd Div. at Tarawa, Saipan, Tinian, Okinawa and went to Nagasaki, Japan with occupational troops. He was aboard 13 different transport ships, making practice landings and landing on enemy fortified islands. When he returned home he married Jean McCollum and had five children: Connie, Donna, Larry, Tim and Kim; eight grandchildren: Craig, Kristi, Carey, Grant, Sean, Hunter, Timmy and Ashley; and three great-grandchildren. He is a painter and is still active as a painter and paint contractor in the Dallas-Ft. Worth area.

BOBBY J. HARRIS, completed boot camp at Parris Island, SC with Plt. 151; 30 days guard duty at Camp Geiger; completed ITR, 20 days boot leave; then reported to 2nd Light Support Co., 2nd Svc. Bn., 2nd Marine Div., FMF, Camp Lejeune, NC in early January 1960 as a private E-1.

On reporting in he was sent to mess duty. After 30 days he was sent to Little Creek, VA for Embarkation School. After a week he was told he was not suited for the class and they sent him home to 2nd Marine Div.

Went to 2nd Marine Div. Red Cross water

safety instructor course for two weeks. He then taught a couple of swimming classes.

Finally after more than eight months in the Corps, he made private first class.

He then went to 2nd Svc. Bn., 2nd Marine Div. Military Subjects School for four weeks. Next, he went to 2nd Marine Div., FMF Personnel and Administration School for seven weeks. Made lieutenant corporal and was shipped out a few days before December 1960.

He never made a Mediterranean cruise and never saw combat. He wants to thank all of the Marines before and after him who served in combat in his stead.

DWIGHT HELLUMS, born Aug. 6, 1921. Enlisted in the service Jan. 14, 1942. Boot training at San Diego, CA, Plt. 113. Entered Co. A, 2nd Amphib. Tractor Bn. from March 1942-September 1944. Wounded Nov. 20, 1943, on Tarawa. Was instructor of Tractor Vehicle Bn. until discharged Jan. 21, 1946, as a sergeant.

Hellums was awarded the American Area Medal, Purple Heart, Asiatic-Pacific Campaign Medal w/4 stars, Presidential Unit Citation w/3 stars, Good Conduct Medal and Pistol Sharpshooter Award.

Memorable experiences: Driving amphibious tractor #15, first wave on Red 2, Tarawa, two days, one night on the beach, wounded.

He and his wife, Helen, have four children: Edmond, Sandra, Larry and Reda; and five grandchildren: Gene, Lora, Shane, Derrick and Christen. Civilian activities include farmer, equipment operator, elevator employee and cattle and tree farmer.

CLEMENT VERNON (CLEM) HENDERSON, born in Orange, TX Jan. 31, 1923, and grew up in south Louisiana. He enlisted in the Marines June 18, 1943, after his sophomore year at Louisiana Tech. After completing three Radio Schools, two in San Diego and one at Camp Lejeune, he shipped out for Saipan  and the 2nd Marine Div. He was part of the second JASCO selected to reinforce the 8th Marine Regt. when it returned to Okinawa. After service in Japan, he was separated from the Corps April 30, 1946.

After graduating from Louisiana Tech, he earned a Master's degree at LSU and did additional graduate study at the University of Arkansas. Henderson spent 30 years at Fair Park High School in Shreveport, LA as a teacher, coach and principal.

Retired, he lives in Natchitoches, LA. He and his wife, Martha, have three sons and four grandchildren. He has located several of his service friends by using Internet directories and spends time each day on the world wide web researching topics of interest to him and a group of retired friends who meet each morning to have coffee, discuss sports, and solve the world's problems.

WAYNE MICHAEL HEWITT II, born July 19, 1966, in Huntington, WV. Grew up and attended L.C. Bird High School in Chesterfield, VA. At the age of 18 enlisted in the USMCR. Entered boot camp at Parris Island, SC in August 1985. Earned a BA degree in history from Virginia Tech in 1989. After completing OCS  was commissioned a second lieutenant in the USMCR in December 1989. Following Infantry School was assigned to 2nd Bn., 2nd Marine Regt., 2nd Marine Div., Camp Lejeune, NC. Soon after taking command of a rifle platoon was sent to Saudi Arabia in December 1990. Participated in Operation Desert Shield/ Desert Storm. In 1992 served as G Co. executive officer aboard the USS *Trenton* and USS *Iwo Jima* during a Mediterranean deployment. Later served as executive officer for Wpns. Co., 2/2. Left active duty in January 1994. Presently a captain in the USMCR.

WILLIAM F. (BILL) HILL, enlisted in the Marines in 1943. He took basic training at Parris Island, SC. After basic he was sent to Hawaii and then to Saipan.

In June 1944, two days into the invasion of Saipan (Marianas), his ankle was injured by a mortar explosion.

The hospital was an old Japanese communications building. One day a priest came in and sat beside him to visit. A photographer came by and took their picture. He told them the picture would be in the newspapers back home.

After the war was over he was stationed in Japan. In September 1946 he was laying in his bunk when one of the guys came in and said, "Hey Hill, your picture is in this magazine." He gave the magazine to Hill and he put it in his sea bag. After four months his time was over and he came home. At home, he put his sea bag in the attic with the magazine inside. The bag and magazine were forgotten.

The sea bag stayed in the attic at his home place for approximately 45 years. His mother was getting frail and suggested he take his things from the attic to his own home. Some months after he took the bag home he decided to check it out. He again found the magazine. By this time it had faded and the pages were showing their age. He took the magazine to a photograph specialist to have copies of the picture made for himself and his family.

A year or so later his wife sent for a book on Saipan. She wrapped it as a Christmas gift. Imagine Hill's surprise as he opened the book and saw his picture in it on page 257!

Hill is the third person from the left in the photo. He would enjoy hearing from any of the other men in the photo. Please write to him at: P.O. Box 272, Millersburg, OH 44654.

JOHN H. HOUSE, born Dec. 22, 1924. Enlisted in the service Nov. 2, 1942. Boot camp at Parris Island, SC. After boot camp to Camp Lejeune. He went to New Zealand to join up with 2nd Marine Div. Left New Zealand and saw action as private first class in Tarawa, Saipan and Tinian. Artillery Forward Observation Team, 1st Bn., 10th Marines, 2nd Marine Div. Received medical discharge Dec. 4, 1944, at Camp Lejeune, NC.

House was awarded the Silver Star, "... in action against enemy Japanese forces on Saipan June 22, 1944 ... launched a hand grenade attack ... to drag the casualty to a safer place ... thereby saving the man's life.

Memorable experiences: Members of the 1st Bn., 10th Marines won a duck in a raffle while in New Zealand. The Marines named the duck "Siwash." When the Marines arrived at Tarawa, they hit a coral reef. Someone threw Siwash overboard. When the Marines reached the beach, Siwash was waiting for them sitting on a coconut log quacking. Later Siwash was featured in *Life* magazine.

House married Melbadeen in 1951. They have one daughter, Cheryl and one granddaughter, Jamie Allison, a Morehead scholar at the University of North Carolina at Chapel Hill.

He is a member of the American Legion, Lions Club, and was a town commissioner for 18 years. Civilian employment as Southland Life Ins. agent for 25 years and owner of his own business for 10 years.

JODIE G. HOWINGTON, born May 17, 1919, in Jackson County, Norwood, GA. Lived and raised on a farm. Drafted into the USMC October 8, 1943. Went to boot camp in San Diego, CA (Plt. 927), took advanced training at Camp Elliott, CA. Departed California in March 1944 for Hawaii. Was assigned to the 2nd Marine Div., 18th Engrs., and departed for Saipan in May 1944. Joined Fox Co., 2nd Bn., 6th Marines on Saipan. Saw action on Saipan, Tinian, Okinawa and in occupation of Japan at Nagasaki. Discharged at Camp Lejeune January 8, 1946, with the rank of corporal.

Married Syble Virginia Chaney Sept. 18, 1941. They have two children, Jane Marie Howington/Barrett and Jodie Grady Jr., and five grandchildren: Courtney Paige Barrett/Howe, Samuel Grady Barrett, Amy Kay Howington/Knox, Brian Wayne Howington and Kevin Scott Howington. Moved to Sinton, TX in 1951. Retired from Mobil Oil in 1983. He and Syble still reside in Sinton.

JOHN J. HRUSKA, born April 10, 1921. Enlisted in the service Nov. 30, 1939. After boot camp at Parris Island he joined the 3rd Def. Bn. with duty at Pearl Harbor April 1, 1940-Dec. 31, 1941, except for period March-October 1941 at Midway Island. Present at Pearl Harbor during December 7th attack. Joined 2nd Marine Div. in Samoa in April 1942, Regt. Wpns. Co. with CPT H.P. "Jim" Crowe commanding. Combat at Guadalcanal and Tinian Island, assault landing with 2-8 on Tarawa and Saipan Islands. Discharged Dec. 31, 1945, with the rank of platoon sergeant from Marine Barracks, Naval Academy.

Awarded the Asiatic-Pacific Campaign Ribbon w/6 Battle Stars and Pearl Harbor Commendation Congressional Medal.

Employed as locomotive engineer 1948-68; construction superintendent 1968-88; and real estate consultant 1988-94. Charter member (1950) 2nd Marine Div. Assoc., past president 1964-65, 20 years service with Memorial Scholarship Board and seven years as chairman. He and his wife, Constance, have two children, Kathleen and Stephen, and two grandchildren, Nicole and Michael.

GRAHAM HUTTON, born July 19, 1922. Enlisted in the service Dec. 11, 1942. Joined G-2-6 in New Zealand. Action in Tarawa, Saipan and Tinian. Went to Okinawa and participated at Nagasaki. Discharged at Camp Pendleton Dec. 11, 1945, with the rank of sergeant. On arrival home to Turner, MT it was 22° below, pretty cool after the hot spots.

Civilian activity as cattle rancher-farmer. Bank director for 17 years. Presently retired, son on the ranch now.

Wouldn't take a million dollars for his experience. Wouldn't do it over again for a million dollars. Treasures his old buddies very highly.

Memorable experiences: Machine gunner. Remembers having one good fox hole; they sent in a tank to fill in a break in the line, in a very

rough area, on side of Mount Topotchau. Every Japanese this side of Tokyo knew this tank was there. He used their pick and shovel to dig a fox hole, luckily, they tried all night to knock it out.

Married 51 years to his Canadian war

bride, Adrienne Richards. They have five children: Mrs. Jim (Phyllis) Fitzpatrick, Mrs. Bill (Chery) Thompson, Mrs. Joe (Linda) Shaw, Mrs. Tim (Karalee) McCoy and Miles (wife, Linda) Hutton; 15 grandchildren: Patrick, Shandi, and Graham Guy Fitzpatrick; Brian, Michael (USMC), and Erin Shaw; Deinna, Billie Jo, Cali, Khrysten, and Cassie Thompson; Lucas and Adrianna McCoy; and Miles John Guy and Lyndsay Hutton; and three great-grandchildren: Dylan Joe, Kendall and Kitana.

TOIVO HENRY IVARY, born Dec. 3, 1918, in Westford, PA. Awarded the Purple Heart and Navy Cross. Ivary attained the rank of captain.

He and his wife, Margaret, have five children:

dren: Eric, Mark, Matthew, Lisa and Daniel. Ivary passed away Jan. 20, 1994, in Berkeley, CA.

HENRY H. JANDL JR, born Aug. 22, 1927. Enlisted in the service June 8, 1949; assigned G-3-10, Camp Lejeune, gunner and section chief.

Discharged June 7, 1952 as sergeant. Awards include Atlantic War Zone, Victory Medal and Naval Occupation.

Semi-retired farmer. He and wife Mary have four children: Elizabeth, Henry III, Frank and Virgina Ann, and two grandchildren, Diana and Henry IV.

FRANK J. JANENDO, born April 9, 1922. He enlisted in the service Sept. 16, 1942 and was discharged in 1945 as private first class (refused sergeant and staff sergeant).

Memorable experience was wiping out enemy machine gun nest before swimming for help amidst sniper fire. Recommended for medal for heroism but never received it.

Civilian employment as machinist, foreman

in construction, book binder, graphic arts, Western Publishing Co. in New York.

His wife Mary and son Frank T. are deceased. He has one daughter Joann Knieger and three grandchildren: Jennifer, Mary and Joseph.

C.E. JARVIS, enlisted in USMC at St. Louis, MO in January 1942. Graduated from boot camp and was assigned to Co. A, 2nd Pioneer Bn., MCB San Diego. After weeks of training went aboard ship where he contacted the mumps and was transferred to Balboa Naval Hospital.

After Balboa assigned to a Casual Co. at MCB San Diego then reassigned to Co. B, 1st Bn., 6th Regt., 2nd MD at Camp Elliott, CA. Boarded the USS *Matsonia* and sailed for New Zealand. He was on patrol Jan. 16, 1943 at Guadalcanal when he was severely wounded in the leg. Sent to several hospitals at various locations and finally to Naval Hospital at Corona, CA.

After a lot of surgery and physical therapy, he refused a medical discharge and was sent to NAS Terminal Island, San Pedro, CA where movie actor, Robert Montgomery, was his CO. His leg wouldn't cooperate and one again he was hospitalized, refused medical discharge (second time) then assigned to Naval Ammo Depot in Indiana. Again his leg acted up and he was discharged at VA Hospital, St. Louis in January 1944.

Began working for the St. Louis-San Francisco RR in February 1944, retired in 1981 and moved to Florida where he spends his time playing golf, fishing and doing volunteer work for the County Sheriff's Dept. and his church.

Married and has three daughters, eight grandchildren and seven great-grandchildren.

ROLAND K. JENNINGS, born in Nodaway County, Missouri in 1926 and graduated from Elmo High School in 1943. He enlisted in the Marine Corps Dec. 23, 1943 and left for active duty Jan. 24, 1944, destination MCRD San Diego, Plt. 90. After boot camp, he was assigned to the First Field Arty Training Bn. at San Mateo Barracks, Camp Pendleton.

His unit, the 58th Repl. Bn., left San Diego May 31, 1944 for Hawaii then the Marianas. He participated in the Tinian Campaign as a member of the 24th Marines, 4th Marine Div. He then joined the 10th Marines before going to Saipan. He saw action at Okinawa and was a member of the occupation forces, serving as a Military Policeman on Kyushu.

Returned to the States in mid-March 1946, and was discharged on the 29th. Later that year he was married to Mildred Wyant. He attended Central Technical Institute in Kansas City studying electronics. After graduation, he was employed as a broadcast station engineer for 10 years, then as a communications specialist for the Dep't of the Army until retirement.

Roland and Mildred have two children, six grandchildren and one great-grandchild.

Hobbies include, amateur radio, portraiture and music.

GILBERT W. (RED) JENSEN, born March 19, 1924 and enlisted in the service July 2, 1942. Boot camp was at San Diego in Plt. 528; at Camp Elliott assigned to D/1/6.

Sailed to Wellington, New Zealand in September 1942 and landed on Guadalcanal, BSI, Oct. 19, 1942. Served in action against the enemy as a heavy machine gunner.

Discharged July 2, 1946 as corporal. His awards include the Good Conduct Medal and Presidential Citation.

Graduated from IIT with degree in mechanical engineering. Rose from research engineer to president (for 17 years) at Roper Industries. Took an early retirement in 1983.

One of his accomplishments was winning a national poetry award. He and wife Eileene have three children: Eric, Craig, Kristine and four grandchildren: David and Kelly Jensen, Valerie and Jeremy Mize.

ROBERT C. JONES JR., born July 27, 1918. Enlisted in the USMC June 15, 1938, New Orleans, LA; went to boot training at San Diego Marine Base and graduated with Plt. 15. Transferred to Sea School, graduated and assigned to the Marine Detachment aboard the USS *Pennsylvania* which was the flag ship of the CIC of the Pacific Fleet.

Spent three years as sea-going Marine, a drill instructor at San Diego Recruit Depot then instructor at San Diego Sea School. Commissioned 2nd lieutenant, July 1942, and assigned to 2nd Marine Spec. Troops which later became 2nd Pioneer Bn., 18th Engr. Regt.

Participated in the landings and battles on Tarawa and Saipan, wounded in both and hospi-

talized for months. Released from AD to the USMCR in March 1946 with the rank of captain. Joined the USMC Retired ranks Jan. 1, 1958 with the rank lieutenant colonel. Awards include the Bronze Star, Purple Heart w/Gold Star, Good Conduct, Asiatic-Pacific, Combat V, PUCs, WWII Victory Medal and Sea Service and Reserve.

Joined the sales staff of the AC Div. of General Motors Corp. where he spent 32-1/2 years, retiring as general service manager of the AC-Delco Div., Oct. 1, 1978.

Married Lorraine Manning Aug. 8, 1942 and they have two children, Karole Lynne Jones-Confer and Robert Jones III; four grandchildren: Robert IV, Carrie, Kelly and Hallie; three great-grandchildren: Robert, Justin and Katelyn. He is a life member of 2nd MarDiv Assoc. and charter/life member of Marine Corps League.

HARVEY KEITEL, born May 13, 1939 and enlisted July 17, 1956. Served with 2/8 and 3/6 at Camp Lejeune. Served with 2/8 for two years and two months and with 3/6 approximately 10 months. In 1958 he participated in Beirut expedition, as a corporal and fire team leader.

Discharged July 17, 1959 as corporal. Awards include the Marine Expeditionary Unit Medal for Beirut landing.

As a civilian he is an actor and producer.

JAMES S. KELLY JR., born in Rushville, IL, June 29, 1921 and graduated from Rushville High School in May 1939 as vice-president of the class. He enlisted in the USMC Sept. 3, 1940; transferred to H&S 2-10 in November 1940, then to H&S 4-10 on April 1, 1940. He served in H&S 4-10 until Dec. 22, 1944, advancing to tech sergeant as battalion motor sergeant.

He saw action at Tarawa, Saipan and Tinian. Served at Quantico Marine Barracks from February 1945-November 1949 as post garage shop chief and became master sergeant on May 24, 1945. Served at Barstow Depot (1949-51) and at Camp Pendleton (1952). Commissioned 2nd lieutenant March 8, 1952 and served in HQ, Washington, DC, Albany Depot in Georgia and 3rd MarDiv in Japan.

Served as company commander of a Truck Company at Camp Pendleton in 1955. Reverted to master sergeant, June 30, 1956 and assigned as Liaison NCO at Benecia Army Depot. Retired May 30, 1960. He worked in Civil Service as a logistics specialist from June 1960-June 1985 at Benecia Depot, Tooele Depot, Rock Island Arsenal and Redstone Arsenal. He worked with government contractors as a logistics analyst until retirement in February 1997 after 57 years in defense work.

Married Nina France in 1942; she died in October 1980. He has three children: Terry, Patricia and Karen. Married Hazel Stephens in

Huntsville, AL in April 1984. Together they have nine grandchildren residing in Pittsburgh, PA; Atlanta, GA; and Huntsville, AL. Being a retired Marine is his greatest joy of life with many highly rewarding memories.

LARRY C. KIMBALL, born Nov. 2, 1924 and enlisted in the USMC Jan. 22, 1943. Boarded SS President Polk at San Diego July 16, 1943 and arrived in New Zealand Aug. 16, 1943.

Participated in landing operations in New Zealand area; Efate, New Hebrides; Tarawa Atoll; Maui, T.H. for amphibious maneuvers. Saw action at Saipan, Tinian, Okinawa and Ie Shima. Atomic bomb was dropped on Nagasaki Aug. 9, 1945. Arrived Nagasaki, Kyushu, Japan on Sept. 23, 1945 for occupation duty until Dec. 6, 1945.

Boarded USS *Sarasota* on December 8th and arrived in San Diego, CA, on Christmas Eve 1945. Received honorable discharge Jan. 11, 1946 with the rank of staff sergeant. Awards include two Silver Stars, two Purple Hearts, Presidential Unit Citation and Asiatic-Pacific w/3 Battle Stars.

Married with three children: Kieth, Patsy and Steve; eight grandchildren: Todd, Katie, Bille, Jenny, Britnay, Amanda, Alyex and Taylor. He is a self-employed cabinet maker (45+ years).

DONAVAN F. KNORZER, born in Hamilton, TX, in 1924. He left school and enlisted in the Marines Feb. 20, 1942. After boot camp at San Diego, he went to American Samoa to join D/1/8.

He saw action on Guadalcanal, Tarawa, Saipan and Tinian. Donovan received the Purple Heart and Bronze Star medals for his service in these campaigns as well as two Presidential Citations. Separated from the Corps Feb. 19, 1946, at MB, U.S. Naval Gun Factory, Washington, DC.

Donovan married Bonnie Brown of Baxley, GA, Jan. 16, 1945, and they have one daughter, Donna Faye Glenn, and one granddaughter, Stephanie Glenn. He returned to school, earned his diploma then worked for the Rural Electric Company for 44 years, retiring as Hazlehurst district operations mgr. of Satilla EMC in Alma, GA, Feb. 1, 1990. Donovan is active in both civic and church affairs and currently lives in Hazlehurst, GA.

ERWIN F. KOEHLER, born June 11, 1920 and died July 25, 1997. Erv was born in Bensenville, IL and grew up in River Grove, a west suburb of Chicago. He left Chicago for boot camp in San Diego, August 1941, where he was a member of Plt. 105.

After boot camp he was a drummer in the Marine Band and performed with the band in the filming of the *Halls of Montazuma*. Erv was with the 2nd Marine Division, B Co., 2nd Tk. Bn. on Tarawa, Saipan and Tinian. He received the Silver Star Medal for conspicuous gallantry while serving as a runner in the capture of Tarawa, November 22-23, 1943.

Erv married Ruth Lippmann in June 1950, and she died November 1965. He married Gladys Burgeson Jacobsen in December 1967 and has one stepdaughter, two grandchildren and five great-grandchildren. He was an ironworker and an antique and art dealer in Oak Park, IL. Erv and his wife resided in River Grove until they retired in 1978 in Sun City, AZ.

JOSEPH F. KOSEK, born Jan. 15, 1922 in northern Wisconsin at Westboro and was raised in Rib Lake, WI. He was in Chicago on Dec. 7, 1941 and enlisted in the USMC Nov. 30, 1942. Assigned to 2nd Spl. Wpns., Rifle Plt., Comm. Section, mechanic and heavy equipment operator.

Left for overseas with 23 Replacement Bn. July 16, 1943 and stopped at New Caladonia on the way to New Zealand. Left New Zealand Oct. 2, 1943 and stopped at New Hebrides on the way to the Gilbert Islands. Saw action at Tarawa, Saipan, Tinian and Okinawa.

After Tarawa they had a nice stay in Hawaii for rebuilding. He was in Japan Sept. 24-Dec. 17, 1945. Was discharged at the Great Lakes Naval Base Jan. 26, 1946 with the rank of corporal. Awards include the Presidential Unit Commendation w/star, WWII Victory Medal, Asiatic-Pacific Campaign Medal w/4 Battle Stars, American Defense, American Campaign and Navy Occupation Medal.

Went to Tech School and worked as a machinist. He is now retired with a lot of memories and is enjoying life. He and wife Loraine have three children: Joe (m. Jan), Dan and Mark; and two grandchildren, Kip (m. Anne) and Koy.

RUDY S. KUTCHAR, born April 14, 1922 and enlisted in the USMC March 3, 1942. He spent 11 months in New Zealand and participated in action against enemy Japanese forces at Tarawa Atoll, Gilbert Islands from Nov. 20-Dec.

1, 1943, at Saipan and Tinian, Marshall Islands, June-August 1944.

Discharged as private first class, Sept. 29, 1945, K-4-10. Memorable experience was when he cast grave marker out of Babit for Capt. P.V. Thompson, killed on Saipan. Grave marker is in a Winchester, VA church.

Spent 18 years as cabinet maker and 25 years with Budweiser Whsl. Retired May 5, 1986. He and wife Justine have two children, Debbie and Craig; and two grandchildren, Erick and Jeff Blackmore.

JOSEPH E. LALICKI, born in DePont, PA on Oct. 26, 1922, moved to New York and enlisted in the Marines on Dec. 8, 1942. Left for Parris Island, SC for boot training and later to New River, NC for rifle training.

Assigned to Camp Pendleton, Oceanside, CA. Later, while he was at Camp Elliott, CA, he met his wife Ann Candela, who came from Michigan to visit her brother Joe.

He left for parts unknown in September 1943, arrived in Wellington, New Zealand and was assigned to G-2-8 60 mm motor, Major Crowe Regiment as a private first class. He saw action on Tarawa and Saipan. He was wounded and received the Purple Heart. He was sent to the USN Hospital in Long Island, New York. He was discharged at the Brooklyn Navy Yard on April 2, 1945.

Joseph moved to Detroit, MI and married Ann on July 6, 1946. They now reside in Warren, MI and are the parents of four children. They also have five grandchildren and one great-granddaughter.

He retired from the postal service Sept. 9, 1979, and now enjoys gardening, traveling and spending time with family and friends.

The memories of Tarawa and Saipan are still vivid in his mind, and he often wonders how he ever survived the war.

WILLIAM T. LANE JR., born Oct. 21, 1931, Atlanta, GA. He attended the Augusta Military Academy in Virginia and with his lifelong buddy, Tony Leone, joined the Marine Reserve in December 1947. In December 1948 he enlisted in the Regular Corps and completed boot training at Parris Island.

Transferred to H&S Co., 2nd Amph. Trac. Bn., Courthouse Bay, Camp Lejeune, NC and

was TAD as a rifle instructor at the rifle range when the Korean Conflict broke out in 1950. He returned to his unit and worked around the clock packing up to go to California to join the units going to Korea. However his platoon was left behind and he was a very disappointed young marine, and to add insult to injury, he was placed on mess duty as his outfit left to the band playing the tune of *California Here We Come*.

They made a battalion out of his platoon and he found himself in Co. B, 2nd Armd. Amph. Bn. where he remained at Courthouse Bay for the rest of his enlistment. He tried to transfer several times but was always turned down. Discharged in September 1952 with the rank of sergeant. His awards include the Sharpshooter, PUC, Good Conduct and National Defense.

He became a police officer in Maryland and rose through the ranks to chief of police, serving for 20 years. He retired with a total of 31 years in law enforcement. He is still serving as a special U.S. Marshal for Courthouse Security.

Married to a wonderful lady and they have been together for over 40 years. She takes a lot of kidding about her name, Lois Lane. They have a son, Edward, who is still single. He joined the 2nd Div. Assoc. and has visited Camp Lejeune with that group several times and has enjoyed it very much. It is true that once a Marine, always a Marine.

JOSEPH J. LAWNICK was born in St. Joseph, MO in 1921. After graduating from high school he enlisted in the Marine Corps in September 1940. After boot camp at San Diego, he was assigned to H&S 2-10 where he stayed until November 1944. Joe was a member of 2-10 when it was incorporated into the 1st Marine Brigade (Provisional) and served in Iceland from July 7, 1941 to March 1942. He saw action on Guadalcanal, southern Solomons, Tarawa, Saipan and Tinian.

Separated from the Corps, Nov. 12, 1946 as a gunnery sergeant, but remained in the USMCR until 1952. Joe married Oryen Johnson, September 1, 1945. They have two sons and a daughter. He graduated from the University of Oklahoma with two degrees in petroleum engineering and retired in 1988 after 38 years in the oil and gas industry. He became a full time volunteer for, the University of Oklahoma.

He is a past president of the University of Oklahoma Alumni Assoc. and in 1979 was the 19th person inducted in the University of Oklahoma Alumni Hall of Fame. He is a member of the University of Letterman's Varsity O Club. He served several years on the National Staff of the 2nd Marine Division Assoc. and in 1992 was presented the association's Distinguished Service Award. He and his wife are grandparents of five children and reside in Tulsa, Oklahoma.

ROBERT STAMM LEE, born Oct. 19, 1916 in West Union, IA, and raised in Grand Rapids, MI. He has one younger brother, John R. "Bill" Lee. He became a sea-going captain in the USMC and fought in WWII and Korea.

Robert graduated from South High HS, Grand Rapids, MI in 1935 where he earned a letter in tennis and a junior warrant as an ROTC 2nd lieutenant. He attended Grand Rapids Junior College and Lake Forest College in Illinois.

He trained 10 days at Quantico; proceeded to Camp Lejeune, NC; then by train to San Diego and on to American Samoa. Promoted to 1st lieutenant and ordered into combat with the 8th Marine Regt. in Guadacanal where he engaged the enemy as company executive officer, Nov. 4, 1942. He fought as acting company commander until he collapsed from loss of 60 pounds and tropical diseases.

Robert was flown out of Guadacanal, Jan. 31, 1943 to hospital at Efate, New Hebrides then by hospital ship *Solace* to a hospital in Auckland, New Zealand. Upon returning to California he was in Balboa Park Naval Hospital and Rancho Santa Fe Rehabilitation Hospital-Burnham Home.

1st Lt. Lee received an honorable discharge from the Corps after 18 months of service. His awards include two Presidential Citations, SOPAC w/Battle Star, American Theater, two Reserve Ribbons and one medal issued by Solomon Island Government.

Married Anne and they have a son, PFC Thomas C. Gravengood, USMC, and a grandson, Sgt. Thomas C. Jensen, USMC.

He thanks God he is a Marine and alive to write this historical note. He is a member of "Ye Knights Of Olde," The Redcoats, a USMC Officers Luncheon Club of Southeastern Michigan, DAV and Grosse Pointe Memorial Veterans Club of Michigan.

HAROLD WILLIAM LYSENE, born March 26, 1924, in Kerora, Ontario, Canada. His mother died in 1929 and Harold and his brother spent the next eight years in a children's home. In January 1942 he was heading for boot camp in San Diego, BAR School, Camp Elliott and Camp Mathews Rifle Range.

Shipped out in June on the *Lurline* with the 22nd Marines for Samoa, Apia and Pago

Pago. Continued training, guard duty and setting up anti-aircraft pits on Wallis Island.

After 16 months left for Hilo, HI to train for shore party duty on Saipan. D+6 joined the 8th as Reserves as mop-ups behind the Regulars. In August was in on the invasion of Tinian for a total of 27 months overseas. Sailed in August 1944 to Hawaii and on to Mare Island. Discharged as private first class at Sand Point, WA, Oct. 15, 1945. Awards and medals include the Pacific Campaign, Good Conduct and Marianas Battle Star.

He married Georgene in June 1948; they have four children: Janet, Mark, David and Leanna; and six grandchildren. He is a retired machinist from Keyport Naval Torpedo Station in Washington. Presently, they are full-time RVers and loving it.

JAMES MACMILLAN, born Aug. 20, 1923, and enlisted in the military Dec. 6, 1942. Boot camp was at Parris Island, SC; 13th Repl. Bn., Camp Lejeune; 1943, Samoa, New Caledonia and New Zealand, B-1-18. Transferred to G-1-6 and saw action in Tarawa, Saipan, Tinian and Okinawa.

Discharged Dec. 12, 1945 at Bainbridge, MD. Awards include Letter of Commendation, Presidential Unit Citation and four Bronze Battle Stars.

Memorable experience was moving inland on Saipan June 15, 1944 and while changing clip in BAR, a Japanese soldier ran out of brush and looked at him. James thought he was going to bayonet him but instead he ran right by him. The soldier was shot by another Marine in the platoon.

Retired in 1981 as a plumber and plumber contractor. James and wife Jacqueline have nine children: Richard, Don, Cheryl, Lee, Jackie, Mike, Gary Robert and Charlie; five grandchildren: Sonya, Don, Jodi, Mike and Jackie; and one great-grandchild, Milo.

EARL WAINWRIGHT MANN, born in Portland, OR Jan. 26, 1917 and moved to Stevenson, WA in 1920, when his father purchased a barber shop in the county seat town.

Enlisted in the USMC Dec. 12, 1941. received an honorable discharge at the end of WWII, then reactivated for the Korean conflict for a short time.

Served at HQ Co. in Wellington, New Zealand during the battle for Tarawa; landed on Saipan six days after the first wave with BGen. Meritt Edson.

Serving as a barber brought him into contact with many Corps notables: Col. David

Shoup, MGen. John Marston, MGen. Julian C. Smith, BGen. Alphonse De Carree, MGen. Joseph C. Fegan, BGen. Edson, BGen. Leo D. Hermle and BGen Thomas E. Bourke.

Mann graduated from Barber School in Portland, OR in 1935 and retired from his barber shop in Stevenson in May 1997.

He was with the 2nd MarDiv throughout WWII and discharged as private first class. He received the American Theater, Asiatic-Pacific and Good Conduct medals.

Mann is the father of three children: Gust, Paul and Katina. Also has five granddaughters.

JOHN R. MARN, born Aug. 15, 1922 and enlisted in the military Nov. 11, 1942. Assignments in the Asiatic-Pacific area, New Caledonia, New Zealand, New Hebrides, Gilbert Islands, Hawaiian Islands, Marshalls, Tarawa and Saipan.

Discharged Nov. 10, 1945 as sergeant, tank commander. Awards and medals include the Purple Heart (Tarawa) and Gold Star in lieu of second Purple Heart (Saipan) and Presidential Unit Citation.

Memorable experience was going into Tarawa with 14 tanks from med. tank battalion and all but his were disabled the first day.

He and wife Shirley have three children: Charlotte, Tim and Sherry; and four grandchildren: Mandy, Tyler, Kelly and Jessica.

WARREN G. MARTENS, born Dec. 21, 1928 and commissioned LTJG, USNR, Jan. 4, 1957. Assignments: 2nd MarDiv, 3rd Bn., 8th Marines, I Co., 2nd Amtrac Bn., Camp Lejeune, chaplain, USS *Tarawa*, USNS Geiger, NAS New York, USS *Compass Island*, USNAVSTA New York.

Discharged June 4, 1965, LCDR, CHC, USNR. He is an ordained minister and a member of Legion of Honor, Chapel of 4 Chaplains; minister emeritus, Reformed Churches, West Nyack and Kerhonkson, NY.

Married Margaret on July 18, 1953 and they have four children: Robert, Daniel, Margaret and Thomas; and eight grandchildren: Michael, Colleen, Christopher, Jessica, Kathleen, Emily, Samuel and Thomas.

DAVID THOMAS MARTIN, born Jan. 29, 1937, Pacolet Mills, SC and joined the USMC Sept. 21, 1955. Assignments include boot camp, Parris Island; ITR with N Co., Camp Pendelton; I-3-3 Japan, which later became BLT 3/3; November 1956-February 1957, stand-by cruise. After a division landing in the Philippines, they moved to Okinawa until July 1957.

Came back to the States and assigned to MP Det, H&H Sq MCAS Beaufort, SC. In June 1958 he was assigned to B Co., 2nd Anti Tank Bn. 2nd MarDiv, Camp Lejeune, attached to H

Co. 6th Marines from September 1958-March 1959 during the Lebanon Intervention.

Discharged Sept. 18, 1959 as corporal (E-4). Awards include the Good Conduct. He is a life member of both the 2nd Marine and 3rd Marine Div. Assocs. and member of Marine Corps Assoc., Marine Corps League and Marine Corps Historical Foundation.

Worked for Kohler Co., Spartanburg, SC over 38 years; also part-time as constable for Spartanburg County Magistrate Court.

He and wife Sarah "Lib" have five children: Donna Martin, Rhonda Harvey, Dawn Bennett, Libby Donald and Karen Manis, and 11 grandchildren: Josh, Dustin and Tyler Harvey; Mindy and Blake Woolen; Kellie and Sidney Bennett; Kaytie and Kelsey Donald; Stacy and Scott Manis.

JOSEPH B. MARTIN, born March 7, 1958 and joined the military April 15, 1976. Completed boot camp with Plt. 288, Parris Island; stationed at NAS Memphis, TN; transferred to Co. G-2-8 at Camp Geiger, rifleman. Graduated 1978 as #3 in class from Scout Sniper School, Camp Lejeune.

TAD Duty, 1978, to 2/8 Rifle-Pistol Team and National Division Shooting Matches, Camp Lejeune; 1978, West Africa/South America Goodwill Deployment (civil disturbance incidents in Monrovia, Liberia, Libreville, Gabon and show of force for President Carter in Lagos, Nigeria; 1978-79 Med Sea Deployment, Joint NATO Ops in Turkey, Cold War flyovers by armed Soviet MiG aircraft; 1979-80, Med Sea Deployment, Iranian Crisis Alert.

Honorable discharge as PFC, Sept 19, 1980; five years Army Guard and Air Guard/AF Reserve Service, 1982-89 (NATO Deployment to Germany and Drug interdiction deployment, Bahamas; USAF AD C-141B loadmaster air crew, five months; honorable discharge as staff sergeant June 21, 1990.

Awards of note include Marine Corps Good Conduct, Navy Sea Service Deployment Ribbon w/Bronze Star, Army Service Ribbon, AF Achievement Medal and Air Reserve Forces Meritorious Service Medal and AF basic Air Crew Wings Badge.

He is single and a member of several veterans organizations and Native American Traditional Pow-Wow Dancer.

JULIUS W. (JULE) MAYHEW, born Dec. 3, 1923 and grew up in Cincinnati, OH. Enlisted in the USMC April 20, 1942. After boot camp at Parris Island, SC, he went to Combat Engineering School in Quantico, VA, then to Camp Elliott, San Diego, CA assigned to A-1-18, 2nd MarDiv. He landed in New Zealand November 1942 and moved to Battalion HQ Co. While there, he was known as "Don."

He saw action in Saipan and Tinian, where he was hurt and hospitalized on Tinian. Returned to the States Dec. 23, 1944 and was stationed at Crane, IN. He was discharged as corporal Dec. 11, 1945. Recalled for the Korean Conflict in September 1950 as sergeant in the Training Aids Art Department at Camp Lejeune.

Graduated from the New York Technical Institute and the Academy of Commercial Art in Cincinnati. He was art director of the General Electric Research Laboratory in Schenectady, NY, 1953-62, then moved to Las Vegas, NV. Married Florence and has two children, Donna and Steve, and six grandchildren and two great-grandchildren. He has fond memories of New Zealand and the people he knew there. After 50 years he returned with his wife and visited with members of the family he had known.

In 1964, Jule started Mayhew, Ltd. (which later became Art Services), an art and printing production company, designing logos, annual reports and brochures for local businesses in Las Vegas, and now works as a graphic arts consultant to McCarran, International Airport.

ROBERT C. MAYNARD, born Aug. 21, 1919 and joined the USMC Jan. 15, 1942. After boot camp in San Diego was assigned to D Co., 1st Bn., 2nd Regt. in the 81 mm Mortar Platoon. The middle of July they boarded the *President Jackson* troop ship and sailed to the Solomon Islands where they landed on Aug. 7, 1942.

Attached to the ship were two Marines he had known in Kansas City, Charley Ward and Charley Wilson. The end of January 1943 the *President Jackson* picked them up and took them to New Zealand. After docking in Wellington it was announced that those who had a clean uniform could go on liberty. After a visit with friends, he was outfitted in a clean set of khakis, dress shoes and cap. When they got to the debarking ramp, the Marine officer inspecting those going on liberty took a look at me and said,

"Maynard, where in the hell did you get that uniform?" "Ways and Means Committee, Sir.". A salute and down the ramp he went.

Discharged Jan. 16, 1946 as corporal. Awards include the Good Conduct, two Presidential Unit Citations, Purple Heart, American and Asiatic-Pacific Theaters.

Employed as manufacturer's representative, wood office furniture for 40 years and is now retired. He and wife Margie have two children, Robert Jr. and Judith (Baringer), and three grandchildren: Christa Maynard and Amie and Nicole Walter.

AUSTIN C. McCLENDON, joined the USMC in 1942 at Texarkana, AR. Boot camp at San Diego. Left Camp Elliott for New Zealand in early 1943; joined the 2nd MarDiv B-1-6; went to Tarawa in November 1943; Saipan, June 1944 where he was wounded by mortar shell and spent over a year in different hospitals.

Memorable experience was arriving at Tarawa late in the evening and seeing the many Marines floating in the tide, some stayed on the beach as the tide rolled out. The landing at Saipan was pretty much the same as Tarawa with the exception that the bodies in the water weren't all dead but were being picked off like sitting ducks.

Joined the USAF in 1950, served in Korea and Japan, 1950-53, and in Vietnam, 1967-69.

While at Camp Tarawa he went to a little town called Hanaka. He has attended many reunions but has never heard anyone mention that town. He would like to hear from anyone who has been there or went on the trip to the Fiji Island where about 30 Marines went with the Navy on an amtrac training mission before leaving for Saipan.

R.H. (MAC) McDONALD, born Nov. 17, 1932, Rockville, CT,, the youngest of three boys. John, his eldest brother, served in WWII and was posthumously awarded the Silver Star for action on Saipan with the 25th Marines, 4th Marine Division. Rick saw action on Okinawa with the 36th Spec. Bn., USN.

Mac enlisted in November 1950 and was a member of Plt. 269 at Parris Island. Following boot camp, he was assigned to the 2nd MarDiv as a member of M-4-10. In October 1952 he was sent to Camp Pendleton for infantry training prior to being sent to Korea on the 27th Replacement Draft. He was assigned to D-2-11 and saw action on the Western Front. He returned as sergeant in November 1953 and was discharged at Treasure Island, San Francisco.

He earned his BS in education from Eastern Connecticut State University in Willimantic, CT and his MS from the University of Connecticut in Storrs, CT.

Married Joan Lee Feb. 27, 1960. They have three children: John, Karen and David. David is a former Marine who served in Operation Desert Storm. Mac and Joan are both retired and reside in Ellington, CT.

WILLIAM F. MCMILLIAN, born April 23, 1914, near Merryville, LA. He enlisted in the USMC, March 13, 1933 and received recruit training at Parris Island. His first assignment was to the Far East in the Philippines. From there he went to sea duty aboard the USS *Fulton* which terminated when the ship burned off the China Coast in April 1934. He then joined the 4th Marines in Shanghai.

Upon return to the U.S. he was assigned to G-2-6 then in its formative stage. The highlight of this tour of duty was the 1937 expedition to Shanghai to defend the international settlement. Later he was transferred to Marine Barracks, Navy Yard, Cavite for a year and then again to the 4th Marines in Shanghai, leaving there aboard the last transport before the Pearl Harbor attack.

On Dec. 7, 1941, he was in Camp Elliott in the 2nd MarDiv. As a platoon sergeant he helped form Co. C, 2nd Tk. Bn. and was with this unit (except for a couple of short intervals) until Tinian. During the Guadalcanal Operation he became a platoon leader of the 2nd Plt. when his lieutenant was killed on Tanambogo.

As Marine Gunner Tank Plt. leader he was in the landings and battles of Tarawa, Saipan and Tinian where he was wounded and evacuated. Upon return to the U.S. and recovery he was assigned to the Marine Trng. Cmd. at Camp Pendleton in the Tank School as tactics instructor.

Having been recommended for a "spot" commission at Saipan, he was commissioned 2nd lieutenant with date of rank Oct. 16, 1944. Promotions came fast and soon he was 1st lieutenant. When he came up in the promotion zone for captain, a technicality was discovered by the Pay Department. Such "spot" commissions were "for duty with the Fleet Marine Force" and the Fleet Marine Force was overseas, he was reverted but quickly promoted to commissioned warrant officer.

In 1948 he competed in the Western Divisional Rifle Match and qualified to compete in the Marine Corps match at Quantico, VA. His next assignment was as maintenance officer of the 1st Tk. Bn. and in this position he made the landing with at Inchon in the Korean War. During the Korean Campaign he also served as a tank platoon leader in several engagements. This time he received a commission without any restriction.

Upon returning to Camp Pendleton he commanded the Tank And Amphibian Tractor Mechanics School Company until his retirement Dec. 1, 1955 as captain (temporary) with permanent rank of commissioned warrant officer 3. His decorations include three Purple Hearts, three Bronze Stars w/Combat V and the Navy Commendation Pendant w/Combat V.

Married to Clara Weaver for 45 years when she passed away in 1989. He has three children: Linda, William H. and David P., and nine grandchildren.

Since retirement he has been a cattleman in Louisiana and held several positions in state government, including representative in the legislature.

LOUIS W. MEASSICK, born Aug. 13, 1926, in Willock, Pittsburgh, PA. Enlisted in the USMC Nov. 5, 1943. Went to Parris Island, SC for boot camp. Was in the 9th Recruit Bn. and made private first class out of boot.

Shipped overseas in March 1944 on the USS *Leon* from Norfolk, VA to Pearl Harbor. Went to Transiet Center then shipped to Co. F, 18th Marine Engrs., April 1944. Boarded USS *Clay* May 1944 and sailed for Saipan. Joined George Co., 2nd Bn., 6th Marines, June 1944. Boarded LST-226 to assault Tinian, July 24, 1944. Went back to Saipan Aug. 8, 1944 to base camp.

Left Saipan in March 1945 on the USS *Hendry* for Okinawa, D-Day, April 1, 1945. Went back to Saipan and sailed on USS *Gage* to Nagaski, Japan, September 1945 for occupation duty. Left Sasebo, Japan February 1946 aboard USS *Monrovia* and arrived at San Diego, CA, Feb. 20, 1946.

Sent to Great Lakes, IL for discharge, March 5, 1946. Met Mildred "Dee" Miller in 1946 and they married Sept. 4, 1948; no children. He joined the USMCR in 1950, D Co. 21st Inf. Bn., Neville Island, PA. Called to active duty September 1950 and shipped out to Camp Pendleton, CA. Was sent home last of November 1950, not physically qualified, and was discharged in January 1951. Awards include Asiatic-Pacific w/2 Bronze Stars, Victory Medal, Navy Occupation Service, Asia National Defense Medal and qualified with rifle and bayonet.

As a civilian he worked as carpenter, construction supervisor, production manager, lumber yard manager, all for Ryan Homes in Pittsburgh.

EVERETT G. MERCER, born March 6, 1922. Enlisted in the USMC Oct. 9, 1942; assignments at Camp Lejeune, American Samoa, New Zealand, Tarawa, Hawaii and Saipan.

Discharged Oct. 15, 1945. His awards include the Purple Heart and Presidential Unit Citation.

Retired tinsmith from Champion Paper Mill; town selectman for eight years; enjoys hunting, fishing, camping and golfing.

Married Genevieve Oliver and they have two children, Robert and Paul, and five grandchildren: Todd, Shawn, Cara, Carly and Kyle.

EDWARD L. MEYER, born March 31, 1925, in St. Paul, MN. He enlisted in the USMC in 1943 and attended boot camp in San Diego. Traveled to Camp Elliott and then went on to New Zealand in July 1943. From there he saw action in Tarawa and Saipan.

On June 16, 1944, he was wounded in action and went to Pearl Harbor Hospital for recovery. After that he worked at the officers mess hall as assistant cook and was promoted to corporal.

Went home on leave in 1945, reported to Camp Perry in Williamsburg, VA and was discharged in Nov. 2, 1945. He received the Purple Heart.

His wife Lorraine is deceased. He has seven children: Bob, Sue, Gary, Patty, Ken, Tim and Cindy, and 13 grandchildren. He is a watchmaker.

ELDON M. (MIKE) MEYER, born Aug. 11, 1921, Forrest, IL and raised and educated in Essexville, MI. Served in the USMC Aug. 25, 1942 to Dec. 30, 1945. Assignments: San Diego Recruit Depot Plt. 703, Radio Operators and Message Center Schools.

Joined HQ Co., 3rd Bn., 8th Marines in New Zealand. Mike earned a Purple Heart at Betio Island, Tarawa and was in Navy hospitals from Aiea Heights (Oahu) to Oak Knoll (Oakland) and Sampson (New York) before Brooklyn Navy Yard and Camp Lejeune.

Played on signal battalion baseball team and helped rehabilitate arm for reassignment to active duty. At Hawaii he headed for Japan invasion when the Atom Bomb was dropped. After short duty on Guam, Hawaii, he was sent to Camp Pendleton for discharge.

Used the GI Bill to gain credentials and doctorate for 35 year career in education. Mike married Frances Snow on Jan. 24, 1948, and they have three daughters, sons-in law and six grandchildren.

WILLIAM R. MEYER, born Nov. 17, 1926 and enlisted in the military Nov. 18, 1943. Assignments: I Co., 3rd Bn., 8th Marines, Saipan, Tinian, Okinawa, Asiatic-Pacific, June 1944-March 1946, auto rifleman BAR.

Memorable experience was being close by when General Buckner was killed. Discharged with the rank of corporal. He received the Good Conduct Medal, Asiatic-Pacific Theater w/2 stars, WWII Victory Ribbon and Presidential Unit Citation w/star.

Employed as ice dealer, 1947-51; head custodian, 1951-89; retired. Now working at Peter's Grocery. Married Doris Meyer and has 10 children: William, Mary, Danny, Michele, Timmy, Denise, Dean, Kathy, Candace and Raymond; 26 grandchildren and eight great-grandchildren.

LEO MICKALOWSKI, born Feb. 27, 1921 and enlisted in the USMC July 20, 1942. Boot camp was at Parris Island followed by Camp Elliott, San Diego, Guadalcanal, Tarawa, Saipan and Tinian.

Discharged with the rank of corporal on Nov. 24, 1945. Attended Bryant College and worked as public accountant. Retired since 1994.

He and wife, Margaret, have four children and five grandchildren.

GLENN E. MILLER, born Dec. 29, 1924 and enlisted in the military July 1, 1943. Went to boot camp at San Diego with Plt. 558. Sailed to Pearl Harbor, HI aboard USS *Langly*; to Big Island on the USS *Calvert*; Eniwetock and Saipan on USS *Funston*; Tinian on LST-166; back to Saipan on LST 820, to Nagasaki then back to the States on the USS *Hudrain*.

Discharged with the rank of corporal and received all the usual awards and medals. Having been trained in camouflage at Camp Pendleton, he selected architecture and interior design as his profession; he was chairman of the Interior Design Committee for the Minnesota Governor's house.

He and wife, June, have two children, Kimerly and Kevin, and four grandchildren: Sarah, Molly, Colin and Charlie.

ROGER J. MILLER, born July 29, 1931, Orange, NJ and was raised in Bloomfield, NJ. Left for Parris Island February 1952 and served with the 2nd 155 Gun Bn. at Camp Geiger and then 2nd Shore Party at Camp Lejeune. Discharged Feb. 4, 1954 as sergeant and entered the active Reserves for brief spell.

Spent 37 years in the food service industry, living in Pittsburgh, PA and various parts of New Jersey, Minneapolis, MN and Irvine, CA. Married Barbara in 1958 and they have four sons: Michael, Peter, Ted and Jimmy, plus six grandkids: Dustin, Ryan, Elizabeth, Erik, Amanda and Kathryn.

The Marine Corps was his college education. To wear the Marine forest green was the proudest thing he ever accomplished in his life. He owes the Marine Corps everything for his happiness, confidence and success in life. May God bless our Corps.

JAMES A. MONTGOMERY, born April 20, 1923, on a farm near Inkster, ND. He graduated from Manvel High School in 1941 and went one year to Mayville State College before enlisting in the Marine Corps Dec. 12, 1942. He went to boot camp with Plt. 1234 in San Diego.

In May of 1943 he joined the 81 mm Mortar Plt. "M" Co., 3rd Bn., 6th Regt., 2nd MarDiv, Wellington, NZ. He saw action on Tarawa, Saipan, Tinian, Okinawa and occupation duty in Nagasaki, Japan from September-November 1945.

He received the Navy and Marine Corps Medal for putting out a fire in a pile of 81mm mortar shells July 22, 1944 on Saipan. After 32 months overseas he was discharged in Chicago, Dec. 13, 1945. He went home and on Dec. 27, 1945 married Kathleen Hansen and they raised three children. Kathleen passed away in 1986.

Jim graduated from Mayville State College in March 1948, taught school in Oregon, Minnesota and California for a total of 38 years. He has been with the Special Education children for 18 years. He is presently married to Barbara and they reside in California where they enjoy 10 grandchildren. He is a member of the 2nd Marine Division Assoc. and has fun reminisc-

ing about old and new times with the group in California and at the yearly national reunion.

VERNON W. MOORE, born May 9, 1925, Victor, CO to Bill and Helen Moore. Enlisted in the military June 19, 1943 in Denver, CO. Stationed at Hawaii, Dec. 25, 1943 to May 29, 1944; wounded on Saipan July 8, 1944; and was at Tinian, July 29, 1944.

Stationed at NAD Puget Sound, Bremerton, WA from February 1945 until his discharge Nov. 9, 1945 with the rank of sergeant. He was awarded the Purple Heart w/Gold Star, Rifleman Sharpshooter, August 1943, and Rifleman Expert, June 1945.

Married Shirley Satran on Nov. 11, 1945; they have three children: Bill, Bryan and Lori; four grandchildren: Blane, Casey, Christopher and Renee; and two great-grandchildren: Alec and Stevie. Self-employed, real estates and oilfield.

KENNETH H. MOSHER, born April 9, 1915 in Palisade, MN on the Mississippi River. Enlisted in the military June 27, 1939. Assignments: boot camp in San Diego, CA; USS *Maryland* (BB-46); Wpns. Plt., B Co., 1st Bn., 8th Regt., Camp Elliott; 2nd Mar. Bde., American Samoa; Sgt. Wpns. Plt., B Co., 1st Bn., 8th Regt., Guadalcanal; G Co., 2nd Bn., 8th Regt., 2nd Mar. Div., New Zealand.

Commissioned 2nd lieutenant in 1943, landed in assault wave at Red Beach 3, Tarawa; landed in assault wave, Rt. Flank of 2nd MarDiv, G Co., 2nd Bn., 8th Regt., Saipan. The remainder of his service was as CO of 1st and 2nd Guard Co. at Camp Lejeune, NC and as staff officer in Trng. Cmd. at Camp Pendleton, CA.

Discharged as lieutenant colonel April 19, 1975. Awards include the Navy Presidential Unit Citation w/3 stars, Good Conduct Medal, American Defense Service Medal w/star, American Campaign Medal, Asiatic-Pacific Campaign Medal w/2 stars, WWII Victory Medal, National Defense Service Medal and Marine Corps Reserve Ribbon.

Chief of Police in California and after retirement moved to Dallas, OR. Married to Myrna for 34 years; three children: Rita, Vernon and Roxanne. Divorced, married to Patricia for thirteen years and two adopted children, Jonathan and Heather from this mar riage; divorced. He has six grandchildren and six great-grandchildren

FRANK T. MURRAY,

joined Marines Feb. 22, 1941 with a promise from recruit major to go into Marine Aviation. He fired expert on the rifle range and turned down a job there because of aviation. He was sent to Camp Elliott in 2-F-2 and made a historical 180 mile hike in record time. Transferred to 1C8 when the war started.

Loaded their own ships, USS Lureline, Matzoni and Monteray, and were the first troops to leave after the war started, Jan. 6, 1942 to Somoa. From there to combat on Guadalcanal until he got malaria and was flown out to New Zealand then to the States. He was offered a medical discharge three times after doing limited duty in Great Lakes, Charleston, WV and Norfolk. The thired time they gave him 80% disability and he went back to Minneapolis, MN to his wife and child.

He and his wife raised three sons and two girls and were very happy. She passed away Aug. 25, 1996. He lives part time in Minnesota and spends winters in Florida. He started flying on his in 1951 and during his lifetime has owned 10 airplanes, using them in his business as a salesman and owner of small company. He has now sold his planes and is retired.

JOHN J. MUSIL,

born March 11, 1929, Chicago, IL. Graduated Crane Tech High, ROTC and enlisted in the service Feb. 7, 1947. Boot camp was at Parris Island, SC; main station, Camp Lejeune, NC; two maneuvers in Caribbean, 1947 and 1949; 1948 Med cruise. Spent five months in Palestine/Israel with the UN under combat conditions, June-October 1948. His main job was to drive observers to hot spots, checking ships for arms shipments, unloading immigrants offshore, taking UN officials to other city and towns, delivering messages and picking up negotiating teams that were out in the field.

Memorable experiences: being stopped by a British tank at a road block manned by Arabs; driving honor guard for Count Bernadette, who was killed at a road block in the Jewish sector of Jerusalem; flying to Cairo Egypt to pick up Dodge trucks at a British base then crossed the Suez Canal, bringing them back to Haifa; being stopped at a road block and rifle was put to his head; leaving Haifa in October 1948 on the USS

Hugh Purvis (DD-207) for Greece then boarded a R5D and flew to North Africa, Azor Islands, Nova Scotia, then home to Cherry Point, NC. The first UN Flag that flew over Haifa (that was on top of the Zion Hotel) is now at the Milwaukee, WI, Public Museum.

Discharged Feb. 6, 1950 as corporal. His awards include the Navy Presidential Unit Citation, Good Conduct, Navy Occupation, National Defense Service, United Nations and Rifle Sharpshooter (still pending is Purple Heart for wound received in Palestine).

Worked 47 years as lithographer and is now retired. He is also a gun and knife collector. Married Helen on Jan. 16, 1950 and they have four children: Kathy, Randy, Debra and David, and four grandchildren: Amy, David, Cory and Jamie.

DAVID M. NESSLEY SR.,

born Aug. 17, 1922. Enlisted in the USMC Jan. 13, 1942, Machine Gun Crewman 604, Rifleman 745. Was stationed at Guadalcanal, Tarawa and Saipan. Served with Co. K, 3rd Bn., 6th Regt., 2nd Div. from boot camp; then 1st Bn., 29th Marines (reinforced January 1942; June 1942-June 1944; April-October 1945, 5th Repl.).

Discharged Oct. 8, 1945, with the rank of sergeant. received Bronze Star, Purple Heart, Presidential Unit Citation and WWII Victory Medal.

Married Norma L. Weber Nessley (deceased). Married Virginia M. Millar Nessley. Has two children, Jan Tully and David M. Nessley Jr.; two step-children, Paul Cosner and Sharon Sellitto; and three grandchildren: Jason and Sarah Tully and Jonathan Nessley. Worked as an electrical equipment repairer foreman, Federal Government Defense Construction Supply Center, Columbus, OH. He is retired.

RICHARD KARL NEUHARTH,

born Sept. 20, 1923, Lodi, CA. Enlisted in the USMC Dec. 12, 1942; attended basic training at San Diego, CA, Plt. No. 1204; Motor Transport School, automotive mechanic; and went overseas to New Zealand July 29, 1943.

Assigned to Co. B, 2nd Motor Transport Bn., 2nd Marine Div. at Wellington, NZ, Aug. 16, 1943; arrived in Hawaiian Islands Nov. 29, 1943; participated in invasion of Saipan June 15, 1944; invasion of Tinian July 22, 1944; Feint

Landing at Okinawa April 14, 1945; and back to Saipan. Landed on Aguni Shima May 8, 1945. Landed on Okinawa May 20, 1945, for final assault. Back to Saipan July 4, 1945. Promoted to corporal Sept. 8, 1945. Landed with the occupation forces at Nagasaki, Japan, Sept. 24, 1945.

Returned to San Diego Jan. 2, 1945. Received honorable discharge at Mare Island, CA, Jan. 27, 1946. Returned to Lodi, CA.

Married Edith Brown June 14, 1947; has three children: Dan, Kurt and Jean; and three grandchildren: Susan, Karl and James. Retired after 45 years in the agricultural chemical and fertilizer field.

ERVIN C. NIELSEN,

born Oct. 19, 1925. Enlisted in August 1943. Was assigned to JASCO and the 2nd Mar. Div. Discharged in January 1946 with the rank of corporal.

Married Bonnie; has four children: Claudia, Carol, Cheryl and Leslie; and five grandchildren: Noah, Lindsey, David, Scotty and Kira. Worked as a lawyer, rancher and photographer.

GEORGE R. NORTHRUP,

born April 23, 1925, Mount Vernon, NY, the son of Albert and Mary Northrup, the youngest of two boys. At the age of 17, he left A.B. Davis High School to enlist in the Marine Corps Reserves in February 1943. Being that Parris Island was quarantined, he was shipped to San Diego where he went through boot camp. From there he went to camp Elliott for infantry training.

In July 1943 he was sent overseas with the 22nd Repl. Bn., where he was assigned to C Btry., 1st Bn., 10th Marines, 2nd Mar. Div., in New Zealand.

He later saw action in Tarawa, Saipan, Tinian, Okinawa and then to Nagasaki, japan for occupation duty. In December 1945 he was sent back to the States after 30 months overseas and was discharged in January 1946.

While making the landing on Tarawa, he chewed tobacco for the first and last time.

He joined the Mt. Vernon, NY, Fire Dept. in December 1950, and retired as a lieutenant in 1973, and moved to Florida. In February 1949 he married Eileen H. Wolf and they raised three children: Christine, Karen and Kurt. All his children are still living in New York state. He drove a Hernando County school bus for 18 years and retired from that in 1992. He is now totally retired. He received the Purple Heart in August 1996, which was received for wounds he got on Saipan, June 20, 1944. He is now single living with his adopted greyhound, Buddy.

WILLIAM L. (BILL) OGDEN, born May 24, 1922, Evansville, IN. He left Evansville for boot camp in San Diego on Sept. 25, 1942, where he became a member of Plt. 900. He left Camp Elliott in the 10th Repl. Draft in January 1943, bound for Guadalcanal but ended up in New Caledonia; then arrived at Wellington, New Zealand on Feb. 14, 1943. He became a member of the 18th Regt. of the 2nd Mar. Div. and saw action on Tarawa, Saipan and Tinian.

Was sent back to OCS in December 1944 and then placed in the Navy V-12 program at Purdue University until WWII ended. He was discharged as a staff sergeant at Great lakes Naval Training Center on Oct. 31, 1945. Joined the Volunteer Marine Reserve in 1947 and was recalled to active duty in May 1951 for one year, serving in the FMF at Camp Pendleton, CA.

Married Isabelle H. Rosser in June 1945 and they have a daughter, Donna, a son, Wayne and seven grandchildren: Michael, David, Debbie, Sherri, Jennifer, Alisa and Shauna. He became a drafting coordinator, designer and a design checker.

GAYLORD R. OHLERICH SR., born Dec. 29, 1922, Belding, MI. graduated from Hillsdale High School, 1941. Enlisted in the USMC March 26, 1942; boot camp, Plt. 325, San Diego, CA; Finished Sea School; transferred into Tank School at Jacques Farm.

He became a tank driving instructor; shipped out as tank commander, Co. B, 2nd Tk. Bn., 2nd Mar. Div. to Hawaii. While there 17 of them were enrolled into the Army ranger and Combat School at Schofield Barracks, HI. After completing the schooling, their unit was quietly snuck down to Nukufutku, Ellis Island, on the outer fringe of the Gilbert Islands, where they defended the CBs who were building airstrips for the invasion of Tarawa.

They returned to Maui, HI. Just before leaving for Saipan, several ships were blown up while loading at Pearl Harbor by saboteurs, also destroying some of the amphibious tractors and their personnel. His outfit was notified that Co. B, 2nd Tk. Bn. was now Co. B, 2nd Amphib.

Tractor Bn., with instructions that the amphibious tractor operated just like tanks on land and water. That was their training. They were then "alligator marines." After Saipan and Tinian they were called "creeping coffins."

He was flown back with the other casualties to USN Hospital at Area HQ, HI. He was placed on limited duty and returned to San Diego where he was transferred to Marine Barracks, Bde. Det., USN Ship Yards, Charleston, SC. He chased court-martialed prisoners from Charleston to the USN Prison at Portsmouth, NH.

Married Helen on Base at Charleston, Aug. 23, 1945. He was discharged March 30, 1946. They returned to Jackson, MI, where he entered the USPS as a clerk carrier; rural carrier; and retired as postmaster at Rives Junction, MI. They have four children: Linda, Gaylord Jr., Pamela and Carla; four grandchildren: Richard, Shawn, Erica and Christy; and three great-grandchildren: Joseph, Lindsay and Brett.

WALLACE OLNEY, born June 17, 1921, Quincy, MI; raised in Battle Creek, MI. Enlisted in the USMC with younger brother in March 1942. Went through boot camp in San Diego, Plt. 322, after which he went through Communication School and joined 4-M-10 at Camp Elliott in June 1942. Sailed from San Diego with 2nd Mar. Div. in November 1942 and saw action at Tarawa, Saipan and Tinian. Returned to the States in January 1945 and was discharged at Quantico in March 1946.

Attended Western Michigan University and worked for 38 years in the paper industry as an industrial engineer and plant manager. After retiring in 1985 he and his wife, Sandra, moved to Leesburg, FL. They have five sons and seven grandchildren.

ROBERT ORR, born Dec. 14, 1923, Philadelphia, PA, the youngest of five children; his father died a month before his birth. Enlisted in the USMC Sept. 23, 1942; attended boot camp at Philippine Islands and Camp LeJeune. More training at New River before a train ride to San Diego; a boat ride to Samoa's; then after a month on Upola boated to the Fiji's; onto Noumea, New Caledonia for three weeks. Sailed to Sydney and Melbourne, Australia; then across the Tasman Sea though five days of a treacherous storm to Wellington, NZ. Surviving that voyage was a reward, but the best reward was becoming a member of the greatest division ever assembled on the face of this planet: 2nd Marine Division.

After Tarawa, Saipan, Tinian, Okinawa and the Occupation of Nagasaki, he was shipped home by the point system. Discharged at Camp Pendleton on Dec. 24, 1945.

Married Marialice Queroli on Oct. 12, 1946. They have been blessed with two sons, Bob and Jack, and their children.

EARL F. (BUD) OTT, born Oct. 26, 1925, Columbus, OH, the only child of Earl and May Ott, Bellefontaine, OH, and from the age of two and one-half years lived in that city. After graduation from Bellefontaine High School in May 1943, he enlisted in the USMC and was ordered to Camp Pendleton, CA, on Oct. 29, 1943.

Completed basic and additional training at Greens Farm as a scout-sniper and deployed to the South Pacific where he was attached to G-26. He scouted many of the islands on intelligence gathering missions and was with the initial landings at Saipan and Tinian here he was wounded on Aug. 2, 1944. He was a patrol leader and a corporal at the time units of the corps. where ordered to occupy Nagasaki, Japan, and was stationed there until honorably discharged Jan. 7, 1946.

Married his high school sweetheart, Delores, March 23, 1948. They are parents of Bruce, a Vietnam era Navy veteran, Beverly Pepper and Barbara Peck; grandparents of nine; and great-grandparents of two. Graduated from Bowling Green State University, Bowling Green, OH, with BS and MS degrees in education; was a classroom teacher, high school principal, assistant and superintendent at Springfield local schools in Holland, OH, where he and Dede reside during summer months. They winter in Fort Myers, FL, since retiring in 1981. He is a member of Mid-Atlantic and Florida 2nd Marine Division Assoc., AASA and active in local and church affairs. He enjoys gardening, fishing and boating and vacations in Canada at the family cottage.

WILLIAM M. OWINGS, born Oct. 31, 1937, Baltimore; raised in Frostburg, MD. Joined the USMCR November 8, after high school, and went to Parris Island in June 1956, with Plt. 171. After boot camp and ITR he was assigned to Delta Co., 8th Marines.

Participated in TRAWX 1-57, in Puerto Rico; was reassigned to A-1-8 in 1958, for MED cruise, during which they landed in Lebanon. Upon returning to Camp LeJeune he re-enlisted and was assigned to H&S Bn., Casual Co. as property sergeant. CRD, San Diego, 1959; returned to Camp LeJeune and was assigned to the 8th Eng. Bn., heavy duty equipment operator. Left the Corps. in April 1963 due to family hardship.

In 1964 enlisted in the USCG. Tours included Florida, Hawaii, Vietnam, Alabama, Massachusetts and New Jersey. Retired June 1, 1978, as a chief boatswains mate.

Now resides in Palm Bay, FL. He is a life member of the 2nd Marine Division Assoc., active in the Florida Chapter. Married to Jimmie Lou Snipes for 26 years; has six children; nine grandchildren; and one great-grandchild.

HAROLD E. PARK, *Photos only, no bio submitted.*

WALTER PARK JR., born Dec. 7, 1924, Atlanta, GA, to Dorothy and Walter Park, a career Marine of 30 years, retiring as a gunny sergeant in 1945 from Camp LeJeune. As a child Walter Jr., lived on Parris Island and was living on the NAB Jacksonville, FL, at the time he enlisted in the USMCR in 1943.

After boot camp at Parris Island he was transferred to Hingham, MA, for a few months of guard duty, then on to Camp LeJeune for training. From there he went to Honolulu into the 4th Div., then as a replacement into I-3-6 for the invasion of Saipan and Tinian. He left Nagasaki, Japan, with the 5th Div. to Camp Pendleton to be discharged in 1946 at Camp LeJeune.

Married Dorothy Carrick in 1946, Baltimore, MD. He enlisted in active Reserves in 1948; was activated in 1950 for the Korean crisis. He has two daughters, Linda and Karen, and two grandsons, Niko and Adrian; and has spent the last 50 years as a land surveyor.

DEAN R. PATRICK, born Oct. 22, 1924, Chadron, NE. Enlisted in the USMC Dec. 15, 1941; was sent to Camp Elliot, CA. After boot camp he was assigned to 1-A-2, the to 1-D-2. Participated in the initial Guadalcanal Operation; landing on Florida, Tanaboga, Guvuta and Tulagi

Islands in August 1942. Went to New Zealand in 1942 and Tarawa where he was wounded.

Returned to Naval Hospital in San Diego, CA. Graduated from Sea School in 1944, assigned to the USS *Idaho*; participated in Iwo Jima and Okinawa battles. Hit by kamikaze at Okinawa. Was in Tokyo Bay during the Japanese surrender ceremonies. Highest rank was private first class. Discharged Dec. 17, 1945, at Great Lakes, IL. Was awarded the Purple Heart and two Presidential Unit Citations.

Attended San Jose State College; participated in Army ROTC and commissioned 2nd lieutenant in 1950; and was sent to Korea. Served in Germany with the 9th Div., 1953-56, and gyroscoped with them to Fort Carson, CO. Was company commander of MP unit when separated in 1957.

Attended Lincoln Law School in San Jose, CA, and became an attorney, practiced in Santa Clara County for 20 years. Married Flora Cunningham, a cadet nurse from Yuma, AZ, in San Diego, CA, June 1, 1946. They have five children: Stephen, Roger, Dennis, Barbara and Donna; and 14 grandchildren: David, Jonathon, Renee, Cari, Jeffrey, Shannon, Nicholas, Steven, Daniel, Benjamin (newborn, deceased 1980), David James, Holly James, Eric James and Sherry East.

NOAL C. PEMBERTON, born Sept. 21, 1923, Bristow, OK. In 1925 his family moved to southeast Kansas, then from there to Colorado in 1941. After graduating from high school he enlisted in the USMC in January 1943. After boot camp at San Diego, Plt. 64, he was assigned to Camp Elliot for extensive training, including scout and sniper at Green's Farm, preparatory to overseas assignment He and other replacements shipped out from San Diego in July 1943 and arrived in Wellington, NZ in August, where he was assigned to F-2-2.

Served with F-2-2 through four battle campaigns: Tarawa, Saipan, Tinian and Okinawa and the Occupation of Nagasaki, Japan. While in Japan he was awarded the Purple Heart for wounds received in action on Saipan in June 1944. Rotated back Stateside on the point system in December 1945 and was honorably discharged at Mare Island, Ca, Jan. 5, 1946, returning home to Colorado Springs, CO, where he still resides.

Married Jessie Ann Mondy July 10, 1948. He likes traveling, sightseeing, fishing and pho-

tographing wildlife. He and Jessie are very active member of the First Southern Baptist Church in Colorado Springs.

ERNEST N. PETRI, born July 23, 1923, Pekin, IL, the son of Nicholas and Blanche Peugnet Petri. He has a brother, Carl (also a Marine) and a sister, Bertha. He graduated from Pekin High School in June 1942 and enlisted in the USMC on November 10, in Chicago.

Took boot camp at San Diego and was sent to the Pacific area in March 1943, arriving in New Zealand in April 1943. He served as forward observer with the 81st Mortar Plt. of Co. HQ-2-8. He was in the first wave of Higgins boats attempting to land on Tarawa. He was in the initial landings in the Saipan and Tinian campaigns and received the Purple Heart for a wound suffered on Okinawa.

He was awarded the Bronze Star Medal w/ Citation by the President for heroic service during those campaigns. The 81st Mortar Plt. received many individual and three Presidential Citations, the most decorated mortar platoon in the history of the Corps. Many of its members were killed.

He achieved the rank of sergeant and was a member of the occupational forces entering Nagasaki shortly after the atom bomb hit that city. He was honorably discharged in Dec. 1945.

He and Mardell Norman of Pekin were married March 9, 1947. They have three children: Mrs. Joseph (Linda) Svec of Chicago, Mrs. Phillip (Jill) Peterson of Kansas City and Joel Petri of Pekin. They have three granddaughters: Julia, Amy and Katie Peterson. He worked as a millwright in a steel plant for 37 years, retiring in 1982. he and his wife reside in Pekin, IL.

BRUCE J. POLAND was born in Long Beach, CA in 1958 and enlisted in the Marine Corps in June 1976. Upon completion of recruit training on MCRD San Diego on Aug. 1976, he reported to the 3rd Marine Division where he served with "K" Company, 3rd Battalion, 9th Marines serving as a rifleman, automatic rifleman, transferring to 3rd Battalion, 4th Marines in August 1977 serving as a fire team leader.

In June 1978, SgtMaj Poland was transferred to 2d Battalion, 8th Marines where he served as a squad leader also serving with "L" Company, 3rd Battalion, 8th Marines serving as a platoon guide. In October 1979, SgtMaj Poland was transferred to "B" Company, 1st Battalion, 6th Marines, serving as a platoon sergeant. In February 1980, SgtMaj Poland was transferred to Marine Barracks Naval Air Station Cecil Field, Florida where he served as a guard section leader.

In May 1982, SgtMaj Poland was transferred to "B" Company 1st Battalion, 3rd Marines, 1st. Marine Brigade, Hawaii. Serving as a Platoon Sergeant, he was later assigned as the NCOIC of the Squad Leaders School, Brigade Schools. In June 1985, SgtMaj Poland was transferred to Infantry Training School, Camp Lejeune, North Carolina. Serving as a Platoon Commander, "B" Company and Tactics Instructor. In August 1986, SgtMaj Poland attended Drill Instructor School MCRD, Paris Island, South Carolina and served as a Drill Instructor and Senior Drill Instructor with "I" Company, 3rd Recruit Training Battalion.

In May 1989, SgtMaj Poland was transferred to Headquarters and Service Battalion, Marine Corps Base, Camp Butler, Okinawa serving as the Company Gunnery Sergeant for "A" Company. In April 1990, he was transferred to the Staff Noncommissioned Academy Okinawa serving as a Squad Instructor, Tactics Instructor, and Drill Master of the Career Course, where he was promoted to the rank of Gunnery Sergeant.

In June 1992, SgtMaj Poland was transferred to 1st Battalion, 8th Marines, "A" Company serving as the Weapons Platoon Sergeant, Weapons Platoon Commander, Company Gunnery Sergeant and Company First Sergeant. He was then selected to be SNCOIC of MTT Gold, Coalition Special Warfare Unit Quantico, VA to deploy to Colombia, South America to establish the NARCO/Counter Drug Riverine Package with the Colombian Marine Corps.

In January 1995, SgtMaj Poland was transferred to the SNCO Academy, Camp Geiger, North Carolina to serve as a Squad Instructor and Basic Warrior Training Instructor. He was then selected to First Sergeant.

In June 1995, SgtMaj Poland was transferred to MCRD San Diego, CA serving as the First Sergeant of "G" Company, transferring in November, 1996 to assume the duties as the First Sergeant of Drill Instructor School. In December 1997, SgtMaj Poland assumed duties as the Sergeant Major of Support Battalion.

In September of 1998 SgtMaj Poland was transferred to 2d Marine Division, Camp Lejeune, to assume his present duties as Battalion Sergeant Major, 2d Assault Amphibian Battalion.

His personal decorations include the Meritorious Service Medal/Navy and Marine Corps Commendation Medal/Navy and Marine Corps Achievement Medal with one Gold Star. SgtMaj Poland is the recipient of the Distinctive Badge of Combat Fluvial Award presented by the Colombian Marine Corps.

He is married to the former Twila Boatright of Kailua, HI. They have two children, Christine and Jake.

GEORGE W. POLLARD

GEORGE W. POLLARD enlisted in the USMC in the fall of 1942. He had finished art school but during the summer still worked on the family farm in Waldo, WI, and in the Waldo Canning Factory. His dad tried to get him a deferral from the draft board in Plymouth but they refused. Enlisting in the USMC and coming back alive turned out to be one of the luckiest breaks in his life. As his dad and mother sent him off, they gave him a New Testament which he carried with him the entire 39 months he served with the USMC.

Being with the 2nd Mar. Div., 2nd Bn., 2nd Regt., and being involved in some of the most brutal combat of any division in the South Pacific during WWII and observing fellow Marines being killed all around him caused him to often think that perhaps that gift from his mother and father saw him through.

He found himself a buck private in Wellington, New Zealand. He had finished his fourth year of art school and could not do artwork enough. As a buck private he was painting USMC generals, ships' captains and the wives of some junior officers who had married New Zealand girls. The currency involved was English pounds. He always refused payments for his work because he never thought he would come back alive, so money did not mean anything to him. However, he did learn two things: how to paint fast and to not be intimidated by important people.

He enrolled in art school night class in a little town north of Wellington called Masterton. After attending a few sessions, his work was good enough that he was asked to be the head professor of the entire art department. This caught the attention of his division commander and he was eventually promoted to staff sergeant and made a combat artist. When not in actual combat he spent his time drawing charcoal montages of combat heroes, using a Coleman lantern as his light source and carrying his materials in a mortar tube. These sketches were sent to hometown newspapers as morale boosters.

He found his first combat on Tarawa, a frightening and everlasting experience. He disembarked from their troop transport at 4 a.m. for their landing and was in a Higgins boat with Time-Life correspondent Robert Sherrod. When they hit the coral reef he transferred into an Amtrak. In both cases their vehicles were bombarded by machine gun and artillery fire. He observed the death of their regimental commander, Col. Amy, their regimental doctor was killed in the Amtrak and as he landed, his closest friend, Forrest Prince, who was right next to him, was shot through the head and dropped into the water beside him. The Japanese bullet had entered his helmet, struck him between the eyes and pierced his entire head. He found the slug in the back of his helmet. On the night before they embarked from New Zealand they had dated two girls from a suburb called Oriental Bay. He knew Prince was from Riverdale, CA, and that his father was a high school principal there. After the war he made several attempts to contact his mother and father and have always regretted that he was unable to do so.

He continued inland with Maj. Ryan and Herm Lewis, a radio operator at that time. He was directed by the major to contact their left flank. Originally he was armed with a carbine rifle which he exchanged for an M-1 from a dead marine. It took only a few moments to realize there was no such thing as a left flank, no right flank, no any flank. The whole episode was like a hallucination. The enemy he encountered he learned later were Japanese marines and very large in stature. In self defense he shot three of the enemy in a matter of seconds.

He found himself in the bizarre situation of witnessing a Japanese running after a marine with a samurai sword and slashing the entire calf of his leg, from the back of the knee to the ankle. As if in a dream, he calmly removed sulfa powder from his cartridge belt, took bandages from his first aid kit, replaced his calf and bandaged it as well as he could.

The whole Tarawa scene was like a psychedelic "Alice in Wonderland" montage of Japanese killing Americans; Americans killing Japanese; a few Japanese in ceremonial robes committing hara-kiri; Japanese snipers tied to palm trees shooting at them; and no front lines, no right flank, no left flank. The juxtaposition of friend and foe was like throwing 1,000 red marbles and 1,000 blue marbles into the air and landing at random, where they landed established who was who.

For several years after the war he was unable to follow public transportation buses fueled by diesel because the smell brought back the smell of diesel fueled Higgins boats mixed with the smell of the rotting flesh of Japanese who had been killed by flame throwers, then washed over with salt water when the tide came in and then baked in the tropical sun.

This was really the beginning and end of combat for him because for the landings on Saipan and Tinian he has no recollection of shooting at anyone.

The occupation of Nagasaki was a delightful experience. No one seemed to be in charge and as a non-commissioned officer, every morning he would requisition a jeep from the motor pool. He and Don Jones, the Japanese interpreter, would tour the entire island, fraternizing with the Japanese and learning to love the people they had been trying to kill for the past three years. He was discharged on Dec. 9, 1945.

Since then he has been fortunate to achieve the status of nationally-known portrait artist. He has painted three presidents, four Supreme Court justices, three Wisconsin governors, congressmen, senators, generals for the Pentagon, hundreds of professional athletes from almost every sporting event in the U.S. as well as Wimbledon, and people from all walks of life. He is the only American artist to have been commissioned to paint Pope John Paul II.

He has often thought what a dull life he might have led if the Plymouth draft board had agreed to his father's request to have him deferred. The second biggest break in his life was when he married his wife, Nan, a well-known illustrator of children's' books, in 1947. They have four children: Sherry Bingaman, Jim, Mark and Paul; and five grandchildren: Kate and Kory Bingaman, Ross and Dean Pollard and Chester Jones Pollard.

WALTER J. POULIOT, born May 7, 1921, on a farm in Tuscola County, MI. Enlisted in the USMC Jan. 24, 1942; attended boot camp in San

Diego, CA; shipped overseas to Tutilia, Samoa, and joined Weapons Co., 8th Marines, HP Crow, captain commanding.

Left Samoa and went to Guadalcanal Nov. 4, 1942. Left Guadalcanal Feb. 9, 1943, and arrived in New Zealand Feb. 16, 1943. Left New Zealand with the 2nd Marine Division and participated in action on Tarawa, Saipan and Tinian. Received the Purple Heart and Bronze Star Medals with Combat V for action on Tinian Island Aug. 1, 1944.

One of his memorable events he remembers is the naval battle on the night of Nov. 13, 1942, while they were on beach defense and had a ring-side seat for the battle and did not know who won until the next day. This was on Guadalcanal. Another experience was landing on Tarawa with the 4th wave. They ran aground 500 yards from shore. They had to wade in pulling their 37 mm anti-tank gun to shore. Two men on the trails and four pushing. They all arrived safely on shore. They were attached to the assault 2nd Bn., 9th Regt., Maj. H.P. (Jim) Crowe commanding. Another event was on Tinian Island on the night of July 31, 1944. They pulled their 37 mm gun to the top of the final ridge just after dark. They were told to expect a counterattack and to push concertina wire in front of their position. The counterattack came shortly after midnight and concentrated on their gun. The six members of their gun crew were killed or wounded but they drove the enemy off. The next day the island was declared secured. He received a Purple Heart and Bronze Star with Combat V for this action.

Was rotated home on points Sept. 7, 1944. Received first 30 day furlough to Detroit, MI, en route to Quantico, VA, Marine Base. Was discharged honorably from Quantico May 3, 1945.

Returned home in 1945; bought a farm in 1946; worked farm for 40 years and worked in foundry for 28 years and retired in June 1983. Married Alice May 6, 1950. They have four children: William Brenda, Richard and Annette; and 10 grandchildren. They still live on their farm near Caro, MI.

JAMES J. POWERS, born in Greenfield, MA, Aug. 14, 1918. Upon graduating high school, he was awarded a football scholarship to Temple University, by "Pop" Warner. In the 1938 football season, he received the prestigious Robert Maxwell Award for his exceptional play in the Boston College game which ended in a 26-26 tie. In the 1938 season's fade-out against the University of Florida, he ran back a kick-off for a 102 yard touchdown helping "Pop" Warner win his final game ending an illustrious 40 year career as coach. In 1940, playing for Temple's new coach, Ray Morrison, he returned the opening kick-off for a 105 yard touchdown against powerful Michigan State; and helped upset the

Spartans, 21-19. This run was the longest in the nation during the football season.

Upon receiving his BS degree from Temple he enlisted in the USMC in April 1942 and was sent to Quantico, VA, for his OCS training. He joined the 2nd Mar. Div. in New Zealand; from there he saw action in Tarawa, Tinian, Okinawa, and in Saipan received the Bronze Star Citation for his effort in defeating the Last Bonsai Attack on the 3rd Bn., 10th Marines.

He was separated from the Corps. in January 1946 as 1st lieutenant; rising to lieutenant colonel in inactive Reserves.

Married; has one son, James J. Jr.; and upon re-entering civilian life, was personnel executive for a machine tool company for over 20 years. In the late 60's he returned to school at the University of Massachusetts at Amherst where he received his masters degree in education. He then taught for over 19 years in the Amherst school system. He and his wife, Nancy Selenko have been ardent supporters of Mary and Don Chappell who were dedicated to encouraging continual camaraderie by so competently spearheading the 3rd Bn., 10th Marines, 2nd Div. reunions which were held in DuBuque, IA.

DENARD S. PRYOR JR., born Oct. 9, 1924. Enlisted in the USMC Oct. 13, 1941. Was assigned to HQ Co., Amphibious Corp., Pacific Fleet, Camp Elliott, Co. B, 2nd Pioneer Bn., August 1942-December 1945. Was sent overseas from Sept. 1, 1942-December 1945. Co. B Pioneers changed to E-2-18 in New Zealand in 1943.

Discharged Oct. 13, 1945, with the rank of private first class. Received the Presidential Unit Citation.

Married Doris; has three children: Patricia, Ronald and Kelvin; six grandchildren and six great-grandchildren. Retired from Moore Business Forms, Inc. after 39 1/2 years. Received the rank of Knight Commander, Court of Honor in the Scottish Rite. Now does lodge work and yard and gardening work.

EDEN A. RANEY, born April 8, 1917. Enlisted July 7, 1941; attended boot camp at San Diego, CA; was assigned to 2nd Eng., Co. A, Camp Elliott, CA, until Oct. 1941 when he was transferred to Eng. Bn., Co. A, to Pearl Harbor; back to San Diego; to Solomons, Aug. 7, 1942; to New Zealand, Feb. 1943; Tarawa, November 1943; to Hawaii, November 1943; camp Tarawa to Saipan, June 15, 1944; to Tinian, Aug. 1944; Mariannas secured, Aug.1944; back to the States.

Landed in San Francisco; trained to San Diego; then 30 day leave furlough; to Camp LeJeune, NC. Boarded troop train for San Diego, April 4, 1945, for San Diego, then transported to Guam. Landed in Guam April 23, 1945.

Joined Co. A, 11th Marines and in July started training for assault on Japan, landing Sept.

15, 1945. Left Flank Yokohama Harbor and was in Demo Flame Thrower Squad 43 and 44 and would have been at Japan Landing. Came home from Guam and discharged Nov. 7, 1945, San Diego, CA.

GERALD J. RAPPOPORT, born Aug. 25, 1925, New York, NY. Joined the Marine Corps.; boot camp at MCBSD; Scouts & Sniper School at Jaques Farm; and then 2nd Mar. Div. Communication School, Wellington, New Zealand. Placed in Hq. 3-8.

He saw combat action on Tarawa, Saipan, Tinian and Okinawa. Received Purple Heart for grenade wound in Saipan. Added a star for a sniper bullet wound the last day of enemy action in the Pacific. He finished his tour of duty in Nagasaki, Japan and was separated from the Corps. in January 1946.

Married in June 1948 and has two children, Bruce and Diane. From 1948-58 he was a development builder. A career change in 1960 brought him into the entertainment business as president of International Film Exchange Ltd. For more than 30 years of extensive travel behind the "Iron Curtain" he represented American motion pictures. His company was the main cultural exchange organization that kept the doors open between United States, the Soviet Union and Eastern Europe. Retired in 1992, he keeps active with different organizations, still in uniform with the Coast Guard Auxiliary, United States Power Squadron and the Marine Corps. League. He and his wife Beulah, reside in Southampton, NY.

DONALD L. RIEB enlisted in the USMC Jan. 8, 1958, and became the 4th member of his family to be a marine. After boot camp at Parris Island, SC, he was assigned to India Co., 3rd Bn., 6th Marines, and shipped out in May 1958 on the USS *Chilton*. The 3rd Bn., 6th Marines, was later incorporated into the 2nd expeditionary service force. After a three month hospitalization, he was returned State side and assigned to Co. F, 2nd Bn., 6th Marines, Camp LeJeune, NC.

Graduated from NCOS in 1960 and was assigned to the Fleet Marine Force aboard the carrier USS *Boxer*. He was separated from service on Jan. 7, 1961, as a lance corporal, but remained in the ready Reserve until 1964. Received the Armed Forces Expeditionary Service Medal, Good Conduct Medal and National Defense Medal.

Married Carol Patterson on Nov. 19, 1961, and has two children, Scott and Allison. He graduated from the State University of New York with a BS degree and a masters degree from L.I. University in Community Mental Health. Presently, executive director of Aid to the Developmentally Disabled, Inc. (ADD), an agency providing residential and clinical services for those with mental retardation and chronic psychiatric disabilities. He and his wife have one grandchild, Carlie, and reside in East Patchogue, LI, NY.

LAWRENCE H. ROANE JR., born December 1933 in Danville, VA. Graduated Plt. 358, 5th Recruit Tng. Bn., Parris Island. Assigned operational communications MOS and served with shore fire control party 3rd Bn., 6th Marines. Team Chief TACP 1st Bn., 1st Marines in Korea and Camp Fendleton. Was honorably discharged a Sergeant in 1956.

From 1956-60 was a student at North Carolina State University. At the invitation of CMC returned to active duty 1961 and served with Btry. H, 3rd Bn., 10th Marines, and supported 2nd Bn. 6th Marines during Cuban Crisis 1962. Served two tours as a drill instructor at Parris Island, two tours of Inspector-Instructor duty, Iowa and California and joint service duty with U.S. Army Strategic Communications Command, Okinawa. Units served with in the 3rd Marine Div., 1st Communication Co. (Provisional) HQ Bn., 1st Amphibious Tractor Bn., 1st Bn., 3rd Marines, 3rd Engr. and 3rd Recon. Bn. (twice). Served with the 1st and 3rd Marine Aircraft Wings and during Vietnam served 34 months in country on three tours 1964, 1967-69 and 1970-71. Transferred to the Fleet Reserve in December 1980.

Graduated from Moorpark College and California State University Northridge. Worked for the Department of Agriculture Forest Service, Kaniksu National Forest Idaho, Angeles and Los Padres National Forest in California and retired from the U.S. Postal Service. Is a life member of the 1st, 2nd and 3rd Mar. Div. Assoc. and a member of the Parris Island Chapter of the Marine Corps. DI Association, South Carolina Chapter 1st Mar. Div. Assoc., VFW, AMVETS, BPOE and Wolf Pack Club.

ROBERT H. ROGERS, born in Geneva, NY, in 1921. Educated in the Geneva schools and Hobart College, prior to full time active duty near the end of his junior college year.

Enlisted in USMCR June 1940. Attended officer training in the summers of 1940 and 1941, after freshman and sophomore college years at Hobart College. Volunteered for active duty starting in April 1942 to attend Basic School at Philadelphia with a commission as a 2nd lieutenant. After graduation in July, assignment was to the 3rd Marines, Camp LeJeune. The 3rd Marines replaced the 8th Marines on Samoa in September with his transfer to F-2-8 coming soon thereafter. The remainder of his overseas duty was with the 8th Marines as a rifle platoon leader on Guadalcanal and company commander of E-2-8 for Tarawa, Saipan, Tinian and Okinawa.

Rotation to stateside duty at Camp LeJeune came Aug. 1, 1945. Relieved from active duty in Dec. 1945. Decorations were the Purple Heart (Guadalcanal), the Silver Star, and Bronze Star.

Returned to Hobart College in January 1946 for completion of his degree in chemistry. Graduate studies followed at Syracuse University and University of Michigan. Served after 1945 in the Stand-by Reserve until retirement in 1959 as a colonel. Summer reserve training was at Camp LeJeune, Quantico, Little Creek, VA, and Fort McClellan's Atomic Warfare School.

Civilian accomplishments included lacrosse All-American 1946, participant in the North-South All Star Lacrosse game, Geneva Hall Of Fame for Lacrosse, Board of Directors of Geneva Chamber Of Commerce and YMCA Of Geneva. His post war years occupations were chemist for Dupont, Newburgh, NY, and a family general insurance business in Geneva, NY, with retirement in November 1994. He and his wife, Pamela Milner, were married in 1953. They have three children and two granddaughters.

PETER J. RONDERO, born Jan. 18, 1926, Holtsville, CA. Married Cora June 13, 1948, and have three grown children and eight grandchildren. Cora is retired from the Pacific-Telephone Co. and he is retired from the U.S. Postal Service.

He enlisted in the USMC at San Francisco, CA, Oct. 17, 1943; graduated from boot camp, Plt. 1058, MCRD, San Diego, CA. Volunteered for the Marine Raider Battalions in January 1944, right out of boot camp. The Marine Raider Battalions were disbanded in January 1945.

Did occupation duty in Japan. The 5th Marine Div. desolved and the troops were transferred to the 2nd Marine Division. Received the Commendation Medal w/V (Iwo Jima), Purple Heart, Asiatic-Pacific Medal w/star (Iwo Jima), American Defends Ribbon, Occupation of Japan Medal, WWII Victory Medal, Good Conduct Medal, Korean War Medal w/4 Battle Stars, UN Service Medal, Korean Presidential Unit Citation, 2nd Commendation Medal w/V and USN Presidential Unit Citation w/5 stars. Was discharged in March 1949 from WWII active duty.

Enlisted in the 12th Naval District USMCR, San Francisco, CA, as corporal in weapons company, March 2, 1949. Called to active duty for the Korean Conflict on Aug. 1, 1950. Made sergeant while in Korea. Came home on points and was discharged from USMCR in March 1952.

Resumed his work in the Oakland Post Office. Retired in 1950 on disability. Life member of the 2nd Marine Div. Assoc.

GERALD E. ROSS, born Dec. 21, 1924. Enlisted Sept. 19, 1941, H-2-8, mortar platoon, Camp Elliott, San Diego, CA.

Went overseas Jan. 6, 1942, to American Samoa for 10 months then to Guadalcanal Nov. 4, 1942; to New Zealand, Feb. 17, 1943; to Tarawa and was in the spearhead invasion and was wounded ; then to Hawaii for more training; then to Saipan and was wounded on the first

day; shipped to Hawaii for two months then to the States to Seattle Naval Hospital, 50 miles from his home. He was there for 10 months and got married.

Discharged in March 1945 to the veterans hospital in Portland, OR, for more than a year for therapy. Received Bronze Star, two Presidential Unit Citations, two Purple Hearts and many more.

He became a logger for four years then went into construction, ready mix concrete, sand and gravel and road construction. Retired in 1981. Has spent 54 years with his wonderful wife, Betty Jo, and has two sons, Vernon Leroy and David Lynn; and four grandsons, three granddaughters and five great-grandchildren to date. He now resides in Maryville, WA.

EDWARD JOSEPH ROWLAND, born March 19, 1922. Enlisted Oct. 3, 1942; was assigned to New Zealand; Saipan; and promoted to sergeant before going on to Tinian. Then went to Okinawa in 1945; Iheya Shima, Aguna Jima, 2nd Marine Div., B-1-8-C-1-18, HQ 1-8.

Discharged on Oct. 10, 1945, with the rank of sergeant. Received the Purple Heart, WWII Victory Medal and Letter of Commendation.

Married Carita Strauch and has three children: Thomas, Carita and Roy; and four grandchildren: Jennifer, Eric, Alec and Mark.

Worked for Bethlem Steel, Baltimore, MD; O.H. Furnace, 1972, furnace man and pulpit operator basic oxygen furnace.

WILLIAM C. SALTZER, born in Orange, NJ; enlisted Nov. 21, 1943, his 18th birthday, the day F-2-2 hit Tarawa. Joined up with the 2nd Div. as a replacement during the Saipan and Tinian operation. Between training, patrols, battalion and division sweeps, was sent to Japanese Language School at Division HQ.

After an exciting side trip to Okinawa he went back to dear old Saipan; then on to Japan and occupation duty; the language school turned out to be good preparation for same. Being the only interpreter left in the battalion he got a lot of exposure: the first was in charge of cleaning out the benjo (head) at Nagasaki; then on to more exotic venues like Kanoya, Shibushi, Iwagawa and Sasebo.

Back to the States as part of the 5th Div.; got his corporal stripes; and discharged in March 1946 at Bainbridge.

Graduated law school from Boston University; admitted to bar in Massachusetts; and commissioned 2nd lieutenant, Army ROTC, 1953. Married in 1951 and has four children and five grandchildren. After some 30 years in various contract law and practice he retired in 1990 and enjoying the boon docks in Maine.

JOHN L. SALZANO SR, born Aug. 28, 1921 and enlisted in the service in the summer of 1942. Sworn in at New York City Sept. 19, 1942 and went to boot camp at Parris Island, SC followed by Camp Lejeune and New River, NC. While on leave he married Jennie and had a full-scale Marine wedding.

Boarded ship at Norfolk, VA for Hawaiian Islands; picked up survivors of Tarawa Campaign and spent a few days in Honolulu then one to Hilo, Camp Tarawa and Saipan. On D+2 the Japanese hit their Co. (B-1-6) where he was wounded and taken to a hospital ship then Aiea Naval Hospital where President Roosevelt came and visited the wounded.

Memorable experience was when he was six to seven thousand miles from home and was visited in the hospital by his younger brother, Philip, and a friend who were on their way to help in the landing of MacArthur at Leyte Gulf in the Philippines. Philip was in the Navy and served on LST 608.

Recuperated at Long Beach Naval Hospital where he met Harry James, Betty Grable, Hedy Lamar, Gloria DeHaven, George Brent, Paul Lukas, Eric Blore. From there to St. Albans Hospital where he met and talked to Jackie Gleason. Discharged from Philadelphia Naval Hospital April 5, 1945.

Has four children: Alexis, John Jr., Donna and Michael; eight grandchildren: Paul Carola, Nicole Freemont, Jennifer Carola, Kimberly Salzano, Patrick Louise, Jenna Louise, Joanna Carola and John Carola. His wife Jennie passed away Oct. 1, 1995. Worked 52 years as tool and diemaker supervisor for Teledyne and is now retired.

FREDERICK A. SAUER JR. completed boot camp at MCRD, Parris Island, SC, in 1947 as a member of Plt. 41 and Plt. 47 after a brief stint in the hospital. After recruit training, he was assigned to E.E. & R.M. School at Great Lakes NTS. After completion of the school he was assigned to the guard company for duty as shore patrolman. In 1948 he was transferred to the 2nd Div. FMF and attached to the 2nd Bn., 2nd Regt. where he was assigned as driver/orderly for the regimental commander, Col. Randall M. Victory.

When the regiment deployed with the 6th Task Fleet, he was detailed as orderly and chauffeur for the commander, Carrier Div. Adm. Forrest P. Sherman.

He was discharged March 10, 1950, as a private first class and returned to Kalamazoo, MI where he completed undergraduate school and was awarded a BA degree from Albion and Kalamazoo Colleges. He next attended Detroit College of Law and was awarded an LL.B. & J.D. degree. He entered upon the practice of law in Kalamazoo. In 1983 he became interested in the USCG and was commissioned a lieutenant commander (O-4) assuming the duties of District Legal Officer and USCG Academy Selection Officer as well as skippering a CG patrol vessel doing SAR and patrols on Lake Michigan. In 1993 he was commissioned as a lieutenant colonel (O-5) in the Michigan State Defense Force and assigned as the commanding officer of the 1st Bn., 6th Regt. in which post he presently serves.

Married to Ann Sauer and has three children: Stephen, a CPA in Atlanta, GA, Stephanie, in business and resident of Jamaica, and Mark, a USN lieutenant serving aboard USS *Spruance* and resident of Jacksonville, FL. He and Ann reside in Kalamazoo, MI.

MICHAEL B. SCAVONE, born Nov. 3, 1924. Enlisted in February 1942 and was assigned to Co. I, 3rd Bn., 8th Marines. Discharged in May 1946 with the rank of staff sergeant. Married Roberta Scavone (now deceased).

GEORGE HAROLD SCHNELLE, born May 28, 1919. Enlisted in the USMC, 2nd Div., Oct. 8, 1940. Was assigned to Pago, American Samoa, Guadalcanal, Wellington, NZ; and participated in action against the enemy on Gua-dalcanal Nov. 4, 1942-Jan. 31, 1943.

Discharged Oct. 24, 1944, with the rank of corporal. Received the Honorable Service Button.

Married Gloria Schnelle and has two children, Pricilla Best (deceased) and Donna Robert; and four grandchildren: Drucilla Best, Kimberly Tang and Jason and Derek Robert. Worked as a plumber and pipefitter and retired with 50 years of service. He passed away December 6, 1997.

BRUCE J. SEWARD, born July 24, 1923. Enlisted Nov. 10, 1942; was assigned to med. tanks; was tank commander; served in the Pacific area July 30, 1943-Dec. 23, 1945; and participated at Tarawa, Gilberts Saipan, Tinian, Mariannas, Okinawa and Ryukyy Islands. Entered Nagasaki the day after the bomb was dropped. Served in cleanup, in the hospitals, etc.

Discharged Jan. 10, 1946, with the rank of

corporal. Received the Purple Heart (Saipan, July 10, 1944), Good Conduct and other medals and battle stars.

Married Nora Jean; has four children: Bonita (deceased), Gale, Vicki and Craig; 10 grandchildren; and seven great-grandchildren. Retired from Illinois Bell Telephone co; was past master of Masonic Order, Ansar Shrine; member of U.S. Air National Guard and U.S. Air Force in Korea in 1951. Was lieutenant and right guide on military type drill team; shrine national drill champ, nine out of 12 years, coast to coast.

JOHN M. SHEEHY, born July 14, 1917, in Montana. He was raised on his parents ranch in the Bear Paw Mountains at Big Sandy, MT. He left Montana for boot camp in San Diego on July 4, 1941. After boot camp he was assigned to the 2nd Engr. Bn. at Camp Elliott. In October 1941 his battalion went to Pearl Harbor, there he was helping to build a camp when the Japanese bombed Pearl Harbor.

His next assignment was Guadalcanal, the Hebrides, New Zealand and Tarawa; then back to Hawaii; to Saipan and Tinian.

Returned to the States in September 1944; then to San Francisco for six months. He was discharged on points May 16, 1945, and returned to his parents ranch in Montana. Married Laura April 28, 1951, and raised one son and two daughters. They have five grandchildren. He is still ranching his Montana Ranch.

CHESTER SHOAF, born Aug. 13, 1926. Enlisted in August 1943; attended boot camp at San Diego, Plt. 914 in 1943; joined 2nd Marine Div., G-2-6; and transferred to Hawaii in January 1944, assigned to machine gun platoon.

Discharged Jan. 8, 1946, with the rank of corporal. Received the Purple Heart (Saipan, June 15, 1944).

Memorable experiences were the 2nd wave landing at Saipan, Tinian and Okinawa; and the Occupation of Nagasaki, Japan.

Married Nancy and has four children: Chester Jr., Karen, Steve and Jeff. Works in management for AT&T.

HARRY SHORTWAY JR., born March 18, 1938. Enlisted March 28, 1956; was assigned to the 8th Marines, 1st Bn. Weapons and 2nd Bn.

Weapons, 1956-58; Parris Island, March 28, 1956; Plt. 113, 3rd Bn.

Discharged March 28, 1958, with the rank of private first class.

Married Fawn and has seven children and 11 grandchildren. Worked as a police officer, Ridgewood, NJ, 38 years; and now a detective sergeant. Played baseball, basketball and football for the 8th Marines, 1956-57.

DAVID L. SIMMONS, born Dec. 4, 1943. Enlisted April 8, 1968; served as administration chief, 2nd Bn., 2nd ITR, Camp Pendleton, CA. Discharged with the rate of E-3.

Married Laura and has two children, Sean and Kelly. Works as a special effects coordinator for movies and television.

JOHN SLAUGHTER JR., born Nov. 15, 1925. Enlisted Nov. 30, 1942; assigned to NSNTS San Diego, CA; USNH, San Diego, CA, Hospital Corps. School; HSNH Puget Sound, Washington. Transferred to Medical Field Service School, Camp Elliott, CA.; 23rd Replacement, BNTC, Camp Elliott, CA; 2nd Ser. Bn., 3rd Mar. Div., FMF in the field, at Tarawa, Saipan and Tinian. Back to USNH Medical Center, Bethseda, MD; called back in Korean War on recruiting duty, downtown Dallas for 14 months. Placed in USNR at USNS, Orange, TX. Placed on inactive duty and moved back to Dallas, TX, in October 1951. Went to Watchmaking School, Houston School of Harology and Tyler commercial College on GI Bill, receiving 63 hours of business.

Stayed in the USNR until discharge with the rank of pharmacist mate 1/c. Received the Pacific Theater Ribbon w/3 Battle Stars, Good Conduct Medal, American Theater Ribbon, WWII Victory Medal, Presidential Unit Citation, Military Merit Medal and Purple Heart.

Divorced in 1982; has four children: John, Patricia, Steven and Leslie; and four grandchildren. He is a certified master watchmaker and jeweler. He has 40 years experience in owning a jewelry store and now has a store in Breckenridge, TX, at the age of 71. He specializes in gold pocket watches; has 200 in stock, the oldest made in 1601 (key wound). He has had a wonderful life and would not take anything for his experiences in WWII, serving the 2nd Mar. Div.

SCOTT SLAUGHTER SMITH, born March 9, 1926. Enlisted Oct. 12, 1942, at San Francisco, CA. Was stationed at MCRD San Diego Base; Camp Elliott; Camp Mathews; assigned to E-2-2, New Zealand, Tarawa, Hawaii, Saipan and Okinawa, as a M1 rifleman (sharpshooter), scout and pointman

Discharged Nov. 1, 1945, San Diego, CA, with the rank of private first class. Received the Bronze Star, Purple Heart, Presidential Unit Citation, Combat, Asiatic-Pacific, WWII Victory, Good Conduct.

Memorable experiences include serving in WWII as a U.S. Marine and making it out alive from the Pacific; last, but not least, coming home!

Married Kathleen; has four children: Michael, Susan, Stephen and Mark; and tow grandchildren, Tammy and John. Civilian activity includes sheriff, security police superintendent, motion picture and television studio policeman, celebrities bodyguard and author, writer and self published.

FRANZ SONI, born April 26, 1947. Enlisted July 22, 1964, I-3-6. He was paralyzed in combat during the Dominican Republic Intervention on April 30, 1965, as part of the initial landing team.

Discharged Oct. 31, 1965, with the rank of private first class. Retired from the USMC. Received the Purple Heart, Armed Forces Expeditionary, National Defense and Good Conduct Medals.

Graduated Bergan Community College, degree in accounting; two degrees from Ramapo College of New Jersey, business administration and history. Worked as an accountant for H.M. Pitman Co., retiring in 1976. Member of Eastern Paralyzed Veterans Assoc., DAV, 2nd Mar. Div. Assoc., Paralyzed Veterans Assoc. and VFW.

Memorable experiences include becoming a U.S. Citizen and traveling to 38 countries; and being a marine Semper Fi and thanks to all Navy Corpsmen who served with the grunts. You're all heroes!

BERTRAND L. SPOONER JR. enlisted in the USMC at Manchester, NJ, Dec. 7, 1942, along with six other enlisted, the seven "Pearl Harbor Avengers." After serving with the 13th Replacement Bn., at British Samoa, and New Caledonia he entered the 2nd Marine Div. in New Zealand in July 1943. With Weapons Co., 6th Marines, he participated in action at Tarawa, Saipan, Tinian and Okinawa. Served with the same company in the Occupation of Nagasaki, Japan. Discharged Dec. 6, 1945.

Employee of the federal government. Started as a clerk in the Veterans Administration Regional Office, Providence, RI. was chief of receipt and dispatch unit; chief, mail section, and assistant chief data processing department. After 17 years with the VA he transferred to the Dept. of Navy at Quonset Point, RI. He was EMA supervisor, then project planner with the data processing department. After retiring from the government service he moved back to New Hampshire. In Northfield, NJ, he owned and operated an antique business, and a out of print and rare book business. In 1987 he sold the Clisby Homestead and moved to Danbury, NJ. He still handles books as a hobby, but has pretty much given up antiques.

Married Virginia I. Bennett, when he returned to New Hampshire in 1945. They have eight children, four boys and four girls. During the Vietnam War his two sons were in the service, one in the Air Force and one with the 1st Marine Div. Three grandsons served in the USMC; two are still in the service; and one grandson and one granddaughter served in the USAF.

ROSS E. STAUFFER, born in Newark, NJ in 1924. After serving a year in the U.S. Maritime Service, with a trip to Casablanca, he enlisted in the Marine Corps. in 1943. After boot camp at Parris Island, SC, he was retained there in the Maintenance Co. because of his experience as an architectural draftsman. Pleading with his commanding officer for overseas duty, he was soon released for Topographical Drafting School, Camp LeJeune; then on to Camp Pendleton; and finally shipped out to join the 2nd Mar. Div. on Saipan; and from there he left for the action in Okinawa.

Shortly after the Japanese surrender, the 2nd Div. landed on the shores of Nagasaki, Japan. He was a member of the Intelligence Section, Hq. Co., 1st Bn., 6th Marines; with the goal of helping to disarm a sector of Kyushu that included the Island of Sekito.

He was separated from the Corps. in May 1946 at the Great Lakes Naval Training Center. He attended school, then became a mechanical design engineer during a career with the U.S. Army Signal Corps. as a Federal employee at Fort Monmouth, NJ. In 1967 he was sent to Vietnam as a scientific consultant where he earned a Commendation Award for attending a search and destroy mission as an observer to find mechanical problems with Signal Corps. equipment.

After his federal retirement in 1972 he worked as a consultant to private companies one of which sent him to Egypt for two years to help supervise the erection of a cement plant in Suez that he helped design. Then finally, permanent retirement in 1985 to Florida where he actively pursues medals in the Senior Olympic Games and holds a county record for the 1,500 meter Official Race Walk. He resides with his wife, Gerta. He has three children, six grandchildren, and two great-granddaughters.

MERRILL M. STEEB, born July 31, 1924, Buchanan County. Educated at St. Joseph Jun-

ior college, Northwest State University and University of Kansas (LL.B. and J.D.). Married April 28, 1949, to Glenrose J. Summers. They have two daughters. Practiced law for 20 years in St. Joseph. Admitted to all Missouri state courts, federal court, U.S. Supreme Court and tax court.

Served in USMC, WWII; U.S. Army, Korean War; and retired from U.S. Air Force Reserve with rank of lieutenant colonel, Judge Advocate General's department. Twice awarded the Purple Heart for wounds in the Pacific Theater, 1941-45.

Joined Co. A, Barracks 29 at MCB, San Diego, June 1941; then to Camp Elliott; then sailed for Samoa on the USS *Lurline*.

Member of the VFW, American Legion, Elks, Masonic bodies and Moila Temple, Eagles, Marine Corps League, St. Joseph Rifle and Pistol Club. Served two years as magistrate. Elected circuit judge in 1976 and 1982.

EARL STOUT, born in 1923, at Long Beach, CA; was raised in Southern California. He joined the Navy in 1942 and after boot camp in San Diego was sent to the new DD-518 Destroyer, USS *Brownson* at the Brooklyn Navy Yard where he helped put it in commission and as one of its first crew.

After duty in the North Atlantic and the Cuba area and to North Africa and Casablanca, he was sent to Hospital Corps School, Virginia and then duty at NAS Corpus Christie, TX. After training there, duty at FMF, Camp Elliott was next. This was followed by the 2nd Regt., 2nd Div. at Camp Tarawa and with the 1st Bn. They trained in rubber boats to enable them to sneak in to Saipan minus D-day and at night. Most of the men were from Tarawa and Guadalcanal, and were all the best men and teachers you could get. They helped them all to have a better edge on getting home and were the best in the world to be with!!!

Received the Navy Cross and the Purple Heart on Saipan and went on to Tinian and then Okinawa, then returned to Saipan and then patrolled and fought the Japanese who led by Capt. OBA, who later gave up years after the last battle.

After duty with the 2nd Marines, Stout did two years at NAS Alameda in Aviation Medicine. This was also the start of a long duty tour with a young lady named Daylene Gill, married in 1946, resulting in two boys and one girl. Stout now lives in Porterville, CA, and after 50 years, still runs his cattle ranch.

HENRY ALFRED SULTENFUSS, born to Frank and Pauline Kenuppen Sultenfuss, both from Texas Pioneer families May 8, 1916, at

Boenne, Kendall County, TX, one of eight sons and one daughter.

Enlisted at Houston, TX, Jan. 4, 1942, received training at San Diego, CA, placed on Co. B, 2nd Pioneer Bn., designation changed to Co. E, 2nd Bn., Nov. 12, 1942. Saw action at Tarawa, Saipan, Tinian and Okinawa from Sept. 1, 1942, through June 28, 1945. Honorably discharged Sept. 15, 1945, San Diego, CA, as staff sergeant.

Worked as a horse wrangler throughout Texas, traveled with the World's Champion Rodeo over the U.S., did construction jobs building highways and dams, mainly 1H10 and Canyon Lake Dam on the Guadeloupe River.

Retired to the hill country, Center Point, TX, where he passed away in the veterans hospital, Kenville, TX. He was never married.

W. EUGENE SWEENEY enlisted in the U.S. Marine Corps Reserve in Oct. 1947 while attending high school in Rochester, NY. His reserve unit was activated for duty during the Korean War by President Truman in Aug. 1950 and served as a communications/radio instructor and administrative clerk with B-1-6 at Camp LeJeune.

In September 1951 Sgt. Sweeney spent six months on a Med Cruise with the 6th Marines making ports of call in N. Africa, France, Italy, Sicily, Sardina, Malta, Crete and Greece. After promotion to staff sergeant he became an assistant to the Battalion Legal Officer prior to his release from active duty in 1952.

In civilian life he was employed 35 years with the Rochester Coca-Cola Bottling Company retiring in 1991 as Director of Customer Relations. He organized reunions for Rochester's Marine Reserve unit in 1975, 1985 and 1990. He is a life member of the 2nd Marine Div. Assoc. and served as president of Florida Chapter SMDA from 1996-98. He now resides with his wife Lorraine in Port St. Lucie, FL.

CHESTER J. SZECH was born in North Chicago, IL, on June 20, 1925. He attended Waukegan Township High School and enlisted in the Navy upon graduation in 1943. He went to boot camp in Farragut, ID, and then to San Diego, CA, where he received training as a hospital corpsman. He was assigned to HQs Co-3-6 and landed on Saipan on June 15th. He went to Tinian, Okinawa, and Nagasaki.

He received a Bronze Star for actions on

Saipan and was discharged on Dec. 13, 1945. He worked in construction before becoming a teacher in North Chicago. He taught for 20 years and then returned to construction work. He retired in 1987.

He has three children: Andrew, Mary, and John; four grandchildren: Clint, Marc, Alan, and Laura; and two great-grandchildren: Charlotte and Kate. His daughter Rachel died in 1992. He lives with his wife, Vicki, in Green Oaks, IL.

FRED E. SZYPULSKI, born June 1, 1924, Milwaukee, WI, to Martin C. and Caroline Szypulski. He was 17 when he enlisted in the USMC on Jan. 17, 1942. Completed basic training at MCB Recruit Depot, San Diego, CA. He attended Telephone School. After graduation he was assigned to H&S Btry., 2nd Spl. Wpns. Bn. at Camp Elliott. He received a belated birthday present, he was promoted to private first class.

In early November 1942, scuttle-butt had it that their unit was being shipped to Guadalcanal. They boarded the USS *President Monroe*, however they ended up at the docks of Wellington, New Zealand. Their camp site was set up at Titahi Bay. Their unit designation was changed to HQ Co., 2nd Spl. Wpns. In early 1943 they shipped out on the USATS Torrens to Hilo, HI. They were bivovaced at Camp POW and Camp Tarawa. Once again their unit designation was changed to HQ Co., Sept. Inf. Bn.

In May 1944 they boarded the USS *Neville* to Honolulu for a short stay. Once again their unit designation was changed to HQ Co., 1st Bn., 29th Marines, but still attached to the 2nd Div. They remained aboard until the end of May and set sail once again. Upon awakening one dark early morning to discover that they were anchored in an island lagoon. On the horizon he could see what seemed to be hundreds of ships. The island they were at was Eniwetok Atoll. None of them had to be told that something big was about to take place.

He celebrated his 20th birthday aboard ship, the cook brought him a small piece of cake, but he was soon to find out that he was to receive another much greater belated birthday present. On the morning of June 15, 1944, after what seemed like months aboard ship, they found themselves at the island shores of Saipan. The good side of his first conflict with their enemy was that he lived to tell about it and that he was promoted to corporal during the battle. In September 1944 they knew what their next destination would be, before they boarded the Alcoa Polaris. Their destination was Guadalcanal to join up with the rest of the 1st Bn., 29th Marines. For some of them, their stay on Guadalcanal would be a short one.

In early November 1944 they boarded the USS *Randall*, a two stacker, for San Diego, CA. In mid December 1944 he received his first 30-day leave in almost three years. He married his high school sweetheart, Josephine Duffy, and more than 50 years later, they are still together. The corps. gave him a nice wedding present. Instead of reporting to Camp Pendleton, CA, after his leave was up, he was directed to report to Great Lakes Naval Base for duty. Six months later he reported to Camp Pendleton in Oceanside, CA. Prior to shipping out again, during some field maneuvers, he was bitten or stung by some unknown critter. He was taken to Santa Margarita Ranch Hospital at camp, then to Long Beach naval, and ultimately Great Lakes Naval Hospital, from which he was discharged from the USMC on Dec. 22, 1945. He never did find out what poisoned his system.

Re-enlisted in the USMC, serving in the 9th Marine Reserve District. Was recalled to active duty in August 1950. He was to report to Camp LeJeune, NC. He was assigned to the 2nd Signal Co. as an instructor. He was discharged from active duty in April 1951.

He calls the above recollections "The Odyssey of the 2nd Spl. Wpns. Bn." Some may label their unit as a bastard outfit, but history did show that their combat unit did vindicate it's self. Corespondent, Robert Sherrod, wrote an article about the 1st Bn., 6th Marines, on Saipan, "their casualties ran 20% higher, but none of them approached the rather appalling losses incurred by an extra heroic 1st Bn., 29th Marines, that faced the fearsome task of taking the 1,554 foot peak of Mt. Tapotchau, the highest point on Saipan. These men never faltered in their assignment. Only about 200 were left where the battle ended."

He worked for Perlick Brass Co. as a machinist for 10 years; then in 1956 he changed jobs and went to work for General Motors, Delco electronics, Oak Crest, WI, as a supervisor. In the early 1970s he was transferred to guide division, Anderson, IN, until 1982 and he retired after 25 years of service. He and Josephine have five children: Fred, Michael (died of cancer), Nancy, Jeff and Lori; six grandchildren: Paul, David, Vicki, Shelli, Rachel and Bridget. They also have one great-grandson, Jay.

DONALD E. TESIERO, born Jan. 28, 1925, Amsterdam, NY, the son of James and Christine Efland Tesiero. They gave five sons to fight for their country: Roy, Jim and Dick were USN; Jack, U.S. Army; Don, USMC; and a brother-in-law, USAF.

He enlisted Jan. 18, 1943; received honorable discharge March 30, 1946. Was sent to Parris Island, Camp LeJeune, San Diego, Marshalls, Saipan, Tinian, Okinawa, Aguma Shima, Iheya Shima, Nagasaki and Sasabo, Japan. Was wounded on Saipan.

Aside from war stores, he believes his most memorable moment was entering Nagasaki with the first troops ashore. the hills were covered with white flags and loud speakers were blasting, not to fear, the Marines will not harm you, and go back to your homes or come for help On the streets were just old people and some children. It was a terrible scene, the people were covered with burns, flesh like melted wax, eyes in awful condition. The total area of destruction was about one-third of the city. He thought back about battle ship row, Pearl Harbor and thought how sad war was.

Discharged March 30, 1946, with the rank of corporal. Received the WWII Victory Medal, American Campaign Medal, Asiatic-Pacific Campaign Medal, USMC Good Conduct Medal, Occupation of Japan, Asiatic Campaign Ribbon w/2 stars, Presidential Citation and Bronze Star.

He owes a lot to USMC and his country. He was a high school dropout with do direction. When he returned home he was too proud to be a nobody. He went back and made up three years of high school and went on to get a BS degree in pharmacy. He later owned his own pharmacy and surgical shop. He proudly flies the U.S. and USMC flags at his country home. He married a wonderful woman, Janet Louise Long, Aug. 2, 1952, and has five great children: Donna (lawyer), Donald (lawyer) who married Kelly who graduated from FL Univ. (landscape architect), Thomas (pharmacist), Dawn (teacher) and James (physicist) who married Robbin who holds various degrees; and seven grandchildren: Janet Rose, Maria, Don, Susan, Lisa, Ronnie and Tommy. In their travels they covered Europe, Arctic and Antarctica, Australia, New Zealand and Russian in 1977.

MELVIN H. THOMAS, born March 24, 1925, in McGregor, TX; worked in Houston shipyard as an electric welder until enlistment in the USMC in March 1943. Attended boot camp, Plt. 220 in San Diego, CA. After combat conditioning and infantry training in Camp Elliott and Pendleton, departed San Diego with the 22nd Replacement Bn. Joined F-2-10 a 75 mm pack howitzer battery of the 2nd Mar. Div. in Paekakariki, New Zealand.

A brother, Bernie, had preceded him and was serving with B-1-2. He was later wounded when B-1-2 landed on Red Beach 1 during the Tarawa invasion.

After training in artillery, participated in action against the Japanese in the battles for Tarawa, Saipan, Tinian, Okinawa and Iheya Shima. Served three months in the occupation of Japan. Received Asiatic Pacific Medal w/4

Bronze Stars, Presidential Unit Citation w/3 Bronze Stars.

Taught basic gunnery at the U.S. Naval Academy during 1946 and 1947. Left the marines, attended Southern Technical Institute and the Institute of Radio Broadcasting and Engineering in Dallas, TX. Worked as free lance announcer and MC for record and live talent programs.

Reordered to active duty for the Korean conflict. After cold weather and combat readiness training at Tent Camp 2 in San Clemente, CA, embarked for Korea, dropping anchor in Pusan Harbor in 1950. Reported to B-1-11 of the 1st Mar. Div., an artillery battery commanded by Capt. Les Proctor, formerly of Austin, TX. Was assigned as scout sergeant, forward observer, serving 1951 on the front lines with the gallant men of F-2-5, and 40 days as artillery advisor to the KMC (Korean Marine Corps). Awarded Korean Service Medal w/4 Bronze Stars, Presidential Unit Citation w/2 Bronze Stars, Republic of Korea Presidential Unit w/ Bronze Star, Silver Star for conspicuous gallantry in bayonet charge against the North Koreans during 1951 action.

Rejoined the 2nd Mar. Div., served as gunnery sergeant of G-3-10 in Camp LeJeune, the Caribbean and the Mediterranean area. Received fourth and final honorable discharge in 1955.

After special training at Kelly AFB, TX, worked as system analyst on the B-52 bombing system. Accepted a position with the Federal Aviation Agency in 1960. After three years in San Juan, Puerto and three years in Miami, FL, was assigned to the Tulsa International Airport, remained in this position until retirement in 1978 after 34 years of government service.

After retirement, authored a book, *Boondocker Ballet*, a fast moving autobiography of what life is like on the front lines with a marine combat unit, and a tribute to the memorable and serviceability of the rawhide *Marine Boondocker*. Published by Dorrance Publishing Co Inc. 643 Smithfield St., Pittsburgh, PA. 15222.

Resides in Tulsa, OK, and has six children, eight grandchildren.

JOSEPH W. THOMPSON, born January 6, 1920, in Pierre, SD. He grew up on a ranch on the lower Brule Sioux Indian Reservation in South Dakota. He graduated from high school in 1939. On July 13, 1942, enlisted in the USMC at Minneapolis, MN, and attended boot camp in San Diego in Plt. 559, then to the Pacific area Jan. 19, 1943. He was in New Zealand with the 2nd Mar. Div., before participating in action at Tarawa and Saipan. He was detailed to Nagasaki after bombing and then to Hawaii and was honorably discharged from the Corps. as a chief cook on Dec. 23, 1943, at Great Lakes, IL, and arrived home to Pierre, SD, on Christmas Day.

Joe was a Native American, a member of the Lower Brule Sioux Tribe and was called "Chief" by his buddies in the Corps.

After his discharge, he attended college and then went in the cattle ranching business. Was a successful rancher until his death from cancer on March 18, 1995. Joe, aka "Jiggs" or "J.W." also loved horses and rodeo and participated in rodeos for many years. He is survived by his wife, Helen, of 57 years, three daughters, eight grandchildren and five great-grandchildren.

RAYMOND U. THOMPSON, born in Sandyville, IA, on April 3, 1929. After serving one year as an Iowa State guard cadet, he enlisted in the U.S. Army, and was given an honorable discharge on April 17, 1945, (under the minority act of 1921). On June 2, 1945, enlisted in the USMC at Omaha, NE. Was real proud that during boot training at Parris Island, SC, and because of prior training and knowledge, was chosen to be squad and later platoon leader and being able to complete boot training with that kind of honor as he had heard how tough and rigorous it was. For him it was a real snap as some of the older fellows were dropping out. He was so proud when they were issued the dress green uniforms after wearing the dungarees for so long, as it felt so good to be dressed up again, they were all promised their PFC stripe.

Then all hell broke loose on Oct. 22, 1945. He was stripped of all his uniforms and equipment and handed what they called their zoot suit along with $25.00 and told to go home to his mother and find his own way home because his mother needs them more than they do.

The Commandant of the USMC had ordered him to be undesirable discharged for fraudulently enlisting and not reporting that he had previous service in the Army, that he should have known the consequences of enlisting again. You bet he knew (he could have gotten his butt shot off); can you imagine what his recruiter would have done if he had told him, he would have kicked his butt all the way down the stairs and through the front door.

Married Dottie on Feb. 27, 1947, in Phoenix, AZ. They have three sons, one of which served two terms in Vietnam with the USMC, and two girls. Employed with Frye Mfg. Company from June 1947 until July 1, 1968; Farmers Mutual Hail Ins. Co., from July 1, 1968 until retirement on June 30, 1994. He was the operating engineer at both companies.

Member of the National Assoc. of Power Engineers as vice-president and education chairman; member of the American Legion, Post 165 at Indianola, IA; member of the Veteran of underage Military Service; also a member of Capitol City Baptist Church.

Ray and his wife Dottie have thirteen grandchildren, and two great-grandchildren. They reside in Des Moines, IA.

EDWARD J. TOMMASI, born April 11, 1920. Enlisted Nov. 22, 1939, trained at Parris Island. Sent to Philadelphia Navy Yard, then to Quantico, Bayonne Naval Base for two years; then to Hawaii; then to initial landing on Saipan, Tinian and Okinawa. Made a fake landing at Iwo Jima.

Was in the initial landing on Saipan, Tinian, Okinawa, Nagasaki, Kuamamoto and Sasebo. Returned to San Diego December 1945 and discharged at New London, CN, 1946. Awarded Combat Ribbons.

While on the Island of Tinian, cooked dinner for movie actress Betty Hutton. While on Saipan, met a priest and became good friends. He informed him some nuns had children in their care that were hungry, so he sent a truck with food to them as he was a mess sergeant.

When this priest came back to the US, he married him and his wife. This marriage lasted 49 years and nine months, she passed away March 16, 1996. They had two girls, Maureen Adams and Coleen Petroski, and one boy, Edward Tommasi Jr. Five grandchildren: John, Megan and Nickolas Tommasi, Katie and Julie Petroski.

JAMES E. TROY, born in Boston, MA, June 13, 1920. He enlisted in the Marine Corps on Nov. 10, 1942, and trained in boot camp at Parris Island. He then was assigned to the 5th Repl. Bn. at New River, NC and was sent overseas to British Somoa.

Upon completion of further training he was sent to Wellington, New Zealand and assigned to H&S 1st Bn., 10th Marines, 2nd Mar. Div. He participated in action against the enemy on Tarawa, Gilbert Islands; on Saipan and Tinian, Mariannas Islands; and at Okinawa, Shima, Ryukyu Islands from April 5, 1943, to Aug. 15, 1945. He was in the initial occupation of Nagasaki, Japan where he was assigned to duty as a provost sergeant. He was awarded the Navy Commendation by Gen. Roy S. Geiger for an operation against the enemy on Saipan where he volunteered to assist in establishing two essential observation posts on a reef 500 yards beyond the front lines, and aided in manning this post for six hours under constant observation by the enemy thereby materially aiding in destroying an enemy landing force.

Plt. Sgt. Troy was honorably discharged on Dec. 6, 1945. He returned to Boston, MA, and joined the Boston Police Department continuing a tradition of law enforcement in his family.

His father James J. Troy, a Boston Police Officer was shot and killed in the line of duty in 1930. He married Rita Lyons on Feb. 10, 1948, and they have five children: James Jr., Kevin, Edward, Rita Troy Scott and Deborah Troy DiBona. They have nine grandchildren: James, Devin, Edward and Eric Troy, Charlene and Jaclyn Troy, John and Jacqueline Scott and Amanda DiBona. He retired from the Boston Police Dept. after 25 years service with the rank of detective.

DONALD C. VANDERLINDEN, born June 11, 1924, in Shakopee, MN. The son of Lewis and Nellie Vanderlinden, he had four brothers and one sister. Enlisted in the USMC Sept. 3, 1941; boot camp in San Diego. Joined the 1st Mar. Div., went overseas, participated in the capture and defense of Guadalcanal and the consolidation of the Solomon Islands.

June 6, 1942, to May 30, 1943; June 6, 1945, to Oct. 31, 1945, Asiatic Pacific Area, Samoa, New Hebrides, Solomon Islands, New Zealand. Had Malaria and was in the hospital, when released joined with the 2nd Marines.

Honorably discharged and awarded the American Defense, WWII Victory, Asiatic-Pacific Theater, American Campaign, Battle Stars.

Employed with Fiberboard, Antioch, CA, plant as a printer April 2, 1946 through time of closure May 1, 1972; owned Van's TV repair.

Married to Adeline for 30 years; has two children and one stepson: Karen Tabler and Donald Jr. from previous marriage, step-son Dennis Sechrest; five grandchildren: Reina Belicha, Joel Caris, Lindsey Tabler, Vita and Amanda Sechrest. Don had a passion for old cars and owned a 1937 La Salle and 1923 Star. Deceased April 24, 1997.

ROY A. VERRET, born Jan. 5, 1923, in Bayou Chene, LA. Enlisted in the USMC July 13, 1941, in New Orleans, LA. Completed basic training at San Diego; assigned guard duty at North Island; then sent to 2nd Mar. Div. Attached to the 6th Regt., then to 8th Regt. Participated in action at Guadalcanal, South Solomon, Tarawa Atoll, Saipan, and Tinian in 1943-44. Participated in atomic test Bikini 1946. Recommended for Navy Cross June 17, 1944, wounded three times. Recommended for Silver Star.

Discharged July 13, 1947, awarded Rifle Marksman, Pistol Marksman, Special Military

Qualification Machine Gun Crewman, Good Conduct Medal four times.

Retired from Abex Corporation March 1990 after 39 years. Hobbies include reading western books, watching college football games.

Married Betty Cochran in 1946. They have two children, Pamela and Joseph who is also a Marine discharged; two grandchildren: Allyson and Susan Marie.

STEVE VICENA, born in 1916 in Panama, IL. He moved to Chicago in 1934 and enlisted from there in the USMC, Jan. 1942. He went through boot camp in San Diego, CA, where he was a member of the 114th Plt. After boot camp, he was sent to Camp Elliott and later to Linda Vista in California.

His unit sailed for Samoa in August of 1942 where he was stationed until sometime in 1944. From there they went to New Zealand. He saw action in Saipan, Tarawa and Tinian. He was in the 3rd Bn., K Co., 2nd Mar.

He will never forget the horror of Tarawa and the stench after the battle. He remembers a time on Saipan when he was cut off from his unit and came upon three of the enemy sitting together in a wooded area. It was there he acquired a hara-kiri knife and pistol.

He received a Purple Heart for wounds received on Saipan. The enemy threw a hand grenade and the shrapnel penetrated his helmet, sending him to a hospital in Guadalcanal.

Recently he went in to have an M.R.I. and the procedure had to be stopped because of the shrapnel in his head, so you see he still carries that part of the war with him.

He came back to the U.S. in 1945 and served out his enlistment as a drill instructor at Parris Island, SC.

In 1950, he was called up in the USMCR at Camp LeJeune, NC for one year, during the Korean conflict.

He currently lives in Panama, IL, with Wilma, his wife of fifty one years. They have two daughters, Lynnette and Sherri, and four grandchildren, Meghan, Erin, Hunter and Jack.

DANIEL A. VILLARIAL, enlisted in the USMC June 11, 1947 from Milwaukee, WI. Graduated Parris Island, SC with Plt. 64 1st Recruit Bn. Assigned to the 2nd Combat Service Group, Camp LeJeune, NC. Made the maneuvers of February 1948 at Iwo Vieques, Puerto Rico from the Navy ship, USS *Fremont* APA-44, was soon transferred to the 21st Marines reinforced for Battalion 21 to the Mediterranean aboard the USS *Marquette* (AKA-95).

On Aug. 24, 1948, landed at Haifa, Israel with 62 other Marines for duty with the UN Peace Keeping Force in Haifa during the Arab-Israelie War.

Returned to the U.S. and transferred back to the 2nd Combat Service Group and then becoming the 2nd Motor Transport Bn.

Discharged June 10, 1950, and recalled September 1950 being assigned to the 2nd Medical Bn. as a jeep driver and 30 cal. machine gun operator, Camp LeJeune, NC, released Sept. 1951.

Settled in Maryland, married Rose V. Jackson, five children: Elaine, Fredric, Karen, Diane and Beverley; 19 grandchildren and one great-grandson.

In 1955, joined the 13th Inf. Bn., USMCR Washington, DC Navy Yard, attained the rank of Sergeant. Discharged from the USMCR 1962, now retired from the Washington, DC Police Dept., residing in Bedford, VA.

RICHARD O. VINEYARD, born March 22, 1924, enlisted Dec. 8, 1941, at the Marine Corp. Depot, San Diego, CA. No boot camp, directly appointed D.I. due to ROTC in high school. Served with 2nd Mar. Div., 6th Regt., SPWPNS Co. Stationed in New Zealand, Guadalcanal, Tarawa, Hawaii and Saipan.

Received a medical discharge on January 18, 1945, for wounds received on Saipan June 16, 1944, with the rank of corporal. Awarded the Purple Heart and all campaign medals including Presidential Unit Citation w/3 Battle Stars.

Business owner for 39 years before retiring; elected city official councilman for four years; Kiwanis lieutenant governor; Kiwanis foundation president; professional race car driver, car builder, driving champion 1948.

Memorable experience was when he was wounded by mortar fire June 16, 1944, he was evacuated to a troop transport ship, doubling as a hospital ship. He believes at this time his helmet was removed and either tossed into a junk pile or maybe reclaimed by someone aboard ship as a souvenir. It had the early style cloth covered helmet inner liner and he had written the names and places his helmet and he had been together. New Zealand, Guadalcanal, New Caledonia, New Hebrides, Tarawa, Hawaii, etc. What a miracle it would be to find his old helmet. He believes his name was either stenciled or printed on the inner liner.

VICTOR O. WADDLE, was in the 2nd Plt. L Co., 3rd Bn., 8th Mar., 2nd Mar. Div.

After they took Saipan, they invaded Tinian. On their way up to the front lines, they stopped in the back yard of some house for quite a while. He looked up in a tree and saw two chickens sitting on a limb.

He picked up a big rock and, believe it or not, knocked those chickens off that limb. One was dead when it hit the ground and the other one took off into the out-house. He caught him, rung off his head and they started picking chicken feathers from those two chickens.

Someone up ahead left a shiny five gallon can with square sides. They cut the ends out with their K-bar knives, dented in one side so the chicken would not roll off, and built a fire inside the can.

They cut up the chickens with those same dirty K-bar knives and placed the pieces on the can. There was no such thing as salt or other seasonings, but they fried them just the same.

As fast as a piece would get reasonably done, someone would grab it and start eating. Would you believe it; It was his idea and his planning with the can and fire, etc., and for all that he was lucky to get one piece of the meat. But it sure beat any "C" rations they ever ate.

CHARLES WILLIAM WALTERS, born Aug. 22, 1922, in Michigan. Enlisted July 5, 1940, in the Marines and went to boot camp at Parris Island. Earned Sharpshooter, pistol expert and bayonet qualified. Next went to Washington, DC, Navy Yard for guard duty until Dec. 7, 1941, then sent to Camp Elliott and on to Guadalcanal, G Co. 2-2, October 1942.

Saw action on Tarawa, Saipan and Tinian. The good Lord took care of him and he was never wounded. Went into E-2-2 Co., Packakariki, New Zealand. After Tinian went home to Williamsburg, VA Naval Depot, life guard duty in the summer and press shop in the winter.

Good and bad times in Zealand included (1) HQ driving three MPs to Livin to keep peace on weekends. (2) Met a farm girl with two horses and they would race (she always won). He wanted her horse and she said no man had ever ridden it. He got on and down the hill it went for a fence. He thought it would jump and wasn't prepared for a sharp turn and that put him into lots of cow manure. What a mess his dress greens were! (3) He lost a great friend with malaria of the brain. (4) He became a loner and went all over New Zealand, Wellington and to Auckland.

Went home and married his hometown girlfriend, Arlene Davis in 1945. He bought a 1936 Plymouth for $85 and had a ball in it. Discharged in 1946 and went to work for Grand Trunk RR, Pontiac, MI, where he worked for 37 years. He and Arlene had three daughters: Sandra Hawthorne, Jane Powell and Teresa Pawley; grandchildren: Linneya Knight, Richelle Spencer, Charles (in Marines for four years), Kecia Poole, Keenan, Kyle, Tammie, Klinton, Larry Wayne, Naomi Dorey, Melanie Christian, Rusty and April; great-grandchildren: Shana, Jori and Kaitlyn.

Belongs to 2nd MarDiv Assoc. and they teach ballroom dancing. Co. E knows them as the last ones off the dance floor.

NORMAN E. WARD, born in 1921, and enlisted May 11, 1942. Boot camp at San Diego, May 1921; Communication School in San Diego, August, September 1942; joined the 2nd Amphibious Tractor Bn., in New Zealand November 1942. The LVTI (alligator) was designed for rescue of downed flyers in the swamps of Florida. The Marine Corps saw the potential of using the tractor as a supply and personnel vehicle. This was its mission on Guadalcanal. The tractor was later seen as the answer to moving troops and supplies over a coral reef in a direct assault on an island like Tarawa.

He was in command of six tractors on the right flank of Red Beach One. His orders were to follow an LCVP guide boat to the reef, then zero in on the point of the island. They were receiving machine gun fire from their right, the Japanese had entered the sunken freighter and had them in a cross fire. They were also receiving fire from anti-boat guns in the cove on Red Beach Two. As they got in closer to the beach, the Japanese were wading out in the water throwing hand grenades, but they were cut down quickly. By this time some of his tractors were on fire and dead in the water. They had taken a lot of hits by machine gun and rifle fire, and had dead and wounded marines in his tractor.

They unloaded and went back out to the reef to pick up marines wading in shoulder deep water. They loaded as many as they could, but there were many more in the water. He figured if he could slow to a crawl they could use U.S. as a shield to get onto the beach. He knows they saved a lot of marines lives but he wishes he could have saved all of them.

When they got to the beach the second time, they unloaded and were going back out when they got hit with a big one, it blew a hole big enough to crawl in and out of the tractor, so from then on they were infantry.

Discharged Nov. 2, 1981, with the rank of major. Awarded the Silver Star, Purple Heart, Letter of Commendation w/Ribbon, Unit Citations. Memorable experience was being commissioned in the field by Col. Drew; being made a

carrier and handcuffed to a satchel and delivering it to Admiral Nimitz in person.

Was in the wholesale building products, wholesale fastener products and builder.

Married Jeanette (deceased) and has three children: Norman Ward Jr., Jana Ward Staoler and Casey Ward; four grandchildren: Megan Staoler, Kirby, Brandon and Travis Ward.

LEO M. WARREN, was born in Benton City, WA. He enlisted in the USMC in February 1943. After boot camp in Plt. 156 he trained at Camp Elliott until embarking for New Zealand, to form the 2nd Marine Div. He was a member of D-2-10, and made three beach heads on Tarawa, Saipan and Tinian, receiving two Presidential Citations.

After being in the Naval Hospital in Hawaii and San Diego, he was stationed at Seal Beach, CA, until discharged on Oct. 25, 1945.

On returning to civilian life was employed for the Atomic Energy Commission in transportation for over 40 years, retiring as a railroad manager.

LYLE WARZEKK, *Photos only, no bio submitted*

ELE W. (BILL) WASSON JR., born Nov. 30, 1924, in Robstown, TX and graduated from Robstown High School in 1942. Graduated from Anderson Airplane School, Nashville, TN in fall of 1942. Enlisted in the USMC in June 1943; boot camp at San Diego; assigned to the 5th Amphibious Corp. K and Hq Co. of 3rd Bn. 8th Mar. 2nd Mar. Div. His first overseas station was Camp Catlin on Oahu.

Was a radio operator in the Saipan, Tinian, Okinawa and occupancy of Japan (Kyushu) campaigns.

Discharged Jan. 1946 as a private first class.

Attended Southwest Photo Arts Institute in

Dallas, TX and simultaneously worked for Western Union Telegraph Co.

Employed by the Detroit Diesel Allison Division of General Motors retiring March 1987 and State Fair of Texas since 1956 (during the state fair).

Married Dolores and they have three children: Peggy, Nancy and Lisa; four stepchildren: Phyllis, David, Douglas and Danny; six grandchildren: Rusty, Randy, Aaron, Amy, Jeremy and Stacey; seven step-grandchildren: Chana, Chad, Heather, Holly, Taylor, Hayden and Tiffany; three great-grandchildren.

HOWARD J. WATTERS, born Feb. 6, 1924, in Bloomer, WI, raised in Iowa. Enlisted in the USMC on Dec. 8, 1941; sworn in Dec. 16, 1941. After boot camp in San Diego was assigned to I-3-9 at Camp Elliott; then to D-1-2, aboard the USS *Jackson*, landed on Florida Island Aug. 7, 1942, next day invasion of Tulagi; months later went to Guadalcanal.

February 6, 1943, arrived in New Zealand to McKay's Crossing; transferred to E-2-2 and in November in invasion of Tarawa; then to Hawaii at Camp Tarawa. June 1944 in invasion of Saipan, wounded second day and awarded the Purple Heart at the hospital in Guadalcanal.

Arriving from overseas in November 1944, while on transfer leave to Dover, NJ, he married Mildred Warner on Dec. 4, 1944. After duty in Dover, NJ sent to Camp LeJeune and then to Camp Pendleton and honorable discharge on March 1, 1946, with the rank of private.

As a civilian became a welder and later a union member of Ironworkers (construction) retired in 1986. Howard and Mildred, parents of Sharon, Susan and Donald; grandparents of Melissa, Lorie, Bonnie, Gena and Gennifer; great-grandparents of seven.

MICHAEL WATTIK, enlisted in the Marines Jan. 2, 1942. His experiences and memories of the 1-D-2, 2nd MarDiv, machine guns and 81 mortars include being sent to Guadalcanal Jan. 5, 1943 to help secure it, then on to Wellington, New Zealand, Jan. 30, 1943 Camp McKays Crossing.

Landed on Tarawa Nov. 20, 1943 and dug in between two pillboxes and behind a two foot sea wall. What a pitiful sight to see all the wounded Marines crawling in the water trying to get ashore. A lot of them died before help came. It was secured on Nov. 24, 1943.

Landed on Saipan June 15, 1944 and secured it July 9, 1944. He was hit with hand grenade shrapnel, but no Purple Heart. Landed on Tinian July 24, 1944 with little resistance and captured quite a few Japanese. Secured it Aug. 1, 1944. Landed on Okinawa April 1, 1945, secured it April 14, 1945.

Out of the 81 Mortars that were in all five battles, he was the last one to leave for the States. He was discharged with the rank of sergeant and received two Presidential Citations and five Bronze Battle Stars.

NOTE: Some of the above dates might not be exact.

ROBERT LESLIE WAUGH, born in Kalamazoo, MI, 1922. Graduated high school then enlisted USMC Oct. 2, 1942. Entered Tank School, Jacques Farm, San Diego, CA. Joined H&S, 2nd Tank Bn. at Hawaii; saw action at Saipan, Okinawa, occupation duty Nagasaki, Japan. Did top secret work for all phases of Okinawa operation.

Honorable discharge Jan. 19, 1946. Became a Michigan police officer. Attended Western Michigan University, Wayne State University, graduating from Art Center College of Design, Pasadena, CA. Spent 32 years in high-level security positions in defense engineering with notable corporations, involving numerous military aircraft, tank, vehicular, electrical and missile projects. Publisher of the *Bogey Wheel* newsletter to WWII 2nd Tank Bn. troopers. Married high school sweetheart, Helen Peters, in San Diego, 1943. Proud parents of daughter Janis, son Rob, and grandparents of six. He and Helen reside in Phoenix and Prescott, AZ.

HAROLD WELSH, *Photos only, no bio submitted.*

WILLIAM M. WENTE, born in Seridan County, KS, Feb. 26, 1924. Was raised in a farming community and was drafted in September 1943 and had the option of serving with the USMC.

Joined the 6th Regt. and was assigned to B Co. shortly after they had returned to Hawaii after the battle of Tarawa. Went in on the second wave on D-Day at Saipan and was with the company then through all the rest of actions and served with the occupation of Japan at Nagasaki

and Sasebo until Dec. 10, 1945, and went aboard ship headed to the States and landed at San Diego three days after Christmas 1945.

Was sent to Mare Island for separation and arrived home around the third week of January 1946. He served the entire time of service as a private and private first class; as a rifleman and Bar-man; and was promoted to corporal the day of his discharge.

Married his high school girlfriend, Sylvia Brown on Dec. 8, 1946. Lived in Emporia, KS, for ten years and moved to Oklahoma with his job in 1957, where he now make his home. They have two sons, David and John and now have five grandchildren and four great-grandchildren.

ROBERT D. WERNEBURG, was born May 13, 1925, in Rotan, TX, and was the only child of William Lorenza and Opal Dry Werneburg. He enlisted with the Marines on Dec. 15, 1942. After boot camp he was sent to Camp Pendleton for artillery training. From there was shipped overseas April 18, 1943. Upon arrival in Wellington, New Zealand he was assigned to D-2-10, a 75 mm artillery unit of the 2nd Mar. Div.

Werneburg saw action on Tarawa, Gilbert Islands, Saipan and Tinian, Marinnas Islands, Iheya Shima and Okinawa Shima, Ryukyu Islands. At the conclusion of the war, he was sent to Nagasaki, Japan and served as an M.P. until he was returned to the states in November 1945.

Robert was awarded the Navy Commendation Medal and discharged as a corporal Dec. 23, 1945.

He was married to Lou Bradley of Mineola, TX, Dec. 23, 194 6. They had no children. Werneburg was in highway construction work a total of 38 years. Prior to his retirement in 1984, he served as C.E.O. and general partner for 29 years for Werneburg Construction Co. He and his wife currently reside in Mineola, TX.

JOHN J. WETTERER, born in Brooklyn, NY, on May 21, 1920. After graduating from high school he worked in a shipyard until he enlisted. His unit left Quantico for the Pacific Theater September 1942. He saw action with the 18th Mar. Engineers, 2nd Div. on Tarawa, Saipan and Tinian.

In 1945, he passed under the Golden Gate homeward bound and was separated from service on July 18, 1945. He returned to New York

and his wife, Elizabeth. Later he was employed in the Customs Service Treasury Department and finally he was appointed to the Federal Court, U.S. Customs Court, where he retired later after 26 years government service.

Betty and John will be married 56 years in August 1998. They have four wonderful children: Janis, John, Robert and Gary, and they are also the proud grandparents of six. They reside in Long Island, NY.

RAY V. WILBURN, born in Aberfoyle, TX, in 1919. He joined the USMC in 1939. He landed on Gavutu in August 1942 and on Guadalcanal in October 1942. He landed on Tarawa in November 1943, Saipan in 1944 and Guam in 1944. He is a member of the "Forgotten Battalion".

He returned to the U.S. in 1944 and returned back overseas in 1945. He landed on Sasebo, Japan, with the 4th Bn., 13th Marines, 5th Mar. Div. and later joined 4th Bn., 10th Marines, in Nagasaki, Japan.

During Korea, 1951-52, he joined 2nd Bn., 11th Marines. He was the sergeant major of 1st Med. Bn., 1st Mar. Div. in Vietnam, 1967-68. He retired from USMC Base, 29 Palms, CA, in 1971. His decorations and awards include the Meritorious Service Medal, Combat Action Ribbon, Presidential Unit Citation w/3 stars, Navy Unit Commendation, Meritorious Unit Commendation, Good Conduct Medal w/9 stars, American Defense Service Medal, Campaign Medal, Asiatic-Pacific Campaign Medal w/5 stars, WWII Victory Medal, Navy Occupation Service Medal, Defense Medal w/star, Korea Service Medal w/stars, Vietnam Service Medal w/4 stars, United Nations Service Medal Republic of Korea, Presidential Unit Citation, Republic of Vietnam Gallantry Cross Unit Citation, Vietnam Unit Citation and Republic of Vietnam Campaign Medal.

He and his wife, Irma, have two daughters, three grandsons and two granddaughters.

JOHN P. WILLIAMS, was born in Elwood, IN, Apr. 27, 1924. Joined the Marines July 24, 1941, and was in the 94th Plt., MCRD, San Diego. He joined F-2-2 at Camp Elliot. Saw action on Tulagi, Guadalcanal, Tarawa, Saipan and Tinian. Was wounded twice and received 2 Purple Hearts. He also served in Korea and Vietnam.

After 30 years Sgt. Maj. Williams retired Aug. 1, 1971. The retirement parade was held at El Toro. He married Mary Allen Oct. 31, 1944. They have six children: Barbara Wallace, Capt. Richard Williams, USMC Ret., Louise Davis, Cmd. John Williams USCG, Judith McInerny and Dennis Williams; 12 grandchildren: Michael, Judith, Jennifer and Rebecca Wallace, Brian and Jon Zanco, Patrick, Christopher and Joseph Williams, Kimberly Alford, Nicholas and Lindsay McInerny. Sgt. Maj. Williams died July 6, 1992. His wife Mary lives in Oceanside, CA.

ROBERT O. WILLIAMS, born Jan. 28, 1922, and enlisted June 6, 1942. Boot camp in San Diego; assigned to H&S-2-10 at Camp Elliott; shipped to New Zealand in October 1942 as support to 6th Marines. Participated in action on Guadalcanal, Tarawa, Saipan, and Tinian. Returned to the USA and stationed at Klamath Falls, OR; then transferred to shore patrol in Los Angeles and Santa Monica, CA.

Discharged June 6, 1946, with the rank of corporal. Awarded a Purple Heart on Tinian.

Memorable experience includes returning to New Zealand in 1978 and to Saipan and Tinian in 1981.

Graduated Woodberry College in 1950 with a degree in business administration. Worked in a number of firms in Los Angeles Area. Retired in 1981 as director of marketing service.

Married Celia February of 1947 and they had one child: Gail; two grandchildren: Jessica and Jordan.

WILEY RAY WILLIAMSON, born Jan. 13, 1924; enlisted in the Seabees July 14, 1942. Left the U.S. in September 1942, headed for Guadalcanal. After that campaign to New Zealand for R&R; then to Tarawa; and then to Hawaii for R&R. Then to Saipan, where he was wounded, and Tinian, with a total of 34 months overseas, returning to the USA in July 1945. Transferred to Co. H, 3rd Bn., 18th Regt., 2nd Mar. Div. Separated from Marines on Tinian and helped build B-29 Base.

Discharged Oct. 11, 1945, with the rank of EM3/c. Awarded the Purple Heart, Asiatic-Pacific Campaign w/4 Stars, Presidential Unit Citation, Good Conduct, WWII Victory Medal and others.

Farmed from 1946 until 1952; employed with the Tennessee Valley Authority 1952 to 1968; Postmaster for the U.S. Postal Service 1968 to 1984. Retired in 1984. Belonged to several clubs and organizations as well as veterans associations, attending battalion reunions each year.

Married Lou Ella and celebrated their 50th wedding anniversary in 1995. They have two children, Shirley Ann and Betty Lou; two grandchildren, Rae Anne and Amy Lynn. He is retired enjoying fishing, hunting, overseeing farming operations.

HERSCHEL J. WILSKY, was born Aug. 10, 1922, at Champaign, IL. He entered service with the U.S. Marines in June 1941. He served at the following military stations and locations: San Diego, CA, Overseas, Camp Pendleton. After boot camp he went with B-1-8 Marines to Camp Elliott, CA.

They left San Diego one month after Pearl Harbor on Matson Liner *Lurline* to Page, Samoa. They later landed on Guadalcanal Nov. 4, 1942. Some Japanese had landed the night before. He recalls the air dog-fights, the malaria, huge night ship battles of Nov. 14-15 as seen from front line hills, scouting for deep patrols, including an ambush of a Japanese officer and private. He was shipped out to New Zealand with malaria and yellow jaundice.

He attained the rank of corporal and was discharged in September 1945. He married Imogene (Jean) Coffin, has two children and three grandchildren. He retired from the University of Illinois Physical Plant as foreman of the brickmasons on March 1, 1988.

CHARLES JAMES WYATT, born in Essex, MO, December 7, 1919. He enlisted in the USMC after high school in Sikeston, MO,

on August 26, 1941, in St. Louis, MO. He was honor man of his platoon, at San Diego boot camp; then was at camp Elliot for further training. He sailed with the 2nd Bn., 2nd Marine Div., Co. G, seeing action at Tulagi, Guadalcanal, then to New Zealand, Tarawa, Hawaii, Saipan and Tinian.

After 28 months he returned stateside on Labor Day in 1944 with 300 famed 2nd Marines. He was awarded a Purple Heart and the division had two Presidential Citations w/Bronze Stars for action at Tarawa and Saipan.

He married Phyllis Dana on Sept. 14, 1944, in Los Angeles and he was discharged in August 1945. They moved to Sheridan, WY, and raised two sons. Jim was recalled from Marine Reserves on Oct. 26, 1950, and served 13 months service in San Francisco, Islais Creek Pacific Parts Depot and discharged as a staff sergeant.

He was a gallery owner; decorator and sales expert. He loved art and was an art collector with his artist wife. He was an avid fisherman and loved fishing in the Big Horn Mountains. He also loved snowmobiling and traveling in their motor home, but most of all loved being a family man. Jim died of cancer March 12, 1995, at age 75. He was the grandfather of seven grandchildren and two great granddaughters.

STANLEY F. ZAK, born March 29, 1916, in Toledo, OH. Drafted into the U.S. Navy; volunteered for the USMC in Cleveland, OH. Spent two weeks in San Diego, got sick, and spent two weeks in hospital and ended up in a platoon with his two cousins, George Herbec and John Jiskra. Transferred to the Fleet Marine Force; went to Tinian, Saipan, Okinawa, Iheya Shima, Aguna Gima. Was wounded on Okinawa and received the Purple Heart.

Was sent to Nagasaki for 4 months, boarded ship in Sasebo and sailed to San Diego. Received discharge Jan. 12, 1946, at Great Lakes, IL.

Married Regina and has two children: James and John; two grandchildren: Mike and Tony. Moved to Pinellas Park, FL, January 1980.

Second Marine Division Association Roster

Editor's Note: This is the most current roster at the time of publication. This roster was submitted by the Association. The publisher is not responsible for errors or omissions.

– A –

Abban, Joseph B.
Abbatoy, William A.
Abbis, Joseph P.
Abbott ,Richard B.
Abbott, Vance
Abbott ,William H.
Abel, Cecil C.
Abell, Gwendolyn
Abels, Joseph W.
Abshire, Isaac N.
Acevedo, Luis M.
Acker, Roger R.
Ackerly, Edward
Ackerman, George W.
Ackley, Raymond L.
Acord, Larry H.
Acrey, Ernest
Acton, David H.
Acuna, Walter P.
Adam, Ernest L.
Adams, Alma
Adams, Hugh E.
Adams, John Q.
Adams, Kenneth M.
Adams, Lawrence P.
Adams, Richard I.
Adams, Vernon L.
Adamson, Jeffrey James J.
Addicks, George A.
Adkins, Ruth
Adlam, Frederick W.
Adler, Rose
Adomaitis, John M.
Adrian, John
Agenbroad, Owen D.
Agosto, Heriberto
Ahern, Barney A
Ahl, Arthur A.
Ahle, Dirk R.
Ahlgren, James F.
Aiello, Marco
Aiello, Norma
Ainsworth, Bradley J.
Airsman, John W.
Aitken, Robert M.
Akin, Marie
Akins, John M.
Akins, Thelma
Albers, Darrell B.
Albers, Norma H.
Albert, Eddie
Albrecht, H Karl
Alcorn, John M.
Aldridge, Ralph C.
Alexander, Alec J.
Alexander, Clarence E.
Alexander, James L.
Alexander, James R.
Alexander, Joseph H.
Alexander, Ray W.
Alger, Bruce A.
Algood, Charles E.
Alico, Anthony A.

Alico, Nicholas G.
Allegretta, Peter T.
Allen, Albert
Allen, Arthur M.
Allen, Carl K
Allen, Clemmy F.
Allen, Donald K.
Allen, Herbert H.
Allen, Richard P.
Allen, Warren O.
Allena, John J.
Allena, Joseph
Allena, Robert
Allison, Charles E "Mike"
Alloway, Ralph F.
Allred, Bill B.
Almeida, Louis A.
Alotta, Roy M.
Alsworth, Paulette
Altman, Sidney S.
Altschul, Sanford
Alvarado, Michael
Alvarez, Francisco M.
Alvis, Wirt C.
Amadio, Joseph G.
Ambrose, Charles E.
Amburgey, Fred C.
Amos, John R.
Anastasia, Raymond A.
Anastos, Nicholas
Anderscavage, Thomas
Anderson, Arne S.
Anderson, Charles M.
Anderson, Charles (Rebel)
Anderson, David L.
Anderson, Donald
Anderson, Donavan E.
Anderson, Fredrick
Anderson, Gladys
Anderson, Harlan E.
Anderson, Howard W.
Anderson, J.L.
Anderson, James H.
Anderson, Neville L.
Anderson, Raymond O.
Anderson, Richard H.
Anderson, Richard C.
Anderson, Robert E.
Anderson, Ross E.
Anderson, Stanley R.
Anderson, Truman D.
Anderson, Virgil P.
Anderson, Wallace N.
Anderson, William A.
Andre, Robert W.
Andrews, Charles D.
Andrews, Frank E.
Andrews, James P.
Andriliunas, Francis
Androvich, Joseph
Andrus, Oliver D.
Andruzzi, Paul R.
Angerome, Salvatore Paul
Anhorn, Robert R.

Annis, Almon A.
Anthonopoulas, Norman J.
Anthony, Mary L.
Anthony, Robert H.
Antich, Stanley J.
Antoine, James B.
Anzalone, Joseph S.
Appel, Merritt L.
Apperson, Mrs. Thomas F.F.
Appleby, David W.
Applegate, Bradley E.
Applegate, James A.
Appleton, James H.
Appley, James M.
Appleyard, James O.
Aptt, George W.
Aquilina, Jennie
Arabian, G.G.
Arellano, Manuel
Arena, Jack
Armenta, John G.
Armes, George C.
Armond, William A.
Armstrong, Adelbert A.
Armstrong, Gerald Allen
Armstrong, Harold G.
Armstrong, Thomas J.
Arn, Richard
Arnault, Donald E.
Arndt, Charles C.
Arne, Philip M.
Arnett, Betty
Arnett, Donald J.
Arnett, George C.
Arnold, John G.
Arnold, M. Wesley
Arnold, Marion D.
Arnold, William T.
Arrand, Michael C.
Arrant, Edmond E.
Arthur, Ernest W.
Artis, Glenn
Artley, David Clinton C.
Artz, George W.
Asbury, Mark "Boomer"
Ash, Lorn R.
Ashley, Audrey E.
Ashley, William E.
Ashton, Jed L.
Ashurst, Emory B.
Ashurst, Saundra Richbourg-
Association, Edson's Raiders
Association, MarCor Aviation
Association, MarCor Tankers
Association, Women Marines
Association, Inc.
Association, 6th Marine Division
Aston, Emily M.
Aston, Leroy
Atkins, Edward L.
Atkins, William M.
Atkinson, Raymond M.
Atwell, William J.
Aubrey, John F.

Aubrey, Mary I.
Aucoin, Bosley J.
Aughtmon, Julian
Auld, Billy G.
Aune, Kenneth J.
Auriemmo, John P.
Austin, Ellis H.
Austin, Max J.
Austin, Robert C.
Averill, Robert J.
Aviles, Manuel J.
Awkerman, Charles C.
Ayala, Arthur L.
Ayala, Pete G.

– B –

Baar, Wilbur L.
Babb, B.F.
Babb, Verlin W.
Babb, Wayne A.
Babcock, Samuel D.
Baccarella, Philip J.
Baccari, Michael J.
Bach, Alfred J.
Bach, Myron P.
Bachman, Alan L.
Bachman, Rosemary
Backus, Clarence M.
Bagans, George R.
Bagdasian, Jacob
Bahe, Aaron A.
Bailey, Brian H.
Bailey, Cletus J.
Bailey, George L.
Bailey, James J.
Bailey, Richard F.
Bailey, Richard P.
Bailey, W. Duncan D.
Bailey, Warren S.
Bailey, Wesley W.
Bain, Herbert J.
Bair, Barbara R.
Bair, Duane W.
Baird, Donald W.
Baisch, Arthur J.
Bakeman, John R.
Baker, Anna M.
Baker, Dick
Baker, Dolores M.
Baker, Douglas A.
Baker, Edward F.
Baker, Edwin F.
Baker, James S.
Baker, Joe G.
Baker, John E.
Baker, Judd D.
Baker, Patrick F.
Baker, Robert C.
Baker, Robert E.
Baker, Robert W.
Baker, Wilbur L.
Bakula, Walter P.
Baldwin, Edward E.
Baldwin, Erna

Bale, Edward L.
Bale, Norman S.
Bales, Otis W.
Ball, Allen A.
Ball, George P.
Ball, Iddo W.
Ball, Martha E.
Ball, William K.
Ballantine, Fredrick W.
Ballas, Mark J.
Balle, Michael J.
Balley, Raymond P.
Ballinger, Eldon M.
Ballou, Charles A.
Baltes, John F.
Bambrick, Robert J.
Bandelier, Charles C.
Banion, Robert J.
Banks, Anthony P.
Bann, Donald W.
Banning, William P.
Banwart, Russell G.
Banyai, Helen
Barak, Ben
Barat, James J.
Barbeau, Kenneth F.
Bardos, Michael
Barker, Betty A.
Barner, Wayne A.
Barnes, Dean S.
Barnes, Helen E.
Barnes, Jackie
Barnes, James
Barnes, Janie
Barnes, Robert "Pete" H.
Barnes, Thomas H.
Barnett, Mildred
Barney, Charles T.
Baron, Richard G.
Barr, Joseph J.
Barrera, Frank J.
Barrera, John
Barrett, Benny B.
Barrett, Bernice L.
Barrett, Froman
Barrett, James L.
Barrett, John R.
Barrett, Paul D.
Barrett, William S.
Barriger, Glenville D.
Barron, Barron
Barron, Eleanor
Barron, Gene M.
Barron, William W.
Barrows, George M.
Barry, William R.
Bart, Donald P.
Bart, Paul A.
Bartels, Harry
Bartels, Roy W.
Bartels, Ruth
Barth, Ernest C.
Barth, Kevin M.
Bartlett, Frances
Bartlett, Harold
Bartlett, Lewis J.
Bartlett, William R.
Barton, Arliss

Barton, Bruce G.
Barton, Graham
Barton, James L.
Barton, Joseph L.
Bartos, Leonard J.
Basford, Henry R.
Bashus, Edward E.
Basore, Max E.
Bass, Helen
Bassarab, Joseph J.
Bassetto, Leo
Bates, James B.
Bates, Thomas W.
Batson, Clifford O.
Battin, Bobby P.
Baublitz, John G.
Baudoin, Edmund J.
Bauer, Lloyd C.
Bauer, Walter W.
Baumgardner, J.R.
Baumiller, Arthur C.
Bavelles, Christopher G.
Baxter, Alpheus L.
Baxter, James
Bayley, Thomas P.
Bazala, Andrew
Beachler, William F.
Beall, Richard C.
Beamer, Francis X.
Bean, Frederick R.
Bearden, William C.
Beardsley, Charles G.
Beardsley, Kenneth E.
Beau, Jerome C.
Beauchamp, Elizabeth
Beauchamp, Peter A.
Beavers, Hal
Beck, Phifer N.
Becker, Hugh C.
Becker, Matthew S.
Becker, Robert A.
Beckman, A.R.
Beckman, Laverne Y.
Beckner, Millard G.
Beckwith, Byron Dela A.
Bedard, Emil R.
Bedard, Linda
Bedford, Warren R.
Bednarz, Charles
Beeba, James
Beele, Philip C.
Beeler, Carl E.
Beem, Floyd J.
Beers, Elden H.
Begelman, Michael
Beggett, Max G.
Begole, Robert W.
Behenna, Charles R.
Behm, Herbert M.
Behrman, Gene
Beighle, Melvin G.
Beisenstein, Roland
Belanger, Stephen E.
Belesky, Michael
Belfiglio, Irma
Belfus, Isaac
Beliveau, George B.
Bell, Cecil E.

Bell, Douglas E.
Bell, Inez
Bell, James P.
Bell, Walter R.
Bellamy, Raymond W.
Belland, Herb L.
Bellanger, Luke V.
Bellini, Frank R.
Belliveau, Andrew J.
Bembry, William L.
Benadom, Everett D.
Benbow, David J.
Bendixsen, Kay R.
Bendzinski, Harry J.
Benedetto, Alfred P.
Benedict, Richard G.
Benelli, John A.
Bengier, John E.
Bennett, Dallas R.
Bennett, Randall R.
Bennett, Rollie G.
Bennett, William W.
Benoit, Bernerd P.
Bera, Thomas E.
Berard, James A.
Berard, Oscar G.
Beresford, Robert B.
Berg, George E.
Berg, Herbert A.
Berg, James R.
Berg, Kenneth L.
Berg, Lois
Berge, Paul J.
Bergen, Andrew J.
Berger, Bernard F.
Berger, John W.
Bergmann, Craig C.
Bergmann, John E.
Berhow, William R.
Beringhele, Joseph M.
Berman, Nat M.
Bermender, Carl L.
Bernard, Alfred A.
Bernard, Margaret E.
Berndt, Ernest F.
Berry, Charley
Berry, David F.
Berry, Douglas E.
Berry, Lloyd
Berryman, Jack H.
Bertelsen, Jens C.
Bertoni, Richard R.
Bertram, William E.
Berube, Arsene J.
Berumen, Frank
Bescher, Anthony G.
Beshansky, Aaron
Besmanoff, Ric Prince
Best, Francis R.
Best, Frank P.
Bethard, Bill
Bethel, Donald E.
Betz, James A.
Betzares, Gus M.
Bevins, Lance V.
Beyer, Monroe G.
Biagi, John A.
Biagiotti, Richard P.

Bianchi, Aurelio R.
Bianchi, Leon E.
Bickel, Raymond J.
Bickel, Robert C.
Bickhart, John W.
Bickley, Norley F.
Bidwell, Gerald W.
Bigelow, Darrell V.
Biggart, John H.
Bigger, Ronald E.
Bigwood, John M.
Bilchak, William
Bilello, Salvatore J.
Billey, Wilfred E.
Bilski, Frances C.
Binotti, Edward A.
Biranowski, Emil B.
Birch, Gray A.
Bird, Donald E.
Bird, Henry J.
Birdwell, Maurice N.
Birge, Sumner F.
Birmingham, Bernard M.
Birnbaum, Saul
Birr, Irving L.
Bishop, Howard H.
Bishop, Kay M.
Bisogno, Frank G.
Bistline, Raymond G.
Bitner, Irene
Bitner, Wesley S.
Bittick, William C.
Bixby, George R.
Bjorneby, John S.
Bjurback, Leif R.
Black, Henry G.
Black, Tom H.
Blackburn, James R.
Blackman, General R.
Blackwell, Dennis
Blackwell, Robert C.
Blahnik, Ted E.
Blair, Joe V.
Blake, Alice Lee E.
Blake, Harry R.
Blake, James R.
Blake, Nell
Blake, Steve D.
Blake, William R.
Blakely, David S.
Blakeman, Corinne
Blanchard, Claude R.
Blanchard, David G.
Blanchard, Wayne A.
Blanchard, Wayne A.
Blank, Harold D.
Blankenship, William L.
Blanton, Donald N.
Blase, Douglas W.
Blasko, Geneva
Blazek, Joseph W.
Bleeck, Herbert
Bleeker, George W.
Bleibdrey, Frank W.
Blenski, Arthur M.
Blessey, Norman J.
Blevins, James H.
Bleyl, Lorraine

Bleyl, Robert C.
Blick, Joseph A.
Blomsness, Dale Q.
Blythe, James E.
Board, Grace A.
Bobchick, George R.
Bochynski, John J.
Bodeur, Raymond E.
Boe, Vern E.L.
Boehmer, Shirley
Boeve, Gerald A.
Bogan, George
Boggan, Jerrell D.
Boggan, William J.
Bogle, Lawrence R.
Bohl, Henry J.
Bohler, Clarence H.
Bohn, Carl E.
Bohn, Claude H.
Bolan, William L.
Boland, George R.
Boland, Glenn H.
Bolen, William D.
Boling, Howard E.
Bolleter, Vernon T.
Bonds, Jack W.
Bonds, Ralph
Bonham, James F.
Bonifazi, Nello A.
Bonner, Lela
Bonner, Robert N.
Bonner, Robert W.
Bonner, Ross
Bontz, Thelma
Booker, Kurt C.
Boone, Eugene M.
Bordon, Remigio G.
Boreman, Gilbert H.
Borgomainerio, Russell J.
Borlase, James R.
Bornes, Carl S.
Bornman, Arthur R.
Bornowski, Freddie H.
Borrell, John (Jack) C.
Bors, Edwin E.
Borsello, Frank F.
Borses, Bill
Borta, Frank W.
Bortko, Walter D.
Bosko, John P.
Bosquette, Elsworth W.
Bosstic, Wilbur E.
Boston, Leeman E.
Boswell, Donald R.
Botkin, Roy A.
Bott, Robert D.
Botta, Brian K.
Boulden, Robert G.
Bourdeau, Howard J.
Bourgeois, Clyde J.
Boutin, Gerard E.
Boutin, Irene M.
Bove, William A.
Bowden, Arvin J.
Bowditch, Robert C. "Jake"
Bowen, Daniel M.
Bowen, Hugh G.
Bowen, Ledell

Bowen, Stanley W.
Bowers, Robert F.
Bowes, Jennifer L.
Bowes, Julia
Bowler, John H.
Bowles, Irvin M.
Bowles, John A.
Bowman, Herman J.
Bowman, Robert B.
Bowser, Max G.
Boyce, Harold L.
Boyd, Edgar A.
Boyd, Granville W.
Boyd, Paul T.
Boyer, Donald R.
Boyer, Harold L.
Boyle, Edward A.
Boyle,, Frances R.
Boyle, Michael A.
Bozeman, Charlie R.
Bozeman, Firmin L.
Braat, John B.
Brace, George A.
Brackett, William F.
Brackney, John J.
Bradbury, David M.
Bradbury, Dorothy M.
Braddock, Joseph C.
Bradford, George W.
Bradford, Herman L.
Bradford, William E.
Bradley, Marvin L.
Bradley, Robert E.
Bradshaw, William
Brady, Hugh G.
Brady, Margaret H.
Brady, Ronald N.
Brady, Thomas M.
Brame, Lucy M.
Bramlett, Betty
Bramlett, Robert J.
Brammer, James R.
Branch, MCRC Archives
Brandman, Jacob J.
Brandon, P.E.
Brandt, Jamie Carroll
Brandtner, USMC (Ret) LtGen
Martin L.
Branstetter, Terry L.
Brasch, Claire C.
Brashear, James A.
Braswell, B.W.
Brault, Richard R.
Braun, Raymond F.
Brawner, Robert L.
Bray, Steven L.
Bray, Vernon C.
Brayton, Wayne N.
Breaux, Edwin H.
Breiding, Fred H.
Brenden, Burton A.
Brennan, James A.
Brenner, Sylvester E.
Brewer, Barney F.
Brewer, Carlene
Brewer, Cecil T.
Brewer, Walter R.
Brewster, Jacqueline A.

Brewster, Ruben G.
Brezillac, Henry S.
Briand, Richard J.
Brezillac, BGen John P.
Bridges, Morris M.
Bridges, Robert R.
Brieger, James F.
Brieske, Robert E.
Briggs, Beverly A.
Bright, Murl
Brigmon, Paul L.
Brinkman, Howard
Brinkman, Walter G.
Briscoe, Edward L.
Brisso, Rodger L.
Brister, Jessie E.
Britton, Albert E.
Britton, Theodore R.
Brockmann, Harold G.
Brockmeier, Leonard H.
Brodbeck, Stephen C.
Brodin, John T.
Brogan, Richard K.
Brokaw, John W.
Brokob, Roger L.
Bromley, Stephen B.
Bromwell, Ronald J.
Bronson, Daniel R.
Bronstein, Richard J.
Brooks, Eugene G.
Brooks, Harry D.
Brooks, Jerry D.
Brooks, John J.
Brooks, Kenneth R.
Brooks, Lou
Brooks, Walter G.
Bross, Robert
Brown, Alvie C.
Brown, Bryan O.
Brown, C. Ray
Brown, C. Rollins
Brown, Cecil G.
Brown, Charles G.
Brown, Clarence S.
Brown, Dale T.
Brown, Dolores C.
Brown, Donald
Brown, Donald M.
Brown, Duane K.
Brown, Earl W.
Brown, Edward A.
Brown, Ernest L.
Brown, Everett D.
Brown, Fred F.
Brown, Harold E.
Brown, Herbert R.
Brown, James J.
Brown, Jean L.
Brown, John E.
Brown, John J.
Brown, Joseph B.
Brown, Lawrence H.
Brown, Leotha
Brown, Lester G.
Brown, Marqueritte R.
Brown, Michael H.
Brown, Robert C.
Brown, Robert J.

Brown, Robert O.
Brown, Ross
Brown, Ruth V.
Brown, Seldon L.
Brown, Thelma
Brown, Vernon J.
Brown, W. Lee
Brown, William I.
Brown, William S.
Browne, Thomas M.
Browner, Ralph L.
Browning, Winfred O.
Brozyna, Stanley
Brubaker, David A.
Brubaker, Richard W.
Bruce, Dale M.
Bruce, David C.
Bruce, Frances
Bruce, Jonathan M.
Bruch, Vernon W.
Brukardt, Herman R.
Brummer, Rose Marie M.
Brunclik, James W.
Brunelle, David M.
Brunke, Ralph L.
Brunn, Billy H.
Bruns, John C.
Brunson, Alvin E.
Bryan, William T.
Bryant, Dare L.
Bryant, Lance M.
Brzezinski, Henry
Buchalski, John F.
Buck, Carl H.
Buck, Gary W.
Buckley, Conrad F.
Buckley, Edna D.
Buckley, Joan
Buckley, Neil H.
Buckley, Paul H.
Buckner, Paul C.
Bud, Emanuel L.
Budd, Ronald T.
Bueltel, Regis B.
Bufalini, Katherine
Buffum, Keith A.
Buhler, Paul H.
Bulik, Albert F.
Bunce, Frank E.
Bundy, Clarence
Bunton, Edwin D.
Bunyan, Maurice J.
Buongiovanni, Vincent
Bupp, Ronald E.
Burchie, Michael T.
Burga, Bruce A.
Burger, Clarence B.
Burger, Neal J.
Burgess, James I.
Burgess, Leroy M.
Burke, B.T.
Burke, Henry J.
Burke, John L.
Burkhead, Robert J.
Burks, Paul C.
Burnett, Emory L.
Burnett, Neal A.
Burns, Daniel D.

Burns, James P.
Burns, Mike P.
Burns, Richard T.
Burns, Robert J.
Burns, William F.
Burns, William J.
Burrud, Bill
Burt, John Richard
Burton, Cecil J.
Burton, Edward J.
Bushnell, Charles H.
Busler, Bradley R.
Bussard, Marie
Butler, Bernard L.
Butler, Carole
Butler, Ernest A.
Butler, James A.
Butler, Joseph A.
Butler, Ralph G.
Butterfield, Milford E.
Buttrick, Robert E.
Butts, Newton
Butturini, Cecil E.
Buzalewski, Joseph T.
Buzhardt, Harry O.
Byington, Francis E.
Byrne, John E.
Byrne, Patrick E.
Byrne, Paul V.
Byrnes, Jerome V.

– C –
Cabot-Hatch, June
Cabral, Herbert E.
Cabrera, Gregorio C.
Cabrera, Joe
Cadwell, Graydon E.
Cagle, Hoyle D.
Cahill, Daniel M.
Cain, Carl E.
Cain, Patrick M.
Calcutt, Wilbur L.
Caldara, Lucian J.
Caldwell, Charles W.
Caldwell, David S.
Caldwell, Rayford D.
Calkins, Donald K.
Callaghan, Wallace O.
Callahan, Charles R.
Callahan, Edward J.
Callahan, June Theresa
Callahan, William H.
Callahan, William Schaadt
Callaway, Franklin L.
Callaway, Walter E.
Calloway, Christopher H.
Calvin, Hayes
Calvin, Jerry L.
Calvit, George A.
Cameron, Joe J.
Cameron, Louis E.
Cameron, Richard A.
Cameron, William H.
Camp, Fred B.
Campagna, Lu
Campaign, Veterans Guadalcanal
Campbell, Alexander J.
Campbell, Donald C.

Campbell, Francis A.
Campbell, James F.
Campbell, James J.
Campbell, Kenneth W.
Campbell, Richard L.
Campbell, Robert J.
Campbell, Virgil W.
Campion, Glenn A.
Camplen, Carl L.
Canale, Julius M.
Cancro, Richard
Candrilli, Ethel
Canfield, Earle G.
Cannon, Ann
Cannon, Jack R.
Cannon, James A.
Cannon, William C.
Cantor, Beatrice
Cantor, Julius
Cantrall, Arthur
Cantrel, Francis J.
Canty, John J.
Caplan, Stan L.
Capps, Clyde S.
Caprio, Harold O.
Caprio, Paul J.
Capuzzo, Lawrence L.
Carangelo, Martin C.
Carazo, Hernan F.
Carbone, Peter J.
Carbonneau, Laurier R.
Carcirieri, M.P.
Cardow, William H.
Carello, Joseph F.
Carey, Colette
Carey, Edward Francis
Carey, Mervyn L.
Carey, Richard E.
Cargile, Cannon C.
Carland, George
Carley, Fred W.
Carley, Ruby
Carlock, Donald E.
Carlsen, Chester O.
Carlson, Howard E.
Carlson, James I.
Carlton, H. Wayne
Carmack, Ivy C.
Carman, Jeff
Carmical, Loris
Carone, Michael J.
Carozza, Patrick
Carpenter, Claude L.
Carpenter, Evelyn K.
Carpenter, Solon R.
Carpenter, William B.
Carr, Louis A.
Carr, Paul A.
Carr, Robert J.
Carrell, Eugene C.
Carrigan, Clifford C.
Carrigan, John D.
Carrington, Clyde F.
Carroll, Don R.
Carroll, Donald L.
Carroll, Grant
Carroll, J P.
Carroll, Thomas R.

Carstens, Harold L.
Carter, Emmett N.
Carter, John A.
Carter, John G.
Carter, Leslie
Carter, Michael R.
Carter, Ray C.
Carter, Raymond E.
Carter, Thomas
Carter, Winton W.
Cartmill, Roscoe S.
Caruso, Matthew J.
Cascarano, John
Casci, Brett N.
Casey, James P.
Casey, Mary N.
Caskey, Charles G.
Casper, George A.
Cass, C.F. Alan
Cassagne, Gilbert J.
Castillo, Alfonso
Castle, Harrison E.
Castleberry, Curtis W.
Castorena, Gilbert
Castro, Richard G.
Cate, Kenneth
Caterbone, Samuel J.
Cavanaugh, C.A.
Cavanaugh, James J.
Cavanaugh, Lawrence A.
Cavanaugh, Lee
Cavell, Gayle
Cayo, Everett A.
Caywood, Walter T.
Cederstrom, Philip
Cerny, Robert S.
Chabo,t Jean L.
Chacho, John J.
Chael, Harrison John
Chaffee, Philip T.
Chaffie, Neil
Chagnon, Joseph V.
Chalmers, Billy B.
Chamberland, Gerald M.
Chambers, James R.
Chambers, Jesse W.
Chambers, John S.
Champagne, Philip E.
Chance, Robert U.
Chandler, Norman A.
Chandler, William H.
Chapiewski, Frank A.
Chapman, Edward J.
Chappell, Vaughn F.
Chapple, William B.
Charette, George F.
Charles, Roy E.
Charles, Theda
Charlton, George W.
Charlton, William G.
Charnquist, Victor D.
Charton, Jimmie Dean
Chase, Donald L.
Chase, James L.
Chatfield, William O.
Chatham, Geraldine
Cheatham, Claborn R.
Cheatham, Clarence Curtis

Cheek, George A.
Cheeks, William R.
Chen, Edgar
Cherry, Geraldine
Cheshire, Lucius M.
Chesny, Daniel E.
Chester, Hugh
Chiasson, Roland M.
Chiavacci, Vaughn J.
Childs, Donald James
Chisa, Adrian B.
Chiudioni, Fausto J.
Chlan, Gary M.
Chosin Few, Inc., The
Choti, William
Christensen, Herman J.
Christensen, Milo
Christensen, Raymond M.
Christensen, Robert H.
Christian, Jim M.
Christie, Richard A.
Churchill, MajGen Walter A.
Chuzum, Arthur B.
Ciaston, William M.
Ciccotello, Leonard A.
Cifelli, James J.
Cing, David M.
Ciotti, Anthony J.
Cipullo, Ray
Cisco, Jeff
Clancey, William P.
Clapp, Warren M.
Clark, Alice
Clark, Carol
Clark, Charles F.
Clark, Denise
Clark, Earnest B.
Clark, Edward B.
Clark, James C.
Clark, Kenneth W.
Clark, Leo J.
Clark, Richard W.
Clark, Robert V.
Clark, Thomas J.
Clark, Thurle B.
Clark, Vida
Clark, William P.
Clark, William A.
Clarke, Charles R.
Clarke, Margie M.
Clarke, Seybert M.
Clasing, Bernard F.
Clausen, Dean W.
Clayton, Bert A.
Claytor, Thomas R.
Clearfield, Joseph R.
Clemens, Emerson H.
Clement, Gerald F.
Clements, Jimmie R.
Clements, Joseph
Clements, Thomas R.
Clements, Tom H.
Clemmons, Philip W.
Clerou, Joe R.
Cleveland, Jonnie Kay
Cleveland, Orville W.
Clevenger, Walter P.
Click, James M.

Click, Robert L.
Clinnick, Mansfield L.
Close, Richard L.
Clough, William H.
Cloutier, Joseph E.
Clover, Ralph H.
Cluka, Daniel
Cobb, Billy F.
Cobb, E. Lynwood
Cobb, Jasper E.
Coble, George R.
Cocoris, George G.
Codispodi, James E.
Cody, Richard L.
Coen, James M.
Coen, Shirley L.
Coffin, William P.
Cogdill, Willard G.
Coghlan, James H.
Cogsdell, Thomas C.
Cohn, Martin L.
Coker, Jack C.
Colby Roger K.
Colclaser, Daniel G.
Cole, Harold J.
Cole, Jack K.
Cole, Richard E.
Cole, Stuart R.
Cole, William O.
Coleman, Francis J.
Coleman, Freddie H.
Coleman, Keith R.
College, Command & Staff
Collier, Arnold G.
Collins, David Ernest
Collins, John J.
Collins, Robert S.
Collins, W H.
Colmar, William C.
Colona, William H.
Colson, Celeste
Columbus, James A.
Colvin, Jacqueline
Comacho, Joseph L.
Combs, Betty
Combs, James E.
Comedy, James
Compton, Ricky J.
Comstock, Harold
Comstock, Harold L.
Conde, Elaine M.
Conde, Gabriel C.
Condit, Frank L.
Condon, John W.
Cone, Charles H.
Congoran, Gilbert N.
Conkey, Doris K.
Conkey, Fred R.
Conklin, Gordon D.
Conley, Donald L.
Connell, Joseph R.
Connell, William P.
Conner, William N.
Conniff, Vincent L.
Connolly, Charles A.
Connolly, James J.
Connolly, James M.
Connolly, John P.

Connolly, Joseph P.
Connolly, Mary G.
Connors, John F.
Connors, Lawrence A.
Connors, Robert
Connors, Thomas A.
Conrad, Jack Wall
Conrad, Pleas H.
Conry, Kevin A.
Consodine, Thomas J.
Conte, Cliff R.
Contessa, Thomas A.
Conti, Anthony
Conway, Daniel J.
Conway, Inez O.
Conway, John T.
Conway, Robert G.
Conwell, Phillip A.
Cook, Arnold E.
Cook, Bill
Cook, Donald L.
Cook, Frederick E.
Cook, Harold G.
Cook, Howard F.
Cook, John A.
Cook, Robert E.
Cook, Robert L.
Cooke, Robert G.
Cooksey, William E.
Cooley, Willard B.
Coonrod, William Angle
Cooper, Herman W.
Cooper, James L.
Cooper, Peter
Cooper, Tomoe
Cooper, Walter E.
Cope, Wesley E.
Copland, Robert John
Copp, Justin F.
Copp, Ralph W.
Coppolino, Joseph A.
Corbett, Benjamin H.
Corbett, James P.
Corbett, Scott S.
Corbett, Tom
Corbitt, Leslie E.
Corcoran, Thomas B.
Corlazzoli, John
Corley, John J.
Corman, Albert
Cormier, F. Earl
Corn, James L.
Cornelison, Elbert B.
Cornell, Ken W.
Cornish, Joseph J.
Corns, Orville E.
Cornwall, Barbara L.
Corriss, Stephen C.
Corriss, Stephen D.
Cortez, Herbert E.
Corzan, John
Cosentino, Charles J.
Cosgrove, Laurence E.
Cosgrover, Robert A.
Costa, Antone F.
Costa, Walter V.
Costello, James T.
Costello, Michael A.

Costello, Robert E.
Cota, Henry J.
Cote, Charles R.
Cotey, Leonard J.
Cotters, George E.
Cotton, James V.
Cotugno, Leonard W.
Couch, Clyde B.
Couckuyt, James R.
Coudayre, James B.
Coughenour, Dale E.
Coughlin, George Francis
Coughlin, John T.
Coughlin, Thomas M.
Coulman, Robert L.
Coulston, Teddy D.
Coulthard, Lavern A.
Councell, Harry W.
Countiss, James C.
Countiss, Sarah M.
Counts, Robert C.
Courage, Bruce W.
Cournoyer, Arthur J.
Courville, Henry C.
Coutermarsh, Ernest R.
Coutu, Charles R.
Covell, Glenn H.
Coverstone, Sue
Covington, William Henry
Cowan, Fred J.
Cowan ,James R.
Cowan, Robert R.
Coward, William L.
Cowart, Robert B.
Cowart, Thelma
Cowart, Woodrow W.
Cowden, Chester J.
Cowper, William H.
Cox, Patrick W.
Cox, Ruth
Cox, Walter T.
Crabb, Francis J.
Crabtree, Richard E.
Craig, Bettye
Craig, Carl
Craig, Everard J.
Craig, Garnel Lee L.
Craig, Jack E.
Craig, James C.
Craig, Marie A.
Crain, Donald M.
Crain, J. Wendell W.
Cramer, T. Franklin
Crane, Clifford Joe
Craven, Murl E.
Crawford, Fayette
Crawford, John A.
Crawford, Muriel
Creech, Jackson D.
Crelia, Lloyd T.
Crenshaw, Guy B.
Crenshaw, Jim C.
Crenshaw, Robert O.
Cressionnie, Jefferson O.
Cretinon, Paul A.
Criley, Brian R.
Crispen, Robert Louis
Crodelle, Vincent A.

Croft, Earl G.
Cromarty, Josie
Crome, Roger H.
Cromwell, L.R.
Crone, Kenneth H.
Cronk, Hugh G.
Cronyn, K. William
Crooks, Boyd H.
Cropp, Alan B.
Crosiar, Ralph Roland
Cross, Edward J.
Cross, Harold F.
Croup, Thomas E.
Crow, Homer C.
Crow, India
Crowder, Emory C.
Cruickshank, Richard A.
Crum, Kenneth G.
Crumb, Albert L.
Crumbie, Watson
Crumlish, John J.
Crumpacker, William E.
Crupi, James J.
Crusey, Philip D.
Cryer, Tyson S.
Cuda, Frank J.
Cuddy, Gertrude M.
Culkin, Thomas J.
Culling, Kenneth E.
Culpepper, Claude W.
Culpepper, Howard O.
Culpepper, Marty
Cummings, Earl E.
Cummings, Robert E.
Cummins, James B.
Cunney, Robert C.
Cunningham, Edwin M.
Cunningham, Harold E.
Cunningham, Jack G.
Cunningham, Robert A.
Cunninghame, Samuel L.
Curatolo, Aldo M.
Curiel, Salvador
Curio, John R.
Curley, Joseph R.
Curran, Edward J.
Curran, James H.
Curran, John P.
Curran, Velma
Currie, Claude
Currier, Carl A.
Curro, Antonino G.
Curtin, Peter M.
Curtis, Jeffrey D.
Curtis, Lewis E.
Curtis, Robert F.
Curtsinger, Jack W.
Cuseglio, Thomas J.
Cushing, Paul F.
Cushing, Robert S.
Cuthbert, John G.
Cutshaw, Orval
Cyr, Gilbert J.
Cyr, Roland C.
Czarnecki, George M.
Czarnecki, Lillian R.
Czeski, Joseph C.
Cziak, James C.

Czimbal, Lawrence W.
Czyscon, Frank P.

– D –

D'Acquisto, Thomas J.
D'Alessio, August G.
D'Amico, Anthony S.
D'Angelico, Guy J.
D'Angelo, Philip
D'Arco, Renato
D'Arienzo, Oscar J.
Dabler, Raymond M.
Dahl, Eddie C.
Dahl ,Juanita D.
Dahlke, Jo
Daigle, C J.
Dailey, Marshall J.
Dailey, Steve E.
Daily, Alvin L.
Daily, Marjorie E.
Dale, Herbert J.
Dale, Laurence R.
Daley, Wayne A.
Dalgleish, Charles K.
Dalrymple, Gerald F.
Dalton, Bill S.
Daly, John G.
Daly, Michael A.
Damewood, Frank C.
Damiaens, Danny
Damiani, John J.
Dana, Jim J.
Dance, Gary A.
Dancey, Don J.
Dancey, Frank J.
Daneker, Brian K.
Daneker, James
Daney, Edward J.
Danforth, Warren W.
Daniel, Clovis E. "Dan"
Daniels, Walter S.
Danis, Armand
Danowitz, Edward F.
Dantin, Maurice
Darling, Norman J.
Darnel, Edna R.
Darnel, Olin K.
Darnell, Robert M.
Daubenschmidt, Albert J.
Davenport, Grover T.
Davidson, Elwayne C.
Davidson, John R.
Davidson, William G.
Davies, George C.
Davies, Loren E.
Davies, Trevor E.
Davies, William J.
Davio, Marjory E.
Davis, Andrea M.
Davis, Byron V.
Davis, Dale W.
Davis, Dale N.
Davis, Daniel Y.
Davis, David J.
Davis, Doris L.
Davis, Harry
Davis, Harvey B.
Davis, James W.

Davis, James J.
Davis, Jerri
Davis, Jerry L.
Davis, Jimmie C.
Davis, Joe R.
Davis, Lamar S.
Davis, Mark
Davis, Pearl
Davis, Richard S.
Davis, Richard H.
Davis, Robert D.
Davis, Sammy S.
Davis, Thomas R.
Davis, Timothy M.
Davis, Virginia
Davis, Wallace M.
Davison, Follis L.
Dawber, Margaret Denise D
Dawson, John R.
Day, Frank H.
Day, George E.
Day, Jean
Day, John Russell R.
Day, William E.
De Angelis, Louis
De Cristofaro, Ted
De Francisci, Thomas J.
De Jong, Raymond L.
De Leo, Geovannino "John" J.
De Marco, Anthony J.
De Maris, John C.
De Martini, Paul A.
De Vera, Armando "Nick" N.
Deal, Charles E.
Deal, Robert A.
Deal, Robert C.
Deal, William F.
Dean, John Y.
Dean, Johnny R.
Deane, William J.
Deardorff, Robert E.
Deardurff, Joe C.
Debell, Jack
Debniak, Willis J.
Debruycker, John
Decker, John L.
Decker, Lloyd R.
Dedic, Robert F.
Degitz, Robert G.
Degrose, Samuel S.
Dehr, Pauline R.
Deighton, Herbert H.
Deitch, Louis
Deitle, Doreen
Deitle, John O.
Deivert, Ruth
Deka, Gene L.
Del Russo, Fred
Dela Cruz, Francisco S.
Delaney, James
Delaney, Jane K.
Delaney, Martin C.
Delaney, Norma
Delaney ,Rev. William H H.
Delatorre, Richard
Delembo, Mary
DeLeo, Joseph B.
Delgado, Juan C.

Delgado, Marvin A.
Della, Vella Michael
Dellarata, William F.
Delmage, Bertram
Delorenzo, James R.
Demler, Donald F.
DeMont, Norman D.
DeMoss, Loucille
Demps, Terrance A.
Dempsey, Daniel P.
Denbrock, Frank A.
Denice, Thomas G.
Denning, Edward J.
Dennis, Otis W.
Dennis, Russell J.
Dennler, Harold A.
Dent, James L.
Dent, Wellborn Watts
Denton, Mark S.
Depew, Jack L.
Derlatka, Theodore
Dern, Harry W.
Des Noyer, Mark S.
Des Rosier, Fred L.
Desano, Henry
Desbiens, Robert J.
DeScisciolo, Larry
Desensi, Anthony J.
Desensi, Vincent J.
Desirello, Kenneth G.
Desmond, Edward J.
Desmond, Francis A.
Dessert, Norman B.
Destaso, James
Dethloff, Harvey F.
Detlefsen, Darrell W.
Devaney, William F.
Deverick, Ronald C.
Devries, Albert
Devries, Charles A.
Devries, John C.
Dewees, Norman E.
Deweese, Max I.
Deweever, Carl C.
Dewey, Carl G.
Dezur, Robert H.
Di Filippi, Joseph L.
Dicke,n Betty F.
Dickerson, John G.
Dickerson, Nelson J.
Dickerson, Robert P.
Dickerson, Virginia
Dickey, Earl L.
Dickey, Shelia
Dickson, David J.
Didlake, Patrick H.
DiDomenico, Ronald N.
Dieckman, Elmer F (Bud) F.
Diehl, Albert H.
Diehl, Shirley B.
Diello, John J.
Dierickx, Phil A.
Dietrich, Arthur O.
Dietz, George
Digiacomo, Anthony V.
DiGiovanni, Paul A.
Diley, Joseph W.
Dilges, Arthur P.

Dilley, Jan C.
Dillman, Norman L.
Dillon, Jacob L.
Dillon, Michael J.
Dilworth, Orvis
Dimitriadis, James C.
Dineen, Thomas F.
Dingler, Christopher J.
Dingley, Robert T.
Dinsmore, Lloyd F.
Dinsmore, Marie Sandra
Disher, Peter Jerome J.
Disney, William J.
DiStefano, Arthur C.
Ditchey, Carl J.
Dixon, Gid N.
Dixon, Henry C.
Dixon, Henry L.
Dixon, Kermit
Dixon, Ray
Dlugonski, Francis A.
Dobson, Paul R.
Dobson, Pauline
Dobson, Richard J.
Docherty, Robert V.
Dodge, Joseph R.
Dodson, Mary
Dodson, Therrell J.
Doebler, George E.
Doepper, Gloria
Doherty, John H.
Doherty, Joseph D.
Doherty, Joseph M.
Dolan, Daniel B.
Dolan, Gerald J.
Dolan, Patricia J.
Dolan, Vincent J.
Dolata, Mrs. Ervin C.
Dolly, Clifford M.
Dolny, Warren S.
Dombkowski, Edward
Dombrovski, Roger T.
Domyan, Andrew J.
Donaghu, Wallace W.
Donahue, John J.
Donald, Clement C.
Donald, Robert
Donaldson, Uhlmon L.
Dondero, Kenneth P.
Donegan, Michael L.
Donelson, Paul C.
Dongweck, Paul B.
Donnelly, Robert M.
Donoghue, Francis X.
Donoghue, Stephen F.
Donovan, Jerome F.
Donovan, Paul T.
Dooley, Philip J.
Dopheide, Nellie
Doran, Joseph M.
Dorf, Paul R.
Doring, Marian W.
Dornberger, Donald A.
Dors, Henry F.
Dortch, Richard F.
Dorzinsky, Joseph
Doskocil, Jean M.
Doskocil, Roger R.

Dotson, Ray E.
Doud, Earl C.
Douglas, Gene W.
Douglas, James A.
Douglas, William C.
Dowdakin, David W.
Dowlearn, Thomas B.
Downey, Bryan S.
Downing, John D.
Downs, Helen I.
Downs, Kathryn
Downs, Mary Kay
Downs, Paul A.
Downs, William B.
Doyle, Dennis M.
Doyle, H. James
Doyle, Philip J.
Doyle, Verla M.
Dozier, Viola B.
Dragan, Denny
Drago, Ronald A.
Dragon, Stephen P.
Dravecky, Harry
Dray, Adrian W.
Dreith, Wilbur J.
Drendall, Harry I.
Dress, Ted W.
Dresser, Robert C.
Drew, Jerry W.
Drews, Adolph A.
Drews, Theodore M.
Driben, Sidney
Driggs, Dick W.
Drinkwine, Florine A.
Driscoll, Ed J.
Drobinko, Ginny
Drobinko, John T.
Drobman, David
Drusky, Raymond D.
Du Pre, Paul J.
Duane, Neil F.
Dube, Joseph A.
Ducoeur, Audrey
Duda, Henry J.
Dudek, Ronald G.
Dudley, George E.
Duffin, Lloyd Urban
Duffy, Michael R.
Duffy, Robert S.
Dugan, Edward D.
Dugan, Martin J.
Duggan, Peter T.
Duke, Albert A.
Dukes, James C.
Dul, Thaddeus J.
Dunbar, Reginald
Duncan, Aloysius E.
Duncan, Antoinette
Duncan, Austin L.
Duncan, Kenneth J.
Duncan, Robert B.
Duncan, William E.
Dunham, Neil V.
Duni, Robert J.
Dunkel, William A.
Dunlap, Edward T.
Dunlap, John W.
Dunn, Barry D.

Dunn, James
Dunn, John J.
Dunn, John E.
Dunn, Kenneth A.
Dunn, Oather J.
Dunn, Robert J.
Dupont, William P.
Durant, Mary
Durboraw, Alvin B.
Durham, Omagene (Rusty) H.
Durkee, Harold E.
Durr, Edmund Lee L.
Durr, Robert W.
Durst, Gloria
Dutcher, Jean
Dutcher, Russell K.
Dutrow, Charles R.
Dwyer, Albert J.
Dwyer, Edward
Dwyer, Thomas F.
Dyar, Willis M.
Dyba, Walter E.
Dyck, Harold C.
Dycus, William A.
Dyer, Robert M.
Dykas, Raymond G.
Dykes, Mary
Dzenkowski, George V.

– E –
Eardley, John Morton M.
Eaton, Horace N.
Eaton, William E.
Eberle, Alvy E.
Eberwein, Charles W.
Eby, Charles R.
Eckert, Frank O.
Eckland, Robert E.
Edblom, Lloyd B.
Edel, August E.
Edgar, John
Edgerly, Royal H.
Edgin, Lester L.
Edmondson, Lloyd G.
Edmonston, James O.
Edwards, James R.
Edwards, Leroy B.
Edwards, Robert G.
Edwards, Ronald L.
Eggleston, Joseph N.
Ehl, Arnold E.
Ehret, Albert J.
Ehrhart, Clause E.
Ehrhart, John R.
Eibl, David L.
Eibl, John L.
Eicher, Jeffrey L.
Eichman, Harry W.
Eichman, Helen M.
Eichner, Andrew J.
Eiker, William E.
Einarson, John
Eisler, John P.
Ekstrom, Martin A.
Elder, William D.
Eldore, Clyde H.
Elkins, James W.
Eller, Roy O.

Ellingsen, Melvin
Elliott, Donald O.
Elliott, Glen E.
Elliott, John F.
Elliott, John T.
Elliott, Leland A.
Elliott, Marvin N.
Elliott, Merrill E.
Elliott, Norma Aspell
Ellis, Donna
Ellis, Fayette
Ellis, Frank J.
Ellis, Fred R.
Ellis, James M.
Ellis, Robert G.
Ellis-Deighton, Joan M.
Ellithorpe, Robert T.
Emeigh, Merl E.
Emerson, Cecil R.
Emery, George L.
Emory, Christopher S.
Endsley, Charles E.
Engel, Eugene E.
Engelhardt, Earl R.
Englehart, Jesse J.
English, Henry G.
English Robert T.
Engstrom, Kenneth W.
Enos, Harry E.
Entzi, Robert
Eoff, Douglas D.
Eranosian, Vahan
Erickson, Eugene W.
Erickson, Eugene A.
Erickson, George T.
Erickson, S.R. Bud
Erne, Earl W.
Erotas, Edward
Ertel, John A.
Ervin, Lawrence J.
Esler, Joseph H.
Esparza, Louie
Estes, Jack E.
Estvanik, Mary H.
Ethington, William M.
Ethridge, John W.
Etsitty, Lucille N.
Etzel, Raymond E.
Eubanks, Fred F.
Evanick, George J.
Evans, Bessie G.
Evans, Carl D.
Evans, Jack L.
Evans, James A.
Evans, James L.
Evans, John W.
Evans, Louis J.
Evans, Paul R.
Evans, Walter M.
Evensen, Lloyd C.
Everett, Eugene E.
Eytchison, Richard M.
Ezzell, Marion

– F –
Fabera, Joseph F.
Facilla, Louis M.
Fackina, Kenneth M.

Fagan, Mildred M.
Faggard, Joseph W.
Failla, James
Faillat, Jean
Faioli, G.
Fairbaugh, Anne
Fairbrother, William E.
Fairest, Shirley A.
Falicki, Sigmund V.
Fallon, Lewis J.
Faquine, Arthur C.
Farais, Martin P.
Farley, David L.
Farley, William H.
Farmer, Francis L.
Farmer, Henri L.
Farmer, James D.
Farnell, Hal S.
Farner, Charles P.
Farnum, William E.
Farrell, James V.
Farris, Clifton G.
Farris, Mary L.
Farster, Bruce C.
Fasano, Michael J.
Fast, Robert J.
Faulkenbery, Jesse R.
Favata, Vincent C.
Favilla, Ralph
Fawcett, James L.
Feck, Mary Lou Driggers-
Feck, Ralph
Federwisch, Roger J.
Feener, Stanley E.
Feeney, Richard J.
Feiner, Richard E.
Feiten, William P.
Feitz, Dave
Fejta, Stanley D.
Feld, Robert
Feldman, W.C.
Fell, David J.
Fellows, Lettie V.
Fels, Joseph
Felts, Dossy B.
Felty, Ralph B.
Fennessey, William M.
Fenolio, Charles L.
Fergerson, Charles L.
Ferguson, Gil W.
Ferguson, John A.
Ferguson, John E.
Ferguson, Lester W.
Ferguson, Richard W.
Ferl, Thomas H.
Fernandez, Ralph P.
Ferrell, Tillman C.
Ferrier, Jim S.
Ferrillo, Andrew
Ferry, Alvin D.
Festing, William F.
Fettis, Emmitt
Fiala, Robert C.
Fick, Jack F.
Field, Earl L.
Fields, Arnold
Fields, Harold L.
Fields, William B.

Fifer, Harry
Figard, Charles R.
Figler, Max
Filipowski, Audy
Filipowski, Kenneth S.
Fillion, Stanley H.
Findlay, John R.
Findlay, Mary B.
Finger, Velma B.
Fink, Eugene P.
Fink, George F.
Finn, John P.
Finneran, John F.
Finney, Charles F.
Finney, Frederick W.
Fioramonti, Robert F.
Fiore, Joseph P.
Fire, Edward R.
Fischelli, Vincent E.
Fischer, Randy W.
Fischer, Raymond J.
Fish, Fredrick L.
Fisher, Annie Ruth B.
Fisher, Carter
Fisher, Catherine
Fisher, James E.
Fisher, Karl E.
Fisher, Robert J.
Fisher, Wayne F.
Fiske, James C.
Fitzgerald, Avis G.
Fitzgerald, E.F.
Fitzgerald, James W.
Fitzgerald, Robert C.
Fitzgerald, Robert L.
Fitzgerald, Thomas J.
Fitzpatrick, Lawrence F.
Fitzpatrick, Tom D.
Fitzsimons, William G.
Fjellman, Robert M.
Fjosne, Wallace M.
Flaherty, Carol A.
Flaherty, Dennis F.
Flaherty, Martin M.
Flaherty, Peter J.
Flaherty, William J.
Flammini, Fred G.
Flanagan, John F.
Flanders, Ward H.
Flannery, Darsie F.
Flatum, Earl F.
Fleckenstein, Myron L.
Fleishman, Richard P.
Fleming, Alan W.
Fleming, Francis P.
Fleming, Gerard J.
Fleming, James R.
Fletcher, Bill K.
Fletcher, Morris O.
Flick, Fred M.
Flint, Alexander
Flint, Robert C.
Florentine, David J.
Flores, Frank C.
Florian, Frank J.
Flory, Stanley T.
Flowers, Miller T.
Floy, Lee R.

Floyd, Paul E.
Flynn, Daniel J.
Flynn, Francis R.
Flynn, Marion R.
Flynn, Patrick A.
Flythe, Cary J.
Foley, James J.
Foley, John L.
Foley, Michael J.
Foley, Patrick M.
Foley, Robert Leo
Folsom, Donald E.
Foltz, Mildred B.
Ford, James R.
Ford, Marlin E.
Fordham, Donald L.
Forencich, Frank J.
Fornal, Robert W.
Fornes, Lawrence V.
Forrest, Stephen David
Fors, Kenneth W.
Forshee, James H.
Fortney, Jack L.
Foselli, Thomas F.
Foster, Frank E.
Foster, Harold L.
Foster, Harry T.
Foster, John J.
Foster, John W.
Foster, William H.
Fountain, Freeman P.
Fowler, Carl R.
Fowler, James A.
Fowler, Sir Michael
Fowles, Leonard J.
Fox, Carlton H.
Fox, Charles S.
Fox, Clyde L.
Fox, David L.
Fox, George J.
Fox, Hershal O.
Fox, Melvin F.
Fox, Mildred M.
Frado, James M.
Fraker, Mary
Fralick, Floyd A.
Francis, Harold D.
Francis, Melvin
Francis, Roland A.
Franco, John
Frank, Josephine C.
Frank, Ralph P.
Frank, Robert E.
Frankevich, Samuel J.
Franklin, John J.
Franklin, Ray M.
Frankovic, Thomas J.
Franks, Warren G.
Fransein, Eldon
Frantz, Robert L.
Franzia, Joseph S.
Fraser, David M.
Fratt, William H.
Fratt, William Perkins
Frawley, Calvin
Frawley, John H.
Frazier, Bill
Frazier, Donald M.

Frazier, Forrest L.
Frazier, John B.
Frazier, Lois
Frazier, Michael M.
Frazier, Philip F.
Frederick, Charles F.
Frederick, Noel W.
Frederickson, Bernard J.
Free, Marguerite
Freeberg, George F.
Freeburg, Gordon N.
Freed, Robert J.
Freels, Alfred G.
Freeman, Don
Freeman, James G.
Freeman, Neva
Freestone, Ferris T.
Frejlich, Walter C.
French, George H.
French, Jack L.
French, Willard E.
Frentrup, Almarie J.
Frentrup, Max O.
Frescoln, Merrill R.
Frey, Francis X.
Frey, Philip Charles
Fricke, Richard A.
Friedsam, Hiram J.
Friel, Edward F.
Friend, Robert G.
Frisbie, Carlton E.
Frisbie, Paul J.
Frise, Muriel M.
Frise, Richard D.
Fritts, Reba L.
Fritz, Delmar W.
Fritz, Marcia
Fritze, Robert W.
Froncek, Leonard J.
Frost, A.V.
Frost, Clarence A.
Frost, Howard E.
Frost, James H.
Frost, William W.
Fruci, Lawrence J.
Fry, Michael C.
Fryer, Fredrick C.
Fugate, Stanley
Fugett, Jean
Fuhrman, Robert
Fuiks, Lois
Fulcher, Tommy E.
Fuller, Herbert R.
Fuller, James E.
Fuller, Patrick E.
Fulmer, Herschel B.
Fulton, Joan
Fulton, Kent G.
Funari, Naldo
Fuqua, Percy V.
Furgal, Michael L.
Furlone, Warren E.
Furman, Richard T.
Furtado, Joseph C.
Fusco, Daniel J.
Fussell, Shirley P.
Futrell, James R.
Fydenkevez, Theodore E.

Fyffe, Carol R.

– G –

Gagan, William J.
Gage, Herbert R.
Gagne, Rev Paul R.
Gagomiros, Eric C.
Gahan, Gary A.
Gahan, Timothy M.
Gaines, James P.
Gaither, Gilbert F.
Gaj, Joseph J.
Gajos, Julia
Galbraith, James R.
Galbraith, Jay M.
Galjour, J.W.
Gallagher, John J.
Gallagher, John T.
Gallagher, John Francis
Gallagher, Joseph M.
Gallagher, Michael J.
Gallagher, William J.
Gallaher, Milburn W.
Gallant, Lucien J.
Gallegoes, Louis A.
Gallo, Dwayne L.
Galloway, J. Stuart
Galvez, Albert A.
Galvin, Tom
Gamble, Frances
Gamble, Maree
Gamble, Orville Ed
Gandy, Bruce A.
Gangi, Charles J.
Gann, Baxter U.
Gann, James Larry
Gannon, John M.
Gante, Peter M.
Garbark, Thomas J.
Garber, Jack D.
Garber, Peter
Garber, William
Garcia, Bonny
Garcia, Francisco
Garcia, Jose C.
Garcia, Max J.
Garden, George T.
Garden, George T.
Gardner, Earl G.
Gardner, Frank V.
Gardner, James A.
Gardner, MajGen Donald R.
Gardner, William
Gare, Ivan D.
Garey, George A.
Garland, Everett D.
Garman, Richard W.
Garneau, Thomas A.
Garner, Thurman P.
Garren, Raymond M.
Garrett, David E.
Garrett, Joy
Garris, Preston F.
Garthright, Jack D.
Gaschler, John
Gaskill, Ray
Gass, Jim J.
Gaston, Percy L.

Gately, Lilla
Gates, Frederick E.
Gates, Richard A.
Gates, Ronald L.
Gaudette, Leonard V.
Gauruder, Stephen
Gauthier, Ward F.
Gavitt, Burton A.
Gavora, Edward S.
Gawel, Louis J.
Gayner, William F.
Gazel, Edward D.
Geades, Harry A.
Geagan, William J.
Geary, John B.
Geary, John F.
Geary, Walter F.
Gee, Don H.
Gehris, Darrell K.
Geiger, Edward
Geiske, John
Gelinas, Robert J.
Geller, Henry P.
Gemmrig, James R.
Genge, Clarinda D.
Genge, George Dobson
Genge, Hugo Victor
Genoff, Ralph W.
Genovese, Joseph Philip
Gentile, James
Gentry, Guy C.
Gentry, James L.
Gentry, John D.
Gentry, John H.
George, Earl A.
George, Robert L.
Gerace, Joseph A.
Gerald, Robert
Gerbino, Agnes G.
Gerbino, Larry
Gerdt, Richard H.
Gergo, Peter
Gerich, Walter
Gerish, Fred W.
Gerker, Edward C.
Gerkhardt, Gerald H.
Gerkin, William R.
Germain, Louis H.
Gerst, William W.
Gervase, Nicholas G.
Geschlecht, Robert W.
Gesin, Ann R.
Geske, Richard H.
Gessner, Alfred H.
Getz, Harold
Geyer, Harlan M.
Gholson, Amon K.
Giambatista, Michael R.
Giardina, Gaetano
Gibbs, Julian B.
Gibney, Richard M.
Gibson, Charles A.
Gibson, Jonathan D.
Gibson, Lee Roy
Giddens, Clarke E.
Gilbert, Glenwood A.
Gilbert, Lyle R.
Gilbert, Victor B.

Gilde, Alfred G.
Giles, Christopher H.
Gilfillan, William E.
Gilker, Donald E.
Gilkey, Allen F.
Gill, John H.
Gill, Philip H.
Gillaspy, Edward V.
Gillen, Frank
Gilleo, Francis A.
Gillespie Jack T.
Gillespie, Jean
Gilliam, James W.
Gilman, Albert B.
Gilmore, Curtis E.
Gilomen, William J.
Gilson, Gradon B.
Gilson, William E.
Gilton, Daniel L.
Gilton, H. M.
Gilton, Keith
Gilton, William P.
Gimpel, Earl R.
Giordano, Joseph F.
Giordano, Joseph N.
Giordano, Salvatore J.
Giovinazzo, Michael
Gipp, Paul H.
Girton, Glenn M.
Giunta, Pat J.
Givens, Jack L.
Gjertson, Russell Norman
Gladbach, Walter L.
Glade, Paul
Gladson, Arnold L.
Gladson, Arnold D.
Glander, Robert J.
Glanzer, Raymond H.
Glasberg, Robert
Glaser, Harold H.
Glasgow, LtGen Harold G.
Glasscock, James T.
Glasser, Leonard B.
Glassmoyer, Donald P.
Glenn, James R.
Glinkman, Leo K.
Glorioso, Joseph S.
Glovacz, Joseph
Glover, Tracy L.
Gluck, Walter T.
Glynn, Thomas G.
Gobar, Hank
Gober, Grady T.
Gober, Una G.
Gobin, Victor K.
Goddard, Cecil L.
Goddard, Daniel
Goddard, Jack
Goebel, Harold H.
Goehle, Paul F.
Goetschel, Kenneth E.
Goforth, Paul G.
Goins, William A.
Golden, Faron P.
Golden, James K.
Golden, John E.
Golden, Louis M.
Golden, Paul F.

Goldstein, Louis S.
Goldstein, Robert
Goldwater, David
Goltz, Seymour
Golumb, Mary Ann
Gomez, Manuel 2
Gomm, Douglas H.
Gomm, Nelson S.
Gooch, Harry
Good, Raymond F.
Gooding, Robert L.
Goodman, Albert L.
Goodrich, George E.
Goodrich, James A.
Goodwin, Jack L.
Goodykoontz, William
Goossens, Joseph P.
Gordon, Abe
Gordon, Alva (Gene) E.
Gore, Richard D.
Gore, Wayne M.
Gorham, Albert G.
Gorham, Opal G.
Gorman, Bill L.
Gorman, Carl N.
Gorman, David C.
Gorski, John A.
Goss, Kenneth E.
Goss, Shirley J.
Gosser, Verlon
Goswick, Ray
Goto, Cecilia
Goton, Beverly A.
Gotzman, Robert W.
Goucher, Richard L.
Gough, James M.
Goul, Sidney R.
Goulding, Robert D.
Goulet, Donald S.
Goz, John L.
Grabner, Charles R.
Grace, Richard J.
Gradin, Edward
Grady, James R.
Grady, John V.
Grady, Leonard S.
Graham, Nila H.
Graham, Robert L.
Graham, William F.
Gramkow, Raymond C.
Granacki, William J.
Grant, Alma P.
Grant, Patrick J.
Grant, Ruth
Grantham, Jack
Grasmuck, Wallace D.
Graul, Frederick C.
Graves, James H.
Graves, Robert C.
Gray, Bill L.
Gray, Glendon C.
Gray, Lamar E.
Gray, Rowland C.
Gray ,USMC Ret Gen Alfred M.
Graziano, Frank A.
Graziano, William J.
Greason, Harry A.
Greco, Anthony

Greco, Anthony
Greco, Peter S.
Greco, Vince
Green, Benjamin A.
Green, Charles L.
Green, Daniel J.
Green, Esther
Green, George J.
Green, George J.
Green, Jesse W.
Green, Leslie
Green, Robert W.
Green, Walter
Greenfield, Thaddeus E.
Greenhalgh, James
Greenwald, Robert
Greenwood, George J.
Greenwood, Robert A.
Greer, Burgess B.
Greer, Dexter E.
Greer, Garland G.
Greer, Leonard A.
Gregg, Joseph C.
Gregor, Christopher J.
Gregory, Ora Lee
Grenon, Raymond H.
Gretch, Judy A.
Grgurich, Joseph H.
Griffin, Elbert A.
Griffin, James M.
Griffin, Larry Paul P.
Griffin, Willmont A.
Griffith, Ann A.
Griffith, Daniel W.
Griffith, Henry A.
Griggs, George R.
Grigsby, Tim L.
Grimm, Raymond M.
Grindel, John W.
Grinstead, Robert J.
Grisdale, Perry F.
Grisham, Otha L.
Grizzle, Bessie
Grobarek, Mary T.
Groeger, James R.
Grommes, Barney H.
Grondzki, Victor J.
Gross, Bernard L.
Gross, Paul H.
Gross, Russell C.
Grotegut, Don J.
Grove, Richard E.
Groves, Jo
Groves, Robert L.
Grubbs, Carolyn B.
Grubbs, Mance D.
Gruenwald, Gary A.
Grummel, Jerome L.
Grund, William F.
Grunst, Ervin P.
Grupp, William A.
Guadagni, Alfred S.
Guarnett, Myron L.
Guba, Edward
Gudger, Troy C.
Guffy, David
Guidry, Lovell P.
Guilford, Eugene W.

Guillory, Anthony C.
Gulich, Adolf E.
Gummere, David C.
Gumnit, Stanley S.
Gundlach, Merle C.
Gunn, John A.
Gunther, Aubrey D.
Gustafson, August F.
Gustafson, Deloris A.
Gustafson, James K.
Gustavson, Gordon W.
Gutekenst, Robert J.
Gutka, John "Jack" T.
Gutzmann, Leslie E.
Guyer, Frederick J.
Guyer, Richard S.
Guyre, Frank
Gwaltney, Albert R.
Gwynne, Alexander T.

– H –

Haack, Edwin G.
Haack, Joseph A.
Haak, Robert G.
Haas, Edward M.
Haberman, Harold F.
Hack, Louise
Hacker, Robert E.
Hackett, Joseph J.
Hackey, Susan Tipton
Hackler, Vann
Hackney, George H.
Haddad, William L.
Haddix, Margaret J.
Haddon, Ralph E.
Hadler, Richard A.
Hadley, Hunter B.
Haeberle, Chris
Haentges, Russell
Haffey, John P.
Hagberg, Clayton H.
Hagen, Janet L.
Hagen, Richard P.
Hager, Caryl E.
Hager, Lero T.
Hagerling, Sidney W.
Haggblom, Harold N.
Haglund, Myron K.
Hahn, Margaret
Hahn, Philip E.
Hahne, William R.
Haig, Douglas P.
Haines, Darlene Y.
Haines, Edward T.
Haines, Edward T.
Haines, Robert A.
Hairgrove, Audrey H.
Hakala, Raymond H.
Halbert, Betty
Hale, Ted R.
Haley, Mary F.
Hall, Arthur Leeroy
Hall, Bruce A.
Hall, Charles W.
Hall, David E.
Hall, Frank
Hall, Glenn J.
Hall, James E.

Hall, John
Hall, Laurence M.
Hall, Raymond O.
Hall, Robert A.
Hall, Robert C.
Hall, Robert O.
Hall, Robert J.
Halle, Fred J.
Haller, Walter L.
Halley, Leonard R.
Hallman, Robert S.
Halloran, John J.
Halls, Charles O.
Halpin, Carl
Hamby, Luther W.
Hamel, Roger G.
Hamill, William D.
Hamilton, Fred W.
Hamilton, Howard B.
Hamilton, John W.
Hamilton, Marilyn
Hamilton, Maurice Dale
Hamilton, Norma Jean
Hamilton, Robert P.
Hamilton, Sam B.
Hamilton, William W.
Hamlin, Stanley M.
Hammel, Eric M.
Hammett, Larry W.
Hammond, Edward T.
Hammond, Thomas C.
Hammond, William P.
Hampton, Philip H.
Hampton, Ronald E.
Hampton, William R.
Hamrick, Junior C.
Hanafin, Jeremiah P.
Hancock, Joe H.
Hancock, Lewis H.
Hanger, Robert C.
Hanley, Timothy J.
Hanlon, Thomas S.
Hanna, Clarence M.
Hanna, Robert L.
Hannon, James M.
Hansen, Jerome F.
Hansen, Thomas L.
Hanson, Gustave V.
Hanson, Otto F.
Hanus, Paul A.
Hardee, James C.
Hardegree, Barry A.
Harders, Robert D.
Hardesty, Lothair Q.
Hardgrove, Harry R.
Hardiman, Matt
Hardiman, Matthew B.
Hardiman, Robert F.
Harding, Frances M.
Harding, John E.
Hardy, Hugh W.
Hardy, Nero W.
Hare, David E.
Hare, Dorothy
Hare, John F.
Hare, William J.
Hargis, Clarence E.
Hargis, John C.

Hargraves, John H.
Harlan, Ellis V.
Harley, Robert W.
Harman, L.L.
Harmon, Richard F.
Harmon, Richard B.
Harms, John E.
Harms, Lora Edna
Harn, Otis E.
Harns, Edward J.
Harper, Charles R.
Harr, Robert D.
Harrell, John M.
Harrill, Danny F.
Harrington, James
Harrington, James E.
Harrington, James J.
Harrington, Michael H.
Harrington, Ted A.
Harris, Albert C.
Harris, Bobby Joe
Harris, Charles W.
Harris, J.E.
Harris, James
Harris, James C.
Harris, Jesse R.
Harris, Marshall E.
Harris, Robert A.
Harris, Robert J.
Harris, Virgil R.
Harris, Wendell G.
Harris, William T.
Harrison, Christell
Harrison, H. William
Harrison, Ray T.
Harrison, William A.
Harrop, Maj
Harrop, William D.
Hart, Carl L.
Hart, Elwin B.
Hartley, Terry L.
Hartman, James G.
Hartman, Jess W.
Hartong, Robert M.
Harvey, Bernard R.
Harvey, William A.
Haskell, Barbara D.
Haskell, Herbert A.
Haskell, Richard T.
Hass, Carl R.
Hatala, John M.
Hatch, Myron G.
Hatch, Norman T.
Hatch, Rodney E.
Hatfield, Charles E.
Hatfield, Kody
Hatfield, Richard D.
Hattendorf, Henry C.
Haubert, Lawrence W.
Hauburger, Robert W.
Hauck, Clinton W.
Hauer, J. Frank
Haugen, Chester M.
Hauk, John W.
Hausske, Albert J.
Havel, Frank R.
Havelka, Kenneth A.
Haver, Richard F.

Havlin, Joseph L.
Hawarah, Kathleen B.
Hawe, Bill E.
Hawk, Paul L.
Hawkins, Armis E.
Hawkins, Charles W.
Hawkins, Earl H.
Hawkins, Paul S.
Hawkins, Robert J.
Hay, Juliet C.
Hay, Walter C.
Hayden, Jack E.
Hayden, Mildred L.
Hayden, Will Lamar L.
Hayes, Mahlon E.
Haynes, Baxter M.
Haynes, Fred E.
Haynes, Juanita L.
Haynes, Linda Strider S.
Haynie, Robert C.
Hazelton, Arthur J.
Hazen, Kathleen
Hazzard, Gerald H.
Hazzard, Milton L.
Hazzard, Richard F.
Heacock, Juan C.
Headley, Roy R.
Heafield, Gordon
Heald, James R.
Healey, Harold L.
Healey, Paul J.
Healey, Richard
Healy, Gerard D.
Healy, Patrick R.
Heaney, Robert B.
Hearnsberger, Brian J.
Heart, Christ W.
Heater, Guy C.
Heath, David S.
Heath, Donald A.
Heath, Robert H.
Hebert, Alfred L.
Hecht, Joseph
Hedderly, James W.
Hedge, Beverly L.
Hedleston, Merlyn T.
Hedloff, Ann T.
Hedrick, Everett J.
Heffernan, John J.
Hegarty, Edward James
Heilbronner, Leroy J.
Heileman, Howard W.
Heimann, John A.
Heiner, John P.
Heinrich, John A.
Heinz, Hans R.
Heinzel, Eugene H.
Heisler, John T.
Helek, Steve
Helenhouse, Donald L.
Hellums, Dwight
Helmey, Majorie
Helms, Ira H.
Helo, Roman J.
Heltemes, Stanley W.
Helton W.C.
Hemmer, Michael W.
Hemmings, Robert L.

Hemstad, Lyle R.
Henderson, Arno A.
Henderson, Clement
Henderson, James L.
Henderson, Robert H.
Hendley, Nita M.
Hendrick, Robert E.
Hendricks, Ira B.
Hendrickson, Henry G.
Hendrickson, Robert H.
Hendrix, Marshall W.
Hengesbach, Robert W.
Henjum, Morris D.
Henkel, Dorothy A.
Henkel, John H.
Henn, Louis C.
Hennessy, Tom A.
Hennigin, William A.
Henry, Brookie B.
Henry, Charles M.
Henschel, Gerald E.
Hensley, Kenneth J.
Hensley, Marilyn L.
Henson, William M.
Henss, Alton Duayne
Henza, Russell E.
Hepford, Robert C.
Herber, William E.
Herbst, Joan
Herleth, David H.
Herman, Bernard J.
Herman, Christopher D.
Hermann, Jacob
Hernandez, Eulalio J.
Hernandez, Ignacio L.
Hernandez, Jack P.
Herndon, Eugene H.
Herr, David F.
Herrick, David C.
Herring, James J.
Herrington, Earl W.
Herrler, Charles F.
Herweck, Arthur C.
Hess, James D.
Hess, John E.
Hess, Roger F.
Hess, Sheldon E.
Hester, Floyd E.
Hester, Wiley L.
Hetrick, Charles W.
Hetzel, Kenneth L.
Heuer, Louis M.
Hewitt, Duane D.
Hewitt, Wayne M.
Hewlett, Edward A.
Heyduck, Billy J.
Heyer, George M.
Hibbard, Wayne O.
Hibbert, Robert G.
Hickel, Kenneth G.
Hickey, Charles D.
Hickey, Martha B.
Hickey, S.M.
Hickman, Edwin L.
Hickrod, George Alan
Hicks, Belle W.
Hicks, Charles L.
Hicks, E. William

Hicks, Kenneth P.
Hicks, Mills
Hicks, Orris I.
Hicks, Richard N.
Hieronymus, Dolores
Hiers, Brill
Higbee, Roland K.
Higdon, Gerald F.
Higgenbotham, Benny F.
Higgins, Arthur E.
Higgins, Byron F.
Higgins, James J.
Higgins, Thomas F.
Highland, Robert O.
Hightshue, James E.
Hile, John D.
Hileman, Jay C.
Hiles, Robert L.
Hilgert, Vincent A.
Hill, Aubrey F.
Hill, Betty M.
Hill, Donald Jacob
Hill, Irwin F.
Hill, Joseph R.
Hill, Lyle E.
Hill, Marshall W.
Hill, Paul C.
Hill, Raymond J.
Hill, Richard T.
Hill, Robert L.
Hill, Ronald G.
Hill, Russell W.
Hill, Thomas T.
Hill, Wallace T.
Hill, William F.
Hillgaertner, William W.
Hillmann, Joseph T.
Hilton, Richard E.
Hinchcliffe, David H.
Hinde, Robert R.
Hindes, Wallace R.
Hindsley, Rolland K.
Hinshaw, Milas C.
Hintze, Willard P.
Hinze, Jerry J.
Hirsch, Marvin
Hiscox, Thomas
Hitchings, Thomas W.
Hite, Ellis K.
Hitt, Wade H.
Hixson, John E.
Hjelm, Eric D.
Hoadley, Kenneth E.
Hoagland, Carmen E.
Hoard, Clarence
Hobaugh, Albert L.
Hobbs, Irene E.
Hobbs, Thomas A.
Hochgertel, John W. "Jack"
Hockinson, William L.
Hocutt, Skippy W.
Hodapp, Arthur W.
Hodges, Thomas V.
Hodges, Tommy E.
Hodges, William L.
Hodin, John V.
Hoeg, Walter W.
Hoehne, Curt O.

Hoenig, John D.
Hoernel, Fowler W.
Hoffer, Gerald E.
Hoffman, Barbara J.
Hoffman, Carl W.
Hoffman, Harvey W.
Hoffman, Reginald L.
Hoffman, Robert B.
Hoffman, USMC Ret MajGen
Carl W.
Hofford, Margaret M.
Hofford, Robert G.
Hofvendahl, Russell L.
Hogan, George N.
Hogan, Gerald P.
Hogan, James E.
Hogan, Richard S.
Hogue, William C.
Hohos, Edward F.
Hojna, Henry M.
Hokkanen, William
Holcomb, Keith T.
Holcombe, Larry D.
Holdeman, W.R.
Holl, Fred L.
Holladay, Howard R.
Hollembeak, Karl L.
Hollenbeck, Floyd G.
Hollenbeck, Gerald D.
Holley, Christian M.
Holliday, Barry J.
Hollingsworth, Dean R.
Holloman, Floyd C.
Holloway, Elizabeth
Holloway, Stanley P.
Hollyfield, Jerry N.
Holmes, Arthur L.
Holmes, Fred
Holmes, James P.
Holmes, John A.
Holmes, Lawrence W.
Holsten, Elmo
Holtsclaw, David C.
Holzer, Betty
Holzheimer, Marvin O.
Homer, James K.
Homer, Karl T.
Homme, Jack E.
Homrich, Bernard J.
Hongisto, Raymond L.
Hook, George C.
Hooke, Walter G.
Hooker, Daniel L.
Hooper, Henry G.
Hoover, Walter J.
Hopey, Lamone J.
Hopkins, Douglas P.
Hopkins, James E.
Hopkins, Paul A.
Hopkins, Timothy A.
Hoptowit, Buddy P.
Horan, Francis X.
Horgan, John F.
Horn, Carl R.
Horn, Ruth
Hornbaker, Lee F.
Horne, William R.
Horner, Richard W.

Hornsby, Joan M.
Horrigan, Elaine B.
Horten, A. Martin
Horton, Eugene
Hortsch, Arthur M.
Horvath, Eugene A.
Horvath, Frank M.
Hosbach, William J.
Hosford, James F.
Hoskins, Ted G.
Hosler, Jerry L.
Hotchkiss, Wesley G.
Hoth, Edward W.
Hotop, Peter G.
Hottle, Jack R.
Houck, Michael F.
Houg, Lawrence A.
Hough, William J.
Houk, James E.
Houle, George A.
House, John H.
Houston, Chip W.
Hovenden, Jack L.
Hovsepian, Archie
Howard, Richard B.
Howard, Roy S.
Howard, Winfred W.
Howarth, BGen James E.
Howell, Lois E.
Howell, Robert L.
Howery, Thomas N.
Howes, Lee F.
Howey, Arden A.
Howington, Jodie G.
Howland, Earl L.
Howse, William J.
Hoyt, Ross N.
Hrella, William P.
Hruska, John J.
Hubach, Gary C.
Huband, Michele Ray R.
Hudgins, Louis R.
Hudman, Clarence W.
Hudman, Jerrell W.
Hudson, Jeanne Wickman
Hudson, Johnie M.
Hudson, Louis O.
Hudson, Virgil J.
Hudzinski, Edward
Huff, Michael T.
Huff, Richard E.
Huffington, Harold S.
Huffman, Fred R.
Huffman, Richard L.
Hufford, William E.
Hughes, Clyde E.
Hughes, David T.
Hughes, Gus
Hughes, Jack W.
Hughes, Mary F.
Hughes, Orville W.
Hughes, Robert E.
Hughes, Ryland J.
Hughes, Thomas H.
Hughes, William G.
Hughes, William D.
Huisinga, Rudolph E.
Huizing, Howard M.

Hulet, Keith A.
Hull, Bruce E.
Hull, Richard F.
Hulsey, George A.
Hulub, Paul R.
Hume, Robert R.
Humphreys, Richard A.
Hundley, Leroy "Redman"
Hunt, Freeman T.
Hunt, James E.
Hunt, Thomas P.
Hunt, Vondane
Hunter, Eno W.
Hunter, Harley Lynn
Hunter, James E.
Huntington, Elmer
Huntoon, Robert L.
Huot, Joseph R.
Hurley, Timothy F.
Hursig, George E.
Hurst, James M.
Huseby, Robert
Husemoller, Dale W.
Husenita, Paul N.
Husted, Albert P.
Hutcherson, Clarence G.
Hutchinson, Donald E.
Huth, Robert C.
Huther, Ralph J.
Hutka, Henry B.
Hutka, Mary L.
Hutsell, Floyd M.
Hutsell, Harry A.
Hutton, Graham H.
Hutton, Harry B.
Hutton, Russell V.
Hyatt, Hershel G.
Hyatt, Juanita
Hyatt, Pauline
Hyde, Arnold B.
Hyde, Betty L.
Hyde, William F.
Hyden, Bernard V.
Hyland, Gladys
Hymel, Kenneth E.
Hymel, Walden S.
Hyson, Edward G.

– I –
Iannelli, Joseph A.
Iding, Charles H.
Ihnot, George F.
Iler, James Posey P.
Ilkiw, Steven
Imholte, Donald C.
Immel, Harrison M.
Inderlin, Anthony J.
Infante, Dominick
Innis, Russell F.
Intaschi, Joseph E.
Inteman, Albert H.
Iodice, Rudolph G.
Iovino, Michael S.
Ireland, Terry R.
Irons, Ralph D.
Irrera, D.A.
Irvin, Roger G.
Irving, Melvin D.

Irving, William H.
Irwin, Jim A.
Irwin, John W.
Irwin, Robert F.
Isleb, Arthur C.
Ivary, Margaret
Iwicki, Ronald M.

– J –
Jabbusch, Arthur J.
Jach, Gloria P.
Jackel, Margaret
Jacklin, Robert J.
Jackman, Robert E.
Jacko, James A.
Jackson, A.B.
Jackson, Barbara J.
Jackson, John W.
Jackson, Martin
Jackson, Robert E.
Jackson, Wilbur B.
Jackson, Willard T.
Jackson, William E.
Jacob, Michael M.
Jacobs, Alex
Jacobs, Donald G.
Jacobs, Donald P.
Jacobs, Marvin L.
Jacobs, Robert D.
Jacobs, William F.
Jacobsen, Donald W.
Jacobson, Albert Vick
Jaggers, David H.
Jakobson, Howard L.
James, Bob W.
James, Glenn W.
James, Harry S.
James, Lummie E.
Jamieson, Mary P (Holly) P.
Jamieson, Robert A.
Jamison, Fred P.
Jamison, Russell E.
Jamison, Thomas V.
Jandl, Henry H.
Janendo, Frank J.
Janik, Joseph J.
Janssen, E. William
Jappe, Fritz J.
Jaquith, George O.
Jarrard, John K.
Jarvis, Calvin E.
Jarvis, William S.
Jasper, Jack W.
Jaworski, Olive G.
Jeanetti, Arnold J.
Jeffcoat, Wallace L.
Jefferies, William L.
Jeffers, George W.
Jefferson, Alonzo Nurman N.
Jenkins, Donald L.
Jenkins, Earl L.
Jenkins, Hardy R.
Jenkins, Harold D.
Jenkins, Louie C.
Jenkins, Morris N.
Jenkins, Vernon L.
Jennings, Roland K.
Jennings, William L.

Jenny, Henry F.
Jensen, George J.
Jensen, Gilbert W.
Jensen, Howard C.
Jensen, Leo J.
Jensen, Robert A.
Jensen, Walter K.
Jersey, Stanley C.
Jessup, Robert G.
Jester, Eleanor J.
Jobe, John H.
Joblin, Lathan
Johns, Kingston
Johnsmiller, Robert W.
Johnson, Arthur
Johnson, Belton H.
Johnson, Bettye M.
Johnson, Bill J.
Johnson, C. Eugene "Gene"
Johnson, Charles E.
Johnson, Charles O.
Johnson, Dennis
Johnson, Donald G.
Johnson, Frank M.
Johnson, George O.
Johnson, Grant J.
Johnson, H. William
Johnson, Herbert E.
Johnson, Hugh K.
Johnson, Ina Mae
Johnson, J.B.
Johnson, James A.
Johnson, James C.
Johnson, James W.
Johnson, James W.
Johnson, Jerry L.
Johnson, John W.
Johnson, Joseph B.
Johnson, Kenneth W.
Johnson, Kenneth J.
Johnson, Marjorie
Johnson, Randall E.
Johnson, Raymond A.
Johnson, Robert E.
Johnson, Samuel E.
Johnson, Stephen T.
Johnson, Thelbert W.
Johnson, Wallace R.
Johnson, Wesley R.
Johnson, William
Johnston, Hazen J.
Johnston, Jack A.
Johnston, James E.
Johnston, Robert B.
Jones, Benjamin R.
Jones, Charles B.
Jones, Charlotte M.
Jones, D. Scott
Jones, Don S.
Jones, E. Eugene
Jones, Edward W.
Jones, Ervin B.
Jones, George L.
Jones, Harvey A.
Jones, James C.
Jones, James D.
Jones, James L.
Jones, Jean

Jones, John C.
Jones, Julius "Deacon" C.
Jones, Kenneth E.
Jones, Knoful S.
Jones, Lee A.
Jones, Marion L.
Jones, Mary R.
Jones, Mary B.
Jones, Mary P.
Jones, Ray C.
Jones, Robert J.
Jones, Robert C.
Jones, Robert E.
Jones, Roy H.
Jones, Victor C.
Jones, Viola M.
Jones, Waller Finley
Jones, Wilbur D.
Jones, William T.
Jones, Willie C.
Jones, Winifred E.
Jordan, Beverley L.
Jordan, Joseph H.
Jordan, Loyd C.
Jorgensen, Laurence P.
Jorgensen, Walter E.
Joseph, Clifford S.
Josif, Paul E.
Jouett, Paul E.
Joy, Daniel M.
Joy, Joseph V.
Joy, USMC Ret BGen James R
Joyce, George E.
Joyce, Patrick J.
Judd, Carroll E.
Judd, Keith R.
Judd, Phyllis M.
Judd, Steve Judge Mollie O
(Shanley)
Judiscak, Jean
Juhan, USMC Ret MGen Jack P.
Juncker, Townsend C.
June, Floyd
Jurkiewicz, Frank J.
Justice, William G.

– K –
Kachurak, Edmund C.
Kaczmar, Stephen R.
Kaeding, Graydon H.
Kaftan, George M.
Kahn, Lauren H.
Kaiser, Leo A.
Kalassay, Theodore A.
Kalber, Howard H.
Kalencik, William P.
Kalinick, Andrew
Kalis, Delores
Kallas, Steve A.
Kameck, Leslie
Kamys, Marie H.
Kane, Harold W.
Kane, Robert A.
Kane, Robert F.
Kania, Frank C.
Kania, Raymond E.
Kapaun, H. Louise
Kapaun, Harold K.

Kaplan, Jerome
Kappel, Frank P.
Kapps, Charles E.
Kapuscinski, John V.
Karakas, Nick K.
Karal, Franklin J.
Karalus, Donald H.
Karr, Margaret L.
Karr, Richard C.
Kastl, Rafael J.
Kastl, Robert T.
Katz, Robert I.
Katzner, Donald M.
Kaucher, John W.
Kaufman, Herman L.
Kaul, John
Kavanagh, Charles J.
Kawka, Helen
Kay, Ronald P.
Kazikowski, Eugene R.
Kazmierski, Stanley
Kazoroski, Ron
Keane, Thomas F.
Kear, Thomas J.
Kearney, Newey F.
Keating, Paul J.
Keaveney, William P.
Keay, Crosby G.
Keck, John A.
Keck, Valerie H.
Keck, Warren
Kee, Fred
Keefer, Albert M.
Keegan, John D.
Keegan, Joseph A.
Keeley, Dean F.
Keeley, James Lee L.
Keeling, Corinne
Keen, Charles D.
Keenan, James T.
Keenan, James W.
Keenan, Joseph
Keenan, Joseph A.
Keene, Edward L.
Keene, Ronald L.
Keeton, Shirley
Keffer, Karl K.
Keitel, Harvey
Kelleher, Edward J.
Kelleher, Eugene
Keller, Elman J.
Keller, Stanley M.
Keller, Thomas E.
Kellett, C. Pete
Kelley, George E.
Kelley, Jessie B.
Kelley, Kevin L.
Kelley, Mildred V.
Kelley, Robert D.
Kelliher, William F.
Kelly, Agnes V.
Kelly, George R.
Kelly, James R.
Kelly, James S.
Kelly, Joe
Kelly, Patrick J.
Kelly, Robert A.
Kelly, Robert T.

Kelly, Walter E.
Kelly, William L.
Kelly, William M.
Kelm, Eddie J.
Kelpine, Oliver G.
Kelsey, James L.
Keltner, Monte R.
Kemp, Henry B.
Kemp, Letty M.
Kempel, Dorothy
Kennedy, Donald G.
Kennedy, James K.
Kennedy, Paul F.
Kennedy, Ralph N.
Kennedy, Thomas L.
Kennelly, Richard J.
Kenner, Beverly Glenn
Kenny, George H.
Kent, Floyd D.
Kent, Kyle C.
Keogh, Howard F.
Kerby, Yale L.
Kerens, Thomas J.
Kerley, James E.
Kerman, Robert L.
Kern, Frank J.
Kerns, Herbert A.
Kerns, James C.
Kerns, John T.
Kerr, Baine P.
Kerr, William P.
Kessel, Aloysius Gabriel
Kessler, Albert F.
Kessler, John R.
Ketchem, Wesley E.
Keys, James D.
Keys, William M.
Keysor, Elvis G.
Kibbey, Betty R.
Kidd, Janet M.
Kidder, William E.
Kiely, William F.
Kiernan, David J.
Kiernan, George F.
Kies, Joseph S.
Kiesner, Merle
Kilakis, Russell E.
Killam, Herman B.
Killeen, William K.
Kilman, Mary Jo
Kilpatrick, William B.
Kimak, Peter
Kimball, Albert F.
Kimball, Lawrence C.
Kime, Robert E.
Kincaid, George E.
Kinder, Charles H.
Kinder, David E.
Kindred, Aubrey A.
King, Alfred D.
King, Clarence W.
King, Douglas
King, Harland F.
King, Judith
King, Kevin D.
King, Perry C.
King, Raymond J.
King, Travis L.

Kingston, Lloyd R.
Kinley, Joy C.
Kinley, Linda C.
Kinley, Robert E.
Kinley, Robert L.
Kinney, Dale A.
Kinney, John F.
Kirby, Evan D.
Kirchman, Donald
Kirchner, Andrew F.
Kirchner, Robert L.
Kirk, Joseph E.
Kirk, Richard D.
Kirkman, Donald I.
Kirkman, William H.
Kirkos, George J.
Kirkpatrick, Bruce F.
Kirkwood, William G.
Kisling, Leroy C.
Klem, Edwin W.
Klemmer, Kurt O.
Kletz, Bruce W.
Klieforth, Raymond C.
Kliem, John M.
Klima, Charles J.
Klimek, Clarence J.
Klingler, Vincent L.
Klink, Marcell G.
Kloak, George E.
Kloss, Thomas H.
Klotz, Charles W.
Knapp, James R.
Knapp, Lucille
Knapper, Solomon
Knauft, David L.
Knight, David M.
Knight, Elliott L.
Knight, Glenn B.
Knight, James A.
Knight, James R.
Knight, Lloyd C.
Knight, Raymond N.
Knippel, Ralph R.
Kniss, Gary J.
Knoebel, Richard C.
Knorzer, Donovan F.
Knudson, Merlin
Knudtson, Verna Emily
Koc, Chester J.
Koch, Carl L.
Koch, Evelyn
Koch, Richard E.
Kochan, Aloysius R.
Kock, George E.
Koehler, Gladys
Koen, Albert E.
Koenig, Alan W.
Koenig, Glenn C.
Koenig, James L.
Koester, Wayne B.
Kogut, Joseph B.
Kohnle, John E.
Kokladas, Ernest W.
Kolman, Merle T.
Koltermann, Calvin V.
Konopatzki, William P.
Kopack, Andrew F.
Kopnik, Peter

Kornblith, Marvin
Korth, Francis L.
Korup, William J.
Kosek, Joseph F.
Kostrzech, Christopher
Kotalic, Dorothy
Kouma, Anthony B.
Kowalchuk, Michael P.
Kowalczyk, Henry
Koziuk, Gregory G.
Kozlowski, Aloysius J.
Kozol, Dr. Solomon M.
Kraemer, Marie R.
Kraettli, Carl J.
Krapf Frank K.
Krause, Arthur W.
Krauss, Clement W.
Krauss, George F.
Kreczmer, Edward J.
Kregenow, Robert
Krehmeier, Herman J.
Krein, Joseph M.
Kremers, Walter S.
Krenke, William R.
Krenke, William R.
Krenz, Clarence W.
Krepps, Claude
Krepps, Royce M.
Krick, Robert K.
Krieger, Robert J.
Kroening, Janet
Kroll, Mitchell
Kruckmeyer, Thomas L.
Krueger, Bernard
Krueger, Bernard
Krueger, James H.
Krueger, Orville E.
Krueger, Orville E.
Krueger, Robert F.
Krulak, Charles C.
Kruse, Mahlon R.
Kruse, Wilbert G.
Krypel, John S.
Kuba, Albert S.
Kuba, Joseph J.
Kubatzki, Walter R.
Kubiak, Lawrence V.
Kucia, John
Kucks, Howard H.
Kudla, Mitchell N.
Kuhens, Denis D.
Kuhn, Leo G.
Kuklin, Edward
Kulesa, Stanley A.
Kuntz, Hillard L.
Kunz, Michael Thomas T.
Kurth, Sara-Ella C.
Kurz, Milton
Kusch, Carl F.
Kutash, Frank J.
Kutchar, Rudy S.
Kutcher, Ernest L.
Kyle, Jean

– L –

L'Abbe, John L.
La Grace, Thomas R.
La Greca, Vincent F.

Labarge, R. Gene
LaBrecque, John H.
Lacey, Daniel T.
Lackey, Harrison E.
Lacomchek, William J.
LaCroix, Russell H.
Ladd, Dean
Ladislaw, Joseph T.
Ladner, Charleston G.
Lafferty, Thomas A.
Laise, William H.
Lakamp, Mildred Sue S.
Lake, Peter F.
Laliberty, Rose
Lalicki, Joseph E.
Lamaster, Clifford H.
Lamb, John A.
Lamb, John A.
Lambert, Christopher J.
Lambert, Wilbert
Lambka, Harvey L.
Lambright, Ruth
Lambros, Alex S.
Lambson, Dale W.
Lambson, Lou Jean M J.
Lammert, Herbert W.
Lammie, William Richard
Lamoreaux, Beverlee J.
Lamoreaux, Ray M.
Lamothe, Lloyd G A
Lampe, Edgar
Lamphere, Elizabeth A.
Lampman, Frank D.
Lampman, Theodore I.
Lampropoulos, Demetrious
Lanam, Esther M.
Lance, Robert E.
Land, Roger D.
Landback, Eldon
Lander, Juanita T.
Landis, Chester S.
Landrum, Bruce D.
Landry, John R.
Landry, John R.
Landry, Joseph P.
Landry, Lucien B.
Landry, Norman T.
Landry, William D.
Landry, William C.
Landsback, Jack S.
Lane, Dolores
Lane, Harold A.
Lane, John E.
Lane, Lillian R.
Lane, Rovie L.
Lane, William T.
Lang,, Gilbert C.
Langdon, Cortland F.
Lange, Lee F.
Langenhan, Ethel
Langford, Randolph M.
Langley, Robert C.
Langston, Jack W.
Langston, Richard I.
Lanier, Grady E.
Lanier, Robert Louis L.
Lank, William R.
Lanning, Mark M.

Lannon, James Morton M.
Lanser, Edward P.
Lantaff, Mary H.
Lantz, Luke
Lanzalotto, Joseph C.
Laporte, Ewing E.
Laporte, Gilbert R.
Lapre', Donald P.
Larabee, John C.
Larkey, Jack W.
Larose, William J.
Larrieu, James A.
Larsen, Robert E.
Larsen, Stanley E.
Larson, Carmella L.
Larson, Imogene
Larson, Jack C.
Larson, Jay E.
Larson, Ole E.
Larson, Vernon D.
Larson, Walter E.
Larzalere, Robert L.
Lasecki, Harry T.
Laskey, James R.
Lasky, Lawrence M.
Lasky, Michael
Lassila, Leslie J.
Latia, Charles
Latkovich, Joe
Latour, Lawrence W.
Latz, Thomas A.
Lauckhardt, Richard A.
Lauderdale, William C.
Lauer, Arthur P.
Laugalis, Shawn M.
Launder, Willis R.
Laurie, Salvatore F.
Lausier, Richard L.
Lavash, Ted J.
Lavelle, Michael T.
Lavers, Albert J.
Lawler, Billy J.
Lawler, Jane
Lawlor, Charles A.
Lawnick, Joseph J.
Lawrence, Charles Ernie
Lawrence, David B.
Lawrence, Stephen A.
Lawshe, Harvey N.
Lawson, David D.
Lawson, Floyd M.
Lawson, John W.
Lawson, Lee E.
Lawson, William M.
Lawton, Walter G.
Layland, Joseph L.
Layman, Douglas H.
Layton, Johnathon C.
Layton, Robert B.
Lazich, George R.
Le Gall, Charles F.
Learn, Timothy G.
Leary, Albert L.
Leary, John L.
Leatherman, Francis R.
LeBlanc, Hedley E.
LeBlanc, Leslie G.
Leblanc, O.K.

LeBlanc, Richard S.
Leblanc, William E.
LeBrun, Robert W.
Leckband, Carl A.
Ledet, David M.
Ledoux, Mark
Lee, Betty M.
Lee, Elena M.
Lee, Gen
Lee, Harvey L.
Lee, Jack K.
Lee, Robert S.
Lee, Walter E.
Leeds, Dan E.
Leek, Myron H.
Lefebvre, Mark A.
Leffel, Leroy W.
Lefurge, Thomas E.
Legan, Deborah I.
Legan, Robert F.
Leger, Alfred J.
Leggett, Manzy F.
Lehman, Richard G.
Lehmann, Burney F.
Leitch, Kevin R.
Leitch, Richard M.
LeMay, Evarist A.
LeMay, Joseph G. R.
Lembke, Arthur P.
Lembke, Frank W.
Lembke, Rose S.
Lemieux, Raymond E.
Leminelle, Ronald T.
Lemm, Elmer W.
Lemon, David L.
Lengyel, John L.
Lenhart, James B.
Lennon, Thomas J.
Lent, Jack T.
Leonard, Edward J.
Leonard, William C.
Leone, Daniel A.
Leonhardt, Carl H.
Lepore, Frances
Leppen, Carla I.
Leppen, Walter K.
Lerdal, Dean A.
Lerman, Maurice G.
Lerman, Maurice G.
LeRoy, Garland R.
Leshinski, Matthew L.
Lesiak, Joseph Z.
Leslie, Louis H.
Lettman, Shirley C.
Leugoud, Alex A.
Levalley, John E.
Levan, Richard
Leviton, Irwin B.
Levy, Franklin L.
Levy, Lewis W.
Lewis, Arthur L.
Lewis, Betty G.
Lewis, Brixey G.
Lewis, Laura E.
Lewis, Ralph W.
Lewis, Richard W.
Lewis, Robert E.
Lewko, William J.
Lewman, E. Kay

Libera, A.J.
Liberty, Bernard
Lichtenthal, Victor N.
Lickteig, Donald J.
Liebermann, William T.
Lienesch, Donald R.
Liepper, Maralin P.
Liggon, Roger W.
Lightfoot, Grady H.
Ligon, Champ
Lillard, Gary W.
Lillestol, Mary Louise
Lilley, Gerald E.
Lillo, Charles J.
Lilly, Charles W.
Lincoln, Roy E.
Linder, David B.
Lindholm, John E.
Lindholm, Norma
Lindlan, Harry
Lindley, Joseph P.
Lindsey, Thomas C.
Lindsey, Weldon A.
Linfoot, William E.
Lingerfelt, Helen
Link, Harold F.
Linkous, Donald E.
Linn, Carl E.
Lint, James R.
Lint, Monique M.
Lipari, Joseph R.
Lippman, Robert I.
Liquerman, Harry
Liszak, Joseph L.
Littell, Kenneth E.
Little, Branden
Little, Richard C.
Little, Robert J.
Little, William B.
Littlefield, Jean
Lively, Roy L.
Livingston, Alfred
Livingston, Lawrence H.
Livingston, Milton Stanley S.
Lizotte, Bernard R.
Lobb, Peggy M.
Lobe, Frank J.
Lobianco, Joseph H.
Lochner, Francis J.
Lockart, Paul E.
Locke, Lyman E.
Lockman, Richard J.
Lockman, Wilma
Lockwood, Robert E.
Lockwood, Ronald H.
Locricchio, Anthony P.
Loftiss, Frank
Loftus, James J.
Logue, Viets S.
Logue, William C.
Lohr, Robert L.
Lombardo, Joseph C.
London, James T.
London, Robert E.
London, William S.
Long, David R.
Long, Erwin D.
Long, Harold G.

Long, Harry R.
Long, Joseph H.
Long, Leonard M.
Long, Margie
Long, Maurry E.
Long, Thomas S.
Lonski, Albert
Lookingland, George W.
Looney, William P.
Lopez, Adolph
Lopez, Alfred
Lopez, Eugene
Lopez, Fred
Lopez, Jay Julian
Lopez, John P.
Lopez, Leonard
Lopez, Lupe
Lopez, Manuel L.
Loppe, Roy E.
Lorbecki, Francis X.
Lorimer, William J.
Lorsch, Howard H.
Loser, Francis T.
Loughran, Michael J.
Love, Huey M.
Love, Lester R.
Lovelace, Norman B.
Lovell, James E.
Lovell, Philip G.
Lovell, Terrance D.
Lovell, Warren P.
Lovering, Francis J.
Low, Roger F.
Lowe, George E.
Lowe, Maurice H.
Lowe, Robert J.
Lowe, Vernon L.
Lowell, Frank R.
Lowers, Bruce L.
Lowes, Norman H.
Loy, John R.
Lubetsky, Albert
Lubinsky, Darrell J.
Luby, Donald E.
Luby, George H.
Lucas, Thomas W.
Luce, Paul A.
Lucero, Patricia
Luciano, Johnnie B.
Lucier, Dennis D.
Lucree, William J.
Ludlam, Wesley H.
Ludlow, Martin R.
Ludwick, William G.
Ludwig, John
Lufkin, Neil E.
Luhan, Charles
Luinstra, Tiny F.
Lujan, J. Mike
Lujan, Michael A.
Luke, Stanley D.
Luker, Patricia
Lukes, Robert L.
Lumetta, Lawrence J.
Lumina, Lawrence "Lou"
Lundahl, Earl E.
Lundy, Joseph
Luneau, Ernest N.

Lupien, Henry F.
Luther, Albert E.
Luther, Joel H.
Lutz, Fred
Lutz, William R.
Lux, Phyllis C.
Lyle, James H.
Lyles, Kenneth G.
Lynch, James F.
Lynch, John J.
Lynch, Joseph E.
Lynch, Thomas J.
Lynn, Bernard W.
Lynn, Bruce N.
Lyons, Charles M.
Lyons, Donald I.
Lyons, Leah D.
Lyons, Louis J.
Lyons, William L.
Lyren, Carl V.
Lysene, Harold W.
Lytell, Orrie L.
Lytle, George R.
Lytle, Walter W.

– M –

Maas, Robert H.
Mabe, Roy E.
Maben, Claude J.
MacCotte,r Hugh B.
MacDonald, William B.
MacEwan, Robert C.
Macey, Albert E.
Machan, Eugene A.
MacIntyre, Douglas J.
Maciolek, Harold F.
Mack, William C.
MacKender, George G.
MacKenzie, Martha
Mackey, Donald M.
MacKiewicz, Anna J.
MacLennan, John M.
MacMahon, Ross
MacMillan, Alice J.
MacMillan, James
MacPherson, Earl
MacPherson, James T.
MacPherson, Sterling J.
MacWilliams, Kenneth J.
Maddalena, Helen
Madden, Jack N.
Madden, L.J.
Mader, Edward C.
Madigan, Paul L.
Madison, Iris
Magee, Donald C.
Magee, Russell E.
Mager, Betty C.
Mager, Bill
Maggard, Danny L.
Magnotti, Louis R.
Magnotti, Mary S.
Magnotti, Mary
Maher, Michael J.
Maher, Philip J.
Maher, Thomas F.
Mahoney, Patricia A.
Mahoney, Willard G.

Maiorka, John
Mairs, Roger L.
Maisen, Edward R.
Major, James E.
Majusiak, Anthony T.
Maker, Bill
Makowski, Bernard C.
Malan, Allan R.
Maldonado, Bill D.
Maldonado, Steven R.
Malek, Nick
Mallah, Robert Arnold
Malley, Anthony C.
Mallon, Douglass D.
Mallon, Joseph A.
Malloy, William J.
Malone, David L.
Malone, Wallace E.
Maloney, Edgar D.
Maloof, Charles
Malovich, Mildred
Mamula, Louis
Mandelkow, David W.
Manderville, Daniel J.
Mangan, Michael J.
Mangos, Charles P.
Manion, H.C
Manley, James D.
Manley, James J.
Manley, John M.
Mann, Earl W.
Mann, Richard C.
Mann, Robert G.
Manna, Paul G.
Manning, Arthur T.
Manning, Charles
Manning, David A.
Manning, Edith B.
Manning, John D.
Manning, Patrick J.
Manning, William G.
Mannino, Alfred A.
Mantel, Hyman
Marascio, Vincent A.
Maratea, Jerome A.
Marcantel, William E.
Marcinko, Chris C.
Marcinkoski, John W.
Marcinkowski, Casimer B.
Marcinkus, Albert R.
Mares, Christopher G.
Mariani, Bruno J.
Marin, Chris J.
Marion, Dale A.
Marion, Elaine
Marion, John F.
Markey, Arthur R.
Markey, Warren L.
Markham, Sue D.
Markley, Walter A.
Markovich, Edward
Marlowe, Philip B.
Marn, John R.
Marnelli, Albert E.
Marquis, Maurice E.
Marron, Thomas
Marrs, John D.
Marsh, Christopher C.

Marsh, John C.
Marshall, Albert J.
Marshall, Donald
Marshall, E. David
Marshall, Frank J.
Marshall, Harry J.
Marshall, Ione R.
Marshall, Jack C.
Marshall, James G.
Marshall, Thomas D.
Martan, James J.
Martens, Rev. Warren G.
Martin, Charles H.
Martin, David T.
Martin, Donald J.
Martin, Francis E.
Martin, Francis J.
Martin, Hazel E.
Martin, Henriette P.
Martin, Jack
Martin, James R.
Martin, Jeanette
Martin, Joe A.
Martin, Johnny J.
Martin, Joseph B.
Martin, Joseph W.
Martin, Lawrence F.
Martin, Lytle A.
Martin, Mary A.
Martin, Nancy J.
Martin, Robert J.
Martin, Stanley B.
Martin, William A.
Martinez, Luis A.
Martinez, Pete B.
Martini, Albert
Martocci, Roderick R.
Marum, Paul E.
Maschmann, Edward R.
Mashburn, Roscoe V.
Mason, Morris D.
Mason, Robert "Bob" E.
Mason, Russell F.
Mason, Virginia L.
Massaro, Frank A.
Masse', Armand A.
Massimin, Robert J.
Mast, Henry R.
Masters, Mike Anthony
Masterson, Patrick J.
Mastin, Peter B.
Mastrangelo, Paul E.
Masztak, Donald A.
Mathews, Edward L.
Mathews, Howard O.
Mathews, Robert C.
Mathis, Don E.
Matjasic, Raymond A.
Matley, "Blackie"
Matson, Roger W.
Matthews, Bert A.
Matthews, George E.
Matthews, Peter J.
Matthews, Richard I.
Matthews, William G.
Matthies, Theophilus
Matthies, Winifred E.
Matthiesen, Jens H.

Mattingley, Arthur A.
Mattingly, Rita Rose
Mattson, Edward C.
Matz, Charles A.
Maul, Betty
Maurer, Donald R.
Mauro, Richard T.
Maxam, William J.
Maxner, Richard B.
Maxson, Lynn R.
Maxwell, Henry F.
May, Alfred
May, Bernice J.
May, Robert B.
Mayhew, Jimmy L.
Mayhew, Jule W.
Maynard, Robert C.
Mazerac, Lawrence A.
Mc Kelvey, Donald E.
Mc Mahan, Claude
McAfee, Robert O.
McAllaster, Helen
McAndrew, Michael H.
McArdle, John J.
McArthur, Keith C.
McAvoy, Edith
McBain, James F.
McBride, Jack W.
McBride, Melvin R.
McBryde, Estes D.
McBryde, Noreen
McCabe, Thomas J.
McCafferty, John E.
McCahill, James E.
McCain, J.M
McCall, Curtis S.
McCallum, Edward L.
McCallum, John P.
McCammon, Claude A.
McCann, James L.
McCardell, Darwin E.
McCarter, Allen G.
McCarter, Wilbur R.
McCarthy, Albert J.
McCarthy, Dagmar
McCarthy, David
McCarthy, Eugene J.
McCarthy, Gerald D.
McCarthy, John
McClain, Charles W.
McClane, Vernon H.
McClard, James E.
McClellan, Elmer G.
McClement, Robert C.
McClendon, Hughetta
McClintick, Russell L.
McClure, Ralph
McConnell, Wm. "Bill"
McConomy, Jason E.
McCord, Byron
McCord, Lloyd R.
McCormick, James E.
McCormick, James R.
McCormick, Vincent D.
McCourt, Berton L.
McCoy, Billy R.
McCoy, Ella Mae
McCoy, Graham F.

McCoy, J.H.
McCrary, Thomas
McCue, Robert A.
McCuen, Allan
McCuen, James K.
McCullagh, Desmond J.
McCullough, Frances
McCurdy, John R.
McCurry, Jim D.
McDaniel, Homer C.
McDaniel, Jacqueline
McDaniel, William H.
McDermott, Clarence E.
McDermott, Joseph F.
McDermott, Michael J.
McDermott, William J.
McDonald, Elliot D.
McDonald, Jack V.
McDonald, Keith R.
McDonald, Paul G.
McDonald, R.H.
McDonald, Roderick W.
McDonald, William F.
McDonnell, Gerald
McDonough, Robert W.
McDowell, Gerald
McDowell, Jack R.
Mce, Paul E.
McElroy, James F.
McElveen, Ernest R.
McElvy, Johnnie L.
McEwen, James V.
McFadden, William L.
McFarlan, Richard H.
McFarland, Everett
McFarland, Malcolm U.
McFarlane, Andrew A.
McFarlane, Donald G.
McGahey, Richard T.
McGee, Horace J.
McGee ,Lawrence H.
McGehee, Bill J.
McGhee, George B.
McGill, Landon G.
McGilvery, Edward F.
McGinn, Edwin J.
McGinn, Harold L.
McGivney, John F.
McGlachlin, WF
McGough, Dudley
McGough, Thomas P.
McGovern, William J.
McGowan, Charles D.
McGowan, Frank L.
McGowan, Madeline M.
McGrath, William B.
McGregor, Helen
McGrew, James R.
McGuigan, John B.
McGuinness, Edmund J.
McGuinness, James L.
McGuinness, John P.
McGuinness, Robert A.
McGuire, John E.
McGuire, Robert P.
McGuire, Terrence W.
McGuire, Thomas J.
McGurk, Francis J.

McHugh, John F.
McHugh, Thomas J.
McIlquham, Ellie
McIlwain, Clifford G.
McInnis, Robert A.
McIntire, Curtis G.
McIntosh, Edward L.
McIntyre, Susan
McKean, Charles P.
McKeen, Harold E.
McKeever, D.W.
McKenna, Daniel J.
McKenzie, Frank N.
McKenzie, Lanore M.
McKenzie, R. Bruce
McKernan, Thomas A.
McKie, Deborah A.
McKinley, Robert J.
McKinney, Raymond E.
McKinney, Virginia
McKinstry, Howard K.
McKinstry, Virginia
McLain, Clyde R.
McLaughlin, Bernard P.
McLaughlin, John J.
McLaughlin, William S.
McLaughlin, William V.
McLeod, Richard T.
McMackin, Douglas K.
McMahon, James N.
McManaman, David E.
McManus, Robert C.
McMichen, William H.
McMillan, Delvin H.
McMillen, George A.
McMillian, William F.
McMinn, Ronald C.
McMoran, Ralph V.
McMullen, Helen
McMullin, Mary L.
McMurdy, Clyde F.
McNally, J.W.
McNally, Patricia
McNamara, Francis R.
McNaughton, Samuel W.
McNeal, Bryan P.
McNeive, Francis T.
McNeive, James F.
McNerney, Frank J.
McNichols, Audrey M.
McNorton, Harrell O.
McNulty, Bill
McNulty, Bill M.
McNulty, Martin T.
McPaul, Bernard C.
McPeak, Matthew R.
McPherson, Don E.
McPherson, Robert A.
McPherson, Wanda
McQuaid, William F.
McQuery, Dave L.
McVay, Clara Marie
McWethy, Daniel V.
McWilliams, Betty Ann
McWilliams, Ray E.
Mead, George F.
Meador, Robert L.
Meadows, Betty S.

Meadows, James I.
Meadows, Richard C.
Meakem, Francis J.
Mears, Roy G.
Meassick, Louis W.
Medaris, Frederick M.
Medford, E. Leslie
Medhus, Melroy (Mel) L.
Medina, Alexander E.
Medus, Allen J.
Meegan, George B.
Meehan, William F.
Mehley, Andrew John
Mehne, Fred D.
Meier, Kenneth F.
Meier, Norman C.
Meier, William A.
Meinders, Harold W.
Meister, William T.
Melanson, Richard C.
Melching, Charles F.
Melchione, Charles M.
Melfi, Edmond E.
Melicher, Roland V.
Melleby, Harold
Mello, Regina T.
Melnyk, Bohdan A.
Memmer, H.J.
Menchey, Robert D.
Menconi, Jeanne
Mendenhall, Edwin N.
Meranda, Vincent P.
Mercer, Dwight R.
Mercer, Everett G.
Merchant, George H.
Mercier, Marie M.
Meredith, Thomas W.
Merkel, Grace
Merker, Robert L.
Merle, Jack G.
Merritt, William M.
Merson, Olen E.
Mesko, John
Messenger, Merlin L.
Messenger, Robert L.
Messia, John
Messier, Thomas F.
Messina, Anthony T.
Messina, Edward D.
Messina, Salvatore W.
Methvin, Bernard H.
Mettler, Charles L.
Metzke, Jean
Meyer, Barbara
Meyer, David D.
Meyer, Edward L.
Meyer, Eldon Mike
Meyer, George F.
Meyer, Herbert A.
Meyer, J.W.
Meyer, Jarett P.
Meyer, Siegfried H.
Meyer, Wilbert D.
Meyer, William R.
Meyerhoff, Robert A.
Meyers, Norman H.
Meyers, William P G
Meza, Richard R.

Micale, Angelo E.
Micek, Joseph G.
Michael, Ronald J.
Michalak, Henry C.
Michaud, Mary Ann
Michelony, Lewis J.
Michuda, Dolores G.
Michuda, Joseph A.
Mick, Henry E.
Mickalowski, Leo W.
Mickelson, William L.
Midas, Frank J.
Middaugh, Randall L.
Middleton, Arthur U.
Middleton, Edgar W.
Middleton, Jack B.
Miears, William D.
Mieir, Steven D.
Mignosa, Gerald S.
Mika, John W.
Mikels, Francis R.
Milano, O.J.
Miles, Charles L.
Milewski, Leo H.
Milford, David W.
Milicich, Stephen
Milla, Leo E.
Millard, David C.
Millen, William L.
Miller, Alfred W.
Miller, Bernard J.
Miller, Calvin O.
Miller, Charles E.
Miller, Cletis M.
Miller, Creed
Miller, Donald R.
Miller, Esther R.
Miller, Floyd M.
Miller, Gertrude
Miller, Glenn E.
Miller, Jackie Lee
Miller, James A.
Miller, John F.
Miller, John H.
Miller, Jon K.
Miller, Kenneth L.
Miller, Louis
Miller, Michael D.
Miller, Paul E.
Miller, Richard J.
Miller, Robert J.
Miller, Robert
Miller, Roger J.
Miller, Shirley M.
Miller, Stanley J.
Miller, Steven D.
Miller, Theodore
Miller, William W.
Miller, Wilma (Gilton)
Milligan, Vernon L.
Milliman, Thomas J.
Millis, Edward H.
Mills, Genevieve
Mills, George R.
Mills, James P.
Mills, William H.
Milne, Enid
Milo, Frank

Milo, Teddy
Milstead, Paul E.
Mingolelli, Raffaella
Minium, Don W.
Minnich, Harold F.
Minnick, Leland L.
Minor, William T.
Mire, David E.
Mireski, Christopher J.
Mitch, Frank B.
Mitchell, Donald Roy
Mitchell, Edward J.
Mitchell, George E.
Mitchell, Gomer E.
Mitchell, James B.
Mitchell, John H.
Mitchell, Joseph
Mitchell, Orville L.
Mitchell, Porter J.
Mizell, Wallace L.
Mizner, Charles S.
Mizzell, George A.
Mobley, Robert F.
Mochon, William O.
Moellering, Ted F.
Moffett, Miller Francis
Mofley, William O.
Mohan, Lorraine S.
Mohs, Ervin L.
Moise, Norman Sydney
Moles, Kenneth V.
Monahan, Bonnie Windrich
Monahan, William J.
Monges, Charles J.
Monroe, James H.
Montalvo, Henry
Montgomery, Edward W.
Montgomery, James A.
Montgomery, Robert R.
Mooney, William J.
Mooneyham, Dora
Moore, Albert
Moore, Donald Franklin
Moore, Edward J.
Moore, Elizabeth
Moore, Frances
Moore, Gerald R.
Moore, Gordon L.
Moore, Gordon E.
Moore, Gurnia M.
Moore, Harold W.
Moore, James A.
Moore, James A.
Moore, James H.
Moore, John H.
Moore, Kenneth E.
Moore, Louie P.
Moore, Louise E.
Moore, Michael D.
Moore, Paul
Moore, Ralph E.
Moore, Rex W.
Moore, Robert E.
Moore, Terri
Moore, Timothy E.
Moore, Vernon W.
Moosher, William R.
Moran, James

Moran, John T.
Morano, Joseph Mordini Leo
Moreau, Francis H.
Morelan, B.R.
Moreno, Joe A.
Morgan, Arthur E.
Morgan, Clifford N.
Morgan, Edward F.
Morgan, Michael A.
Morgan, Michael K.
Morgan, Monroe
Morgan, William J.
Morgen, Gerald E.
Moriarty, Timothy J.
Morio, Edward J.
Morley, Paul J.
Morrell, Marybeth
Morrett, Patricia E.
Morrett, Wesley D.
Morrill, Frank L.
Morris, Charles W.
Morris, Elizabeth H.
Morris, Harold W.
Morris, John N.
Morris, Joseph P.
Morris, Nanette J.
Morris, Thomas B.
Morris, William D.
Morrison, James J.
Morrison, Thomas J.
Morrissey, James J.
Morrow, John P.
Morrow, Richard J.
Morton, Richard V.
Moseley, Cecil R R.
Moser, Edgar R.
Moses, John N.
Moses, Sidney L.
Mosher, Kenneth H H.
Mosier, Duane F.
Mosley, Henry Wayne E.
Moss, William B B.
Mouradjian, Margaret M.
Mowrey, Lenora O.
Mucha, Joseph F.
Muchnok, Frank J.
Muckel, Daniel K K.
Mudd, Charles F.
Muelhausen, Elmer R.
Mueller, Joseph N.
Mueller, Rudolph T.
Muffler, Joan N.
Muffler, Robert J.
Muha, Stanley J.
Muhlbach, Robert C.
Muir, Hayden N.
Mulhern, Paul J.
Mulkey, Jess O.
Mullen, Edward D.
Muller, Eugene F.
Muller, Mary Elizabeth
Muller, Steven A.
Muller, William J.
Mulligan, Francis R.
Mulligan, James P.
Mulligan, Peter J.
Mullin, Robert J J.
Mullins, James R R.

Mullins, Larry D D.
Mulvihill, Francis P.
Mulvihill, Matthew J.
Mumford, Marshall N.
Mungenast, Thomas C.
Munk, Raymond F.
Munn, Sumner T.
Murcott, Margaret K F.
Murdock, John B.
Murphey, Rev. William J.
Murphy, Bernard D.
Murphy, Cecil J.
Murphy, David B.
Murphy, Dennis J.
Murphy, Edward P.
Murphy, Edward F.
Murphy, Eugene T.
Murphy, Harold F.
Murphy, John M.
Murphy, John A.
Murphy, Paul O.
Murphy, Robert T.
Murphy, Stephen W.
Murphy, William
Murphy, William F.
Murphy, William D.
Murray, Frank T.
Murray, Gordon A.
Murray, James J.
Murray, Michael J.
Murray, Russell E.
Murray, Thomas F.
Murrell, Marshall G.
Murry, Ova A.
Murtaugh, James O.
Musil, John J.
Musser, John R.
Mutti, Charles C.
Myer, Marvin E.
Myers, Edward
Myers, Gemma
Myers, Gordon F.
Myers, James A.
Myers, Joseph J.
Myers, Merle L.
Myers, Ralph L.
Myers, Robert William
Myslicki, Edward

– N –
Nabers, Earskin J.
Nace, Albert J.
Nadeau, Armand J.
Nadolny, George R.
Nagel, Clarence S.
Nagel, Robert C.
Nagel, Ruth
Naile, James H.
Nailor, Richard A.
Nance, Vernon V.
Napoli, Leon J.
Nardello, John R.
Nardone, Edward W.
Nash, Gordon C.
Nash, Richard W.
Nason, Ary E.
Naumov, Nicola F.
Nava, Charles H.

Naylor, Howard N.
Nazzaretto, John
Neal, John P.
Neal, Mary Emily
Neal, USMC Gen Richard I.
Nebesne, Stephen
Neblitt, Frederick L.
Nedelka, John T 2
Needham, Gerald P.
Nehring, Nona June
Neigh, Earl B.
Neill, Dorothy M.
Neill, Esther M.
Neill, John
Neilson, Glendon L.
Neitman, Eugene W.
Neller, Bob
Nellis, Charles F.
Nelson, Arthur L.
Nelson, Arthur P.
Nelson, Boyd
Nelson, David R.
Nelson, Ernest P.
Nelson, Glenn W.
Nelson, Herbert E.
Nelson, Irving E.
Nelson, Jack E.
Nelson, Jacob M.
Nelson, James H.
Nelson, James J.
Nelson, Mack W.
Nelson, Robert W.
Nelson, Shelton R.
Nelson, Shirley
Nelson, William O.
Neomany, Joseph G.
Nereim, Robert L.
Nesbella, Michael B.
Nesbitt, William A.
Nessley, David M.
Netreba, Dorothy E.
Neuharth, Richard K.
Neveu, Kenneth J.
Nevgloski, Edward T.
New, Robert M.
Newbauer, Robert L.
Newbill, Patrick S.
Newby, Roy
Newcomb, Richard K.
Newcomb, Vance A.
Newell, Eugene F.
Newman, Preston E.
Newsom, Frank A.
Newton, Alvin W.
Newton, Harvey S.
Ney, Ray F.
Nicely, John D.
Nicholas, Ralph W.
Nichols, Carl W.
Nichols, Clyde
Nichols, Mary Jane
Nicholson, Arthur J.
Nicholson, Edsel W.
Nicholson, John L.
Nickel, Leo F.
Nickerson, William A.
Nicoloff, Roy M.
Niebur, Leon J.

Niehoff, Harry H.
Nielo, Andrew J.
Nielsen, Alvin
Nielsen, Erwin (Bud) C.
Nielsen, Peter W.
Nielsen, Peter W.
Niemczyk, Bernard R.
Nigg, Anthony A.
Nigrelli, Louis A.
Nilsen, Donald A.
Nilssen, Elda M.
Nixon, Grady C.
Nixon, Howard J.
Nixon, Iris
Nixon, John P.
Nixon, Mary D.
Nixon, William W.
Nobile, Philip P.
Noble, Emery J.
Noble, Robert J.
Nolan, Terence E.
Nollau, E. Wilson
Noonan, George C.
Nord, Jerome A.
Nordyke, Felix A.
Norman, Richard C.
Norrell, Henry G.
Norris, Billy R.
Northern, Thomas K.
Northrup, George R.
Norton, Dale R.
Norton, Lawrence M.
Norwig, Ralph F.
Norwood, Robert M.
Nosewicz, Nicolaus M.
Noss, Carl A.
Noubarian, Harvey S.
Novak, Elna V.
Novak, Thomas A.
Novella, Francesco
Novitski, Andrew J.
Novitszki, Alex
Novotny, Randy
Nowacki, Stanley V.
Nowak, Thomas V.
Nowik, Thomas E.
Noyes, Leonard
Nunn, Larry C.
Nutting, Mary
Nuzzo, Nofeo
Nygaard, Kenneth J.
Nygaard, Kenneth J.
Nygren, Wallace E.
Nystrom, Arthur N.
Nystrom, Kenneth W.

– O –

O'Barr, Prentice E.
O'Bell, Francis A.
O'Brien, Betty A.
O'Brien, Curtis M.
O'Brien, Daniel T.
O'Brien, Edward H.
O'Brien, Francis B.
O'Brien, John T.
O'Brien, William J.
O'Bryan, Craig S.
O'Bryan, Edward A.

O'Connell, James F.
O'Connell, James F.
O'Connell, Joseph E.
O'Connell, Thomas J.
O'Connor, James E.
O'Connor, John M.
O'Connor, John P.
O'Connor, Laura C.
O'Connor, Pat
O'Connor, Thomas M.
O'Conor, John R.
O'Dell, Ollie F.
O'Donnell, Herbert J.
O'Donnell, Thomas J.
O'Donnell, Thomas P.
O'Donnell, Virginia Lee
O'Hara, Francis R.
O'Hara, James F.
O'Hara, Thomas L.
O'Kane, William J.
O'Keefe, Walter H.
O'Kelley, John L.
O'Leary, John F.
O'Leary, John F.
O'Leary, Michael E.
O'Loughlin, Frank
O'Loughlin, John K.
O'Mara, James R.
O'Neal, Thomas E.
O'Neil, William J.
O'Neill, Kevin B.
O'Reilly, James K.
O'Reilly, Paul T.
O'Reilly, Robert E.
O'Rourke, George
O'Rourke, James M.
O'Rourke, Leonard J.
O'Toole, Thomas J.
Oakes, Kenneth K.
Oakley, John W.
Oaks, Hans C.
Oare, Dale D.
Obenhuber, Lawrence C.
Obermiller, Harold L.
Oblachinski, Stanley
Odell, John M.
Odom, Marion W.
Ogard, Alton N.
Ogden, William L.
Ogg, Harry Russell
Ogilvie, James A.
Ogle, James T.
Ogletree, B.A.
Ogrean, Walter D.
Ohlerich, Gaylord R.
Ohly, Donald E.
Oja, Oliver G.
Ojala, William R.
Olandese, Bernice
Oldfield, W.B.
Oldham, Clarence W.
Olds, Margaret L.
Oleary, Anne P.
Olensky, Arthur
Oliver, William G.
Olmsted, Gae
Olney, Clifford L.
Olney, Wallace E.

Olsen, Clyde N.
Olsen, Edward G.
Olson, Dale D.
Olson, Dennis H.
Olson, Donald O.
Olson, Donald W.
Olson, Howard A.
Olson, Howard W.
Olson, Isabelle Cook
Olson, Robert J.
Olson, William H.
Oman, Richard
Oorbeck, John C.
Oprea, John
Optekar, Peter S.
Orendorff, Louis J.
Orlicek, Matilda Rose
Orlove, Paul M.
Orlove, Seymour B.
Orman, Robert T.
Ormsby, Vaughn E.
Oros, Ernest L.
Orozco, Pascual U.
Orr, Lewis V.
Orr, Robert
Orsock, John W.
Ort, Don R.
Osborn, Clifford J.
Osthagen, William A.
Ostrander, Gary E.
Oswald, Virginia I.
Otillio, Hilary W.
Ott, Christopher L.
Ott, Earl Franklin
Otto, Martin M.
Ouart, Glenn M.
Over, Florice
Overstreet, George W.
Owen, Arthur Eddie
Owen, Kenneth L.
Owen, Wayne L.
Owens, Ben T.
Owens, David F.
Owens, Donald J.
Owens, Jack K.
Owens, Morris C.
Owings, William M.
Ownbey, Lois O.
Oxford, Kenneth G.
Oxley, David E.

– P –

Pace, Angelo
Pack, Jon Hermon
Pack, Samuel E.
Packard, Levi R.
Pacsmag, Glennys
Padalino, Robert J.
Paddock, David E.
Padeletti, Joseph C.
Padilla, Manuel D.
Padrnos, Valerian
Page, Michael L.
Pahutski, John M.
Paige, Terry F.
Palio, John
Palio, Joseph F.
Paliotti, Joseph

Palm, Ruth E.
Palmer, David E.
Palmer, Dennis A.
Palmer, Irl E.
Palmer, Morton
Palmer, Robert J.
Palmere, Raymond M.
Palumbo, Leonard
Pander, Catherine
Panetta, John J.
Pankratz, John
Pankus, Victor J.
Paparizos, Dimitrios A.
Papcsy, Robert W.
Pappani, George W.
Pappterson, Karl R.
Parasmo, Louis R.
Pardaen, Daniel J.
Pardue, Hubert R.
Paris, Ralph E.
Pariseau, Dennis J.
Park, Eugene Owen
Park, Harold E.
Park, Walter
Parker, Benjamin F.
Parker, Frank A.
Parker, Jack
Parker, John M.
Parker, Lane D.
Parker, Merrill O.
Parker, Robert
Parkes, Charles P.
Parkinson, Walter C.
Parkinson, Zenda M.
Parks, Carl E.
Parks, Daniel L.
Parks, William "Billy" S.
Parlier, Charles R.
Parma, Shirley
Parque, Richard A.
Parrish, Cecil J.
Parrish, William E.
Parry, Hugh L.
Parsell, George
Parson, Stanley
Paschall, Frederick G.
Pase, Charles P.
Pasquale, Alfred V.
Pasquavelli, Sam
Passacantando, Michael D.
Passet, William J.
Pasternak, John J.
Patrick, Clifford D.
Patrick, Dean R.
Patrick, Rolland J.
Patridge, Robert T.
Patterson, Carl S.
Patterson, Jeanette
Patterson, Philip R.
Patterson, Robert N.
Patterson, Stacey A.
Patterson, Wayne T.
Patterson, William H.
Pattock, Robert J.
Patty, Clyde J.
Paul, Albert W.
Paul, Jeffery A.
Paul, Philip M.

Paulhamus, H.M.
Paulick, Walter S.
Pauline, John W.
Paulson, Paul
Pauly, Anthony H.
Pavlinich, Thomas George
Payne, Benjamin J.
Payne, Cecil H.
Paynter, Stewart W.
Peachman, Howard D.
Peacock, James N.
Peake, Clyde C.
Pealer, Donald D.
Pearcy, William J.
Pearson, Clarence N.
Pearson, Harriett
Pearson, Richard A F
Peavler, Donald R.
Pecheone, Raymond F.
Pecher, Robert J.
Peckenschneider, Larry W.
Peckham, Marie
Peeker, William B.
Peeples, Henry C.
Peick, Charles F.
Pekrun, John A.
Peltier, Carl H.
Pelvit, Dolores
Pemberton, Noal C.
Pendergast, Helen
Pendergast, James G.
Pengra, Oren J.
Penn, George B.
Penn, Jesse B.
Pennell, Thomas J.
Pennings, Edmund F.
Pepper, Elizabeth
Perchard, James F.
Pere, David
Perez-Rivera, Guillermo
Perkins, James E.
Perkins, Lee C.
Perkins, Wendell V.
Perkins, William C.
Perry, Angelo P.
Perry, David S.
Perry, Don F.
Perry, Gregory C.
Perry, John M.
Perry, Raymond G.
Perry, Ruth H.
Person, Edward T.
Perullo, Gregory L.
Perullo, Louis P.
Peter, Frederick H.
Peters, Donald A.
Peters, Ivor C.
Peters, John E.
Peters, John W.
Peters, Oscar A.
Peters, Thomas A.
Peters, W.G.
Petersen, George C.
Petersen, Kenneth O.
Petersen, Martin T.
Petersen, Roy P.
Peterson, Henry
Peterson, Richard C.

Peterson, Vernid E.
Petit, John S.
Petras, Frank W.
Petri, Ernest N.
Petricca, Rose L.
Petrie, Jack R.
Petro, Peter G.
Petroline, Charles
Petronzio, J.A.
Pettit, Edward M.
Pettit, Oliver A.
Petty, Arthur O.
Petty, Huie W.
Petty, Lois
Petty, Marion R.
Petzold, Howard H.
Pfeifer, Wallace G.
Pfeiffer, John J.
Pflieger, Edward J.
Pharr, James H.
Phelan, Alice M.
Phillips, Claude K.
Phillips, Harry H.
Phillips, Irvin R.
Phillips, John A.
Phillips, John C.
Phillips, John J.
Phillips, Stanley J.
Phillipson, Robert V.
Phipps, Bernard C.
Picarello, Michael R.
Picillo, Philip G.
Pickens, Darrell A.
Pickett, Leroy
Pickett, Ralph E.
Pickler, David H.
Picou, Joseph D.
Pidich, Charles D.
Pieper, Marguerite A.
Pierce, B.L.
Piercy, Samuel J.
Pierczynski, John B.
Piering, William J.
Pierini, Robert J.
Pierre, George
Pierson, Connie L.
Pike, Douglas A.
Pike, Lawrence V.
Pikel, Allen E.
Pikur, Thomas
Pilant, Robert L.
Pimental, John A.
Pincola, Charles R.
Pinge, Harry J.
Pinkerton, Paul E.
Pinkerton, Vernon T.
Pinkham, Mary E.
Pinna, Wilfrido C.
Pino, Fernando E.
Pinske, Elaine
Pinter, Joseph A.
Pinto, Rudolph J.
Piper, Raymond
Pipes, Walter H.
Pipitone, Frank Mario
Pisacane, Anthony F.
Pisapia, Michael A.
Piser, Stanley P.

Pishock, S.J.
Pitard, Ernest E.
Pitkin, John E.
Pittari, Angelo J.
Pitts, Forrest M.
Placker, Wallace W.
Plaehn, Rose M.
Plain, Gordon J.
Planchon, Donna J.
Planchon, Irvon
Plese, Edward
Plocica, Carl J.
Plourde, Raymond N.
Plumley, Arnold
Plumley, Arnold
Poche, Hollis H.
Podunavac, Ray
Poeta, Raymond A.
Poff, Barry L.
Pogozelski, John F.
Pogue, Hartman H.
Poivey, Joseph F.
Polanchyck, Russell A.
Policastro, John F.
Polick, Edward R.
Poling, Harry E.
Polis, Elna
Polk, Marjorie M.
Pollard, George
Pollock, Stephen D.
Polverino, Samuel
Poman, Elmer E.
Pomfret, John J.
Pond, Elizabeth K.
Pond, William A.
Ponti, Dorothy E.
Pontiff, Alvin H.
Pontiff, Myrna R.
Pontiff, Steve D.
Pontones, Joseph A.
Poole, Parker
Pope, Charles C.
Pope, John W.
Popov, Peter W.
Portemont, John
Porter, Charles D.
Porter, George R.
Porter, Jack
Porter, Nancy
Porterfield, H. Mark
Portrey, Gary J.
Post, Mary Lou
Post, Melvin P.
Postero, Martha R.
Posthumus, Ivan J.
Potkonski, Edward F.
Potochniak, Daniel B.
Potter, Donald
Potter, Earl C.
Potter, Lem C.
Potter, Percy P.
Potts, David C.
Potts, Robert D.
Potts, Thurman I.
Pouliot, Walter J.
Poulos, Bill L.
Powell, Wanda W.
Powers, George Frank

Powers, Jack H.
Powers, James J.
Powers, Rodney A.
Powlus, Gerald D.
Prather, Chester C.
Prather, Claude R.
Pratt, Elwin H.
Pratt, Lawrence H.
Praught, Benet A.
Praul, George A.
Prejean, Alexandria
Prentice, Elmer A.
Presbruhi, Michael J.
Presley, Evelyn E.
Press, Frances
Pressley, Larry L.
Preston, George W.
Preston, Hugh A.
Pretto, John F.
Pretty, Roy N.
Prewett, Robert H.
Prezioso, Rudolph
Pribanick, Helen
Pribanick, Mathew Milan
Price, Ernest R.
Price, Louise B.
Price, Lucy
Price, Thurman R.
Priess, Albert B.
Priestly, Kenneth L.
Prieto, Pete R.
Prill, Howard L.
Pritchett, Henry W.
Privette, Richard B.
Probart, Richard D.
Procter, Henry J.
Prokop, William F.
Prosser, James H.
Prosser, William S.
Provost, Herman L.
Prow, Joseph R.
Pruitt, David T.
Pryor, Denard S.
Pryor, Robert L.
Przybylo, Joseph A.
Puckett, Robert E.
Pudelek, Chester A.
Pudelek, Karen L.
Pugh, Freddie R.
Pugh, Kathleen
Pukatch, John
Puleo, Charles J.
Pulkkinen, Waino R.
Pulley, James L.
Pumphrey, John J.
Purdy, Ellen Ray
Purinton, Robert H.
Purser, Harry C.
Puttmann, Stanley E.
Putzier, Willard C.
Pyeatt, Charles F.
Pyle, Robert G.

– Q –
Qualteri, John N.
Qualters, Terrance P.
Quarternik, Kenneth V.
Querry, Jake E.

Quigley, Walter J.
Quine, Clifford G.
Quinn, Jack J.
Quinn, John P.
Quinn, Joseph L.
Quinter, Charles M.

– R –
Rabbers, Gordon L.
Rabidoux, Charles F.
Rabka, Fred F.
Raciti, James W.
Rader, Hawk
Radigan, Edward F.
Radochonski, John C.
Radtke, Harlan C.
Radtke, William G.
Rae, Frank M.
Rago, Antone F.
Ragonese, David E.
Raiano, Luke A.
Raiber, Dr. Richard
Raines, Lawrence D.
Rainey, Albert C.
Rainey, Roger J.
Rains, Bruce
Raitman, Ronald B.
Ralph, Virginia A.
Ramberg, Roy L.
Ramella, Walter J.
Ramey, Margaret M.
Ramos, Thomas
Ramsey, Lucretia
Ranck, Charles A.
Rand, William T.
Randall, Edwin W.
Randall, Olga I.
Randell, Ernest L.
Randolph, Bernard R.
Randolph, Earl S.
Randolph, James A.
Raney, Eden A.
Rao, Vito M.
Raper, John V.
Rapley, David R.
Rappoport, Gerald J.
Rasbury, Avery Guinn
Rasbury, Linda L.
Rasco, Edna Lee
Ratcliff, Joseph M.
Ratcliff, Russell W.
Ratliff, Curtis L.
Ratner, Gene
Raumschuh, Charlotte
Rauscher, Jacob J.
Raver, Allen J.
Rawlings, Thomas L.
Ray, Johnson
Ray, Marvin A.
Ray, Robert A.
Ray, Robert P.
Raymond, Manuel J.
Reagan, Louis V.
Ream, John I.
Reames, Edsell C.
Reardon, Eugenia
Reasner, Garnet B.
Reaves, Gerald O.

Reck, Robert T.
Record, Thomas E.
Rector, Roscoe E.
Reddick, Robert A.
Redding, Alan
Redinbaugh, Ivan W.
Redoway, Michael W.
Redsicker, Robert G.
Redus, Thomas L.
Reed, Charles J.
Reed, John E.
Reed, Lee J.
Reed, Richard
Reed, Rolland H.
Reed, Wilson H.
Reed, Wyland K.
Reedy, Garland W.
Reedy, George M.
Reef, Mark E.
Rees, Mary Ann
Reese, Daniel J.
Reeve, Louis E.
Reeves, Donald E.
Reeves, Jesse F.
Reeves, Robert C.
Reeves, Todd A.
Regan, Robert E.
Reguli, Kenneth P.
Reich, Betty
Reichert, Leo E.
Reid, W.K.
Reifsteck, Lewis F.
Reilley, Paul F.
Reilly, Bernard W.
Reindl, Robert E.
Reinier, Kenzie L.
Reints, Benny E.
Reis, William A.
Reitz, Howell N.
Remar, John A.
Rembert, David C.
Renko, Joseph
Renna, Joseph F.
Renton, Raymond J.
Rentoul, Dawn G.
Renzi, Elaine
Reppas, Michael R.
Ressler, William J.
Retallick, William F.
Retzer, Willard
Reuting, Rodney
Reutter, Glen A.
Revolinski, Margaret
Rew, Charlotte
Rexrode, Frank H.
Reynolds, Bailey H.
Reynolds, Max G.
Reynolds, Robert F.
Reynolds, William E.
Rhatigan, John F.
Rhea, Guy S.
Rhea, James M.
Rhine, Wesley (Wes) E.
Rhoads, Rodney F.
Rhoden, Jack E.
Rhodes, Carl E.
Rhodes, Duane L.
Rhodes, Samuel H.

Rhodus, Hugh E.
Rhymes, Thomas R.
Rhyne, Robert L.
Rice, Joseph B.
Rice, Lawrence F.
Rich, Robert A.
Richardson, Dalton W.
Richardson, Jack E.
Richardson, Kenneth E.
Richardson, Malcolm A.
Richardson, Marguerite G.
Richardson, Perl
Richardson, Rodney C.
Richardson, Willie F.
Richer, Beverly M.
Richey, Robert E.
Richmond, Earl H.
Richmond, Stoughton
Richter, Carl E.
Richter, Eugene O.
Rickabaugh, George A.
Rickards, Clifford C.
Riddle, James D.
Rider, James W.
Ridings, Mrs Eula
Rieb, Donald L.
Riehl, Jeanette
Riehl, Lawrence L.
Rigg, Edward J.
Riggs, Bernard J.
Rightmer, William C.
Riley, Frederick W.
Riley, James W.
Rinaldi, Samuel E.
Rinder, Warren W.
Ring, Stanley C.
Ringgold, James W.
Rings, Frederick G.
Rinzel, Ambrose R.
Ripley, John W.
Ripley, Robert A.
Risvold, Larry B.
Ritch, Walter A.
Ritchie, Alta O.
Ritchie, Laurence
Ritchie, Violet B.
Ritchko, Arthur
Ritter, Carney L.
Ritter, Jack D.
Rivera, Jose A.
Rivers, Edwin L.
Rix, Dorothy F.
Rizzo, Carmen L.
Rizzo, Philip
Roach, Joseph D.
Roach, Sandra
Roane, Lawrence H.
Roark, Ray W.
Robbins, James A.
Robbins, Murray W.
Roberts, Archibald
Roberts, Claude L.
Roberts, Douglas M.
Roberts, Finch L.
Roberts, Fred
Roberts, Harvey H.
Roberts, Jackie L.
Roberts, John D.

Roberts, John M.
Roberts, Rev. William F.
Roberts, Robert B.
Roberts, Thomas W.
Roberts, William F.
Robertson, Charles E.
Robertson, Floyd S.
Robertson, JW Peyton
Robertson, Margert
Robertson, Ralph
Robertson, Spann
Robertson, William J.
Robichaux, Rev. George Simmons
Robideau, Robert E.
Robinson, Doyle H.
Robinson, Harry F.
Robinson, Lawrence N.
Robinson, Thomas R.
Robinson, William L.
Robishaw, Joseph H.
Roblyer, Lenore
Roche, Edward C.
Roche, Maurice P.
Rockhold, Paul E.
Rockhold, Sarah J.
Rockwell, William G.
Roden, Joan D.
Roden, John J.
Roden, Ralph
Rodenbaugh, Dorothy
Rodenberg, Alton T.
Rodewald, Gerald G.
Rodgers, David J.
Rodgers, Hueit
Rodgers, James Q.
Rodgers, Thomas M.
Rodrigues, Ernest F.
Rodriguez, Gary C.
Roe, Evvard N.
Roe, Thomas W.
Roemer, John W.
Roesing, George A.
Roetter, Nelson C.
Rogal, William W.
Rogers, Daniel S.
Rogers, Donald E.
Rogers, Donald J.
Rogers, Donald Allen
Rogers, James M.
Rogers, James W.
Rogers, James L.
Rogers, John S.
Rogers, Paul R.
Rogers, Robert H.
Rogowski, John B.
Rolette, Howard S.
Rollings, Wayne E.
Rollins, Fred
Rollins, Gen
Rollins, Geoffrey R.
Rollins, Markham F.
Rollins, Pat
Rollins, Rex R.
Romaniak, Theodore F.
Romanko, Stephen J.
Romano, Nick W.
Romano, Ruth
Romanzo, John J.

Ronck, Wilfred A.
Rondero, Peter J.
Rondino, Nicholas A.
Ronnan, Edward A.
Ronning, Edna
Ronquillo, Marcos M.
Rood, John C.
Roop, James R.
Root, Chester E.
Root, William L.
Rorke, John P.
Rosa, William D.
Rosacker, Calvin L.
Rosales, Charles
Rose, Angelo F.
Rose, Lena T.
Rose, Levi T. Bud
Rose, Seymour M.
Rosenbaum, James T.
Rosenblum, Joan
Rosenstein, Bernard J.
Rosenthal, David H.
Rosenthal, Maurice M.
Ross, Aurele J.
Ross, Edgar V.
Ross, Gerald E.
Ross, Robert D.
Ross, Rolland L.
Rosser, Alice M.
Roth, James P.
Rothar, Harry J.
Rothschild, Charles G.
Rotolo, Eugene J.
Rotton, Luther C.
Roulo, Robert S.
Rourke, Harry E.
Rouse, Mahlor C.
Roush, Roy W.
Rovinsky, Stanley
Rovnak, Joseph W.
Rowe, Herbert J.
Rowe, John F.
Rowe, Lewis C.
Rowe, Robert E.
Rowe, Thomas J.
Rowe, William C.
Rowell, Carroll V.
Rowland, Edward J.
Roxburgh, Vivian M.
Royahn, Betty
Rozich, Frank J.
Rubin, Mannie J.
Rubino, Arthur A.
Rubinsohn, B. Marcus
Ruby, Jack H.
Rucco, George J.
Ruch, William L.
Ruchin, Bernard G.
Rudee, Milton
Rudolfi, Angelo L.
Rudolph, Curt W.
Rudolph, Philip M.
Rudzinski, Richard J.
Ruffin, George C.
Ruffner, Van N.
Ruhmshottel, Philip E.
Rummel, Lyman B.
Runge, Charles E.

Runion, T.L.
Ruocco, Ralph Frank
Rupel, Charles E.
Ruperd, Charlotte
Rupp, Christopher A.
Ruppert, Paul M.
Ruse, Dorothy M.
Rushcamp, Fred J.
Rushing, Edwin Karl
Rushing, Morris E.
Rushton, William G.
Rusk, Harold W.
Russ, Johnny O.
Russell, Charles A.
Russell, David C.
Russell, Harry W.
Russell, John S.
Russell, Maxine
Russo, John A.
Russo, Richard J.
Russo, Richard Anthony
Rustic, Edward
Rutherford, J.T.
Rutter, Thomas G.
Ryan, Francis J.
Ryan, Gerald K.
Ryan, James
Ryan, John W.
Ryan, John S.
Ryan, John V.
Ryan, Michael P.
Ryan, Robert J.
Ryan, Robert Elison
Ryan, Robert Eugene
Ryan, Ronald W.
Rybacki, Edward R.
Rydell, Everett E.
Rydell, Everett E.
Ryder, Ernest W.
Ryder, Ernest W.
Rydzeski, Larry V.
Rydzinski, Raymond P.
Rymer, Luther T.
Rypkema, Bert F.
Rzab, Peter E.
Rzewnicki, John J.

– S –
Sabin, George W.
Sablan, David M.
Sachlatzer, Robert K.
Sachtleben, James L.
Sacora, Gerald D.
Sadler, Jeannette
Sadowski, Edward G.
Sager, Charles J.
Sakaris, James J.
Sakin, Sy
Salefski, Eugene H.
Salerno, Joseph O.
Sallen, Urban F.
Salmons, Timothy D.
Salsbury, Edward F.
Saltrick, Charles W.
Saltzer, William C.
Salzano, John F.
Salzillo, John S.
Sampson, Oralee

Sand, Harry R.
Sandager, Harold H.
Sandburg, Carol R.
Sandburg, Rodney A.
Sanderford, Woodrow Gerald
Sanders, Gerald H.
Sanders, Glen J.
Sanders, Harry L.
Sanders, Howard H.
Sanders, Leroy W.
Sanders, Robert J.
Sanders, William H.
Sandquist, Warren D.
Sands, Jack M.
Sanford, Eugene D.
Sanford, Wellington D.
Sanford, William H.
Santese, Benjamin E.
Santos, Reginald B.
Sapienza, Francis A.
Saraf, John L.
Sarazin, Raymond P.
Sarkisian, Harry M.
Sasser, Ralph C.
Satterfield, Mark D.
Sattler, John F.
Saturnus, Helen
Sauer, Frederick A.
Sauer, Robert G.
Sauls, Henry C.
Saunders, Court A.
Saunders, Floyd W.
Saunders, Joseph B.
Saunders, Ritchie C.
Savage, Leon E.
Savitz, Morris
Sawchik, William
Sawka, Eugene J.
Sawulski, Eugene J.
Sawyer, John D.
Sawyer, Wayne O.
Saxton, Max M.
Sayers, Ralph E.
Scalcione, John F.
Scalf, Raymond M.
Scalisi, Marion S.
Scally, James M.
Scarano, Wayne V.
Scarborough, Sidney H.
Scarfo, Roy
Scarn, Anthony J.
Scavone, Michael B.
Schack, Robert F.
Schade, Gustav M.
Schaeffer, Philip B.
Schafer, Hal R.
Schaffer, Jean
Schaffhauser, George J.
Schaible, Al B.
Schang, Arthur C.
Schaudel, George L.
Schectman, Arnold B.
Scheetz, Lyle F.
Scheffler, William T.
Scherer, John M.
Schersand, Cecil B.
Schervinski, Zygmont J.
Schey, William E.

Schieber, Fritz A.
Schiewe, William P.
Schiller, Donald W.
Schilling, Ira R.
Schintzius, Edward A.
Schlef, William K.
Schley, Walter H.
Schloss, Philip A.
Schmeelk, Steve H.
Schmelzer, Virginia
Schmick, Walter C.
Schmidhamer, Barbara
Schmidt, Alfred J.
Schmidt, Robert K.
Schmitt, Matthew
Schmitt, Val J.
Schmitt, William E.
Schneggenburger, Donald
Schneider, David W.
Schneider, Don L.
Schneider, John H.
Schneider, John "Jack" E.
Schneider, Lloyd C.
Schneider, Raymond H.
Schneider, Richard L.
Schneider, Willard J.
Schneider, William M.
Schneidmiller, Floyd L.
Schnelle, Gloria L.
Schnippel, Eugene H.
Schnitker, Jacqueline
Schnug, Edward
Schoenherr, Robert J.
Schoolfield, Clarence E.
Schou, Robert C.
Schouviller, Floyd H.
Schramm, Michael J.
Schreiber, Paul
Schroan, Lee
Schroder, Donald E.
Schroeder, Clifford D.
Schubert, Edward F.
Schultheis, Anthony H.
Schultz, Daniel T.
Schultz, David D.
Schultz, Donald T.
Schultz, Harry
Schultz, Henry E.
Schultz, Hugh "Jim"
Schultz, Lavada Scott
Schultz, Ned E.
Schultz, Robert H.
Schultz, Shirley
Schulz, Donald C.
Schulze, Ralph
Schumann, Jack A.
Schuster, Bernhardt
Schwab, John J.
Schwartz, Alan W.
Schwartz, Douglas W.
Schwartz, Frank J.
Schwartz, Isabel
Schwartz, Leland Dwight
Schwartz, Lorraine
Schweighardt, Robert W.
Schwenk, Adolph G.
Schwenk, Keith A.
Schwenn, William F.

Sciba, Victor J.
Scidmore, S. Bruce
Sciechowicz, Chester M.
Scinto, George
Scotson, Eric A.
Scott, Charles B.
Scott, Earl A.
Scott, Eleanor
Scott, Hugh
Scott, Monte L.
Scott, Richard I.
Scott, Sterling E.
Scott, Steven D.
Scott, Thomas B.
Scott, Thomas E.
Scott, W.M.
Scott, Wilson R.
Scovill, Roger P.
Scrivens, Eugene G.
Scroggins, Suda
Seale, James H.
Seaman, Richard J.
Searfoss, Lloyd S.
Searle, Milton H.
Sears, Gordon M.
Sears, Ronald F.
Sebetto, Raymond A.
Seborowski, Veronica
Securo, Vincent M.
Sedlak, Alberta H.
Sedoski, Chester A.
Seebode, Marjorie
Seek, Robert L.
Seeler, Jack R.
Seelye, Ernest M.
Seep, Phil
Sefl, Earl R.
Segina, John M.
Sehi, Earl H.
Seibel, Elaine
Seier, Perry R.
Seifried, Carol
Seiler, Bertie M.
Selavka, Michael B.
Self, Horace
Sellers, Dodd
Sellick, Winston R.
Selzer, Jacob J.
Semler, John C.
Senger, Ruth
Senich, George
Seppala, Gary M.
Seppi, Gino James
Seprish, David J.
Serdar, Eli D.
Setser, Mac S.
Severance, Dave E.
Severns, Dale J.
Sevick, Richard E.
Seward, Bruce J.
Seymour, Eldridge E.
Sgambati, Joseph P.
Shaffer, Anna
Shaffer, David
Shaner, Timothy P.
Shank, Carl
Shank, George M.
Shank, Lucy Prado

Shanks, Clarence A.
Shanley, David B.
Shannon, James K.
Shannon, John P.
Shapen, George T.
Shapiro, Arlene Siegel
Shapiro ,Esther
Sharafinski, Marcy
Sharib, Daniel M.
Sharp, Arthur G.
Sharp, James J.
Sharp, Joel E.
Sharp, Thomas W.
Sharples, Robert B.
Sharpless, Garland L.
Shatos, Ralph J.
Shaw Allen S.
Shaw, Barry M.
Shaw, Charles L.
Shaw, Connie
Shaw, Elbert W.
Shaw, Robert L.
Shawaryn, Eugene T.
Shea, John T.
Shea, Joseph L.
Shea, Robert B.
Shearer, John A.
Sheehan, Charles R.
Sheehan, John H.
Sheehan, Raymond C.
Sheehy, John M.
Sheehy, Terrance W.
Sheets, Thomas E.
Sheffield, William M.
Shell, USMC Ret BGen G R E
Shelton, Donald C.
Shelton, Rex V.
Shelton, Weldon L.
Shepard, George H.
Shepherd, Jerry R.
Shepherd, Michael A.
Sheppard, Donald J.
Sheppard, Marvin H.
Sheridan, John F.
Sherlock, Robin A.
Sherman, Henry K.
Sherman, Walter L.
Sherwood, Bruce A.
Sherwood, Edward
Shields, James P.
Shimek, Joseph L.
Shimkus, Tony A.
Shine, Robert J.
Shinn, Thomas G.
Shipley, Helen L.
Shiptoski, Paul J.
Shirley, Everett W.
Shivetts, Michael E.
Shoaf, Chester W.
Shoemaker, Robert J.
Shone, Thomas
Shook, Juel C.
Short, Albert J.
Short, John J.
Short, Thomas F.
Shortway, Harry
Shoup, Zola D.
Shultz, Herbert L.

Shultz, Robert F.
Shumaker, J.C. "Shu"
Shuper, Joseph
Shuttera, Laverne F.
Shuttera, Vincent
Shymansky, Stephen W.
Siciliano, James G.
Sickinger, Daniel L.
Siebel, William S.
Siepert, Terrell K.
Sigafoos, Stuart D.
Siggia, Joseph V.
Siglin, Lester A.
Sill, Wayne R.
Sills, Donald C.
Silva, Edmund F.
Silveira, Edward J.
Silvestri, Edmund J.
Simard, Paul J.
Simerman, Wayne A.
Simmons, Charles William
Simmons, David L.
Simmons, Gerald C.
Simmons, John V.
Simmons, Lee
Simmons, Richard A.
Simmons, Roy
Simon, Albert
Simone, Joseph E.
Simonson, Arthur K.
Simpson, Charles A.
Simpson, Edna Mary
Simpson, Elmer E.
Simpson, Gordon E.
Simpson, Leslie Gordon
Simpson, Lois A.
Simpson, V.R.
Simpson, W.C.
Simpson, Warren H.
Sims, John R.
Sims, Ray Vaughn M.
Sinclair, Ronald F.
Sincock, William F.
Sinder, Mike
Sines, Gerald E.
Sines, Lee Ora
Sines, Leonard W.
Singer, Robert F.
Singletary, Josie A.
Singleterry, Bill D.
Singleton, John H.
Singleton, Kenneth W.
Singleton, Patrick
Singleton, Richard S.
Sinnott, Hugh P.
Sipes, Calvin R.
Siriani, Joseph G.
Sissom, Raymond
Siverson, Paul W.
Skacan, Peter
Skaritka, Paul
Skeldon, Philip C.
Skibinski, Bernard E.
Skilton, Francis H.
Skinner, Bonnie L.
Skinner, Franklin E.
Skinner, Kathleen G.
Skinner, Richard F.

Skow, Howard E.
Skrade, Robert H.
Skrivseth, Kenneth B.
Skweres, Frank Michael
Skwirowski, Robert
Slater, James D.
Slaughter, George R.
Slaughter, John
Slaughter, Ralph C.
Sligh, Thomas M.
Slivocka, Frank R.
Sloan, Frank B.
Sloan, George O.
Slominski, Robert L.
Slone, James W.
Sloto, Milt
Slouf, Raymond B.
Slowe, Norman B.
Slutz, William L.
Small, Lawrence L.
Smalley, Byron W.
Smart, John M.
Smiley, Chester H.
Sminkey, Thomas G.
Smith, Albert J.
Smith, Allene
Smith, Charles A.
Smith, Charles W.
Smith, Charles B.
Smith, Daniel M.
Smith, Dannie G.
Smith, Don L.
Smith, Edward Joseph
Smith, Ella
Smith, Frank D.
Smith, Fred O.
Smith, George R.
Smith, George B.
Smith, H. Tom
Smith, Harold E.
Smith, Harold T.
Smith, Helen M.
Smith, Henry C.
Smith, Irving J.
Smith, Jack W.
Smith, James F.
Smith, Jean D.
Smith, Jim C.
Smith, Joemax
Smith, Joseph D.
Smith, Kathleen Edens
Smith, Kenneth G.
Smith, Laurence A.
Smith, Lowell Wayne
Smith, Marvin R.
Smith, Nathan R.
Smith, Neil D.
Smith, Neil G.
Smith, Norman H.
Smith, Patricia M.
Smith, Paul P.
Smith, Ralph R.
Smith, Ray L.
Smith, Reginald O.
Smith, Richard C.
Smith, Richard D.
Smith, Richard E.
Smith, Robert E.

Smith, Robert L.
Smith, Robert P.
Smith, Ronald C.
Smith, Ronald L.
Smith, Ross E.
Smith, Scott Slaughter
Smith, Sharon B.
Smith, Vivian
Smith, William E.
Smith, William G.
Smith, William M.
Smith, William Dodson
Snelders, Arthur O.
Snell, William E.
Snellgrove, John "Jack" H.
Snelling, Shirley
Snider, Jimmie J.
Snoddy, Sam H.
Snow, Robert E.
Snyder, Charles M.
Snyder, Dean H.
Snyder, Jack E.
Snyder, James W.
Snyder, Jerry L.
Snyder, John W.
Snyder, Ralph W.
Snyder, Robert L.
Sobol, Eli H.
Sobol, Joseph F.
Socie, George R.
Soderbloom, Gerald E.
Sofranko, Frances
Sokoly, Dorothy M.
Solomon, Charles B.
Solomon, Cleo
Soltman, Donald E.
Somerville ,Jeanne H.
Sommerville, Richard D.
Soni, Franz
Sooter, Charles A.
Sooter, Jean J.
Sooter, Will J.
Soper, Melvin A.
Soper, Philip
Sorensen, Laverne C.
Sorge, John R.
Sosolik, Waldemar C.
Sotelo, Neston
Soucie, Gilman William
Soules, Emmett L.
Souza, Betty
Souza, Joseph W.
Souza, Manuel
Spach, Curtis A.
Spagna, Francis L.
Spahn, Ernest R.
Spahn, James L.
Spahr, Ryder S.
Spain, Arley R.
Spanovich, Steve
Sparkman, Woodrow G.
Sparks, Patrick A.
Sparrow, James A.
Speake, Paul E.
Spears, James W.
Specht, Joseph P.
Specht, Robert A.
Speed, John A.

Speer, Gary
Spehn, William H.
Speights, Robert J.
Spence, Allan J.
Spence, Joseph S.
Spencer, Carolyn V.
Spencer, Donald A.
Spencer, Doyle F.
Spencer, Gordon E.
Spencer, John
Spencer, Michael A.
Spencer, William E.
Spicer, Ethel
Spooner, Bertrand L.
Spooner, Richard T.
Sposito, Joseph J.
Sprague, Daniel M.
Sprague, Walter B.
Spraker, William G.
Springer, Ralph G.
Spry, Philip A.
Spurlock, Edgar T.
Spurr, Kenneth L.
St. Clair, William J.
St. John, William V.
Stacy, Robert A.
Stacy, Walter A.
Staffieri, Anthony
Staffieri, John P.
Stafford, Dave
Stafford, Eleanor C.
Stahel, George E.
Stake, Stanley N.
Staker, Frances
Stam, Paul B.
Stambaugh, Harold W.
Stamper, Maxwell H.
Stancel, George J.
Stancel, Robert J.
Stanfel, Stephen J.
Stanford, Kenneth D.
Stanley, Daniel S.
Stanner, James L.
Stansky, Ardys
Stanson, Betty M.
Stanton, Arthur J.
Stanton, George F.
Stanton, Robert W.
Staples, Patricia Crawford
Stark, Robert Dale
Starkey, James A.
Starkey, Leland A.
Starks, Joe
Starr, Jackie
Starzynski, Paul M.
Stasio, Dr. Anthony S.
Stasio, Mary F.
Staton, Gerald
Stauffer, Ross E.
Staugaitis, John
Steck ,Lewis J.
Steding, Gerhard D.
Steeb, Merrill M.
Steed, Leonard B.
Steed, Patricia H.
Steele, Debbs R.
Steele, Orlo K.
Steele, William F.

Steffens, Fred F.
Stegemerten, Walter W.
Stegemoller, Ernst F.
Stein, George E.
Stein, Richard R.
Steinke, Gilbert H.
Stentz, Clifton E.
Stephan, Clarence L.
Stephens, Don W.
Stephens, Elmer E.
Stephens, Hilda
Stepp, Randy L.
Stern, Caroline
Stern, Sidney Somerset
Steuernagel, William B.
Stevens, Carl E.
Stevens, Clayton L.
Stevens, John H.
Stevens, William E.
Stevenson, Harold J.
Stevenson, Robert D.
Stevenson, Virginia
Stevenson, W. Kendall
Stewart, Albert L.
Stewart, Chester C.
Stewart, Earl E.
Stewart, Everett E.
Stewart, Frank R.
Stewart, Harding J.
Stewart, Mark R.
Stewart, Richard G.
Stickler, Russell L.
Stidham, Jeffrey A.
Stiles, Curt H.
Stinson, Kenneth Kinney
Stith, Paul J.
Stock, Paul R.
Stock, Ray G.
Stockstill, Billy J.
Stodgell, Erika
Stoffer, Donald E.
Stohldrier, Chris W.
Stokes, Joseph M.
Stolarski, Mark Anthony
Stoldt, Robert J.
Stoll, William C.
Stone, Arthur F.
Stone, Charles D.
Stone, Christopher D.
Stone, David E.
Stone, Elmer J.
Stone, John E.
Stone, Richard L.
Stonebraker, Russell O.
Stonebraker, William B.
Stoner, Ramona Bright
Stoppie, Andrew
Storer, Alfred L.
Storm, William G.
Stornello, James V.
Story, Lester D.
Story, Robert D.
Stoumbaugh, James R.
Stout, Dale O.
Stout, Earl L.
Stout, Rita K.
Stout, Ward K.
Stout, Wesley D.

Stovall, Bill
Stover, James C.
Stowell, James E.
Strack, Steve P.
Strader, Calvin L.
Strasser, Robert E.
Strate, Rex V.
Street, Phil A.
Streeter, Marguerite M.
Streever, William A.
Streubel, Lloyd E.
Strickland, Kenneth W.
Strickland, William M.
Strider, C. Davis
Strider, Carroll D.
Strider, Harry E.
Strider, Sybil C.
Strinden, Duane N.
Stringer, Willie F.
Stringham, Lawrence W.
Strohm, George
Strong, Garland A.
Stronsick, Ivan L.
Stronsick, Victoria M.
Strother, William R.
Stroud, Virgil L.
Stroud, William F.
Struhar, Robert A.
Struss, Lyle E.
Stuart, Gordon W.
Stuart, Jon C.
Stubblefield, Robert E.
Stubbs, Peter F.
Studd, Donald P.
Stueber, Theodore H.
Stum, Donald M.
Stundon, John P.
Stygles, Allen G.
Stygles, James E.
Stygles, John Henry
Styron, George F.
Suane, Remy L.
Suddarth, Margaret V.
Sudduth, Eugene T.
Sudduth, Joseph F.
Suggs, William A.
Sukowatey, Edward W.
Sullivan, Daniel P.
Sullivan, James B.
Sullivan, James M.
Sullivan, John J.
Sullivan, John L.
Sullivan, John W.
Sullivan, Joseph
Sullivan, Leo G.
Sullivan, Marion
Sullivan, Mark J.
Sullivan, Pat N.
Sullivan, Raymond J.
Sullivan, Robert C.
Sullivan, Robert E.
Sullivan, Wendell T.
Sullivans, John D.
Suma, George
Summa, Anthony J.
Summar, Alverta
Summar, James L.
Summar, Verta F.

Summers, Eleanor J.
Summers, Harvey M.
Sumpter, O.E.
Sunder, Michael C.
Supplee, Dorothy
Surovy, Emil J.
Surridge, Floyd J.
Suszczynski, Frank A.
Sutay, J. Bruce
Sutherland, Frank L.
Suttmiller, Howard
Sutton, Glen W.
Sutton, USMC BGen R H
Sventeck, Richard J.
Swackhamer, Robert E.
Swaney, Emory R.
Swango, Melvin F.
Swanson, Carl M.
Swanson, Ernest R.
Swanson, Gordon R.
Swanson, Leonard P.
Swanson, Leslie R.
Swanson, Swan Bertil
Sweeney, Anne J.
Sweeney, Donald E.
Sweeney, Lionel T.
Sweeney, W. Eugene
Swenson, Ernest
Swift, Roy F.
Swilley, Bennie F.
Swisher, John M.
Swiston, Stanley J.
Switalski, Edmund J.
Switken, Michael J.
Switzer, Richard W.
Swoboda, Nina Mae
Swofford, James E.
Sydlaske, Daniel W.
Symons, Vernon F.
Syms, Joseph E.
Syverson, Wayne A.
Szabo, Alexander A.
Szabo, William A.
Szarafinski, Edward A.
Szech, Chester J.
Szerszen, Benedict B.
Szilasi, William J.
Szmed, Thomas S.
Szypulski, Fred E.

– T –
Tabakian, Arthur J.
Tabor, Gene R.
Taff, George S.
Taft, John J.
Talbot, Robert N.
Taliaferro, Charles P.
Taliferro, Charles B.
Talkington, Grace
Tall, Anthony D.
Tallent, Pauline
Talley, Robert P.
Talty, Joe L.
Tango, Alfred W.
Tanis, Cornielius
Tankersley, Hubert J.
Tanner, J.W.
Tanner, John D.

Tappen, John R.
Tarbrake, Charles E.
Tarkowski, Lambert J.
Tarrant, Brian P.
Tartaro, Salvatore J.
Tassey, Vernon W.
Tassone, Paul S.
Tatarakis, Mitchell
Taubert, Lenore E.
Taubert, Richard F.
Taureck, Otto D.
Tauscher, Gilbert K.
Taylor, Adrian W.
Taylor, Brandon D.
Taylor, Cathlinn
Taylor, Darrell L.
Taylor, Donald F.
Taylor, Douglas O.
Taylor, Edward
Taylor, George W.
Taylor, Harry J.
Taylor, Henry R.
Taylor, Jacob R.
Taylor, James C.
Taylor, James W.
Taylor, Joseph F.
Taylor, Larry S.
Taylor, Mae C.
Taylor, Matthew G.
Taylor, Merrill E.
Taylor, Richard L.
Taylor, Sidney B.
Taylor, W.E.
Taylor, William N.
Teague, Erwin A.
Teague, Jack
Teague, Jackson B.
Teal, Darrell G.
Teckmyer, Frederick C.
Tedford, George D.
Teegarden, Homer L.
Teising, Basil
Teldeschi, Paul J.
Tellish, Louis J.
Telshaw, Clarence A.
Templeton, Helen
Tennant, Sidney E.
Tennant, Sidney E.
Termini, Melvin J.
Terruso, Paul F.
Terry, James A.
Terry, John M.
Terwilliger, James L.
Tesiero, Donald E.
Tessmann, Herbert W.
Tetzlaff, Elden C.
Teutschel, Charles A.
Teves, Everett
Thalassites, L.G.
Thaler, Thomas F.
Tharp, Louise E.
Thatcher, Robert A.
Thaxton, Peggy L.
Thaxton, Thomas Roy
Thayer, Alvin E.
Thayer, Arthur V.
Thayer, Ronald A.
Theis, Charles E.

Theis, Norman
Thibault, Mary
Thielman, Ed P.
Thisius, Alvin C.
Thisius, Merlyn N.
Thomas, Benjamin H.
Thomas, Betty K.
Thomas, Clinton R.
Thomas, Frederick W.
Thomas, Gerard F.
Thomas, John
Thomas, Melvin H.
Thomas, Ruth R.
Thomas, Terry F.
Thompson, Donald L.
Thompson, Harry A.
Thompson, Helen R.
Thompson, James A.
Thompson, James L.
Thompson, James T.
Thompson, Jean N.
Thompson, John B.
Thompson, Kenneth E.
Thompson, Leon H.
Thompson, M. Samuel
Thompson, Michael P.
Thompson, Rev. Dr. Herbert H.
Thompson, Robert H.
Thompson, Victor L.
Thompson, Virginia
Thompson, William H.
Thompson, William R.
Thompson, William L.
Thomsen, Earl A.
Thomson, Charles F.
Thomson, Gaylord S.
Thomson, Madge H.
Thon, Audry M.
Thon, Howard M.
Thore, Marietta
Thornton, George F.
Thornton, James L.
Thornton, John A.
Thornton, Nelson E.
Thrall, Arthur
Thurber, Richard E.
Tice, William T.
Tichy, Robert G.
Tiemann, Frank J.
Tierney, Michael R.
Tierney, Thomas A.
Tift, John H.
Tiller, Paul O.
Tilley, David L.
Tilton, Margaret M.
Timbers, Larry J.
Timm, Marshall T.
Timpany, William J.
Timperio, William T.
Tinsley, Jessie D.
Tipton, Nancy
Tipton, Scott W.
Tipton, Thomas N.
Tirocchi, Carlo
Tishma, Vladimir "Tish"
Tisseker, George E.
Toal, Joseph V.
Tobin, Patrick A.

Todd, Robert M.
Tokash, Joseph D.
Toland, Edward M.
Tolbert, Charles L.
Tolerton, Leon G.
Tolley, Victor F.
Tomczyk, Richard
Tomey, Ronald
Tomko, John J.
Tomlin, Leo J.
Tomlinson, Morris Wayne
Tomlinson, Thomas L.
Tommasi, Edward J.
Tompkins, Rathvon Mcclure
Tomporowski, Thaddeus C.
Toms, Edward H.
Tonet, Earl
Tooley, Floyd J.
Topham, William J.
Topping, Thomas R.
Torgerson, Don B.
Tormey, John
Torres, Jose V.
Torstenson, Richard J.
Touchstone, Realious L.
Tower, Mary A.
Towlson, William J.
Townsend, Velma A.
Townsend, Weldon O.
Tracey, Thomas B.
Trafford, Mary
Trainor, William E.
Trauger, Ronald M.
Trauth, Walter B.
Trautman, Henry
Travis, Edwin J.
Traylor, Harry B.
Traylor, Melvin A.
Trembly, Emil L.
Trephan, Michael R.
Trero, William S.
Trimble, Lee S.
Trippler, Dewey A.
Trites, H. Patrick
Trojanowski, Richard S.
Trovillion, John P.
Troy, James E.
Troy, Thomas C.
Troyanek, Edward F.
True, Blanche
Trusler, George J.
Trzaskalski, Adam J.
Tsareff, Thomas C.
Tubbs, Clifford M.
Tuck, Richard H.
Tucker, Derwood C.
Tucker, Evelyn
Tucker, Harry C.
Tucker, James C.
Tucker, John R.
Tucker, Joseph R.
Tucker, Keith C.
Tucker, Ronald E.
Tucker, Thomas S.
Tucker, Virginia M.
Tufts Eugene H.
Tulack, Gregory
Tuohy, John P.

Tupper, Lawrence F.
Turk, George J.
Turko, Steve E.
Turley, Gerald H.
Turner, Dave P.
Turner, John G.
Turner, Wayne E.
Turpin, Kenneth
Turrini, Angelo B.
Turse, Carmella
Turse, Frank
Tuter, Otis R.
Twardzik, Louis F.
Twarok, Stanley M.
Twitchell, Robert R.
Tworek, Conrad J.
Tyldesley, Audrey M.
Tyldesley, Walter E.
Tyler, Berton C.
Tyler, Wiley W.
Tyson, Francis David

– U –
Uehling, William V.T.
Ulics, Joseph S.
Ulino, Donald
Ulsh, Ammon J.
Umstead, George H.
Underdahl, Paul A.
Unruh, Jonathan M.
Upton, William C.
Urban, Barbara L.
Urban, Robert L.
Urbanik, Theodore M.
Urbaszewski, Richard
Uris, Leon
Utter, James R.
Uyehara, Kimberly J.

– V –
Vadell, Joseph A.
Valdez, Steve F.
Valentia, Henry R.
Valentine, Norman N.
Valk, Dawn A.
Valley, Ida Marie
Van Acker, Ella Mae E.
Van Amburg, David E.
Van Bibber, Burl E.
Van Buren, Thomas D.
van der Els, E. Matt
Van Duzor, John T.
Van Dyke, George D.
Van Dyke, John C C.
Van Dyke, William E.
Van Ee, William J.
Van Etta, Michael L.
Van Horne, Charles W.
Van Horne, Judie T.
Van Horne, Richard F.
Van Houten, George D.
Van Keuren, Robert E.
Van Kirk, James F.
Van Laningham, Jo
Van Liew, John B.
Van Loan, Richard C.
Van Note, Gerald E.
Van Riper, USMC MajGen P.K.

Van Sleet, Myles F.
Van Wie, Duane A A.
Vance, Orville L.
Vance, Randolph H.
Vance, William E.
Vandehaar, Oren W.
Vandenbout, Philip A.
Vanderbilt, Albert L.
Vanderhoeff, Thomas
Vanderlinden, Adeline
Vandermeulen, Conrad
Vandevender, James V.
Vandrilla, Jacob B.
Vanfleet, Joseph O O.
Vanosten, Howard J J.
Vanwinkle, Raymond S S.
Varay, Lois Jane E.
Vargo, Peter J.
Varnadore, Leslie L.
Varney, Merle E.
Varuola, William J.
Vassallo, Michael
Vatrano, Tom J.
Vaughn, Donald R.
Vaughn, Keith M.
Vehrs, William F F.
Velar, John A.
Venables, Jack T.
Ventura, Robert E.
Vera, Pete E.
Verno, George J.
Verret, Roy A.
Verschoor, Paul F F.
Versteeg, Lester I I.
Vessell, William A.
Vest, Morris L.
Veylupek, Joseph C.
Vian, Gerald E.
Vicena, Steve E.
Vickers, William H.
Vida, Paul W.
Vielhauer, William C.
Vigliatura, John F.
Villanueva, Angel P.
Villarial, Daniel A.
Vincent, Elizabeth J.
Vincent, Nat H.
Vineyard, Richard O.
Virgin, George E.
Visek, Rodger J.
Vita, Louis A.
Vitek, Charles F.
Vittitoe, Hagan
Vlach, Margaret A.
Vlastelica, Paul
Voeltner, Harvey C.
Voight, William T.
Volkman, E.
Russell, L.
Volkman, Robert L.
Volpe, Victor V.
Voorhees, Madeline E.
Voorhees, Robert E.
Vorgang, Blaine D.
Vorlander, Joan C.
Vorwalle,r Richard N.
Vought, Kimber E.
Vought, Richard D.

Voumard, Edward D D.
Voyer, George J.
Voyles, Charles W.
Voyles, Myrtle L L.
Vrana, Emery J.

– W –
Waalen, Earl O.
Wachsmuth, Frances C.
Wachsmuth, Jerome "Jerry" C.
Waddell, Charles
Waddell, James C.
Waddell, Mary C.
Waddle, Victor O.
Wade, Edward K.
Wade, Horton E.
Waeckerle, Herbert H.
Wagner, Edward F.
Wagner, Irving J.
Wagner, John S.
Wagner, Robert C.
Wagner, Thomas A.
Wagner, Virgil E.
Wahlberg, Gilbert L.
Waite, Edward
Waite, Florence L.
Waite, Vernon J.
Wakefield, Davies E.
Wakefield, Douglas J.
Wakefield, Margaret
Wakeman, John W.
Wakuluk, William
Waldman, Robert F.
Waldman, Robert F.
Waldner, Anne C.
Waldo, Clyde C.
Waldron, Edison A.
Waldron, Michael W.
Waldrop, Barbara G.
Walker, Alvin J.
Walker, Brian G.
Walker, Cleveland L.
Walker, George A.
Walker, Ronald L.
Walker, Thomas
Walker, Walter C.
Walker, Wanda D.
Walkingstick, Charles M.
Wall, Henry L.
Wall, Joseph M.
Wall, Wayne J.
Wallace, Arthur
Wallace, G.A.
Wallace, Henry
Wallace, Richard D.
Wallace, Walton M.
Wallace, Warren L.
Wallach, Stanley E.
Wallin, William E.
Wallner, Joseph R.
Walls, Billy G.
Walls, Paul F.
Walneck, Rudolph J.
Walp, Donald W.
Walsh, Gerald F.
Walsh, John J.
Walsh, John J.
Walsh, John P.

Walsh, Michael
Walsh, Thomas J.
Walter, Francis R.
Walter, Francis R.
Walters, Charles Wm
Walters, Elmer Louis
Walters, Robert E.
Walters, Upton Joseph
Walther, Robert G.
Wambach, William A.
Warble, Herbert D.
Warblow, Gaylord H.
Ward, DeWayne C.
Ward, George Gordon
Ward, H. Clay
Ward, John P.
Ward, L.G.
Ward, Macaulay
Ward, Norman E.
Ward, Richard F.
Ward, Robert A.
Warner, Dean R.
Warnke, Clara
Warren, Leo M.
Warren, Michael A.
Warren, Wells B.
Warren, William C.
Warren, William F.
Warren, William D.
Warzeka, Lyle Leo
Wascom, Haynes J.
Washington, James R.
Washington, William L.
Wasicek, George R.
Waskom, Wendell M.
Wasson, Dennis P.
Wasson, Ele W.
Waters, George W.
Waters, Georgia L L.
Waterworth, James R.
Watkins, Keith W.
Watson, Bennie O.
Watson, Berkley G.
Watson, Edward
Watson, Francis J.
Watson, Frank H.
Watson, Leonard G.
Watson, Nolan A.
Watson, Robert E.
Watson, William R.
Watters, Clarence A.
Watters, Howard J.
Watters, Robert E.
Watters, Robert E.
Watters, William L.
Wattik, Genevieve L.
Wattik, Michael
Watts, Charles R.
Waugh, Isaac D.
Waugh, Robert L.
Wayman, Kenneth H.
Waymire, Melvin G.
Weaner, John W.
Weatherford, Raymond D.
Weaver, Albert H.
Weaver, James E.
Weaver, Murray C.
Weaver, Ralph "Bo" L.

Webb, Dorothy G.
Webb, William C.
Webber, Robert L.
Weber, Donald G.
Weber, Edward J.
Weber, Francis S.
Weber, John H.
Weber, Joseph F.
Weber, Lee R.
Weber, Lew E.
Webster, Robert
Webster, Walter A.
Weckerly, Frank W.
Wedlock, Stanley L.
Weech, Richard W.
Weekly, Dean V.
Weeks, Maury (Lee) L.
Weeks, Maury (Lee) L.
Weems, Paul T.
Wegert, Ronald W.
Weide, Don O.
Weide, Janet
Weightman, Eugene B.
Weikel, Virgil L.
Weiman, George Wallace
Weishaupt, William H.
Weixeldorfer, Daniel G.
Welch, Andrew Jarvis
Welch, Dennis E.
Welch, Donald R.
Welch, James J.
Welch, Robert T.
Welch, Sara Jane
Welch, Stephen A.
Welch, William R.
Weldon, Howard P.
Welkos, Warren D.
Wellemeyer, Leon F.
Weller, Wallace E.
Wellman, Goldie F.
Wells, Arthur W.
Wells, Bruce I.
Wells, Monroe H.
Wells, Robert P.
Welsh, James L.
Welsh, John L.
Welsh, Lee H.
Wenger, Al
Wenger, Robert W.
Wente, William M.
Werneburg, Lou
Werner, Robert P.
Wescott, Edward C.
Wesley, Joseph A.
Wesley, Steve T.
Wessel, Theodore F.
West, Gen
West, Jimmie M.
West, Joan
West, Oscar J.
West, Roy F.
Westbrook, Robert R.
Westcott, Craig M.
Westerman, Patricia E.
Westwick, E.R.
Wetherell, George J.
Wetterer, John J.
Weyker, John R.

Whalen, Charles C.
Whalen, Harold Thomas
Whalen, Irvin O.
Whalen, Thomas
Whaley, Wilbur W.
Wharton, John R.
Wheaton, Howell N.
Wheeler, Florence M.
Wheeler, Richard P.
Wheeler, William L.
Wheelock, Orville J.
Whetstone, William O.
Whipple, David L.
Whipple, Mary
Whitaker, Hoyt M.
Whitcher, Arthur B.
White, Albert R.
White, Donald E.
White, Edwin W.
White, Harold H.
White, Jeanette F.
White, John A.
White, John H.
White, John R.
White, Thomas J.
Whiteaker, Jeanette
Whitehead, Alfred E.
Whitehead, Burnes R.
Whitley, Marshall G.
Whitlow, Merton O.
Whitman, Robert P.
Whitmore, Wayne L.
Whitney, Dwain E.
Whitney, Raymond V.
Whittaker, George A.
Whittington, James D.
Whitton, Donald M.
Wholey, Joseph V.
Wick, Richard W.
Wickersham, Rev. George W.
Wideman, Synotte L.
Widman, Elmer R.
Wiegel, Carl
Wieland, William H.
Wieleba, Richard
Wiertella, Donald R.
Wiest, William T.
Wightkin, William J.
Wilbanks, Danny C.
Wilbert, Earl G.
Wilburn, Ray V.
Wilcox, William D.
Wilde, Shirley
Wildermuth, Patricia
Wiley, George K.
Wilhelm, Robert E.
Wilke, Edward F.
Wilkerson, Clayton T.
Wilkins, Claud H.
Wilkinson, Sibyl M.
Wilkus, Frank J.
Will, Alan B.
Will, Gerald K.
Willard, W.W.
Willett, Jay R.
Willhite, Charles E.
Williams, Arthur R.
Williams, Carl

Williams, David A.
Williams, Donald R.
Williams, Edwin C.
Williams, Fowler S Rocky
Williams, Fred W.
Williams, Helen T.
Williams, Howard L.
Williams, James E.
Williams, James T.
Williams, John J.
Williams, Joseph E.
Williams, Margaret B.
Williams, Mary I.
Williams, Maxie R.
Williams, Parkes T.
Williams, Robert D.
Williams, Robert O.
Williams, Robert W.
Williams, Ted O.
Williams, Thomas F.
Williams, Thomas C.
Williams, William G.
Williamson, Alan S.
Williamson, Elmer R.
Williamson, Russell J.
Williamson, V.L.
Williamson, Wiley R.
Willis, Donald W.
Willner, Arthur Lee
Willson, Minard
Willson, Robert C.
Wilsey, Roland D.
Wilsey, William R.
Wilsky, Herschel J.
Wilsky, Jean
Wilson, Bill
Wilson, Charles L.
Wilson, Cullis Rayford
Wilson, Daniel F.
Wilson, Donald M.
Wilson, Donald F.
Wilson, Donna
Wilson, Donophan
Wilson, Earl J.
Wilson, Fred R.
Wilson, Garland C A
Wilson, Henrietta
Wilson, Irvin R.
Wilson, Jean A.
Wilson, John J.
Wilson, Joseph G.
Wilson, Patricia J.
Wilson, Paul T.
Wilson, Tyson
Wilson, Wilbur W.
Wilson, William G.
Wimer, Leland J.
Win'E, Todd R.
Winall, William Bradford
Winburn, Charles E.
Windell, Clyde
Wines, Gary F.
Winfrey, Lloyd Vaughn
Winn, Clyde H "Jack"
Winner, Erin
Winslow, Agnes
Winslow, Donald R.
Winter, Daniel I.

Winters, Jerry L.
Winters, Robert
Winters, William G.
Winterstein, William E.
Wirtshafter, David
Wirtz, William J.
Wischmeyer, Ralph Eugene
Wise, John D.
Wiseman, John T.
Wismann, L.W. Pete
Witasick, Bernard E.
Witek, Mark
Withee, Burton R.
Witkowski, John C.
Witowich, Michael
Witte, Alvin H.
Wittern, William V.
Wittsell, Kenneth E.
Wojcik, Walter T.
Wojnarowski, Leonard S.
Wojtas, August J.
Wolcott, Earl Stan
Wold, Victor H.
Wolfe, Charles F.
Wolfe, Jacob M.
Wolfe, Kenneth E.
Wolfe, Margie
Wolford, L.S.
Woll, Irene
Womac, Hershal D.
Wood, Amb John
Wood, David D.
Wood, Jean
Wood, Keith R.
Wood, Loeta M.
Wood, Robert H.
Wood, Tony R.
Wood, Warren P.
Wood, William L.
Woodard, Addison L. "Woody"
Woodcock, Warren
Woodhouse, Edward W.
Woodin, William B.
Woodman, Cecil W.
Woodman, Charles
Woods, Billy J.
Woods, Charles J.
Woods, James W.
Woods, Wesley E.
Woodsmall, Billy L.
Woodward, James A.
Woodward, Leeman E.
Woodworth, Grace
Wooley, Arthur L.
Wooley, Clifton S.
Woolum, Joe D.
Wootten, Eugene K.
Work, William H.
Worman, Roy K.
Worsley, James M.
Wortman, Clara V.

Wray, Marvin G.
Wright, Dean W.
Wright, Eric L.
Wright, Laverne
Wright, William J.
Wright, William L.
Wroblewski, Ronald W.
Wroten, Leroy M.
Wroten, Raymond L.
Wumkes, Eilert L.
Wuschke, Michael F.
Wuschke, Robert D.
Wyatt, Beatrice
Wyatt, Phyllis
Wyckoff, Jennifer A.
Wyckoff, John E.
Wyckoff, Louis O.
Wycoff, Ralph I.
Wynn, Leonard L.
Wysmulek, Edward H.
Wysocki, Betty
Wysocki, Charles
Wyzywany, Stephen

– Y –
Yancey, Lonnie E.
Yancey, Maude E.
Yanero, Richard F.
Yanniello, Anthony
Yarbrough, Eldon R.
Yarbrough, John D.
Yates, Davis F.

Yates, Randall R.
Yavenue, Richard N.
Yearby, Carl W.
Yeddo, Roy J.
Yerem, Andrew
York, Thomas E.
Yott, Paul L.
Youd, Douglass S.
Younce, Dorothea
Young, Carl
Young, Chester
Young, Dale M.
Young, Elizabeth
Young, Gavin H.
Young, James R.
Young, Mark A.
Young, R.K.
Young, Vincent W.
Youngbird, Edmund
Youngs, Clifford F.
Younie, Milo E.
Yowell, Ronny L.

– Z –
Zabala, Matthew
Zaborowski, John J.
Zachary, William E.
Zack, David L.
Zack, Richard J.
Zahn, Roy
Zahn, William A.
Zajic, Raymond

Zak, Stanley F.
Zane, Ellen M.
Zang, Opal
Zaporski, Erwin F.
Zappia, Dominic C.
Zechman, Irvin F.
Zegers, Vernon R.
Zendle, Abraham
Zettlemoyer, Glenn E.
Zidik, Donald J.
Zidik, Joseph S.
Ziegler, Allan R.
Zieziula, John J.
Zihar, Carolyn V.
Zimmerman, Gerald J.
Zimmerman, Leora D.
Zimmerman, Mary Marie
Zingarelli, Louis
Zingaro, Joseph P.
Zinni, Jules
Zirakian, James M.
Zito, Anthony R.
Zito, Edward J. Sr.
Zotter, John G.
Zouyras, Gus
Zuber, Vincent W.
Zuehlke, Rosalind
Zullo, Louis A.
Zurfas, Robert J.
Zurn, Robert C.
Zwiegel, Frank

Hawaii.

INDEX

New Zealand, S.S. Smith USMC 1943 2nd Anti Tank BN.

Top Left: New Zealand, S.S. Smith USMC 1943 2nd Anti Tank BN.

Lower Left: Saipan, June 1944.

Lower Middle: Saipan, June 1944.

Below: Pete Barnes picture on Guadacanal, upper extreme left with shorts on.

Printed in the USA
CPSIA information can be obtained
at www.ICGtesting.com
JSHW060054150824
68134JS00032B/2731